THE OLD OREGON COUNTRY

ON A SEA-OTTER HUNT
From John Meares, *Voyages* (1790)

THE
OLD OREGON
COUNTRY

A HISTORY OF FRONTIER TRADE,
TRANSPORTATION, AND TRAVEL

OSCAR OSBURN WINTHER

DEPARTMENT OF HISTORY
INDIANA UNIVERSITY

UNIVERSITY OF NEBRASKA PRESS
LINCOLN

First Bison Book printing March, 1969

Most recent printing shown by first digit below:

4   5   6   7   8   9   10

Bison Book edition reprinted by arrangement with the author

TO MY BROTHERS

"Commerce is a noble calling. It mediates between distant nations, and makes men's wants . . . . bonds for peace."

WILLIAM ELLERY CHANNING (1841)

PREFACE

Today the Pacific Northwest possesses a distinctive character as one of several sections of our nation. This region's geography, people, and economy have an individuality which blends with and yet stands apart from the rest of the United States. Like other sections, the Pacific Northwest cannot escape its past. Long known as the Oregon country, it was once thought of as one of the most remote and inaccessible frontier areas in the Western world. The region first unfolded its secrets to explorers and fur traders in whose footsteps came in quick succession missionaries, adventurers, pioneer farmers, miners, and businessmen. To all these the Oregon country presented a serious logistic problem. High, rugged mountains, inland waters, deserts, forests, ocean, snow, ice, rain, mud, heat, and magnificent distances thwarted the normal growth of community life and contact with the outside world. The battle to overcome these imposing physical obstacles in order to exploit the rich natural resources of the Oregon country and to establish orderly methods of commerce and travel comprise the major themes of this book. It is a saga of man against Nature; it is a story of adventure, indomitable courage, endurance, and brilliant business ingenuity and enterprise. This book is in part the history of men and events that have given vigor, confidence, buoyancy, and a proud consciousness of the past to people who today make up Canadian and American civilization in British Columbia, Oregon, Washington, Idaho, western Montana, and, to be precise, a bit of western Wyoming.

To personal experiences in the region I owe my first and lasting interest in the subjects here discussed; to friendly help and co-operation of many persons and institutions I owe a debt of gratitude for placing materials at my disposal for the preparation of this book. The manuscripts and printed materials, which, in the final analysis, comprise the most essential sources for this history, were widely scattered. The collections of greatest quality and quantity were found in the Bancroft Library of Western History at the University of California; the Henry E. Huntington Library at San Marino, California; the Archives of the Oregon Historical Society Library, Portland, Oregon; the Oregon Collection at the University of Oregon Library; the Northwest Collection at the University of Washington Library; the Stanford University Library; the Library of Congress; the Robert S. Ellison Collection, Indiana University Library; the Montana Historical Society at Helena; the Archives of British Columbia at Victoria, B.C.; and the Economics Records Library at Reed College, Portland. Helpful materials were also gathered from the William Robertson Coe Collection, Yale University; the University of Montana Library, Missoula; the Library of Oregon State College, Corvallis; the California State Library, Sacramento; the Portland Public Library; Division of Archives, Ottawa; the Seattle Public Library; Hudson's Bay House, London; the private collection of Donald Bates in the Board of Trade Building at Portland; the files of the *Portland Oregonian* at the office of this newspaper; the files of the *Ashland Tidings* in the office of this newspaper (other newspaper files were used in various libraries); the files of the Federal Writers' Project at Portland; Los Angeles Public Library; New York City Library; and the Indiana State Library at Indianapolis. To the personnel of these many institutions I am deeply indebted for their making materials readily available, and for their many courtesies.

I am indebted for help and encouragement to Professor Walter G. Barnes and the late Professor Robert C. Clark while at the University of Oregon, and Professor Edgar E. Robinson, Stanford University. The late Judge F. W. Howay, historian of British Columbia, and Dean Harold W. Bradley, Claremont Colleges, kindly read and offered criticisms on chapter ii; Miss A. M. Johnson, Hudson's Bay Company, London, chapter iv; Professor Walter N. Sage, University of British Columbia, chapter v. I am also appreciative of courtesies extended me by Mr. Leveson Gower at the Hudson's Bay Company headquarters, London. My brother Sophus kindly read the manuscript for style. Frances Hathaway Hyde, research assistant, and Wanda Kotschek Wilson, graduate assistant, rendered valuable help. Nellie Pipes McArthur, formerly at the Oregon Historical Society, Miss Madge Wolfenden, acting archivist of the British Columbia Archives, Mrs. Edna M. Parratt (formerly of the Bancroft Library), Miss Mary Isabel Fry of the Huntington Library, and Ronald Todd, librarian of the Northwest Collection at the University of Washington, were among those who were helpful in my search for materials. I am, moreover, under continued obligation to the Indiana University Library staff, and especially to Dr. Robert A. Miller, director; Dr. Cecil K. Byrd, assistant director; Miss Geneva Warner, curator of special collections; and Miss Kathryn Troxel, cataloguer of special collections. Not only were libraries and historical societies generous in offering use of their illustrations, but so too were Mr. Donald Bates, Portland, and Bernice Band, Sacramento. Miss Frances Krauskopf kindly assisted in compiling the index. Lastly, I am grateful to Mary, my wife, who was my companion on the many jaunts West, my best critic, and my high chief typist.

The out-of-state research was necessarily done during summers over a period of ten years. The costs involved for both research and publication could not have been met without the generous subventions, which included grants-in-aid from the Social Science Research Council made directly by the Council and also through a Stanford University local committee, a grant-in-aid from the Henry E. Huntington Library, Indiana University faculty research fellowships, and other research grants from Indiana University and the Indiana University Foundation.

Some of the subjects and materials included herewith have already been used for published articles in *The Oregon Historical Quarterly*, *The Pacific Northwest Quarterly*, and *The Pacific Historical Review*. And inasmuch as trade (notably fur trade) and transportation are a part of the general history of the Pacific Northwest, I incorporated such portions as seemed appropriate into my book, *The Great Northwest*, published in 1947 by Alfred A. Knopf, Inc. In the latter case it is hoped that the more extended and detailed treatment here, with accompanying documentation, will be of added value to the readers. Permission from the editors of the periodicals mentioned above and from Mr. Alfred A. Knopf to make use of such materials is gratefully acknowledged.

OSCAR OSBURN WINTHER

BLOOMINGTON, INDIANA
October 1, 1949

TABLE OF CONTENTS

PART FOUR. THE MONOPOLY ERA

BIBLIOGRAPHY

INDEX

LIST OF ILLUSTRATIONS

LIST OF MAPS

PART ONE

THE FUR TRADE

CHAPTER I

PRIMITIVE OLD OREGON

Three centuries of bounding activity in the new world failed to lift a veil of ignorance surrounding the region known as the old Oregon country. To the average man of President Washington's day this land mass bordering on the North Pacific was simply some more of the great, mysterious Western wilderness. And to explorers and learned geographers Oregon simply meant a sprawling area of unexplored land sandwiched in between the Czar's Russian America and Spain's newly founded Alta California. By the time of American independence sailors of many nationalities had become intimately acquainted with most points, harbors, and coves along nearly all North American shores, but some of them were just in the process of finding out something about that foggy, rocky coast of a region to which various spellings of the name Oregon were applied.[1]

Absence of accurate knowledge about the old Oregon country during the three centuries separating Christopher Columbus and President Washington does not mean there had been no intervening contact with the region. There is evidence that during these first years of Pacific Ocean navigation Spanish galleons were blown ashore on the Oregon coast, their crews meeting disaster upon jagged rocks that then, as now, lined the water's edge and stood like sentinels guarding the mountain walls that stretched with so few good harbors from icy Russian America to sunny Spanish Alta California.[2] But if the facts on such inadvertent contacts remain obscure, there are numerous early Spanish voyages that come within the range of definitely recorded history. In 1603, for instance, Martín de Aguilar, Spanish pilot of the Vizcaino expedition, passed and noted Cape Blanco on the forty-third parallel north latitude. It was not, however, until the final quarter of the eighteenth century that interest in the North Pacific had widened to the point that ships of many nationalities, including Spanish, came to this remote part of the world with exploration and trade motives. The Spaniards Juan Perez and Bruno Heceta, the Englishmen James Cook, John Meares, Charles Barkley, George Vancouver, Peter Puget, and others made many dis-

---

[1] Charles H. Carey, *A General History of Oregon* (Portland, 1935), I, 8–16. According to Carey, the name "Oregon," or anything approximating that spelling, did not appear on any known map until Major Rogers first used the word in 1765. Among early-day spellings were Ouragan, Ourigan, Origan, and Oragan.

[2] J. Neilson Barry, "Spaniards in Early Oregon," *The Washington Historical Quarterly*, XXIII (January 1932), 25–28.

coveries, gave names to numerous places along the coast, and in other ways became familiarly associated with this untamed country during the climactic years that either immediately preceded or were contemporaneous with the discovery (or perhaps rediscovery) of the Columbia River by the American Robert Gray in 1792.[3]

It would appear that the data collected during these three long centuries are considerable, but the amazing fact remains that by 1792 the maps purporting to represent the coastline of present-day Oregon, Washington, and British Columbia were amazingly inaccurate. Some of these show the nonexistent Strait of Anían, or the Northwest Passage; others indicate imaginary inlets such as "Mere de l'Ouest" and "Entrance de Martín d'Aguilar"; while still others reveal the as yet unentered Columbia bearing such varying names as "River of the West," "Rio de Aguilar," "Rio de los Estrechos," and "Ensenada de Heceta."[4]

What of the vast interior of the Oregon country? Spanish *conquistadores* had penetrated far north into the Mississippi Valley and into the southern Rocky Mountains. Swarthy-complexioned Spanish *pobladores* and Franciscan padres had founded their ranchos, pueblos, and missions as far north as the Sacramento Valley in Alta California, and a presidio had been established at San Francisco Bay. But for all their amazing energy, these far-ranging, landlubbing, as well as seagoing, Spaniards fell short of planting the flag of His Most Catholic Majesty over the great expanses of the Oregon country.[5] Likewise, before 1792, the Russians, pushing eastward across Siberia and into North America (Alaska), failed to reach Oregon's mountainous terrain.[6] So too did the French in their steady cross-Canadian marches into the Western wilds.[7] The Verendryes reached a point in 1743 now known as Pierre, South Dakota,[8] but there is no evidence that they, as subjects of the French government, ever crossed the Continental Divide. As for the British, it was not until 1793, one year following Gray's entrance of the Columbia River, that courageous Alexander Mackenzie, a Scot under British authority, was the first to thread his way across the continent, reaching the Pacific

[3] Henry R. Wagner, *Spanish Voyages to the Northwest Coast of America in the Sixteenth Century* (San Francisco, 1929), entire; Robert Carlton Clark, *History of the Willamette Valley* (Chicago, 1927), pp. 70–87; F. W. Howay, ed., "The Spanish Settlement at Nootka," *The Washington Historical Quarterly*, VIII (July 1917), 163–71.

[4] Charles H. Carey, "Some Early Maps and Myths," *The Oregon Historical Quarterly*, XXX (March 1929), 14–32.

[5] Herbert Eugene Bolton, *Outpost of Empire* (New York, 1939), pp. 11–19; Charles E. Chapman, *A History of California: The Spanish Period* (New York, 1936), pp. 383–97.

[6] F. A. Golder, *Russian Expansion on the Pacific, 1641–1850* (Cleveland, 1914), chap. 9.

[7] The full story of British western advance will be told in the pages following.

[8] Lawrence J. Burpee, ed., *Journals and Letters of Pierre Gaultier de Varennes de la Vérendrye and His Sons* (Toronto, 1927), p. 17.

shore at the mouth of Bella Coola River in present British Columbia.[9] But while Mackenzie had made this significant first crossing, it remained for other English subjects, notably David Thompson (1800–1811) and Simon Fraser (1805–1809) to develop practical east-west pathways to the Columbia and Fraser river basins.[10]

Meanwhile the Americans contributed their bit toward lifting this veil of mystery when, during 1803–1806, Captains Meriwether Lewis and William Clark likewise crossed the Continental Divide via the head-waters of the Missouri River and Clark's Fork and trudged their way down the Columbia River to its mouth, spent a winter at what is now Seaside, Oregon, and then went back to St. Louis from which place they had come. Successful as was the Lewis and Clark Expedition, it remained for the fur traders, whom the two American captains did much to encourage, to find what became the greatest and most practical and popular of all the routes to the West—the Oregon Trail.[11]

No amount of overland exploration could minimize the cold fact that the Oregon country was sadly isolated by sea and land from the settled portions of North America, and from the world at large. To reach the Oregon country by sea from any point of settlement was tedious and dangerous, and three to six months (depending upon the mode of travel) were involved in passage over either the Canadian or the American trails. The overland trails were also dangerous. They led across parched plains and deserts, across broad and swift-flowing rivers, into tangled forests, and over treacherous mountain passes that rose from three to eight thousand feet above the level of the sea.

Popular interest in the Oregon country followed discovery and exploration, and it was intensified as information (both reliable and unreliable) on the region's resources and climate became more widely circularized. What had been a moderate inquisitiveness immediately following the Lewis and Clark Expedition emerged into feverlike excitement during the decade of the 1840's. Among the first publications to stir interest in Oregon was Patrick Gass's *A Journal of the Voyages and Travels of a Corps of Discovery* (Pittsburgh, 1807) which was followed by the publication of the official records of the Lewis and Clark Expedition seven years later. Protestant missionary circles were in-

[9] Alexander Mackenzie, *Voyages From Montreal, on the River St. Laurence, Through the Continent of North America* (London, 1801), entire. See also Lawrence J. Burpee, *The Search for the Western Sea* (New York, 1936), II, 415–49.

[10] J. B. Tyrrell, ed., *David Thompson's Narrative of His Explorations in Western America, 1784–1812* (Toronto, 1916), Part II. Hereafter cited as *David Thompson's Narrative.* See also Burpee, *The Search for the Western Sea,* II, 536–66.

[11] T. C. Elliott, "The Earliest Travelers on the Oregon Trail," *The Quarterly of the Oregon Historical Society,* XIII (March 1912), 71–84.

formed of the region through the columns of its newspapers: Boston's *Missionary Herald* and *Zion's Herald*, and New York's *Christian Advocate and Journal*.

Beginning about 1830 the general literate public found available to it an ever increasing number of published narratives. One of the first publications that received wide notice was Hall J. Kelley's *A Geographical Sketch of that Part of North America, Called Oregon* (Boston, 1830), Kelley having admittedly prepared his sketch "for the benefit of the friends to the *Oregon Colonization Society.*" He described the country (though he had not been there) as one where the mountains are "peculiarly conspicuous and sublime," where the climate is "salubrious," and where the country is "better furnished with natural facilities for the application of labour." He pointed out how much more valuable for settlement was the Oregon country than, say, the Floridas, New Orleans, and much of Texas. Kelley urged people to go to Oregon and he stressed the point that "The settlement of the Oregon country, would conduce to a freer intercourse, and a more extensive and lucrative trade with the East Indies." "Commerce," he added, "would break away from its present narrow and prescribed limits, and spread into new and broader channels, embracing within its scope China, Corea, the Philippine, and Spice islands, Japan and its provinces." Kelley concluded his observations by stressing that settlers going to Oregon would find an American republic ready to "protect and cherish" them and "thus enlarge the sphere of human felicity, and extend the peculiar blessings of civil polity, and of the Christian religion, to distant and destitute nations."[12] Kelley continued his one-man educational program. A second edition of his *Geographical Sketch* appeared in Boston, 1831, and that same year Kelley also produced *A General Circular to All Persons of Good Character, Who Wish to Emigrate to the Oregon Territory* (Charlestown, 1831). Other booklets and circulars were to follow.[13]

The pioneer advocate of Oregon in the Congress of the United States was Dr. John Floyd, representative from a western Virginia district. He entered Congress in 1817 and three years later he introduced a resolution in that body which called attention to the rights of the American government in the valley of the Columbia River. Discounting the failure of John Jacob Astor, he called attention to great profits to be made from the fur trade; he reminded his listeners of Oregon's rich timber resources; and, long before Portland was born, he prophesied loudly and vocifer-

---

[12] Hall J. Kelley, *A Geographical Sketch of that Part of North America, Called Oregon* (Boston, 1830), pp. 3, 17–19, 79–80.

[13] F. W. Powell, "Bibliography of Hall J. Kelley," *The Quarterly of the Oregon Historical Society*, VIII (December 1907), 375–86.

ously that a city would emerge at or near the mouth of the Columbia which would some day become a world mart, if not a modern Tyre. Dr. Floyd failed at this early date to stir Congress to action such as was to come a quarter of a century later, but to him goes the credit for having aroused Washington officialdom to an interest in the Oregon country, and for being the first to propose actual occupation of the Columbia River Basin.[14]

In 1836 Washington Irving's facile pen produced the two-volume work *Astoria*, which found a wide reading audience; whereas such publications as Alphonso Wetmore's *Gazetteer* (1837), Samuel Parker's *Journal of an Exploring Tour Beyond the Rocky Mountains* (1838), and Zenas Leonard's *Narrative* (1839) made it clear, as Archer B. Hulbert expressed it, "that the American public acquired in 1830–40 a goodly fund of information concerning the West."[15]

Among the first during the decade of the "Fabulous Forties" to describe and to perpetuate interest in Oregon and the West was John C. Frémont. Frémont's writings, though of not unquestioned accuracy and purpose, enjoyed wide popularity. Moreover, newspapers and magazines in both England and America repeatedly carried sensational copy on Oregon; and with the great annual migration over the Trail, beginning in 1841, the name "Oregon" came to be spoken by nearly every American man, woman, and child in the United States.[16] To most Americans Oregon, by the 1840's, was manifestly destined to become a possession of the United States. "Their ploughs turn its sods, their axes level its timber," wrote *Hunt's Merchants' Magazine* in 1846 about those who had gone to the Willamette Valley, and "No power on earth, nor all the powers of the earth, can check the swelling tide of the American population. . . . ."[17]

If in Washington's day the Oregon country had been a vague geographical expression, it had become, by the time of President James K. Polk, an area with well-understood dimensions, physiognomy, character, and spirit. To interested nations the Oregon country was definitely that region west of the Continental Divide, north of the forty-second degree north parallel, and south of the now historic fifty-four forty. Expressed in political terms this region embraced present-day Oregon, Washington, Idaho, that part of British Columbia lying west of the Divide, and western portions of Montana and Wyoming. This is an area one-fifth

---

[14] Charles H. Ambler, "The Oregon Country, 1810–1830: A Chapter in Territorial Expansion," *The Mississippi Valley Historical Review*, XXX (June 1943), 7–24.

[15] Archer Butler Hulbert and Dorothy Printup Hulbert, eds., *The Oregon Crusade* (Denver, 1935), V, xiii–xvi.

[16] Allan Nevins, *Frémont: Pathmarker of the West* (New York, 1939).

[17] *Hunt's Merchants' Magazine*, XIV (May 1846), 436.

the size of the present continental United States. It had become recognized for what it is: a land and water mass rich and amazingly varied in its geological formations, topography, soil, climate, and resources. Boxed in, as it were, by towering mountains and sea, its five hundred thousand square miles of surface are further segmented by low-lying but rugged ranges, most significant of which are the Cascades that stretch, unbroken except by the Columbia River gorge, from California into British Columbia. West of this range above which rise majestic, snow-capped, volcanic peaks, the ocean winds bring abundant moisture (in some parts as much as twelve feet annually) to the Willamette-Puget trough and Umpqua, Rogue, and other valleys that are snugly hidden among the green, forest-carpeted mountains. The eastern portion of the Oregon country contrasts with that of the western. It is a country of arid and semiarid plateaus broken by numerous mountain spurs that seemingly buttress the Cascade and Rocky Mountain ranges.

Far to the north in what was once New Caledonia are found still more rugged uplands, two ranges which form, as one writer puts it, a "rampart to the east and to the west," and it is from there that the Fraser and other torrential streams carry the drainage to the sea.

Reaching fingerlike far into present-day British Columbia and linking together, as it were, the three main segments of the old Oregon country, is the mighty Columbia River (the great "River of the West") about which there had been such speculation for centuries, the river on whose greenish, swiftly flowing waters so much of that region's livelihood has and always will depend.

Scattered throughout the Pacific Northwest on the eve of white intrusion were an estimated 180,000 Indians grouped into about 125 tribes. The character and habits of these aborigines were conditioned in no small measure by the varied climate and by the physical terrain in which particular groups found themselves. The coastal Indians were most numerous, had the richest culture, and were very sedentary in their ways of life. They were relatively fixed in their living habits, and had an aristocratic society supported in part by slavery and by a money economy. By comparison, the natives living east of the Cascades—the Plateau Indians—were more itinerant. To these had come during the eighteenth century the horse; consequently, with added means of getting about, the incentive to roam received further impetus. The Plateau Indians were influenced greatly by coastal tribes, but the culture pattern of the inland groups was relatively simple. Simple too was the culture pattern of the Great Basin peoples, some of whom were found in the Oregon country.

The Great Basin tribes also fell heir to the horse which greatly increased their range of activity.[18]

Whether settled or shifting, whatever their culture patterns, the Indians must be regarded as the first traders, trappers, hunters, and travelers in the Pacific Northwest. Each tribe had its own economy, but it was interrelated with other tribes, and without exception some trading and traveling was a part of everyday life. The red men kept no written narratives of their workaday existence before the arrival of their white brethren, and it is to the anthropologists and the earliest white visitors that one must turn for information regarding the lives of Oregon's first inhabitants.

The Indians dwelling on the North Pacific Coast relied very heavily upon fish and shell foods for their permanent livelihood. To a limited degree this was also true of inland groups (they made extensive use of salmon), although to them meat, grasshoppers, camas, berries, pine nuts, and roots were staple foods. For the Coast Indians the fishhook, spear, sieve, scoop net, and dugout were essential equipment; for the Plateau and Basin, the bow and arrow, the knife, and snare were the weapons and devices most indispensable. The Coast Indians preferred to live in simple, but often sturdy, well-constructed rectangular plank houses; those of the Plateau favored the conical, skin huts as a place in which to live; those of the Basin region a domed, mat-covered structure.

Everywhere there is evidence of linguistic and material culture diffusion, and this may be taken as partial evidence that communication had long existed among the tribes of the Pacific Northwest. For instance, in the making of their beautiful checkered, twilled, and coiled baskets, the raw materials (if not the designs) were often imported from sources outside the area. If not absolutely dependent upon each other's produce, it is apparent that the Indians found some trade in goods both desirable and enjoyable.[19] Barter among neighboring tribes was a daily affair, but the exchange of goods between the natives of one region with those of another was usually done during specified seasons and at designated places. The autumn was a favorite time for many tribes to come together, and choice places along the Columbia River for such rendezvous were the Cascades, the Dalles (the site of the present city of The Dalles), Celilo Falls, and Kettle Falls. Yakima and Sprague river valleys and numer-

---

[18] Oscar Osburn Winther, *The Great Northwest* (New York, 1947), chap. 1; Pliny Earle Goddard, *Indians of the Northwest Coast* (New York, 1924), p. 25; Harry Turney-High, "The Diffusion of the Horse to the Flatheads," *Man*, XXXV (December 1935), 184; Joel V. Berreman, "Tribal Distribution in Oregon," *American Anthropological Supplement*, XXX (1937), 7–8; Cora Du Bois, *The Feather Cult of the Middle Columbia* (Menasha, Wisconsin, 1938), p. 17.

[19] Otis T. Mason, "Aboriginal American Basketry," *Annual Report of the Smithsonian Institution, 1902* (Washington, D.C., 1904), pp. 220, 440.

ous other places scattered throughout the region could be added to the list of traditional trading spots.

Taking for a time reference the eve of the Lewis and Clark Expedition, one then would have observed large numbers of friendly natives from the upper Columbia coming annually to Celilo Falls and to the Dalles. They usually gathered on the right bank of the great river to avoid their enemy, the Snake Indians. They brought with them the horse, their latest and most highly coveted acquisition.[20] Brought in on the backs of horses, but likely, too, on the backs of women, were quantities of wild flax, camas, flints, horns, and skins of assorted varieties.

From below the Dalles there also came to these trading places large numbers of Chinookans whose pouches were well filled with *higua*, or shells, used as money. *Higua* commanded a high return in terms of goods. Alexander Ross, clerk and historian at Fort Astoria, makes the statement that he once saw a new gun offered for six such shells, and refused. In addition, the Chinookans brought with them bits of iron and copper acquired from shipwrecks along the Oregon coast.[21] Processed fish, such as dried smelt, salmon, and sturgeon, were also among goods offered for trade by the Chinookans.

Unless the year had proved a failure, salmon was usually available to the upper as well as the lower Columbia River inhabitants, and unlike any other fish, pink salmon meat was for most Indians a principal food. For this reason the salmon was held in reverence. Rituals were observed regarding its use, taboos surrounded it, and its place in mythology was an important one.[22] Fishing for salmon could also be done at Celilo Falls, and since these fisheries belonged to the Wasco Indians, the selling of permits was in itself a factor in the trade. Women at the rendezvous could be seen busily engaged in processing the salmon into pemmican. First the meat was dried, then pulverized by being pounded between stones.[23] Unsalted, the pemmican was placed in baskets lined with salmon skins, pressed, tied, again wrapped, and corded. Each package weighed about ten pounds. So ingeniously were these processes performed that whoever bought the product would have found the contents well preserved and tasty several years later.

Smelt were usually laid side by side in varying numbers (heads and

[20] Leslie Spier, ed., *The Sinkaietk or Southern Okanagon of Washington* (Menasha, Wisconsin, 1938), p. 74. Before the horse, trade followed water routes more rigidly. The horse simplified cross-country travel and stimulated overland trade.

[21] T. A. Rickard, "The Use of Iron and Copper by the Indians of British Columbia," *The British Columbia Historical Quarterly*, III (January 1939), 48.

[22] Erna Gunther, "An Analysis of the First Salmon Ceremony," *American Anthropologist*, n.s., XXVIII (October–December 1926), 605, 617.

[23] Not to be confused with pemmican of the plains which was generally made from dried buffalo meat.

tails alternating), fastened together by a thread, and then dried and smoked. In this form they were much in demand, and found their way into the remotest corners of the country.

Conspicuously present at the Columbia River rendezvous were the Nez Percés and Cayuse Indians. These were well known as hunters, and they and other tribes from near the Rocky Mountains brought dried horse, bear, buffalo, and deer meats (venison), skins from these same animals, various kinds of grasses used in basketry, and also horses on the hoof. The Klikitats were famous weapon makers, and their handiwork, offered in trade, also was much in demand.[24]

To the valley of the lower Sprague River and along the shore of Upper Klamath Lake came each October the neighboring Klamath, Shasta, Modoc, and Pit Indians;[25] from greater distances came the Warm Springs and the Snakes. On the lake shore, and within sight of conical Mount Pit,[26] bartering festivities were engaged in with great intensity.

Trade among these Indians was often accompanied by a good deal of carousing and gaiety. As such the natives were not unlike the white traders whose predilection for play and carousing at their own Rocky Mountain rendezvous is well known. Dancing, gambling, horse racing, and stealing were all a part of this annual fair. "Wait a moment," wrote an old Oregon pioneer, "and you will see some desperate gambler bring up his last stake, hoping to retrieve his losses—a beautiful captive woman, perhaps, taken in some hostile raid, intended for his private harem, but to win his horses back he pledges this squaw."[27]

Elsewhere within the old Oregon country there were similar trading festivities. A great variety of goods changed hands; always foods, especially fish, dried meats, and *wappatoo* (a potatolike root) were offered for trade. So too were weapons used in the hunt and in war. In the conduct of trade, either at the rendezvous or in everyday dealings, or later when the white men came, Indians were accomplished traders. They were keen, shrewd, and cunning. Meriwether Lewis, who wrote from firsthand observations, told how, for instance, bartering was done among the Clatsops. "They begin by asking double or treble the value of their merchandise, and lower the demand in proportion to the ardor

---

[24] Alexander Ross, *Adventures of the First Settlers on the Oregon or Columbia River* (London, 1849), pp. 94–96. Hereafter cited as Ross, *Adventures*. See also Mason, *op. cit.*, p. 440; S. A. Clarke, *Pioneer Days of Oregon History* (Portland, 1905), I, 110, 123–25; Elliott Coues, ed., *History of the Expedition Under the Command of Lewis and Clark* (New York, 1893), II, 785–90. Hereafter cited as *Lewis and Clark Journals*.

[25] Modoc, Shasta, and Pit Indians were from northern California.

[26] Later called Mount McLoughlin in honor of Dr. John McLoughlin, Chief Factor for the Hudson's Bay Company in the Columbia District.

[27] Clarke, *Pioneer Days of Oregon History*, I, 121.

or experience in trade of the purchaser; if he expresses any anxiety, the smallest article, perhaps a handful of roots, will furnish a whole morning's negotiation."[28]

In trade women played a conspicuous role. Slaves did the drudging labor, but wives and daughters prepared most items for sale or barter. And since virtue among the latter was not priceless, their female charms, or what passed for such, were also marketable, though at no exorbitant price. Even a chief would boast of obtaining a "paltry toy or trifle in return for the prostitution of his virgin daughter," wrote Alexander Ross.[29] Lewis characterized a Chinook or Clatsop "beauty" as "one of the most disgusting objects in nature," yet they, and in fact most other Indian females, "solicit the favors" with approbation. Though "ill-shaped" and breastfallen, such persons, he wrote, were as likely as not to be "the medium of trade, the return for presents, and the reward for services." Among all the tribes, wrote Lewis, "a man will lend his wife or daughter for a fish-hook or a strand of beads"; and to refuse the offer was regarded as a great offense both to the one who made the offer and to the female as well.[30]

Historically, at least, the many Indian tribes inhabiting the Puget Sound area were in a class by themselves. These rather strong, squat, broad-faced, seminaked natives of present western Washington, together with the Nootkas farther north, were the first to come into active contact with the white sea-otter traders whose ships began assiduously to comb the North Pacific waters during the closing years of the eighteenth century. Like the Chinookans of the Columbia River area, Puget Sound Indians placed much reliance upon fish as a food, although roots and wild game were to them desirable supplements. Spears, bows, and arrows were their weapons in warfare and in the hunt, and they relied heavily upon dugout canoes as a means of travel. Blankets woven of dog hair added much to their comfort during the winter months, but the blankets, as well as the long white shells obtained off Cape Flattery, came to be regarded generally as standard units of value in their inter-tribal trade.[31]

Puget Sound Indians were particularly fond of potlatches. At these festive get-togethers a great quantity and variety of edible and non-edible goods changed hands, although in no commercial sense. On such

---

[28] *Lewis and Clark Journals*, II, 785, 787.   [29] Ross, *Adventures*, pp. 92–93.

[30] *Lewis and Clark Journals*, II, 778–79.

[31] Goddard, *Indians of the Northwest Coast*, pp. 58–59, 68. North of Puget Sound, whale was widely used as a food. [Edward Bell], "H.M.S. *Chatham* Journal, 1792." Transcript of MS, Archives of British Columbia, Victoria, B.C., p. 65. R. L. Olson, "Adze, Canoe, and House Types of the Northwest Coast," *University of Washington Publications in Anthropology* (Seattle, 1929), II, 1–38.

occasions there was much display of riches and of liberality. In an effort to outdo in generosity any of his guests, a chief often gave away slaves, canoes, clothing, skins, and foods. Such giving away was a measure of a man's wealth, although in reality the giver expected as much or more in return when it was his privilege to be guest.[32]

The North Pacific coastal Indians were in the habit of enslaving their captives. Accordingly, slaves were regarded as property and they became popular offerings in trade.[33]

It was with the Nootka Indians that Captain Cook established contact when on his famous third voyage which took him into North Pacific waters. Cook was soon followed by others whose favorite trading spot was on Nootka Sound in Vancouver Island. Like their southern neighbors, the Nootkas were comparatively short and plump. And like a good many of the coastal Indians who spent so much of their lives in cramped positions in canoes, they tended to have malformed legs, feet, and ankles. Their faces were flat, eyes small and dark, and their hair was long and black or dark brown in color.

The sturdy rectangular plank houses in which the Nootkas dwelt were none too warm in winter, and for articles of dress the inhabitants relied strongly on blankets. At first these were of native manufacture, but later of white importation. Among the Nootkas salmon and herring were staple articles, and whales were hunted for food whenever they made an appearance in home waters, as they frequently did during the months of May or June. In these more northerly waters were also found the sea otters. These the Nootkas hunted by means of canoes and harpoons, the heads of which consisted of barbed bones. Sea-otter skins, some fish, and *olachen* oil the Nootkas offered in trade. *Olachen* was an oil taken from small candlefish caught by net during March and April. It was a favorite cooking oil because it could be kept without spoiling, and for this reason was much in demand locally and by outside tribes. It was shown partiality at potlatches. Many of the trails across Vancouver Island, and others extending northward on the mainland and along the Bella Coola River (the latter followed by Mackenzie), were known as grease trails because they were the paths over which *olachen* oil passed to the interior.[34] In short, trade in the old Oregon country began long before the white men came. The Indians were expert in the art of trade, and were not easily duped by their white brethren who expected much for very little.

[32] Goddard, *op. cit.*, pp. 132–33.

[33] H. H. Bancroft, *The Native Races* (San Francisco, 1883), I, 210–18; Goddard, *op. cit.*, pp. 25, 85; William C. MacLeod, "Economic Aspects of Indigenous American Slavery," *American Anthropologist*, n.s., XXX (October–December 1928), 638–49.

[34] Goddard, *op. cit.*, pp. 17, 68, 73.

CHAPTER II

A LINK IN THE CHINA TRADE

On the tangled network of natural waterways that form China's Pearl River Delta are situated the cities of Canton, Whampoa, Macao, and Hongkong. For centuries these cities have constituted a vital gateway to China's hinterland. During the eighteenth century Canton, ninety miles inland, was the best known and most important of the delta cities. As early as the third century B.C. it had been incorporated into the Chinese Empire, and at least intermittently had been a mecca for foreigners. Arabs had preceded the Europeans, and still earlier Parsee merchants traded in this colorful river port. Canton had been singled out somewhat because in an effort to reduce contacts with "foreign barbarians" to a minimum conservative Chinese had reluctantly designated this city as one open to outside trade. And because of the foreign character of the city, Canton was often referred to as the "Ulster of China."

Near the wharfs stood the factory, or post, of the famous British East India Company. To it the English government had granted a trade monopoly in the waters between the Cape of Good Hope and Cape Horn. On Factory Street, the longest of Canton's narrow thoroughfares, were located "factories" of numerous foreign nations. It was here, as well as on shipboard, that sea captains from the Occident carried on a brisk trade with the hong merchants of China. During the late eighteenth century British silver, secured in India from sale of home manufactures, and American ginseng, sandalwood, and furs were among the many items offered the Chinese in exchange for their tea, silk, and a great variety of other oriental goods.[1]

It was in connection with this same Chinese trade that the old Oregon country first became linked with the emerging trans-Pacific commerce. Among the foreign articles highly prized by the hong merchants of Canton were sea-otter skins, which, as it turned out, were first to be hunted in the waters off Vancouver Island, Alaska, and the Aleutians.

Operating under the flag of Russia, it was Vitus Bering and his men who discovered the commercial value of the large and beautiful sea-otter furs. And throughout the middle and late eighteenth century dar-

---

[1] James Cook and James King, *A Voyage to the Pacific Ocean* (London, 1784), III, 434. Volume III was written by Captain James King. See also Sir William Foster, *England's Quest of Eastern Trade* (London, 1933), pp. 324–25; Payson J. Treat, *The Far East* (New York, 1928), pp. 57–58; *Encyclopædia Britannica*, fourteenth edition (London, 1936), IV, 771–72.

ing Muscovite traders braved the fog-bound and treacherous waters of
the North Pacific in search of pelts.[2]

In the meantime there occurred Captain James Cook's visit to the
North Pacific. Cook had left England on his third and last voyage of discovery during the same month and year that the Americans declared
their independence. His explorations took him to the mid-Pacific where
on January 18, 1778, he discovered the Sandwich Islands.[3] From there
the Cook expedition sailed northeastward and during early March Cook's
ships *Resolution* and *Discovery* cast anchor at Nootka Sound on the west
coast of Vancouver Island.

While in these waters Cook's men took some sea-otter skins aboard
for which, much to their surprise, they found a good demand at Canton.
Wrote Captain James King:

The whole amount of the value, in *specie* and goods, that was got for the furs, in
both ships, I am confident, did not fall short of two thousand pounds sterling; and
it was generally supposed, that at least two-thirds of the quantity we had originally
got from the Americans, were spoiled and worn out, or had been given away . . . . .[4]

This discovery by Cook's men, that a sea-otter trade might well prove
highly profitable, in time caused other English shipmasters to depart
for the coasts of British Columbia and Alaska. The first of such trading
voyages was made in 1785 by Captain James Hanna with a crew of
twenty in the sixty-ton brig *Sea-Otter*.[5]

The year following Hanna's voyage witnessed the entrance of eight
English trading vessels in this new Pacific trade. Six of them returned
safely with cargoes totaling $100,000 in value. Two of these vessels
were outfitted at Bombay and sailed under the direction of Captain
James Strange. The journal and letters of Strange are added evidence
that he was engaged, as he phrased it, in a "lucrative branch of commerce."[6]

Among other English sea captains prominently identified with this
newborn trade was Captain Charles William Barkley, whose·ship, the
Imperial Eagle, in 1787 masqueraded under the Austrian flag. And

---

[2] Adele Ogden, *The California Sea Otter Trade* (Berkeley, 1941), chap. 1.

[3] The Sandwich, or Hawaiian, Islands, became important as a supply center in the trans-
Pacific trade. See Harold Whitman Bradley, *The American Frontier in Hawaii* (Stanford
University, 1942), chaps. 1–2, 5.

[4] Cook and King, *A Voyage to the Pacific Ocean*, III, 437. The publication of this book had
much to do with the spread of information concerning the sea-otter trade.

[5] A. Grove Day, "The Earliest Explorer-Traders of the Northwest Coast," *United States
Naval Institute Proceedings*, CLVII (December 1941), 1678; F. W. Howay, ed., "Letters Con-
cerning Voyages of British Vessels to the Northwest Coast of America, 1787–1809," *The Oregon
Historical Quarterly*, XXXIX (September 1938), 310.

[6] Day, *op. cit.*, pp. 1678–81; James Strange, "Narrative of a Voyage to the North West
Coast of America, 1786–1787." Transcript, Archives of British Columbia.

equally important was John Meares who arrived in North Pacific waters in 1788, only to become involved with the Spanish in a jurisdictional dispute over Nootka Sound. Numerous as the British traders were, those not sailing under the jurisdiction of either the East India Company or the South Sea Company were placed at a grave disadvantage in view of the monopolistic control exercised by those two powerful trading concerns. Rather than be regulated by the monopolies, many English shipmasters preferred to operate under foreign flags rather than under the British banner.[7]

Captain John Meares was regarded by some of his contemporaries as a liar and a thief, and some present-day historians place no great reliance upon his words. The fact remains that from the pen of Meares has come one of the most lucid accounts of how the mighty sea otter was caught by skilled native hunters, the killing of which was a far more hazardous operation than whaling. Meares wrote:

For this purpose, two very small canoes are prepared, in each of which are two expert hunters. The instruments they employ on this occasion are bows and arrows, and a small harpoon. . . . . Thus equipped, the hunters proceed among the rocks in search of their prey. Sometimes they surprise him sleeping on his back, on the surface of the water; and, if they can get near the animal without awakening him, which requires infinite precaution, he is easily harpooned and dragged to the boat, when a fierce battle very often ensues between the otter and the hunters, who are frequently wounded by the claws and teeth of the animal.

Most commonly, points out this annalist, the animal is pursued for hours. Under such conditions the strategy was to maneuver the canoes to a position where the otter might be caught swimming below the surface of the water. When this was accomplished the hunters stood in readiness with arrow and harpoon to shoot the very moment that the animal raised his head above the water. A most dangerous situation existed if the otter happened to be overtaken at a time when it was caring for its young. ". . . . the parental affection supersedes all sense of danger; and both the male and female defend their offspring with the most furious courage, tearing out the arrows and harpoons fixed in them with their teeth, and oftentimes even attacking the canoes." Catching the seal and sea cow was also tricky business, but less precarious. For this purpose the natives constructed decoys, "so exact a resemblance of nature, that the animal takes it for one of his own species." And then upon the approach of the deceived animal, the natives would let go a barrage of arrows from their hiding place.

In this manner, then, the prize fur-bearing animals were killed,

[7] F. W. Howay, "International Aspects of the Maritime Fur-Trade," *Proceedings of the Royal Society of Canada*, Third Series, XXXVI (1942), 62–63. The East India Company was entitled to supervise an English voyage, control the crews, and manage the sale of furs.

after which their skins soon found their way to the trading vessels where they were stowed away for eventual passage to China.[8]

While the English were thus pushing forward new frontiers of Pacific commerce, there was being born, on the western shores of the Atlantic, the United States of America. As British subjects the American colonists for generations had been skilled woodsmen and shipbuilders. They were, moreover, envied as seamen; and the pursuit of trade, particularly in New England, had always been an essential part of their workaday life. While under the British crown the Americans had endured many regulations of their trade, but they had also enjoyed important privileges and opportunities. When independence came the new United States found its commercial status greatly altered. No longer could the Americans share as Englishmen in the empire trade, and from then on they were obliged to look elsewhere for new markets. It was in the search for these new markets that many an adventurous sea-thinking merchant of Salem, Newport, Boston, New York, and Philadelphia turned his thoughts first toward the Orient and then in the direction of the North Pacific.

Scarcely was the ink dry on the Treaty of Paris when Robert Morris wrote to John Jay: "I am sending some ships to China." And on February 22, 1784, only eleven weeks after the last British warships cleared New York Harbor, the first American ship, the *Empress of China*, sailed out past Staten Island, squared her sails, and set her course for China. She was loaded with a cargo of ginseng, which is a medicinal root of dubious value.[9] The first appearance of the Stars and Stripes at Canton created no little excitement. French, Dutch, and Danish sea captains assisted in the mooring. Samuel Shaw, the American vessel's supercargo, was reputedly told by a British officer at Canton that the English regarded "the war to have been a mistake" and that they welcomed the American flag "to this part of the world." During May 1785, Shaw brought his vessel safely back to New York, its owners $30,000 the richer. They had made 25 percent on their investment over a period of fifteen months.[10]

Meanwhile Elias Hasket Derby of Salem ordered his ship, the *Grand Turk*, to follow in the wake of the *Empress of China*. From this

---

[8] John Meares, *Voyages Made in the Years 1788 and 1789, From China to the North West Coast of America* (London, 1790), pp. 260–61. Sea-otter hunting methods are also explained in Ogden, *op. cit.*, pp. 3–14.

[9] A yellowish root belonging to the sarsaparilla family. Americans at times received as much as ten dollars per pound for this root. And for ginseng bearing a fancied resemblance to human beings, superstitious Chinese would pay an added premium.

[10] Sydney Greenbie and Marjorie Barstow Greenbie, *Gold of Ophir: The China Trade in the Making of America* (New York, 1937), pp. 31–34. See also [New York City W.P.A. Writers' Project], *A Maritime History of New York* (New York, 1941), p. 79.

time forth the youthful American republic was headed toward what was to become a brisk and profitable trade with the Orient, a trade that increased in volume with each passing year. So extensive did this new trade become that during the year 1789 alone no less than fifteen American vessels are purported to have called at the port of Canton.[11]

It was amidst alert and bustling sea life such as this that attention became directed to the words and writings of a young Connecticut Yankee, John Ledyard. After but four months at Dartmouth College, where learning to be a missionary was not to his liking, this none too diligent Groton-born lad had taken to wandering, first among the Six Nations Indians, and then to sea. He reached London just when Captain Cook was making preparations for his third voyage around the world. And "nothing could more exactly accord with the native genius and cherished feelings of Ledyard," reflected his illustrious biographer, Jared Sparks, than "becoming connected with this expedition."[12] Cook hired Ledyard and made him corporal of marines in which capacity he sailed from London on July 12, 1776, around Good Hope to the Dutch East Indies, thence to New Zealand,[13] from which place the famous English explorer began his long cruise to the North Pacific. Captain Cook seemingly admired Ledyard and he is referred to in Cook and King, *Voyage*, as "an intelligent man, for the purpose of gaining information."

Like other members of Cook's crew, Ledyard had been impressed by the interest which Chinese merchants had shown in sea-otter skins brought in from the North Pacific. He returned to Huntington Bay, Long Island, aboard a British man-of-war at the close of 1782. The following year Ledyard published a journal supposedly based on his experiences, and then turned with bursting enthusiasm to his task of interesting American merchants in the great possibilities of the North Pacific–Chinese fur trade.[14] He urged the merchants not to sail eastward to China as they were doing, but westward! Previous experience with Cook had convinced Ledyard that profits might well be made from a voyage fitted out expressly for the North Pacific–China trade.[15]

[11] Samuel Eliot Morison, *The Maritime History of Massachusetts* (Boston, 1921), pp. 44–46; Arthur H. Clark, *The Clipper Ship Era* (New York, 1910), p. 120; George Granville Putnam, *Salem Vessels and Their Voyages* (Salem, Massachusetts, 1925), pp. 10–13, contains a representative manifest of shipments from Canton destined for the United States for 1790; Bradley, *The American Frontier in Hawaii*, pp. 13–14; "John Green," MS (in possession of Josephine Green Emmerich, Baltimore, Maryland).

[12] Jared Sparks, *Life of John Ledyard, the American Traveller* (Boston, 1847), pp. 49–50.

[13] Cook and King, *A Voyage to the Pacific Ocean*, I, 14 ff.

[14] John Ledyard, *A Journal of Captain Cook's Last Voyage to the Pacific Ocean and in Quest of a North-West Passage Between Asia & America* (Hartford, 1783).

[15] Sparks, *Ledyard*, pp. 172–74.

Ledyard found the Americans interested but not immediately willing to risk the ships and capital necessary for such an undertaking. But in time an announcement came from Boston that Joseph Barrell, Samuel Brown, and Charles Bulfinch, of Boston, Crowell Hatch from near-by Cambridge, the already familiar and wealthy John Derby, of Salem, and John M. Pintard, of New York City, had combined resources to enter the trans-Pacific fur trade. At a cost of $50,000 these gentlemen outfitted two vessels, the now historically famous *Columbia*, a fully rigged ship of 212 tons burden, and the sloop *Lady Washington*, of 90 tons.

Under command of John Kendrick and Robert Gray, respectively, the two vessels cleared Boston's harbor on September 30, 1787. In less than two weeks after the adjournment of the Constitutional Convention at Philadelphia there was inaugurated a new and fitting American adventure of great future significance. In a public lecture on the North Pacific fur trade years later, the renowned William Sturgis vividly recalled to his audience this "extraordinary undertaking," and he told that a medal commemorating the event had been struck off. On one side of the medal were engraved the words "Columbia" and "Washington," while on the reverse appeared the names of the merchant adventurers who financed this pioneering enterprise.[16]

A year elapsed before Kendrick and Gray arrived on the Pacific Coast, at which place the two captains traded vessels. Both ships were used in the fur trade; and while the course of the *Lady Washington* cannot be traced with certainty, it is believed that she, like the *Columbia*, reached Canton. Captain Gray resumed his westward course, and in 1790 returned to Boston with a cargo of partially damaged tea. His sturdy vessel was the first to carry the American banner around the world.[17]

Losses had been incurred in this first American venture into the fur trade, but with minor changes[18] the backers were determined to try again. This time Gray was to be in full command, and on September 28, 1790, the *Columbia* sailed from Boston, once again bound for the North Pacific. On board was a cargo worth $25,000; there were 2,000 bricks, 135 barrels of beef, 60 barrels of pork, 1,500 pounds of gunpowder, 5 hogsheads of New England and West Indian rum, and quantities of tea, sugar, chocolate, and miscellaneous items, much of it for the Indian trade, such as copper sheets, "Barr Iron," "Iron Hoops," "Chissells,"

---

[16] Frederic W. Howay, ed., *Voyage of the "Columbia" to the Northwest Coast, 1787–1790 and 1790–1793* (Boston, 1941), pp. vi–viii; [E. C. Cowdin and William Sturgis], "The Northwest Fur Trade," *Hunt's Merchants' Magazine*, XIV (June 1846), 534.

[17] Howay, *op. cit.*, p. xviii; Bradley, *The American Frontier in Hawaii*, p. 15.

[18] Derby and Pintard disposed of their shares to Gray and others.

"blue duffil," "scarlet coating," buttons by the gross, and scores of other things.[19]

The year 1791 was devoted to trade. Gray and his men wintered at Clayoquot Sound, Vancouver Island, during which time they built a sloop named the *Adventure*. From the logs and narratives of John Hoskins, Robert Haswell, and John Boit, all associated with this expedition, one learns much about this American adventure. In Haswell's Second Log, for example, one reads for 1792 what might well be an exaggeration: "The ship during the cruise had collected upwards of 700 sea otter skins and 15 thousand skins of various other species."[20]

Even though sea-otter skins were those singularly favored, it is noted in Hoskins' *Narrative*:

The skins are bears, wolves, foxes, rein, fallow and moose deers, land otters, raccoons, brown minks, martins, beavers, wild cats, grey rabbits, the large grey and small brown squirrels common in our country and mice. The fallow deer, wolves, (which are grey) raccoons, squirrels and martins are found in great abundance
. . . . .

So much for the land fur-bearing animals. Equally important were the amphibious seals and sea otters, for as Hoskins correctly asserts, it was the traffic in the latter that "induced us to visit this coast." Hoskins' *Narrative* contains this description of the sea otter:

. . . . this animal when young is of a dirty white with long course hair which being hauled out leaves a short chestnut coloured fur   its colours change through its natural gradation of life   as it grows older the fur grows thicker blacker and longer with less hair till it arrives at its maturity having the belly and head at this time of a yellowish white   after this as it still continues to grow older the longer hairs or fur are tipt with white until it becomes of a beautiful silver grey. . . . . this animal in shape much resembles the seal   it has a very good set of teeth which are remarkably white and much valued by the natives   the largest skin of this animal that I saw measured six feet two inches from the end of the nose to the tip of the tail . . . . .[21]

It was during the next spring, May 11, 1792, that Captain Gray brought the sturdy little *Columbia* across the bar of the "Great River of the West" which Gray named after his ship. Important as was Gray's discovery (if not discovery, then first exploration of the mouth of the Columbia), his job was to collect furs. Having secured his cargo, Gray again sailed on to China and on July 29, 1793, sea-conscious Boston witnessed the *Columbia* sailing into harbor.[22] "On her first voyage, the *Columbia* had solved the riddle of the China trade," reflects Samuel Morison; "On her second, empire followed in the wake."[23] In ever

[19] Howay, *op. cit.*, pp. 448–64.   [20] *Ibid.*, p. 337.
[21] *Ibid.*, pp. ix–x, 282–83.   [22] *Ibid.*, pp. ix–x.
[23] Morison, *The Maritime History of Massachusetts*, p. 51.

increasing numbers American windjammers, no larger than those commanded by Columbus three centuries before, braved the perilous waters at the Horn and, always at the mercy of the elements, plowed their way to the Oregon coast. The area in which they operated extended, in general, from the mouth of the Columbia to Cook's Inlet and out among the many islands that buttress the mainland.

Trade with the Indians was always carried on "alongside, or on board the ship, usually anchored near the shore," related Sturgis, who knew this business well. Because of the dangers involved, only the native chiefs and otherwise important Indian personages were at first admitted on board. Individual successes varied with the season and with the amount of competition, and for that reason the time occupied on the coast was from one to three years. But once the captain was satisfied, off he sailed to Canton and there exchanged his cargo "for the productions of the Celestial Empire, to be brought home or taken to Europe, thus," to use again the words of Sturgis, "completing what may be called *a trading voyage.*"

This, to be sure, was a labor of excitement, if not of love. Men thrilled at the sight of beautiful furs as they were taken aboard ship; and with a nostalgia for those good old days Sturgis later expressed the opinion that "excepting a beautiful woman and a lovely infant," he regarded the sea-otter skin as the most attractive object that could ever be placed before him.[24]

It would be pointless here to describe each and every venture in this trans-Pacific trade. It continued to increase until about 1805; thereafter a marked decline set in. During 1801–1802, for example, there were 15 vessels of all nationalities operating in the North Pacific, and no less than 15,000 sea-otter skins were collected. Returns on these operations naturally varied, but there are instances on record where $40,000 capital investment yielded $150,000 within the usual time allotted for such an undertaking, while still another investment of $50,000 gave a gross return of $284,000. By the turn of the century, however, sea-otter skins that once brought as much as $120 apiece sold in China for $20 apiece.[25]

---

[24] *Hunt's Merchants' Magazine*, XIV (June 1946), 533–34; Nathaniel Portlock, *A Voyage Round the World* (London, 1789), pp. 228–29.

[25] *Hunt's Merchants' Magazine*, XIV (June 1946), 537. The American, William Sturgis, who in 1804 traded in this area with a vessel owned by J. and Thomas Lamb, made a profit of $73,034.32 on this one venture. Sturgis did the novel thing of trading ermine skins for those of the sea otter. He also had with him about 650 gallons of New England rum which he used to good advantage in his trade with the natives. He may not have been the first to trade with liquor but it is believed no one had before him used it with such wholesale abandon. Later Sturgis made a sizable personal fortune out of the Northwest trade. See F. W. Howay, ed., "William Sturgis: The Northwest Fur Trade," *British Columbia Historical Quarterly*, VIII (January 1944), 11–12. See also J. F. G. De La Pérouse, *A Voyage Round the World* (London, 1799), II, 287–88.

At first the sea-otter trade was entirely British. But as noted, Americans entered the field in 1789, and within a decade had all but driven off their British competitors. Most of the American vessels were from Boston, and for the period after 1800 Boston had a virtual monopoly on the American North Pacific trade. To New Englanders this coastal fur trade became important because it provided a medium of exchange in Canton with which to buy Oriental goods for sale on the American, or home, market.[26] And when sea otters became scarce in the North Pacific, traders focused their attention upon California where, by special connivance with governmental officers, they could continue their operations along familiar lines.[27] What is most important in the history of the Pacific Northwest is that the sea-otter trade established this heretofore little-known hinterland as an important commercial link in the commerce of the world. Out of this sea-otter trade came, also, a shift in the claims to the sovereignty over the Oregon country. Russia's claims were extended to Alaska; those of Spain all but vanished; those of the United States and Great Britain became paramount, and disagreements arising therefrom were eventually settled by treaty in 1846.[28]

The final phase of the trans-Pacific sea-otter trade was brought on by the impact of the Napoleonic wars and the War of 1812. British men-of-war roamed the high seas, and ships of nationalities at war with England were not safe. British and Russian vessels, however, continued to operate in Pacific waters, and until 1812 American merchantmen were there also. Particularly active were the trading houses of J. and T. H. Perkins, J. and Thomas Lamb, Edward Dorr and Sons, Boardman and Pope, George W. Lyman, and such individual traders as Captains Jonathan and Nathan Winship, Joseph O'Cain, George Washington Eayrs, and others. Contact between the Pacific Northwest and Canton was retained, and increasing in importance were the Sandwich Islands and, in a surreptitious manner, the coastal towns of Alta California. News in 1812 of the outbreak of hostilities between the United States and England, however, dampened the spirits of Yankee traders, many of whom hastened to tie up in neutral ports to escape attacks by British fighting ships.[29]

The revival of trade in the Pacific which inevitably followed the re-

---

[26] Frederic W. Howay, "A List of Trading Vessels in Maritime Fur Trade, 1785–1794," *Transactions of the Royal Society of Canada*, Third Series, XXIV (May 1930), Sec. II, 111–12.

[27] Ogden, *The California Sea Otter Trade*, chaps. 5–6.

[28] Howay, "International Aspects of the Maritime Fur-Trade," p. 78.

[29] Bradley, *The American Frontier in Hawaii*, chaps. 1–2; Ogden, *The California Sea Otter Trade*, chaps. 2–5; Kenneth Wiggins Porter, *John Jacob Astor* (Cambridge, 1931), I, 129 ff.; Harold W. Bradley, "The Hawaiian Islands and the Pacific Fur Trade, 1785–1813," *The Pacific Northwest Quarterly*, XXX (July 1939), 283–85.

turn of peace in 1815 shifted the spotlight from the North Pacific Coast[30] to California and southwestward to the Sandwich Islands. California sea otters which before 1815 had escaped wholesale slaughter were thereafter hunted with greater intensity. The hides, horns, and tallow of the large and roaming California herds were in demand by Yankee traders in exchange for New England manufactures, and sandalwood from the mid-Pacific islands which previously had been frowned upon by the Chinese was to enjoy a brief but booming market in Canton.[31]

While these shifts transpired, there emerged from behind the scene in the old Oregon country a potentially great inland fur trade. For many years to come it was around this new and lucrative business that much of Oregon's history was to revolve.

---

[30] Recent evidence shows that the sea-otter trade also extended southward in the Oregon country from Vancouver Island to Gray's Harbor. See Victor B. Scheffer, "The Sea Otter on the Washington Coast," *The Pacific Northwest Quarterly*, XXXI (October 1940), 371–88.

[31] Howay, "International Aspects of the Maritime Fur-Trade," pp. 77–78.

CHAPTER III

THE NORTH WEST COMPANY

The historian Francis Parkman sets the scene: ". . . . if the wilderness of ocean had its treasures, so too had the wilderness of woods."[1] There it was, deep in the seemingly impenetrable forests of the New World, that the picturesque trader armed with gun, scalping knife, and trading truck wandered across hill and dale in search of pelts. In New France and in the colonies of the English, Dutch, and Swedes the rough, rugged and usually illiterate fur trader was constantly and prominently in the vanguard of frontier expansion. He often became an important tool in the hands of diplomats seeking to extend political boundaries, and his commercial activities often weighed heavily in bringing on bloody imperialistic conflicts that involved political control of the New World.

Important as was the fur trade throughout North America, it was in Canada both under French and British guidance that it reached its greatest scope and development. At first carried on in a haphazard manner, fur trade there very early came under large company management, a change readily explained by the fact that operations in the interior demanded a greater outlay of goods and equipment than could easily be provided by the average trader.[2] Also in New France the state very early assumed considerable direct supervision over fur-trading activities, whereas in the region of Hudson Bay the English Crown and Parliament very largely delegated their authority to those who actually managed the trade.[3]

The presence of both English and French companies in Canada naturally resulted in cutthroat competition and military strife that was ended only when the French were ousted from North America by the English in 1763. English political mastery of Canada quickly resulted in Anglo-Saxon domination of the fur trade. Capital and supplies shifted from Paris to London, and English businessmen were quick to expand their existing American operations both from Hudson Bay and the Hudson River in order to embrace the former French-Canadian West. Actual field operations were luckily continued by French Canadians who had perfected the trading techniques.[4]

---

[1] Francis Parkman, *Pioneers of France in the New World* (Boston, 1901), II, 52.

[2] Harold A. Innis, *The Fur Trade in Canada* (New Haven, 1930), chap. 2.

[3] "Charter of the Governor and Company of Adventurers of England Tradeing into Hudsons Bay," May 2, 1670. Photostat, Public Archives of Canada, Ottawa, Canada. Hereafter cited as "Hudson's Bay Company Charter."

[4] Innis, *The Fur Trade in Canada*, chap. 3.

To cope with the disrupting influences of the Seven Years' War powerful fur interests in the St. Lawrence Valley directed their attention to the Far West. The North West Company which they organized for this purpose probably began on a very informal basis in 1775, but by 1788 tangible agreements had been made. The Company, operating as a simple partnership, included in its organization such already well-known men as Benjamin and Joseph Frobisher and Simon McTavish, Peter Pond, Alexander Mackenzie, David Thompson, and Simon Fraser. Peter Pond, an explorer and trader during 1775–1778, was the first of the North West Company men to venture into the Lake Superior and Grand Portage region and to penetrate into northwestern Canada. "To Pond," writes his biographer, Harold Innis, "must be given the credit of being the first white man to cross the Portage la Loche and of discovering the Athabasca River and Lake Athabasca." The Company's significant development of the Athabasca district was directly based on the foundation laid by Pond.[5]

After Pond came the Scot, Alexander Mackenzie, also operating under the auspices of the North West Company. His extensive explorations in the Great Slave Lake region led him in 1789 to the Arctic mouth of the river now bearing his name. During 1792–1793, again under the direction of the Company, Mackenzie, with Alexander Mackay, six French Canadians, and two Indians, journeyed on from the Peace River to the Pacific Ocean. Thus Mackenzie became the first to lead a party across the North American continent, more than three centuries after its discovery. For this and other feats he was knighted by the King of England.

For several years the North West Company operated as a loose association of certain fur traders who agreed among themselves not to become connected with any other company, to establish at Montreal offices which would handle the importation of essential supplies from England, and to market such bales of fur as drifted in from Grand Portage. This post would serve as a field depot for the area west of the Hudson Bay watershed, a region the Company designed to pre-empt. For a time business ran smoothly, but in 1796, partly as a result of the Jay Treaty which called for British abandonment of Northwest posts, a rift occurred among the partners. So serious did the disagreements become that dissident elements withdrew to form, under the rebel leadership of Alexander Mackenzie, what has variously been called the New North West Company, Sir Alexander Mackenzie and Company, and, more popularly, the X Y Company.

---

[5] Gordon Charles Davidson, *The North West Company* (Berkeley, 1918), p. 15. Harold A. Innis in notes to author. Athabasca is also often spelled Athabaska.

Bitter and unrelenting rivalry grew out of this schism, as each group strove for supremacy. The loser, however, was neither contestant, but rather the impartial Indian on whom, during a two-year period, no less than 195,000 gallons of liquor were expended by the rivals in pursuance of the fur trade. Luckily for both whites and Indians, in 1804 the death of the obstreperous Simon McTavish made a reconciliation of contending factions possible. In 1821 the North West Company was merged with the Hudson's Bay Company to place under unified control the fur trade of half a continent.[6]

To relate the complete history of the North West Company would be to go beyond the province of the present study. Suffice it to say that its march was a westward one that led unhesitatingly in the direction of the Oregon country which lay beyond the Great Divide.[7] Scarcely had the imaginative and industrious Mackenzie reached the Pacific in 1793 when he conjured up grandiose schemes for the early establishment of an ocean-to-ocean overland trade and for the eventual merging of the great fur business of Canada into one gigantic whole. Before the lapse of a year Mackenzie's brilliant ideas had found favor in official circles and they were being relayed in a report by Lieutenant-Governor J. Graves Simcoe of Upper Canada to the Lords of the Committee of the Privy Council for Trade and Foreign Plantations in London:

The Traffic which may be carried on by this rout [overland to the Columbia], will undoubtedly strike your Lordships as a matter of great importance, but it appears from the observations of Mr. McKenzie who seems to be as intelligent as he is adventurous, That to carry on this Commerce to National Advantages, the privileges & rivalship, the claims & monopoly of great commercial Companies must be reconciled & blended in one common Interest.

Mackenzie was somewhat of a prophet, for within a quarter of a century his vision of overland trading routes and of unified management of the fur trade was to become a reality.

Moreover, Mackenzie foresaw, according to Simcoe, the necessity of establishing posts in the Pacific Northwest, at least one on "Cooke's [Columbia] River" and another at the southerly limit of the British claims which "would probably secure the whole Traffic."

Lieutenant-Governor Simcoe in this report to the Lords went even farther than Mackenzie in his dreams of a new empire. He foresaw

---

[6] [F. Wentzell or Roderick Mackenzie], "Sketch of the Indian Trade of Canada," (n. p. 1809), Photostat, Archives of British Columbia. Original in Royal Colonial Institute, London. Hereafter cited by title only. See also Davidson, *op. cit.*, pp. 73–80; W. Stewart Wallace, ed., *Documents Relating to the North West Company* (Toronto, 1934), pp. 143–57. Hereafter cited as *Documents Relating to the North West Company.*

[7] Harold A. Innis, *Peter Pond* (Toronto, 1930), chap. 4.

not only the extension of fur operations to the Pacific Coast, but the great governor even envisaged a tie-up of the Columbia River region with the already established trade of the empire. "The East India Company, who possess the Privilege of the Chinese Market," he wrote, "It is to be presumed, would find the Utility of these Establishments & he seems to apprehend the diminution of the Quantity of Silver sent by China in Consequence of the encrease of the Fur Trade would be a national advantage." Simcoe envisaged Canada as a mighty portage which stretched from Hudson Bay to the mouth of the Columbia River, and saw the necessity of tying together the British trade of Canada with that of the Far East. This, he declared, was a matter of "importance to Great Britain, as a maritime Power—& possibly, in the case of necessity, might be of consequence to the safety of Upper Canada."[8]

To Duncan McGillivray, nephew of the recalcitrant Simon McTavish and clerk of the North West Company, must go some credit for actually turning dreams into reality, and for pushing field operations farther toward the Pacific area. It was under his direction that Fort Augusta on the Sturgeon River in Alberta was established in 1795. It was he who four years later established Rocky Mountain House within the very view of the towering Rockies themselves. Thus was the way prepared for David Thompson who came to Rocky Mountain House from where in 1800 he and McGillivray began explorations that led directly to the establishment of North West Company posts in the upper reaches of the Columbia River.

Leaving Rocky Mountain House in the autumn of 1800 Thompson and McGillivray explored a route which took them to a point twenty miles east of Banff. From there they returned to their base of operation, and the following year the two men set forth in a different direction finally reaching a spot in the Rockies that satisfied them as to the existence of practical trading routes to the Pacific slope.[9]

Here matters rested until 1807 at which time the challenging news of the Lewis and Clark Expedition reached the British North West Company officials and stirred them to renewed action. Then it was that the meticulous David Thompson, still operating under instructions from McGillivray, journeyed farther westward. On this expedition Thompson

---

[8] J. Graves Simcoe to Lords of the Committee of the Privy Council for Trade & Foreign Plantations, September 1, 1795, *The Correspondence of Lieut. Governor John Graves Simcoe,* edited by E. A. Cruikshank (Toronto, 1925), III, 68–69.

[9] Arthur S. Morton, ed., *The Journal of Duncan M'Gillivray of the North West Company* (Toronto, 1929), *passim*; Arthur S. Morton, "The North West Company's Columbian Enterprise and David Thompson," *Canadian Historical Review,* XVII (September 1936), 271–73. It is the opinion of A. S. Morton that the Lewis and Clark Expedition had no direct influence upon David Thompson's Columbia River enterprise in 1807, although news of the American expedition reached the ears of the partners in 1805. See *ibid.,* p. 278.

went through what afterward was known as (Joseph) Howse Pass in the Rocky Mountains and located the headwaters of the Columbia and the North Saskatchewan rivers. And it was from this point that Thompson pioneered his way down upper Columbia and Kootenai (or Kootenay) rivers.

During the summer of 1807 David Thompson had begun construction on what became known as Kootenai House, located one mile below the outlet of Lake Windermere on the Columbia (at the mouth of Toby Creek) in what is now the southeastern part of British Columbia. This post has the distinction of being the first within the area drained by the great Columbia River. In the locality Thompson set up his thermometer and spent the winter. But in April of the following year (1808) he set out with canoes and reached the portage of the Kootenai River. He descended that stream, and on May 6 Thompson was at Kootenai Falls which are near the present town of Libby, Montana, to which place in October he sent his clerk, Finan McDonald, with men and canoes full of trading goods to establish a fort. McDonald reached this place in November and began construction of leather lodges which were also to become known as Kootenai House, a post destined to have many future locations. McDonald was there joined by James McMillan and the two Nor'westers inaugurated a brisk trade with the Indians of the vicinity. By the end of 1808, therefore, the Nor'westers had established two posts, both named Kootenai, and located on opposite sides of the present international boundary line.

Thompson resumed his post-founding activities during 1809, in which year he built Kullyspell House on the eastern shore of Lake Pend d'Oreille at present Hope, Idaho; also Saleesh House, three miles above Thompson's Falls on Clark's Fork in present western Montana. Then during 1810 Spokane House was established on the Spokane River, about ten miles northeast of the present city of Spokane. It was built by Finan McDonald and became the fifth North West Company post in the Columbia Department.

Disconcerting to the energetic Thompson was the news in 1810 that the Piegan Indians had become belligerent and had blocked the Howse Pass over which his supplies were being sent. In the face of this situation Thompson cast about for a substitute crossing of the Continental Divide. Such a place, and a better one at that, was discovered about fifty miles farther north. It became known as the Athabasca Pass, and it was of great importance to future development of the fur trade.

In addition to having laid the foundation for the development by the Nor'westers of the fur trade of the Columbia Basin, Thompson, by his careful survey of the country through which he moved, had laid out a new and practical line of communication which in the years to come was to be vital to the fur trade of the Pacific Northwest.[10]

When on their way to establish the Hudson's Bay Company in Oregon in 1824, Sir George Simpson and Dr. John McLoughlin crossed the precarious Athabasca Pass discovered by Thompson. From Simpson's *Journal* one may glean some idea of what that crossing entailed. Simpson wrote:

. . . . Wild & Majestic beyond description; the track is in many places nearly impassable and it appears extraordinary how any human being should have stumbled on a pass through such a formidable barrier as we are now scaling and which nature seems to have placed here for the purpose of interditing all communication between the East and West sides of the Continent.

At its very summit was a basin which emptied into streams going in opposite directions, and which, adds Simpson:

may be said to be the source of the Columbia & Athabasca Rivers as it bestows its favors on both these prodigious Streams, the former falling into the Pacific . . . . the latter after passing through Athabasca & Great Slave Lakes falling into the Frozen [Arctic] Ocean . . . . .[11]

Thompson's work did not end here, for during the latter part of 1811 he returned to the Big Bend country where he busied himself at Spokane House. Meanwhile his fellow trader, David Stuart, moved north from Okanogan to the north branch of the Thompson River where in 1812 he established Fort Kamloops which provided a valuable and natural, as well as an only, link between the Columbia Basin and New Caledonia. Thompson next belatedly made his way down the Columbia River to its mouth in the hope that he might establish a post there ahead of the Astorians of whose plans he had been apprised. He arrived at the Pacific on July 15 or 16, 1811, only to find the American banner flying above Fort Astoria. After a brief stay Thompson began his homeward journey. He reached Montreal in August 1812, thanking "good Providence" for having brought him and his men safely past the dangers, not of the wilderness, but of enemy Americans with whom his country was now unhappily at war. The great surveyor, explorer, map maker, and fur trader had failed to outflank the Astorians, but the time was not far off when the fortunes of war enabled his company to acquire Fort Astoria and

---

[10] *David Thompson's Narrative*, pp. lxxxvii–xciii; T. C. Elliott, "The Fur Trade in the Columbia River Basin Prior to 1811," *The Washington Historical Quarterly*, VI (January 1915), 3–10.

[11] Frederick Merk, ed., *Fur Trade and Empire: George Simpson's Journal* (Cambridge, 1931), pp. 33–34; W. D. Vincent, *The Northwest Company* (Pullman, 1927), p. 13; Davidson, *The North West Company*, pp. 98–100.

thus to realize Thompson's coveted dream, a fur-trading post at the mouth of the mighty Columbia River.[12]

While David Thompson was pushing the interests of the North West Company deep into the Columbia River Basin, the equally audacious Simon Fraser and John Stuart were moving forward in another direction. In 1805 the partners ordered these two men to proceed up the Peace River, cross over via the Parsnip and the Pack rivers to the headwaters of what became the Fraser River (but then Jackanut), and there establish still other Company posts. This country, lying between the forty-ninth and fifty-eighth parallels, became known as New Caledonia, a region which, except for the Mackenzie expeditions and coastal seaotter operations, was hitherto very little known.

In the prosecution of his instructions Simon Fraser and his fellow officer, John Stuart, established a base at Rocky Mountain Portage and there erected a crude-looking post known as Rocky Mountain House. From there they moved over the summit to McLeod Lake where in the fall of 1805 construction of Fort McLeod was begun. This was the first trading post to be built west of the Rocky Mountains and in what is now British Columbia. Fraser and Stuart returned to their base to winter, and in the spring of 1806 the two men, after first returning to Fort McLeod, moved on to Stuart Lake where work on Fort Nakasleh (afterwards Fort St. James) was begun. From there they proceeded to Fraser Lake where they founded Fort Natleh, or Fort Fraser. Then, anxious to thwart the Americans, Fraser and his men in 1807 moved on to the confluence of the Nechako and Fraser rivers (thinking the latter stream might be the Columbia) and there established Fort George. It was from this point that the courageous explorer and builder set forth the next year on the perilous trek down the turbulent Fraser River. To his everlasting chagrin he learned that the stream he followed was not the Columbia, but another which now bears this famous explorer's name.[13] A trail was then cut extending from Fort McLeod to Fort St. James, and as such it became the first of its kind in the future British Columbia province.[14]

In 1809 Fraser left New Caledonia, somewhat sick of his western rambles. He had placed in charge John Stuart who, with headquarters

[12] Davidson, *The North West Company*, p. 100.

[13] Simon Fraser, "Letters from the Rocky Mountains, 1806–1807," Transcript, Archives of British Columbia. John Stuart was the uncle of the first Lord Strathcona whose role in Canadian history was a conspicuous one. See also T. G. Marquis, "The Period of Exploration," *Pacific Province*, I (Toronto, 1914), 52–54, 57; F. W. Howay, W. N. Sage, and H. F. Angus, *British Columbia and the United States* (Toronto, 1942), p. 18.

[14] Arthur G. Doughty, ed., "First Journal of Simon Fraser from April 12th to July 18th, 1806," *Dominion of Canada Report of the Public Archives for the Year 1929* (Ottawa, 1930), pp. 109 ff.

at Fort McLeod, stayed on until the Hudson's Bay Company incorporated New Caledonia with the Columbia district.[15] At the very time of Fraser's departure news reached the partners that John Jacob Astor planned to establish a post at the mouth of the Columbia.[16] That this created a stir among the New Caledonians there is ample evidence. Accordingly John Stuart, assisted by the interesting and genial Daniel Harmon, lost no time organizing the fur trade in this remote transmontane segment of the Northern Department and to make of this trade a profitable business venture.

Throughout the period during which the North West Company operated before the merger with the Hudson's Bay Company no satisfactory intercommunication existed except between the regions developed by Thompson and Fraser, respectively. And since each was approached through widely separated Rocky Mountain passes, the Company, as shown in the Minutes for 1808, established separate administrations for the two regions. Fraser's New Caledonia remained a part of the contiguous Athabasca Department, the Company's choice and exclusive preserve, and thus enlarged this district to include the lands westward to the coast, bounded on the south by the watershed between the Fraser and the Columbia rivers and on the north by the Russians, whatever that could mean. Thompson's domain, on the other hand, became the separate Columbia Department, and in its ultimate area embraced the entire Columbia River watershed (including the Snake River) and the northern part of present-day Utah tossed in for good measure. The country between the lower Columbia and Fraser rivers remained a sort of no man's land, but farther to the east, at the confluence of the north and south branches of Thompson River, the two vast administrative units were brought into contact by the establishment there of Fort Kamloops. At this point, too, the transcontinental trails converged to link the entire Pacific operations with those east of the great Rocky Mountains.[17]

The Minutes for 1809 show that David Thompson was the sole clerk for the Columbia Department, but the next year John McDonald was elevated to share that position with Thompson. So far as the administration of the Columbia Department is concerned, the Minutes are silent except for one important matter, namely the acquisition of Fort Astoria. On

---

[15] Marquis, *op. cit.*, pp. 56–57; Alexander Begg, *History of the North-West* (Toronto, 1894–95), I, 117–18. Hereafter the official designation Columbia Department will be used in referring to the Company's West Coast organization.

[16] [Nathaniel Atcheson], *On the Origin and Progress of the North-West Company of Canada* (London, 1811), pp. 34–35.

[17] *Documents Relating to the North West Company*, p. 254. The editor, W. Stewart Wallace secured these Minutes from Hudson's Bay House, London. See also W. Kaye Lamb's Introduction to *The Letters of John McLoughlin, From Fort Vancouver to the Governor and Committee, First Series, 1825–38*, edited by E. E. Rich (Toronto, 1941), Vol. I. Hereafter cited as *McLoughlin's Fort Vancouver Letters*, first series.

July 11, 1814, a meeting of the partners assembled at Fort William (old Kaministikwia). The Minutes read:

. . . . the first Business introduced was the transactions in the Columbia last Winter & Fall, ... no material objection was made to the terms on which the Purchase from the Pacific Fur Company had been made, except as to the Payments, the near period at which they are fixed being considered highly advantageous to the Concern . . . . . The Advantages derived from the Arrangement were deemed considerable, by means of it the Posts were supplied for the Winter . . . . and it greatly facilitated the getting out of the Country our Competitors the American Fur Company . . . . .

The Minutes further reveal that now at last plans could be made for a sea approach to this area and "If a favourable connection could be made with an American House—it was the general opinion—it should be adopted for facilitating the Business in China."[18]

Thompson's journal gives the earliest and the best account of this pioneer fur-trading venture in Oregon's inland regions. Plans called for immediate action in order to forestall, not only American competition, but also that of the ever alert and ever encroaching Hudson's Bay Company. At first pelts and supplies were to be moved to and from supply bases east of the Rockies with the hope that the Pacific Coast bases subsequently might be provided. With these considerations in mind, Oregon's first inland fur-trading operations began.

From the very start David Thompson never overlooked a chance to trade, but it was not until the summer of 1809 that full-fledged operations got under way. The Saleesh Indians were selected that summer as the best prospects and Thompson wrote on July 14, 1809, how, under the charge of Finan McDonald, he had sent forth a canoe, "it's cargo four pieces of Merchandise: weighing 320 lbs. four, nine gallons kegs of greese (the melted fat of the Bison) and five bags of Pemmican, each of ninety pounds, with five men, a less number could not stem the current."[19] It was in the process of these operations that Kullyspell House was built—"a strong Log building for the Goods and Furrs, and for trading with the Natives."

By September, trade was in full swing. Guns, ammunition, and iron-headed arrows that could really pierce the thick-skinned bison and not break off as the stone ones did, were dispensed to the native hunters in exchange for hides and furs; while iron objects such as awls and needles were demanded by the squaws who also came to the post to trade. Thompson's narrative for the winter of 1809–1810 refers to constant

[18] *Documents Relating to the North West Company*, pp. 260–61, 282–83; [Wentzell or Mackenzie], "Sketch of the Indian Trade," p. 22.

[19] *David Thompson's Narrative*, p. 407.

trading of North West Company merchandise for furs, horses, and fresh and dried meats. Thompson came to love the Saleesh and called them "a fine race of moral Indians." Thompson returned to Rainy Lake, presumably with his pelts, and there he and his men once again "made an assortment of goods wherewith to load four Canoes for the furr [sic] trade of the interior country."[20] They recrossed the summit and once again the trade was resumed, although it was on this particular trip that Thompson personally traveled on to the mouth of the Columbia River.

In New Caledonia trading began under similar circumstances. Here, as in the Columbia Department, relations with the Indians began peacefully. The prospects for trade with them were from the outset good, although the Nor'westers found it difficult to induce the Indians to exert themselves beyond what was required for day-to-day living. Only as the natives developed a craving for liquor did the "incentive to industry" become increasingly noticeable.[21]

The manner in which trade was conducted has been vividly recorded by Ross Cox who knew the business well. To the fort would come a party of Indians "loaded with the produce of their hunt." Having placed their skins upon the ground the Indians, says Cox, would "squat themselves in a circle" and after their chief or leader had lighted "the calumet of peace," and other ceremonies had been indulged in, the real business of trade began. Each Indian had his skins divided into piles or lots. For one pile he would demand a gun; for another he would ask for ammunition; for still a third, perhaps a copper kettle, an axe, a blanket, or a knife. "The trading business being over," adds Cox, "another general smoking match takes place; after which they retire to their village or encampment."[22]

Friendly as relations between the Nor'westers and the Indians may have been, the white traders continued to suffer from lack of supplies incurred by the great distances that separated them from the bases of supply. The traders could take with them only the bare necessities of life, utilizing most of the available space for trading truck, and for this reason they were compelled to live off the country.

The native fare consisted chiefly of salmon, fresh or dried, and the traders, too, became very dependent upon the annual run of this delectable pink fish which to this day remains an important economic factor in the life of the region. Just how much the salmon meant to both the traders and Indians alike is well revealed in the instructive *Journal* of

---

[20] *Ibid.*, pp. 410–22, 438.

[21] Arthur S. Morton, *A History of the Canadian West to 1870–71* (Toronto, n.d.), p. 473.

[22] Ross Cox, *Adventures on the Columbia River, Including the Narrative of a Residence of Six Years on the Western Side of the Rocky Mountains* (London, 1831), II, 88–90.

D. W. Harmon, long a Company clerk in New Caledonia. Writing on September 13, 1810, Harmon commented on the report that "salmon, this season, do not come up the rivers of that region, as usual. As this kind of fish forms the principal article of food, both for the Natives and white people, it is apprehended that they will all be under the necessity of proceeding towards the Pacific Ocean, until they find a people who have been more favoured by Providence."[23] And again, writing from Fort McLeod, August 2, 1811, Harmon expressed his concern over the delay of the salmon run. "Unless the salmon from the sea, soon make their appearance, our condition will be deplorable."[24] This overanxiety was probably conditioned more by shortage of food stores than their distrust in the salmon whose habits and antics are amazingly regular. And sure enough on August 22 the first salmon appeared: "joyous intelligence to us all."[25]

Not only were these first New Caledonians dependent upon native foods, but also upon a precarious line of communication with their home base. Not infrequently, as in the fall of 1807 and again in 1811, supply canoes failed to arrive so that the field men were left stranded in the trade for skins.[26] On November 16, 1811, Harmon informs us that at Fort Stuart alone no less than seven thousand fish had been caught, but that supplies from the Peace River again failed to come through, making it necessary for Harmon to cross the Rockies in December in an effort to recoup them.[27]

While life was hard, it was also tempered with many successes. Stuart and Harmon continued their cordial relations with the Indians (chiefly carriers) and Harmon at least demonstrated his sincerity by living happily with an Indian squaw who bore him several children. And when after years the time came for Harmon to return to civilization he wrote that he considered himself "under a moral obligation not to dissolve the connexion, if she is willing to continue it."[28]

Forts Stuart and McLeod continued for years to be the chief posts, with Rainy Lake as the headquarters to which Stuart happily went every summer with the annual catch of beavers, otters, lynxes, skunks, fishers, martens, muskrats, foxes, wolves, bison, and other kinds of skins and hides. Every effort was made to make each post as self-sufficient as possible, and for that reason some berries of the region were gathered and some farming, or at least gardening, was done.

Self-sufficient as were these Pacific Coast outposts, their dependence

---

[23] Daniel Williams Harmon, *A Journal of Voyages and Travels in the Interiour of North America* (Andover, 1819), p. 185.

[24] *Ibid.*, p. 205. [25] *Ibid.*, p. 206. [26] Morton, *Canadian West*, p. 473.

[27] Harmon, *Journal*, pp. 213–14. [28] *Ibid.*, pp. 270, 284.

upon Montreal and the East generally was inescapable. The difficulties involved in communication with home bases were such as to stagger the imagination. To cover the distance from Montreal to Fort McLeod involved at least a hundred days of steady and intensive canoe, foot, and horseback travel. As a general rule travel was done by brigades of four large birch-bark canoes, each carrying from three and one-half to four tons and manned by eight or nine skillful Canadian *voyageurs*. By going up the Ottawa and by cutting across to the Huron River, the nine-hundred-mile trek to Sault Ste Marie was made in thirty days; whereas an additional nine hundred miles to the general rendezvous at Grand Portage were covered in half that time. From Grand Portage the route varied, depending on whether one went to the Columbia River region or to New Caledonia. But in any event, another six weeks to two months —often more—were employed in boating and portaging an additional three thousand miles, which was the added distance to the Pacific Coast posts. The total distance, then, from Montreal to Fort McLeod was approximately 4,800 miles.[29] The time involved was never exactly the same because the rate of travel depended on the weather. When crossing lakes, for instance, the canoes were generally rigged with square sails, and a strong or favorable wind would greatly boost the speed.

The goods comprising the cargo were usually done up in bales of about ninety to one hundred pounds each, with from seventy to eighty bales in each boat. Bateaux and cargo alike had to be portaged frequently, and in the less severe rapids the men would have to walk along the bank and pull their heavily laden boats by means of ropes. The latter method was known as "tracking." Once on the Pacific slope, pack horses as well as canoes were employed for interpost transit, but horses were not as readily available as might be supposed. For instance, the trader Alexander Ross states that when reaching Fort Okanogan on his way upstream from Fort George following the Astoria purchase, "everything was at a dead stand for want of pack-horses to transport the goods inland, and as no horses were to be got nearer than the Eyakema [Yakima] Valley, some 200 miles south-west, it was resolved to proceed thither in quest of a supply: at that place all the Indians were rich in horses." Not until the more advanced stages of the fur trade were horse or ox-drawn carts used rather widely to facilitate portaging and for the transportation of goods across the plains.[30] Difficult and hazardous as were those extremely long hauls, some attempt was made at regularity and punctuality. In time the West Coast traders came to rely with confidence on the ar-

---

[29] *Ibid., passim*; Begg, *History of the North-West*, I, 297.

[30] Alexander Ross, *The Fur Hunters of the Far West* (London, 1855), I, 19; Begg, *op. cit.*, pp. 297–98.

rival of the winter express. And later, when operations became even more routinized, light canoe service between Fort George, at the mouth of the Columbia River, and Montreal came to be referred to as the Hundred Day Express.[31]

It early became apparent that, efficient as was the overland express, direct access to and from the sea would be a condition for remaining in business in the Oregon country. Such an opening to the sea offered marvelous possibilities, the chief of which would be direct contact with both England and China.

It was toward this end that the partners directed their efforts. The problems facing them were difficult and delicate. It was the opinion of one of their own historians, writing in 1809, that American adventurers on the West Coast had mistreated the Indians who were now hostile. "But this prejudice," he added hopefully, "will yield to the superior convenience of a hatchet & a gun, over a sharp stone and a bow and arrow . . . . and to the kindness and fair dealing of those who intend to make permanent establishments among them."[32]

Three years after these remarks were written an opportunity presented itself, one which officials of the North West Company could ill afford to resist. War broke out between England and the United States. The English government which heretofore had refused a request to forestall the Astor enterprise now hastened to order H.M.S. *Phœbe* at Portsmouth to escort the Company ship *Isaac Todd* and other merchant ships, to which fleet was subsequently added H.M.S. *Raccoon*, to proceed to the mouth of the Columbia River and there take possession of Astor's trading post. The *Raccoon*, being a faster sailing vessel, moved on ahead. Facing the prospect of encountering either armed attack, or at least a blockade by an overwhelming British force, the Astorians, who already had experienced very hard luck, chose to accept an offer from the North West Company to buy Astoria. On October 16, 1813, the deal was consummated and the American post formally passed into the hands of the British fur-trading company. Many questions were afterwards raised with regard to the validity of this transaction, but for all practical purposes the North West Company had now realized Mackenzie's dream of eighteen years before.[33]

As if to anticipate the foregoing achièvement, John Stuart at New Caledonia was seeking some direct water communication between Stuart Lake and the Columbia River, thereby binding the two Pacific Coast districts more closely together. Looking forward to the day when New

[31] Davidson, *The North West Company*, p. 220.
[32] [Wentzell or Mackenzie], "Sketch of the Indian Trade," p. 22.
[33] Morton, *Canadian West*, pp. 504-7.

Caledonia would thus be joined with its southern neighbor and have a window to the sea, Harmon on May 13, 1813, wrote: ". . . . we shall, for the future, obtain our yearly supply of goods by that route, and send our returns out that way, to be shipped directly for China in vessels which the company, in that case, design to build on the North West coast."[34]

In making this statement Harmon failed to note one serious obstacle to the future development of his company's maritime trade, namely the powerful East India Company and the South Sea Company, both of which monopolies would impose serious impositions upon all British vessels not of their ownership that sought to venture into the China trade. All efforts on the part of the North West Company to reach an accord with its paternalistic British rivals failed, and finally in desperation the Canadian fur traders resorted to a subterfuge by making arrangements (following the Peace of Ghent) with the American firm, J. and T. H. Perkins Company of Boston, for handling the Columbia Department's outside trade. Not bound by the restrictions of the British monopolies, the Boston firm was free to carry goods at will to all ports of the world then open to American trade. Accordingly it undertook to carry North West Company supplies to Astoria where such cargoes were exchanged for furs, which in turn were carried from this Columbia River port to Canton where the money received from sales of furs was in turn spent for teas and other Oriental goods taken back to Boston and sold on the American market. Thus it was that many furs from the Columbia Department now moved westward to China instead of, as formerly, eastward to England; and in contrast to the situation prior to 1813, this new trade proved to be extremely profitable, not only to the partners of the North West Company, but to the American consignees as well. Until the merger in 1821 this happy arrangement remained uninterrupted.[35]

While the development of the maritime trade was unquestionably the chief change brought about by the purchase of Astoria, there is also evidence that the range of the inland trade was widened to include the rich Willamette and Snake valleys, relatively little exploited except for the limited contacts which the Astorians may have had with the Indians there.[36]

It is regrettable that there are no complete figures of the amount

---

[34] Harmon, *Journal*, p. 228.

[35] *Hunt's Merchants' Magazine*, XIV (June 1846), 537–38; Marion O'Neil, "The Maritime Activities of the North West Company, 1813 to 1821," *The Washington Historical Quarterly*, XXI (October 1930), 243–67.

[36] Ross, *The Fur Hunters*, I, 100 ff., 248 ff.; Vol. II, chap. 10.

and value of the Columbia River and New Caledonia trade. That a great variety of goods reached the Columbia is apparent, included among which in 1814 were wearing apparel, felt hats, butter, cheese, pickles, sauces, suet, candles, gunflints, gunpowder, guns, military stores, saddlery, fishing tackle, playing cards, stationery, tobacco pipes, wrought brass, copper, iron, etc. The official value of the goods shipped from England to the Pacific Northwest amounted to £1,738 9s. 10d. Each year brought more of the same kind of goods and many additions, including such articles as musical instruments, sails, carts, and wagons, having in 1818 an official value of as much as £20,730 14s. 2d. and a declared value of £22,847 6s. 2d. During 1819 and 1820 the figures again declined.[37]

The trouble, so far as the Columbia Department was concerned, was that the value of supplies shipped or packed into this distant region was such as to erase a desired balance of trade. Reports made in 1821 and after to the future Hudson's Bay Company by Governor George Simpson on post conditions within the District were such as to leave grave doubts as to the advisability of even continuing operations there. "We understand," wrote Hudson's Bay Company officials to Simpson in 1822, "that hitherto the trade of the Columbia has not been profitable, and from all that we have learnt on the Subject we are not sanguine in our expectations of being able to make it so in the future." Certain it is that the Columbia District had been inefficiently run, and as one trader phrased it, "a losing Concern to the N. W. Company."[38]

In 1821 the North West Company ceased to exist in name. By merging with the Hudson's Bay Company the North West concern had much to contribute by way of tangible assets, personnel, and business skill. By this time the North West Company operations on the Pacific slope had, as we have observed, become considerable. The trade of New Caledonia had at last become profitable and that of the less profitable Columbia District, while incurring heavy expenditures, gave promise of great future expansion in the Snake and Willamette valleys, and perhaps even into Alta California. From the larger and more lasting point of view, the North West Company must be credited with having opened the inland Oregon country to trade and settlement.

---

[37] Davidson, The North West Company, pp. 221–23, notes 100, 103.

[38] McLoughlin's Fort Vancouver Letters, first series, pp. xv–xvi.

CHAPTER IV

COMPANY OF ADVENTURERS

From out of the American back country there arrived in England in the middle 1660's two very interesting French explorers. They were Pierre Esprit Radisson and Médard Chouart, known as Sieur des Groseilliers. They were in the service of the British, had explored and traded in the upper Mississippi River region, and now had come to report to His Majesty, King Charles II's government, that a great area, rich in furs, lay north of Lake Superior and could be reached through Hudson Bay.

It is believed that the enthusiastic reports of these men led to the formation on May 2, 1670, of the now famous and aged Hudson's Bay Company, or, as the charter reads: "The Governor and Company of Adventurers of England Tradeing into Hudsons Bay." Granted by the direct patronage of the King, the charter gave these "adventurers" "the sole Trade and Commerce of all those Seas, Streightes, Bayes, Rivers, Lakes, Creekes, and Soundes, in whatsoever Latitude they shall bee, that lye within the entrance of the Streightes commonly called Hudsons Streightes." This charter, moreover, granted to the "Governor and Company, and their Successors," the sole trade, commerce, and mineral rights.[1]

In addition to all the foregoing rights and privileges, the company was empowered to pass laws, impose penalties and punishments, to sit in judgment on all civil and criminal cases in accordance with English law, and, moreover, it could employ armed force, appoint commanders, and build forts. As if this were not enough, the Governor and Company could require of His Majesty's armed forces assistance in the enforcement of the powers granted in the Charter.[2]

King Charles II of England personally handed the charter of this new company to his cousin, Prince Rupert, who accepted it for himself and seventeen other nobles and gentlemen, among whom was the powerful Duke of Albemarle, the Earl of Shaftesbury, and Sir George Carteret. Being in this manner born to the purple, it is fitting that through the years a heraldic coat of arms has been the symbol of the Hudson's

---

[1] "Hudson's Bay Company Charter." Photostat, Indiana University Library, Bloomington, Indiana.

[2] *Ibid.*; George P. Scriven, *The Story of the Hudson's Bay Company* (Washington, D.C., 1929), p. 9; Eldon Max Wales, "The History of Hudson's Bay Company." Master of Arts Thesis, 1929, Indiana University Library, Bloomington, Indiana, pp. 14–16.

Bay Company. This armorial insignia consists of an argent shield on which are surmounted the red cross of St. George and, fittingly enough, four black beavers. To further accent the business in which the company has been engaged, there is at the crest of this shield a cap with turned-up ermine, and sitting on the cap is a fox. On either side, and supporting the shield, are two elks. At the bottom is written the motto: *"Pro pelle cutem."*[3]

From this highly auspicious beginning the new company continued, though at first very slowly, to prosper and to expand. In 1749 it could claim only four or five forts and about 120 employees. For that reason it faced, but nevertheless weathered, a severe attack in Parliament based on the charge that the Company was a "non user" of its charter. So long as the French were in control of Canada the Company suffered many heavy losses, but when in 1763 the French were driven out, the door was opened for other encroachments, chief among which were the Montreal traders who were eventually to form the North West Company.

Following the actual formation of the North West Company the competition, especially along the boundary line west of Grand Portage, reached the point where indecencies knew no bounds. Indians were demoralized with liquor, the fur-bearing animals were killed without regard to future supply, and Nor'westers and Hudson's Bay men not infrequently resorted to outright killings in order to further their respective ends.[4] Probably the most conspicuous instance of this life-and-death struggle was the so-called Red River settlement feud. In 1811, the Hudson's Bay Company granted in fee simple to Lord Selkirk (then owning enough shares to control the parent company) 116,000 square miles on the Red River of the North. This territory comprised parts of present-day Manitoba, Saskatchewan, Minnesota, and North Dakota. On this land Selkirk promptly founded a colony (1812) that lay athwart the very crossroads used by the Nor'westers in the conduct of their Far Western trade. That resistance to such a move would come was inevitable. During the summer of 1814, while the War of 1812 was still dragging on south of the border, bigwigs of the North West Company met at their usual western rendezvous which was Fort William on Lake Superior. Their decision was that Selkirk's colonists must go. ". . . . Nothing but the complete downfall of the colony will satisfy some by fair means or foul," wrote Alexander Macdonell, a Nor'wester.

---

[3] Robert Watson, *The Hudson's Bay Company* (Toronto, 1928), p. 7. This representation of the coat-of-arms is used at the present time in the advertisements of the Hudson's Bay Company. The idea back of the motto is that traders risk their own skins in the procurement of the skins of animals.

[4] For a brief sketch, see A. Neville J. Whymant, "Hudson's Bay Company," *Encyclopædia Britannica* (London, New York, 1929), XI, 861.

During the summer of 1815 violence broke loose. To use the words of Douglas MacKay: "Crops were trampled down; barns were burned; shots were fired from the bushes at night. Macdonell was fighting it out. . . . ." Then came recriminations from the Selkirk men. In 1816 Selkirk, with a private army of about one hundred ex-soldiers, Swiss mercenaries, and colonials, prepared to move against the Nor'westers, but not before the latter had succeeded in literally wiping out twenty-one settlers that were still at their homes near the confluence of the Assiniboine and Red rivers.

The merciless slaughter of these settlers has become known as the Seven Oaks Massacre. This unhappy affair aroused English political circles, and investigations followed. With the death of both Lord Selkirk and Sir Alexander Mackenzie in 1820, plus the threats of revocation of company charters or licenses, an opportunity for a thoroughgoing settlement of differences presented itself.[5]

Fights, kidnapings, highjacking, dueling, and other mutual recriminations continued for a while, but the final upshot of the Seven Oaks Massacre was a merger of the two rival concerns. At the urgings of Lord Bathurst, the colonial secretary, negotiations were begun in London for a merger in 1820. It was with grave misgivings and mutual suspicions that conversations were entered into, but each side felt convinced that no other course could possibly save the respective vested interests involved. On March 26, 1821, a final deed of co-partnership, one built upon the original Hudson's Bay Company charter, was agreed upon. It was to be good for twenty-one years. The name Hudson's Bay Company was to be retained; that of the North West Company dropped. For a period of twenty-one years the concern was to continue to be a monopoly guaranteed by an act of Parliament. But unlike the original charter of 1670, the area involved would not be limited to that draining into Hudson Bay, but would embrace as well the entire Canadian West, including the Oregon country. The vast territory over which the new Hudson's Bay Company would have administrative, as well as trading powers, involved an area approximately equal in size to the present continental United States.[6] This territory would be divided into four great parts, namely: (1) the Northern Department of Rupert's Land, which up to 1825 included New Caledonia; (2) the Southern Department (the James Bay area, southward to provinces of Upper and

---

[5] Douglas MacKay, *The Honourable Company* (Indianapolis, 1936), chap. 9; Morton, *Canadian West*, pp. 578–622.

[6] "Agreement for carrying on the Fur Trade by the Hudson's Bay Company exclusively under the Terms within mentioned," E. E. Rich, ed., *Colin Robertson's Correspondence Book, September 1817 to September 1822* (Toronto, 1939), pp. 302–27. See also "Deed Poll," *ibid.*, pp. 327–44; Alexander Morris, *The Hudson's Bay and Pacific Territories* (Montreal, 1859), p. 12.

Lower Canada); (3) the Montreal Department, embracing Upper and Lower Canada (and later Labrador); and (4) the Columbia District (subject to the control of the Northern Department), which embraced the Columbia River Valley, and after 1825, the Canadian Pacific slope, or New Caledonia.

Moreover, the Deed Poll of the new company provided that the shares would be prorated among Hudson's Bay Company and North West Company proprietors and the wintering partners—a three-way split. Total gains in any one year would be divided into one hundred shares, of which forty would go to the wintering partners in North America. These forty shares in turn were to be divided into eighty-five shares, fifty going to the former North West Company men and the remaining thirty-five going to Hudson's Bay men. Each factor was to receive two shares, each trader one share.

In an effort to prevent further violence, Parliament also passed in 1821 "An Act for regulating the Fur Trade, and establishing a Criminal and Civil Jurisdiction within certain Parts of *North America.*" This Act calls attention to the past misdeeds of the late rival concerns, how these companies were "productive of great Inconvenience and Loss," how they did "great injury to the native *Indians,*" and committed "Breaches of the Peace, and Violence extending to the Loss of Lives, and considerable Destruction of Property." But henceforth the powers of the courts of Upper and Lower Canada would extend, with certain reservations, to the territories granted to the Hudson's Bay Company. Within the Oregon country, British rights would be shared with the United States.[7]

For all the compromises, reservations, and restrictions the new merger turned out to be a fortunate one for the late London and Canadian companies. It enabled the reorganized Hudson's Bay Company not only to retain its previous privileges but new ones were added. It paved the way for expansion and for carrying on the fur trade with greater efficiency and profit and over a much wider area than had hitherto been possible. The Deed Poll, for one thing, set up efficient machinery of government that lasted for half a century. Under its provisions the governors of each department called annual meetings of their chief factors (together comprising a local council) to discuss and map out local operations, which were carried out under the central direction of the Governor, Deputy Governor, and Committee in Lon-

---

[7] *Charters, Statutes, Orders in Council, etc. Relating to the Hudson's Bay Company* (London, 1931), pp. 93–102; [Hudson's Bay House], *Hudson's Bay Company* (London, 1934), pp. 23–24; Innis, *The Fur Trade in Canada*, pp. 285–87; MacKay, *The Honourable Company*, pp. 158–64.

don in whose hands final authority was vested. Under the direction of the Deputy Governor, Nicholas Garry, who in 1821 came to North America, appointments were made and organizational details of the concern were ironed out.[8]

Probably the most important organizational change made subsequent to the merger occurred in 1822 when two governors were appointed to administer the four territories. William Williams received the appointment to the Southern and Montreal departments; George Simpson was assigned to the Northern Department and Columbia District. The two field governors were responsible to the Governor and Committee. Then in 1826 Williams was recalled and George Simpson was made governor of both the Southern and Northern Departments; and in 1839 he was made Governor-in-Chief of the entire American operations of the Hudson's Bay Company, responsible, of course, to the Governor and Committee in London.

George Simpson, whose birth in Ross-shire, Scotland, about 1787, was illegitimate (the son of George, eldest son of Reverend Thomas Simpson), had been reared and well educated by kinsfolk. Employment with a London mercantile firm eventually led to his becoming associated with the Hudson's Bay Company in which organization, thanks to his brilliance and the friendly influence of Andrew W. Colvile, a partner in the firm, Simpson's rise was meteoric. Simpson, writes Frederick Merk, "had the imaginative vision of a Clive; he drew his plans on a scale that was continental" and as such "he combined a grasp of detail that was extraordinary."[9] Today as the Hudson's Bay House views its own history, Sir George Simpson still remains a pivotal personality in those critical transition years. "In him," write Hudson's Bay officials at London, "a clear orderly mind and a driving ambition were sustained by a physical vitality which carried him buoyantly through life."[10]

For three years following the merger George Simpson devoted most of his energies to the expansion of the fur trade east of the Rocky Mountains, but by no means did he ignore what to him was a great challenge, the development of a master plan with respect to Old Oregon.

Before the merger the Hudson's Bay Company had done little but explore the possibilities of trade in the Far West. Representing the firms during 1810–1811, Joseph Howse had, however, crossed the Rocky

[8] Merk, *Fur Trade and Empire*, pp. xii–xiii; MacKay, *The Honourable Company*, pp. 165–74.

[9] Merk, *Fur Trade and Empire*, p. xviii. See also E. E. Rich, ed., *Part of Dispatch From George Simpson Esqr Governor of Ruperts Land to the Governor & Committee of the Hudson's Bay Company, London* (Toronto, 1947), pp. xii–xiii.

[10] [Hudson's Bay House], *Hudson's Bay Company*, p. 25; Arthur S. Morton, *Sir George Simpson* (Portland, 1944), chap. 1; Walter N. Sage, "The Place of Fort Vancouver in the History of the Northwest," *Pacific Northwest Quarterly*, XXXIX (April 1948), 87.

Mountains at a pass now bearing his name. He had done so at the risk of being killed either at the hands of the warring Piegan Indians or by rival Nor'westers. Howse had ventured as far west as the Flathead country and he returned with glowing accounts of his experiences in which the dangers of his journey were not emphasized. Why should they have been? He brought back thirty-six bundles of furs on which he gleaned a profit of 75 percent. But with the exception of this isolated exploit, the new Hudson's Bay Company was obliged to draw upon the experiences of those who had represented the North West Company in the Pacific Northwest.[11]

Even after the merger some doubts were entertained about the legality of operation in the Oregon country. By an act of Parliament, July 2, 1821, the charter of the reorganized Hudson's Bay Company was liberalized and exclusive sanction was granted to conduct the fur trade "Westward of the Stony Mountains."[12]

Accordingly the energetic Simpson began to form his plans of organization. Never in doubt about New Caledonia, a fact-finding committee of four men, three of whom had been partners of the North West Company, were appointed immediately by the Council of the Northern Department to go to the Columbia District and report back on the state of affairs existing there, and in addition to these four men Simpson dispatched the trustworthy Archibald McDonald in the capacity of an accountant.[13]

Meanwhile, letters and reports began reaching Simpson, and somewhat optimistically he wrote the Governor and Committee in London, July 31, 1822:

From the result of Columbia Outfit 1821/22 the prospect is rather more flattering than hitherto, however large profits can scarcely be expected, yet by aeconomy and perseverance and following up measures which are found to be practicable, combined with a favourable Market for the Furs, the Trade might support itself, provided always, that no formidable opposition from the Americans assail us . . . . .[14]

---

[11] Morton, *Canadian West*, pp. 496–97.

[12] *Charters, Statutes, Orders in Council, etc. Relating to the Hudson's Bay Company*, pp. 93–102. This grant did not, of course, imply exclusion of the Americans.

[13] *McLoughlin's Fort Vancouver Letters*, first series, p. xv. Those first sent to the Columbia District were Chief Factors John Haldane and John Dugald Cameron, and Chief Trader James McMillan, former partners of the North West Company, and Chief Trader John Lee Lewes, veteran Hudson's Bay man. Others who were dispatched to the Oregon country before the formal establishment of the Hudson's Bay Company there were Samuel Black, Peter Skene Ogden, and John Work. Ogden and Work, especially, were to become important figures in the history of the Pacific Northwest. See Henry D. Dee, "John Work: A Chronicle of His Life and a Digest of His Journals." Master of Arts Thesis, 1943, University of British Columbia, Vancouver, B.C., p. 6. See also published form, Henry D. Dee, ed., *The Journal of John Work, January to October, 1835* (Victoria, 1845).

[14] George Simpson to Governor and Committee, July 31, 1822, in Merk, *Fur Trade and Empire*, pp. 184–85.

Reports continued on the whole to be affirmative and on July 12, 1823, one finds Simpson stating in a memo dispatched to the authorities of the Columbia District that trade there "may not only defray its expenses, but yield moderate profits if strict economy and exertion are exercised and there is no opposition."[15]

No doubt contributing to the making of final plans and decisions was an agreement entered into early in 1824 between the East India Company and the Hudson's Bay Company in London whereby the latter would sell the trading monopoly 20,000 beavers and 7,000 otter skins in 1824 and a similar number the following year.[16] This deal would not only relieve the London market but would lessen dependency upon J. and T. H. Perkins Company which, as has been noted, had acted as middleman for the North West Company.

In order to expedite communication between the Columbia District and the East, Norway House, to the north of Lake Winnipeg, was to replace Fort William as the scene of the annual council. Also definite plans were laid for sending John Work to Spokane House, and further arrangements were made for outfitting Alexander Ross to lead a trading brigade into the Snake River country during the summer of 1824. All this took place while diplomatic negotiations were going on relative to the political disposition of the territory; and although a final settlement was by no means reached, the withdrawal of Russia to 54° 40' north latitude was a reassuring sign.[17]

The year 1824 was, therefore, one of decision with respect to British interests in the Oregon country, and once having decided to carry on in the Columbia District, the Governor and Committee at London acted with great promptness and dispatch. The Company purchased the brig *William and Ann* and ordered it to proceed to northern Pacific waters; it ordered the construction of new headquarters somewhere on the north side of the Columbia River; it urged that the Snake River trade should be prosecuted with renewed vigor, lest Americans capture this commerce; and, lastly, it was to the tough and energetic George Simpson that the Company turned for a successful execution of the policies agreed upon.[18]

August 15, 1824, found George Simpson still at York Factory (the Company's great depot in Hudson Bay) where he had met with the Council and where final plans for the West Coast operations had been

[15] Simpson to the Chief Factors of the Columbia River District, July 12, 1823, in *ibid.*, p. 198.

[16] *Ibid.*, p. 207.

[17] Dee, "John Work," p. 6; William Schooling, *The Hudson's Bay Company* (London, 1920), p. 31.

[18] *McLoughlin's Fort Vancouver Letters*, first series, pp. xxii–xxiii.

mapped out. Extreme haste was now necessary if he were to cross the Rocky Mountains before the heavy snows of winter would block his passage. He had hoped vainly for the arrival of another ship from London bearing additional instructions, but now, at last, the deadline had passed, and the voyage was begun. Traveling by canoe, Simpson was accompanied by James McMillan, chief trader and one familiar with the Columbia River region; also by eight *voyageurs*, an Indian guide, and a personal servant.

Twenty days earlier Simpson had dispatched his previously appointed Chief Factor for the Columbia District. This was Dr. John McLoughlin, a man whose dominant and vivid personality was to leave a lasting imprint upon the history of the Oregon country. He had been born October 19, 1784, on the south bank of the St. Lawrence River in the Province of Quebec (about 120 miles below the city of Quebec), and was a mixture of Irish, Scotch, and French-Canadian blood. Little is known of his childhood except that he had been baptized a Catholic, grew up on a farm, received training, such as it was, in medicine at Quebec, and at the still youthful age of nineteen was licensed by the Lieutenant-Governor of Lower Canada to practice medicine and surgery. Meanwhile the young M.D. had met influential persons, among them the old tyrant, Simon McTavish, who induced McLoughlin to enter the service of the North West Company which, it will be recalled, was then on the verge of being reorganized. Until the merger eighteen years later, Dr. McLoughlin continued to serve the Nor'westers first as physician and then as actual trader east of the Rocky Mountains. And while he may have found it possible to combine the art of healing with that of fur trading, it was as a trader that McLoughlin showed great skill. It was in the latter capacity that he continued to serve until 1821 when as one of his company's representatives he was sent to London to arrange for the merger with the rival Hudson's Bay Company.[19]

Not too much is known of McLoughlin's private life. Already the father of a son by an Indian squaw, McLoughlin, about 1812, married in fur-trader fashion the half-breed widow of the hapless Alexander McKay by whom she had borne four children, and who as a result of her union with McLoughlin bore an additional four. Personally Dr. McLoughlin was of striking appearance. He was six feet, four inches tall; he was rawboned, well proportioned, and strong. His eyes were piercing; his flowing, prematurely white hair hung down over his massive shoulders. He was dignified but impetuous, and to use the words

---

[19] *McLoughlin's Fort Vancouver Letters*, first series, pp. xxix–xlviii; MacKay, *The Honourable Company*, pp. 175–77.

of H. H. Bancroft, ". . . . he was fitted to govern men both by awe and love."[20] This, then, is the man upon whom Governor Simpson pinned his hopes for the Columbia District about which the Honourable Company had grave misgivings.

McLoughlin was no dawdler, but on September 26 the swiftly moving Simpson party overtook McLoughlin near the Athabasca River, and writing of this strange meeting in the wilderness Simpson has left us, in his journal, another of the many vivid pictures of the colorful Dr. McLoughlin.

[He] was such a figure as I should not like to meet in a dark Night in one of the bye lanes in the neighborhood of London, dressed in Clothes that had once been fashionable, but now covered with a thousand patches of different Colors, his beard would do honor to the chin of a Grizzly Bear. . . . . his own herculean dimensions forming a tout ensemble that would convey a good idea of the high way men of former Days.[21]

By November 8, 1824 (having made the trans-Canadian journey from York Factory to Fort George at the mouth of the Columbia in eighty-four days), Simpson and McLoughlin were ready to revamp their vast Columbia District. A new fort was to be built at Belle Vue Point on the north side of the Columbia River on what Simpson believed would be permanently British soil. The post to be erected there was to be named Fort Vancouver in honor of the great explorer, and it was to replace Fort George as headquarters for the District.[22] Fort Nez Percés (Walla Walla) was to be shifted; Spokane House was to be abandoned, or rather replaced by what was to be Fort Colvile near Kettle Falls, seventy-five miles farther north; Kootenai House and many other posts were slated for a thorough revamping; and, as circumstances dictated, other new trading posts should be added to those already within that region.

Simpson was not slow to order a general streamlining of the administrative setup by eliminating excessive personnel and wasteful practices and by mapping out important expeditions such as those involving the Snake country. Moreover, the Governor proposed that agriculture, stock raising, and salmon fishing should supplement the fur trade much more than had previously been the case; and it was his command that the coastal and trans-Pacific trade should be made a very important part of the Company's operations in the Columbia District. Simpson

[20] H. H. Bancroft, *History of Oregon* (San Francisco, 1886), I, 29–30; Richard G. Montgomery, *The White Headed Eagle* (New York, 1934).

[21] Merk, *Fur Trade and Empire*, p. 23.

[22] [Hudson's Bay House], *Hudson's Bay Company*, p. 31. Simpson stood ready to surrender all lands south of the Columbia to the United States.

personally remained in the District throughout the entire winter of 1824–1825, helping Chief Factor McLoughlin to inaugurate the new regime. By March 19, 1825, the new Fort Vancouver (which post was subsequently rebuilt on higher ground) had been completed and appropriately christened.[23]

Simpson's immediate task had been accomplished. He returned to east of the Rockies, visiting en route posts along the Columbia River— Walla Walla, Okanogan, and Spokane House. He further discussed plans with the chief traders. But before he left, Simpson had ordered that the Columbia River Valley and New Caledonia, separate districts under the North West Company, were now to be merged into one administrative and operating unit, the working out of which plan, however, was left in the hands of his capable Chief Factor McLoughlin. Under him were to serve many shrewd and brilliant traders. Among them were Peter Skene Ogden, James McMillan, James Douglas, Alexander R. McLeod, John Warren Dease, Archibald McDonald, Francis and Edward Ermatinger, and John Work.[24] These and several others were to be important in the early history of the old Oregon country.

For more than two decades McLoughlin remained the Chief Factor of the Columbia District, and not until the end of his services in 1846 did the Honourable Company retreat before the rising tide of the American immigrants under whose dominance much of the region was due to fall. It was with great energy and perseverance that the "White Headed Eagle" (for such did the Indians call McLoughlin) carried out the ambitious program that the imaginative Governor Simpson had so courageously conceived.

Immediate steps were taken, first, to unite New Caledonia with the Columbia River Basin into one co-ordinated administrative and trading unit under the direction of the Northern Council, and, secondly, to expand the fur trade. Toward these ends Chief Trader James McMillan, Simpson's friend and companion, set out to examine the heretofore unexploited lower Fraser River. And still further endeavors brought an opening, without hindrance from once hostile Indians, of trails which connected the new headquarters of Fort Vancouver with the potentially rich Puget Sound country.[25]

Meanwhile, the Company gave its attention to the important matter of the number, position, and character of fur-trading posts around which its business would naturally revolve. In this role the Fort Vancouver

[23] Merk, *op. cit.*, p. 124.

[24] *Ibid.*, pp. 125–42; Robert E. Pinkerton, *Hudson's Bay Company* (London, 1932), p. 267.

[25] Carey, *History of Oregon*, I, 241–42; Clark, *Willamette Valley*, pp. 162–64; Morton, *Sir George Simpson*, pp. 125–26.

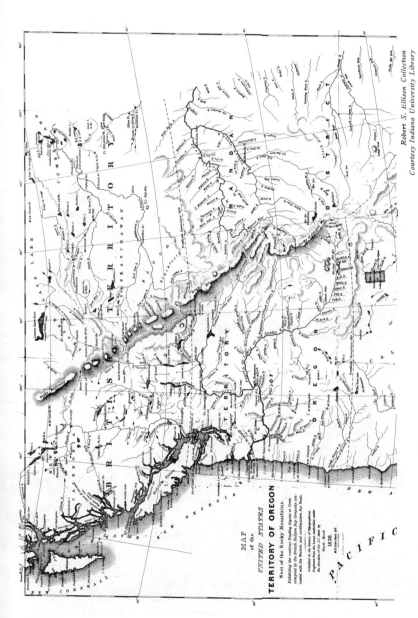

Map of the Oregon Country (1838) Showing Location of Important Fur Trading Posts

FORT NISQUALLY GATE. A RESTORATION

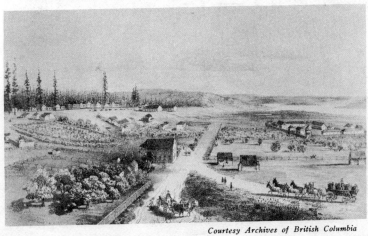

FORT VANCOUVER IN LATER DAYS

headquarters were designed to be the hub toward which all trails eventually led and in relation to which all other posts remained subsidiary. From Fort Vancouver brigades set forth; from it were issued orders affecting operations in even the tiniest outpost in some isolated river valley hundreds of miles away. To it flowed the coveted bales of furs; to it gravitated would-be settlers, visiting dignitaries, scientists, and travelers to whom the fort offered relief and comfort. To the weary overland traveler, it was a haven; to those who came exhausted from a long sea voyage, it was a home.

Fort Vancouver continued to grow in physical proportions, and when at its height in 1845 it consisted not only of stockade areas, but of a sizable village. The fort proper, according to John Dunn, was shaped like a parallelogram, with dimensions of 150 by 250 yards, "enclosed by a sort of wooden wall, made of pickets . . . . closely fitted together, twenty feet high, and strongly secured on the inside by buttresses." There was the customary bastion (placed at the northeast corner) where "twelve-pounders" commanded both fort and village areas. Some "eighteen-pounders" were located in the center of the stockade to support the bastion battery. Within was a court around which were arranged numerous strong wooden buildings, "designed for various purposes—such as offices, apartments for the clerks, and other officers—warehouses for furs, English goods, and other commodities—workshops for the different mechanics; carpenters, blacksmiths, coopers, wheelwrights, tinners, &c. . . . . There is also a schoolhouse and chapel, and a powder magazine, built of brick and stone." In the center of all this stood the governor's residence with its popular dining hall and public sitting room. Immediately outside the fort to the north was an orchard; and on the other three sides, cultivated fields. A road which passed by the southern side of the fort was connected with others which reached the village a few yards to the west and the Columbia River a half-mile away to the south. Fort Vancouver was, as Dunn concludes, "the grand mart and rendezvous for the Company's trade and servants on the Pacific."[26]

Lieutenant Charles Wilkes, commander of an American naval exploring expedition, called at Fort Vancouver the summer of 1841. The headquarters made a profound impression on him. His account of the physical plant agrees in essential detail with Dunn, but Wilkes adds the human touch. He tells of operations there, of McLoughlin's hospitality, the long table in the large dining hall, and of the "abundance of

---

[26] John Dunn, *The Oregon Territory, and the British North American Fur Trade* (Philadelphia, 1845), pp. 100–102; see map, *McLoughlin's Fort Vancouver Letters*, third series (Toronto, 1944), opposite p. 48.

good fare." Fort Vancouver, wrote Wilkes, "is a large manufacturing, agricultural, and commercial depôt, and there are few if any idlers, except the sick. Everybody seems to be in a hurry, whilst there appears to be no obvious reason for it."[27] In the vicinity of the fort were also expansive farm lands devoted to a diversified agriculture and to the grazing of large herds of cattle, sheep, and horses. As will be shown later, agricultural activities were to become an important part of the Company's economy. To use the words of Walter N. Sage, Fort Vancouver became "a veritable hive of industry. It was the nerve center of British trade west of the Rockies."[28]

With regard to the outposts, it had been Simpson's opinion from the start that the newly reorganized Company should salvage whatever North West Company property there was of value. Now that New Caledonia was a part of Columbia District, Forts McLeod, St. James, Fraser, George (B.C.), Kootenai, Flathead, Kamloops, Okanogan, and Nez Percés were the important North West Company establishments retained in the new organization. Many of these posts were still in fair condition when McLoughlin took command in 1824, and served as useful establishments for several years thereafter. Fort George (formerly Astoria) was, however, to operate on a very small scale and it was to fall into disrepair, while Spokane House was completely abandoned.[29]

To the number of posts retained the Company added, besides pivotal Fort Vancouver, many others that facilitated an expansion of operations to the farthest reaches of the Oregon country. At Simpson's instigation Fort Colvile was founded in 1825 to replace the North West Company's Spokane House. This new post was located near Kettle Falls, about forty miles south of the present international boundary line and about the midway point on the 1,400-mile course of the Columbia River. John Work was detailed to supervise the construction of its first small unit, to which many buildings were subsequently added. When in 1846 an inventory of the Colvile properties was taken there were listed no less than nineteen separate buildings ranging from a store twenty-five by sixty feet to a pigeon house nine by nine feet. All were surrounded by

---

[27] Charles Wilkes, *Narrative of the United States Exploring Expedition, During the Years 1838, 1839, 1840, 1841, 1842* (Philadelphia, 1845), IV, 328–29. The Fort was occupied by the Hudson's Bay Company until 1859 when its license expired. In 1860 the United States Army declared the buildings unfit for use and burned them. Louis R. Caywood, "The Archeological Excavation of Fort Vancouver," *Oregon Historical Quarterly*, XLIX (June 1948), 116.

[28] Sage, "Fort Vancouver," *op. cit.*, p. 97; Wilkes, *op. cit.*, IV, 333–38; Clark, *Willamette Valley*, pp. 197–201.

[29] Data on individual post histories is scattered and difficult to obtain. Many post records are still in the possession of Hudson's Bay House in London and have not been released for publication. From the archives of local historical societies and from special monographs, however, some pertinent facts concerning these posts can be obtained.

a protective stockade. Like Fort Vancouver, Fort Colvile, with its 340 acres under cultivation, its blacksmith and carpenter shops, flour mill, and bake house, was to all intents a self-sustaining unit.[30]

Attention was also directed to the lower Fraser River where Dr. McLoughlin's trusted aide, James McMillan, arrived with a party on June 27, 1827, to begin construction of what was to become the important Fort Langley. McMillan chose a site on the left bank of the Fraser, twenty-eight miles upstream. It took but six weeks to build a stockaded structure 120 by 135 feet, according to the journal of Archibald McDonald who became its chief trader and whose duty it was to develop the coastal trade. Because of the hasty workmanship, the post deteriorated rapidly, and in 1839 it was rebuilt two miles farther upstream only to be destroyed by fire the following year. It was again rebuilt and was still serving as a post a half-century later.[31]

The next post of any importance was Fort Simpson, built in 1831 and located on the Nass River about twenty miles from its mouth. Three years later it, too, was relocated, in this case at the north end of Tsimpsean Peninsula. For several decades to come Fort Simpson operated as a profitable trading establishment.[32]

To describe each post separately would be repetitious, for as the British Commander Richard C. Mayne observed: ". . . . all Hudson Bay posts are much alike." Six to eight houses serving as lodgings for officers and men, mess halls, a trading store, workshop, and storage places, were here compressed within the square wall from fifteen to twenty feet high. In two of the four corners, and rising above the walls, were wooden and usually octagonally shaped bastions. Openings on all sides were large enough to accommodate six- and twelve-pounders and thereby the entire surrounding countryside was within the range of cannon fire.[33]

One such post followed another in the fulfillment of McLoughlin's

---

[30] J. Orin Oliphant, "Old Fort Colville [*sic*]," *The Washington Historical Quarterly*, XVI (January 1925), 29–45. See also O. B. Sperlin, "Washington Forts of the Fur Trade Regime," *ibid.*, VIII (April 1917), 108. To avoid confusion, note that fort should be spelled Colvile (named for Sir Andrew Colvile); the town which eventually replaced the fur trading post is spelled Colville.

[31] Malcolm McLeod, ed., *Peace River* . . . . ; *Journal of the Late Chief Factor, Archibald McDonald*, by Sir George Simpson (Ottawa, 1872), p. 38; Denys Nelson, *Fort Langley, 1827–1927* (Fort Langley, B.C., 1927), pp. 7–12; Robie L. Reid, "Early Days at Old Fort Langley," *The British Columbia Historical Quarterly*, I (April 1937), 71–72; "Correspondence Relating to Fort Langley from the Hudson's Bay Company's Archives, 1830–1858." Transcript, Archives of British Columbia.

[32] "Fort Simpson Correspondence, 1859–1871." Transcript, Archives of British Columbia; H. H. Bancroft, *History of the Northwest Coast* (San Francisco, 1886), II, 635.

[33] R. C. Mayne, *Four Years in British Columbia and Vancouver Island* (London, 1862), pp. 117–18.

dream of a network of posts that would stretch from the Columbia River far north to Russian Alaska. In 1833 Fort McLoughlin was built on Milbanke Sound.[34] The next year witnessed the building of Fort Boise on the Snake River a few miles from the mouth of the Boise River. Near it was Fort Hall on the big bend of the Snake River, which was acquired from Wyeth by the Hudson's Bay Company in 1837. Both these posts enhanced the Company's trade in a region hitherto reached by brigades only, and they also served to deter competing American traders from entering the Oregon country from the East. But ironically enough, the day was already at hand when both Forts Boise and Hall were to become important landmarks, not necessarily for American traders, but for long lines of westbound American immigrants.[35]

With respect to American immigration into the Willamette Valley, McLoughlin was a realist. He early became convinced that the future of the fur trade lay north of the Columbia. To be sure, the Chief Factor maintained a small post on the Umpqua River; he sent brigades far south into California; and he even sent W. G. Rae to Yerba Buena to establish a post opened May 1841. But the advance of the Hudson's Bay Company in Old Oregon was predominantly northward. This being so, the day would inevitably come when the interests of the Hudson's Bay Company would clash with those of the Russians. Even before the Hudson's Bay Company moved west of the Rocky Mountains, the Russian Czar, in a ukase, had declared that all lands north of the fifty-first parallel belonged to Russia, and he forbade foreigners to come within one hundred Italian miles of her coast. This led to the convention and agreements of 1824–1825 involving Russia, Great Britain, and the United States, which established 54° 40′ as the southern extent of Russian territorial claims.[36]

Agreement in matters of sovereignty naturally brought with it limitations on trading companies of the countries involved. It was in the face of such limitations that Governor George Simpson and Rear Admiral Baron Ferdinand Wrangell of the Russian American Fur Company signed an important agreement at Hamburg, February 6, 1839, respecting trading operations in the border area of Alaska. Beginning with 1840 the Russians agreed to cede to the Hudson's Bay Company for exclusive trade for a period of ten years the waters and land from 54° 40′ north to Cape Spencer. In return the British company agreed

---

[34] *McLoughlin's Fort Vancouver Letters*, first series, p. xc; see also note 39 below.

[35] Annie Laurie Bird, *Boise* (Caldwell, Idaho, 1934), chap. 4; Carey, *History of Oregon*, I, 279.

[36] Thomas A. Bailey, *Diplomatic History of the American People* (New York, 1940), pp. 180–82, 190.

not to trade in the remaining Russian territory, and further agreed to pay annually to the Russian American Fur Company as rent 2,000 land-otter skins. The Hudson's Bay Company further agreed to sell at specified prices to the Russians an additional 5,000 skins and quantities of agricultural produce such as flour, peas, barley, salted beef, butter, and hams.[37]

This agreement led in 1840 to the establishment by James Douglas of Fort Taku (or Durham) on lands leased from the Russian American Fur Company. It also led to the leasing by the Hudson's Bay Company in the same year of Fort Stikine, also within this same area, and today the site of Wrangell, Alaska. Formerly this post had been called Redoubt St. Dionysius and had been built in 1834 to forestall British advances into that region.[38]

The first American immigrant train arrived in the Willamette Valley in 1841. The Hudson's Bay Company saw this as the handwriting on the wall, and accordingly gave added impetus to its northern developments. Under the direction of James Douglas, Fort Victoria was established on the southern tip of Vancouver Island in 1843. It was strategically located, and six years later it replaced Fort Vancouver as headquarters for the Columbia District. In 1848 Fort Yale was founded at the head of navigation on the Fraser River, and during the following year Fort Hope was located twenty miles farther downstream. Also in 1849 Fort Rupert was established at the northern end of Vancouver Island; 1852 saw the founding of Nanaimo as a coal-mining enterprise on the eastern shore of this large island. As time went on still other forts were established, and to this very day the Hudson's Bay Company maintains no less than two hundred trading posts in northern Canada, some of which are within the boundaries of what was once called the Oregon country.[39] In addition to trading posts, the Company also created agricultural establishments about which more will be said in subsequent chapters.

---

[37] "Agreement Between the Hudsons [sic] Bay Company and the Russian American Fur Company, 1839." Transcript, Archives of British Columbia.

[38] *McLoughlin's Fort Vancouver Letters*, second series (Toronto, 1943), pp. xii, xxx, 8 n.

[39] Ernest Voorhis, comp., *Historic Forts and Trading Posts of the French Regime and of the English Fur Trading Companies* (Ottawa, 1930), *passim*; B. A. McKelvie, "The Founding of Nanaimo," *The British Columbia Historical Quarterly*, VIII (July 1944), 169–88. For information relative to the individual posts, the author is indebted to Miss Madge Wolfenden, Acting Archivist of the Archives of British Columbia, and to Nellie B. Pipes McArthur, formerly Librarian of the Oregon Historical Society, Portland, Oregon. The dates of founding, dates of relocation, and of abandonment are often obscure and contradictory in available records. See also J. Neilson Barry, "Early Oregon Country Forts: A Chronological List," *Oregon Historical Quarterly*, XLVI (June 1945), pp. 101–11. The list erroneously dates the founding of Fort McLoughlin as 1827. The correct date is 1833. See *McLoughlin's Fort Vancouver Letters*, first series, p. xc.

Taken as a whole, Hudson's Bay Company trading posts in the Columbia District were strategically placed along rivers, bays, and the coast. In general, it may be said that they answered the requirements of the trade. The structures, varying in number at each fort, were sturdily built and in most cases fortified and armed to meet the needs of the particular region in which they were located. The posts were stocked with a great variety of supplies, and were essential not only in the conduct of local trade but also in the operation of Company brigades which covered a wide area. The posts were the physical instruments so necessary to fullest development of the fur trade.

CHAPTER V

"PRO PELLE CUTEM"*

Once a fur trading post had been constructed, adequately fortified, stocked with trading truck, and manned by a trader and a requisite number of clerks and apprentice clerks,[1] the doors were opened for business with the Indians. The trader acted cautiously; he was always careful not to admit more than one or two Indians at a time. And this the trader did with the benefit of readily available firearms and a partition between himself and the customers. Actual trade, however, was preceded by an exchange of gifts.[2] Pieces made of wood, bronze, or other material, and corresponding in number with the pelts delivered, served as money, and were good for the purchase of articles, the value of which was described in terms of a standard beaver skin.

At first the Company hesitated to offer its choicest articles for exchange. In his first letter to the London office, dated October 6, 1825, McLoughlin expressed his intentions of unloading upon the natives "Several articles which are a dead Stock on our hands." The Chief Factor had blankets and "fine Guns," but he hoped to put off the exchange of such valuable articles as long as possible.[3] Eventually Hudson's Bay blankets, their value fluctuating, became favorite articles of trade; from available account books some idea may be had of the articles offered by the Company in trade. In the 1840–1841 Fort McLoughlin inventory of such supplies one finds an amazing assortment, viz.: Indian awls, needles, scissors, thread, Canton beads, blankets of varying description, ball vest buttons, combs, yard goods, colored cock feathers, files, looking glasses, Indian guns, wire gun worms, powder horns, silk handkerchiefs, fishhooks, pocket knives, scalping knives, copper and brass kettles, finger rings, soap, axes, lanterns, frying pans, spoons, vinegar, molasses, carbonate of soda, and sundry other articles.[4]

Conversely, the same Fort McLoughlin account book lists the type, number, and estimated value of the skins received during this fiscal year,

* It has been previously explained that this was the motto of the Hudson's Bay Company. It means simply: "Skin for Skin." For the pelt, in other words, the trader often risked his own skin.

[1] An employee of a Hudson's Bay Company post was expected to begin as an apprentice clerk and serve in this capacity for five years; thereafter, the succession was: a clerk, trader, chief trader, and chief factor. See Schooling, *The Hudson's Bay Company*, p. 32.

[2] Clark, *Willamette Valley*, pp. 182–83.

[3] *McLoughlin's Fort Vancouver Letters*, first series, pp. 3, 17–18.

[4] "Fort McLoughlin Account Book, 1840–1841." MS, Henry E. Huntington Library, San Marino, California, pp. 3–7.

as well as other fiscal years. During the 1840–1841 fiscal year this post received the skins of no less than 1,111 beavers, 829 minks, 194 black, brown, and grizzly bears, 477 martens, 300 land and sea otters, 97 lynxes, and a smaller number of raccoons, fishers, rats, and wolverines, the total value of which was placed at £2,330 1*s*. 2*d*.[5]

In some instances chief traders allowed a limited amount of credit to individual customers, but most frequently this was accorded only to Indians employed at or around the post. The Fort Nisqually account books contain several entries of such arrangements as, for example, the following excerpt.[6]

Began Working 15th Septr.

Silah [Indian's name]

1842	To	
Octr. 1	1	Small . . . . Chev^t Skin
	1	Sinew
	1	oz Blk Thread
	1	foot Twist Tobacco
	10	Ball G Powder
15	1	ft. twist Tobacco
22	1	Needle
	2	Hanks Thread
	1	Indian Capot 3½ Ells cape

. . . .

Dec. 20   2 ft. Comn. Blue Stroud (went off Jany 1843)

This Indian deserted 1st Jany 1843—if he is seen about the place hereafter, he should be made to work—for two months to earn the above—

Each chief trader was expected to keep, in addition to account books, a "Journal of Occurrences." It is from records such as these that varied and interesting glimpses may be had of the everyday activities at the trading posts. At Fort Nisqually the chief trader was Dr. William Fraser Tolmie, about whom more will be said later. Much of Dr. Tolmie's "Journal" relates to agricultural operations at Nisqually, but entries such as these reveal the casual manner in which a trader acquired his annual accumulation of furs:

Oct 26th Monday [1835] . . . . A few Indians arrived with some skins to trade.

This day I have entered on my forty first year eighteen of which I have passed in the Indian Country. Thanks be to God I am still in sound health[7]

. . . .

[5] "Fort McLoughlin Account Book, 1840–1841," p. 29.

[6] "Fort Nisqually Account Book, 1841–1842." MS, Henry E. Huntington Library, p. 15.

[7] "Fort Nisqually Journal of Occurrences, 1835–1836." MS, Henry E. Huntington Library, p. 34. Hereafter cited as "Journal of Occurrences," Nisqually.

Nov. 12 Thursday . . . . *Astsay lem* arrived and traded 3 Beavers & two Otters . . . .[8]

Decr. 31 Thursday . . . . The Trade of this month much better than anticipated . . . .[9]

And again one year later:

Decr. 20th Tuesday [1836]. Last evening four Yackamaws arrived with the Frenchman. They have brought a few skins. . . . .[10]

Sept. 30 Saturday [1837]. This day traded with the Klallums, very few furs. . . . .

Trade of the month poor.

55 Large Beaver	115 frm Cords
12 Small do.	2 Wolves
1 Bear.	280 frm Iyouquois
39 Otters	1 Horse
1 Fur seal	615 ps D. Salmon
11 Racoons	4 animals
34 Musquash.	26 fresh Salmon[11]
23 Chev Skins	

To the north, in New Caledonia, the trading followed much the same pattern, although there (except on the coast) the Company was without competition or interference from the Americans, whose numbers steadily increased in the southern and western parts of the Oregon country. But even in the north, writes Walter N. Sage, "The gathering of these peltries required much tact and ingenuity." At Fort Langley extra precautions were frequently taken by transacting business along the riverbank rather than within the stockade; and only those Indians with beaver skins to trade were permitted within the walls of the fort. British warships were seldom in the North Pacific waters and there was no standing army to offer protection, so the Company forts had to rely upon their own strength whenever resistance was offered by the natives.[12] Likewise, Indians' fighting among themselves affected the trade as indicated in the following letter from Chief Factor Donald McLean to James Douglas in January, 1859: "Furs are not coming in so plentifully as could be wished owing to a feud among the Aboriginies which renders each party fearful of hunting at any distance from their respective Villages."[13]

The most certain way for the Hudson's Bay Company to be assured

---

[8] *Ibid.*, p. 37.   [9] *Ibid.*, p. 46.   [10] *Ibid.*, "1836–1837," p. 18.

[11] *Ibid.*, p. 60. The "frm Iyouquois" probably means fathoms of shells.

[12] Walter N. Sage, "Life at a Fur Trading Post in British Columbia a Century Ago," *Washington Historical Quarterly*, XXV (January 1934), 14–15: "Autobiography of Roderick Finlayson, 1818–1891." MS, Archives of British Columbia.

[13] F. Henry Johnson, "Fur-trading Days at Kamloops," *The British Columbia Historical Quarterly*, I (July 1937), 174–75.

of a supply of skins was to send their traders and trappers to the sources of supply : the streams, the valleys, and the hills of the hinterland. The less enterprising natives could not be relied upon to put sufficient zest into their hunting and trapping. They met personal requirements. Why should they do more? Neither could the Indians be depended upon to bring all their pelts to the post for trade. And, moreover, what was there to prevent American competitors from going directly to the Indians and to the field in their quest for the coveted furs? For these reasons (and also because general transportation routes were essential) Hudson's Bay men added new trails to those previously used by Nor'westers and sent over them bands of hunters, trappers, and traders in search of furs. And to make such expeditions into the hinterland feasible, it was also necessary to organize brigades, the functions of which were to transport supplies from the main depots such as Fort Vancouver to outlying posts. It was from the hinterland posts that trading expeditions set forth and returned; and again, it was from such places that brigades conveyed the bales of furs back to the main depots for final shipment to London. The routes over which these caravans traveled were known as brigade trails.

Most vital of all the brigade trails was the one first established by the North West Company to connect its Fort St. James headquarters on Stuart Lake with its Montreal life-line on the one hand, and with the Columbia River on the other. From Fort St. James in the north to Fort George (Astoria) at the mouth of the Columbia there accordingly emerged a route of commerce over 1,500 miles in length. The upper third of this route from Fort St. James to Fort Okanogan on the Columbia was a winding overland course which to this day is referred to as the Hudson's Bay Brigade Trail.[14]

When in 1846 the established Oregon boundary line severed this vital route, Chief Factors James Douglas and John Work (in that year appointed Chief Factor) managed to stake out a western extension of the trail which led from Fort St. James over exceedingly rugged mountains to the easily navigable portion of the Fraser River. Near the mouth of this river stood Fort Langley, suitable as a supply base. "Confidentially," wrote Douglas and Work to their Company's London office, "expect to have everything in readiness for the passage of the Brigades by the new route in the summer of 1849. We will thereby escape the exactions of the United States Government, and have it in our power to supply the

---

[14] The upper part of this route from Fort St. James to Fort Alexander was a water route; from there to Fort Okanogan it was overland; from Okanogan to Fort George (Astoria) the course was again water, namely the Columbia River. F. M. Buckland, "The Hudson's Bay Brigade Trail," *The Sixth Report of the Okanagan Historical Society, 1935* (Vernon, British Columbia, 1936), p. 11; F. W. Howay, "British Columbia Brigade Trails," *The Beaver*, Outfit 269 (June 1938), pp. 48–51.

Interior with British goods free of import or transit duties."[15] In this plan they succeeded, and for many years thereafter Fort Langley became the jumping-off place for the northern brigades.[16]

There were several other trails, perhaps less sharply laid out, over which fur-trading expeditions ventured into such areas as the Snake River country, the Thompson River country, the region of the Great Salt Lake, the Willamette and Umpqua valleys, the Oregon coast, and even far south into Spanish California.

A fur-trading brigade was made up of a motley crew of humanity. The number in a brigade varied anywhere from about fifty to four hundred, and there were usually as many horses as there were people. Certain types of personnel were invariably present. Running the show was, generally, the Chief Trader or at times the Chief Factor. In order to bear certain marks of distinction the commander was usually dressed in a broadcloth suit, white shirt, and high collar, and invariably he wore a high beaver hat. The chief trader carried with him the fire bag containing his flint and steel, touchwood, and tobacco. Then there were the hunters, trappers, traders, clerks, storekeepers, and an assorted number of Indians—whole families of them—whose job it was to care for the horses, to handle provisions, trading goods, and other essential equipment.

"A beautiful sight," reminisced Malcolm McLeod, "was that horse brigade, with no broken hocks in the train, but every animal in his full beauty of form and colour, and all so tractable—more tractable than anything I ever knew in civilized life."[17] Out ahead were the hunters in search of meat and the next camp where there would be feed and water. Next came the person in charge, followed by the indispensable piper who played on his bagpipes to the mile-long procession. There was a packer by each horse, and a carefully loaded pack on the back of each animal, held properly in place by straps around the horse's belly and made tight with the diamond hitch. Trudging along in the rear were the families of the packers.[18]

Points of departure varied, depending upon the destination of a particular brigade. And if it left from Fort Vancouver bound inland, the first long stretch to Fort Okanogan (usually involving sixty days) was made in large clinker boats and canoes. Horse brigades also departed from these headquarters, namely the southbound troupes. The time for leaving Fort Vancouver was in the very early spring. Though on a

[15] "Fort Langley Correspondence," *The British Columbia Historical Quarterly,* I (July 1937), 191–93.

[16] James Douglas to Sir George Simpson, August 7, 1855. Archives of British Columbia; Johnson, *op. cit.,* pp. 177–78.

[17] Quoted in Howay, "British Columbia Brigade Trails," p. 51.

[18] Buckland, *op. cit.,* pp. 14–15.

smaller scale than previously described (about fifty to sixty in the party)
it was not without its color and excitement, especially for those who had
spent long, dreary, and monotonous winter months at some isolated post.
At the headquarters, wrote Dunn, the blacksmiths were "busily engaged
making beaver-traps . . . . storekeepers making up articles for trade,
and equipping the men . . . . packing up provisions . . . . ."[19]

To George Simpson there was little of romance about the brigades.
To him the brigades were absolutely essential to the fur trade, but the
people comprising these outfits were irresponsible human wretches, "the
very scum of the country and generally outcasts from the Service . . . . ."
They were, he added, "the most unruly and troublesome gang to deal
with in this or perhaps any other part of the World . . . . ."[20] Douglas
was equally unflattering when in a letter to Simpson he commented on
how "exceedingly riotous and unruly" the Fort Langley brigade had been
during the summer of 1848. He wrote that the group had caused "a great
deal of trouble" and that some had deserted and returned to the fort,
where they had been punished. At best, life with the brigades was hard,
cruel, and hazardous.[21]

In the employment of brigades and expeditions, the Hudson's Bay
Company far outstripped its predecessors, although the Nor'westers had
previously sent caravans into the Umpqua and Snake River valleys.
However, beginning with an expedition led by A. R. McLeod in 1826,
the Hudson's Bay Company brigade made an annual trip into the Umpqua Valley and subsequently across the Siskiyou Mountains into the
great interior valley of California as far south as the Tulares.[22]

Very important was the trade in the country of the Snake Indians,
and to them both Simpson and McLoughlin gave much attention. The
first North West Company trading expedition had entered this Oregon
back county in 1818, and for five years thereafter the region had been
revisited by the Nor'westers. Following the reorganization, Peter Skene
Ogden, son of a Quebec admiralty court judge and United Empire
Loyalist, was designated as Chief Trader in charge of the Snake country trade. Simpson feared American penetration into this region, and it

---

[19] Dunn, *Oregon Territory*, p. 108; Clark, *Willamette Valley*, pp. 184–85; Bancroft, *History of Oregon*, I, 46–47.

[20] Merk, *Fur Trade and Empire*, p. 45.

[21] James Douglas to George Simpson, March 12, 1849, "Correspondence Relating to Fort Langley, From the Hudson's Bay Company Archives, 1830–1858." Transcripts, Archives of British Columbia. See also *McLoughlin's Fort Vancouver Letters*, second series, pp. 57, 108.

[22] Ross, *The Fur Hunters*, Vol. II, chap. 10; Clark, *Willamette Valley*, p. 190; Alice B. Maloney, "Hudson's Bay Company in California," *The Oregon Historical Quarterly*, XXXVII (March 1936), 11–19; *Journal of John Work*, p. 59. John Work and Peter Skene Ogden also led parties into California. T. C. Elliott, "Peter Skene Ogden, Fur Trader," *The Quarterly of the Oregon Historical Society*, XI (September 1910), 229–78.

was his idea that Ogden should pursue the trade there for all that it was worth.[23]

On December 20, 1824, Ogden left Flathead Post with a formidable party of seventy-five men, mostly half-breeds, fully equipped with 25 teepees, 80 guns, 364 beaver traps, and 372 horses. The party moved eastward to the Missoula and Bitterroot rivers, across the Continental Divide to the very headwaters of the Missouri, and onto American soil. On its return the brigade struck the Salmon and Snake rivers, and subsequently moved as far southward as to become the probable discoverers of the Great Salt Lake. From this inland sea the Ogden party turned homeward. They moved north in the general direction from which they had come, but ultimately returned to headquarters in November 1825, by following the course of the Snake River.

Ogden entered the region at a time when American traders were also there, but even so the returns from this first year's catch amounted to 3,090 beaver skins, and the profits were encouraging enough to prompt Dr. McLoughlin to repeat the experiment.[24] Ogden subsequently made four more expeditions into the Snake country. In so doing he put fur trading in this area on a very profitable footing for over two decades. The sphere of Ogden's activities was gradually extended, for in 1828 he cut far southward from the Snake River to the Great Salt Lake, the Humboldt River, and back by way of the Pit River in northern California with a catch of furs that netted him a profit of £3,141 3s. 5d.[25]

Interior expeditions led by John McLeod, William Connolly, John Work, and other prominent traders, regularly penetrated the country of the Flathead, Cayuse, Nez Percés, and the Blackfoot Indians. Such journeys were invariably dangerous and the Company took every reasonable precaution against Indian attack. Simpson once went so far as to suggest to McLoughlin that John Work would do well to marry a Cayuse squaw (expenses to be paid by the Company), and that as a sort of good-will messenger she should accompany him on his journeys through the Cayuse country. That Work faced many dangers is revealed in a letter he wrote to his friend and fellow trader, Edward Ermatinger, following one of his expeditions: "I am happy in being able to inform you that I enjoy good health, and am yet blessed with the possession of my scalp which is rather more than I had reason to expect." Referring to his trip of 1831, Work

---

[23] Dee, "John Work: A Chronicle of his Life and a Digest of his Journals," p. 11.

[24] *McLoughlin's Fort Vancouver Letters*, first series, p. lxvi.

[25] "Returns, Columbia District and New Caledonia, 1825–1857." MS, Archives of British Columbia. This is in notebook form and was known to fur traders as a "skin book." Frederick Merk, "Snake Country Expedition, 1824–25," *The Oregon Historical Quarterly*, XXXV (June 1934), 99–107. Ogden's journal of this first expedition has been lost. [Hudson's Bay House], *Hudson's Bay Company*, p. 32.

added: "This last my friend has been a severe years duty on me, all my perseverence and fortitude were scarcely sufficient to bear up against the danger, misery, and consequent anxiety to which I was exposed."[26]

In their search for furs the brigades made direct contact with Indian tribes scattered throughout the back country. By means of this penetration Indians were often stimulated to trade when otherwise they might not have bothered. Members of the brigade also did some trapping and hunting of their own.

Complete records of the many expeditions are not extant, but those available show how extensively they added to the number of furs gathered directly at the scattered posts. The Fort Vancouver "Skin Book" (record book) gives the returns for all the Snake River expeditions from 1826 to 1852. The first party venturing into this region returned with 2,744 beaver skins, about equal the annual take in that year at Fort Colvile, and roughly two-thirds the number of beaver skins taken in at the Fort Vancouver headquarters. Two decades later the returns of the Snake River brigade were 1,454 beaver skins, as compared with only 962 at Fort Colvile, and 1,460 at Fort Vancouver. Many of the other brigades did not do so well, but neither are the returns from some of the small outlying trading posts impressive.[27]

Concerning the rugged coastal area, a grand scheme was evolved by Simpson and carried out by McLoughlin. Small craft were to operate along the coast in search of pelts. In the conduct of business they would make contact with posts that were accessible by water. The furs acquired in the smaller boats would then be transferred to the larger supply vessels which carried the cargo either to England or perchance to Canton and other points. Arrangements for marketing furs at Canton were to be made through the East India Company.

These were the plans. The Nor'westers had accomplished very little, if anything, in this type of trade, and alas, the Yankee traders had all but monopolized the North Pacific waters. But the new company was not so easily dissuaded; and with land-based operations, it "ought," wrote Simp-

---

[26] *McLoughlin's Fort Vancouver Letters*, first series, pp. 356–58, lvii; William S. Lewis and Paul C. Phillips, eds., *The Journal of John Work* (Cleveland, 1923), p. 179; John Work, "Journals." MSS, Archives of British Columbia. Work made an enviable record as a brigade and expedition leader. The following indicates the wide range of his activities: crossed the continent, 1823; in the Columbia Valley, 1823–1824; with McMillan to the Fraser River, 1824; in the Spokane area, 1825–1826; at Fort Colvile, 1826–1830; first Snake expedition, 1830–1831; Flathead and Blackfoot expedition, 1831–1832; Sacramento and Umpqua expedition, 1832–1834; on the Northwest coast, 1834–1835; and finally he settled down at Fort Simpson and Fort Victoria, 1836–1861. See Dee, *op. cit., passim*; the journals of many of Work's expeditions have appeared in edited form from time to time in the following periodicals: *British Columbia Historical Quarterly; California Historical Society Quarterly; Oregon Historical Quarterly; Washington Historical Quarterly*. See in addition to works previously cited: Alice Bay Maloney, ed., *Fur Brigade to the Ventura* (San Francisco, 1945); Dee, *The Journal of John Work*.

[27] "Returns, Columbia District and New Caledonia."

son, "to be able to put down all competition on the Coast."[28] And, chimed in McLoughlin: ". . . . it can be made a profitable Business" and "we can Secure it to our Country provided we are favoured with the same advantages in turning our Furs to account as our Competitors."[29]

Moreover, the Company meant to lose no time in the execution of the ready-made plans for the development of this coastal trade. Scarcely had the crude doors of Fort Vancouver swung open in 1825 when Chief Factor McLoughlin received instructions to assign the supply ship *William and Ann* (she had arrived at Fort George on April 16) to coastal reconnaissance. Her captain, Henry Hanwell, was unfortunately both incompetent and dilatory, at least so said McLoughlin, and little or nothing was accomplished during this first season. As for Captain Hanwell, his crew and the *William and Ann* were all lost in an attempted crossing of the Columbia River Bar four years hence.[30]

The hopefulness with which the coastal trade was first viewed was dampened by the seeming inability of the Governor and Committee in London to respond to the Chief Factor's insistence on: (1) more ships over which he, McLoughlin, would have complete authority; and (2) an extra year's supply of goods from England. If sufficient trading materials were on hand at Fort Vancouver, McLoughlin argued, then local trading operations could begin early in the spring without first awaiting the arrival of the annual supply ship from abroad. Not until 1828 did the London office attempt to meet these demands, at which time a plan was made to allocate three ships to the business of the Columbia District, two of which were to make annual voyages to and from London, the third to remain on the coast.[31] In principle this plan was carried out and such ships as the *Ganymede*, the *Isabella* (both of which unhappily shared the fate of the *William and Ann*), the *Dryad*, the *Eagle*, the *Columbia*, the *Lama*, and the *Nereide* were sailing vessels, averaging about two hundred tons each, which at times served in this North Pacific trade.

Moreover, smaller vessels were built to be used exclusively in the local river or coastal operations. One of these was the sixty-ton schooner *Vancouver* built at the fort for which it was named. It was ready for service in 1828 and it was used until 1834. Then there was the seventy-ton schooner *Cadboro*, built in London but sent to the District with the *William and Ann* in 1827, and it served as a permanent supply ship. She was first based at Fort Langley, and for a long time to come the sturdy little *Cadboro* became familiar to nearly every coastal port. Also built at

[28] Merk, *Fur Trade and Empire*, pp. 78–80, 86.

[29] *McLoughlin's Fort Vancouver Letters*, first series, p. 18.   [30] *Ibid.*, pp. lxix, lxxvii.

[31] *Ibid.*, p. lxxiv. See also Burt Brown Barker, ed., *Letters of Dr. John McLoughlin Written at Fort Vancouver 1829–1832* (Portland, 1948), p. 6.

Fort Vancouver was a twenty-five- to thirty-ton sloop, the *Broughton*, used exclusively for river service. And in a class by itself was the steamer *Beaver*, launched in England in 1836. The full story of the *Beaver* will be told subsequently. Suffice it to say here that in spite of McLoughlin's initial objection to a steamer for the coastal trade, this vessel gave notable service to the Company for many years to come. On the whole, McLoughlin favored vessels of the two-hundred-ton class for his coastal operations. Ships of this size, he felt, would command great respect from the natives with whom the trade was carried on.[32]

As for the forts, equally essential for the coastal trade, much has already been said. Fort Vancouver, though located inland, was as much the central entrepôt for coastal operations as it was for those pertaining to the hinterland. Forts Stikine, Taku, Langley, Simpson, McLoughlin, and Nisqually were among the most important in a chain of forts established in proximity to coastal or Puget Sound waters from Russian Alaska to the mouth of the Columbia. So important were these land bases that in 1834 the Doctor ventured the statement, and gave figures to support it, that "we can carry on the trade of the coast to more advantage by establishing posts than by vessels and that four posts when established will be kept up at less expense than one Vessel . . . . ."[33]

This, then, comprised the physical arrangements for the Company's great push to the shores of the Pacific. It had become a very costly undertaking in terms of pounds sterling, men, ships, and materiel. But the whole venture was soundly managed. Though carried at a loss at first,[34] and never yielding tremendous profits per se, the "coasting trade" had far-reaching ramifications. It facilitated the expansion of salmon fishing and lumbering, future key industries of the Pacific Northwest. It threw open the gates to far-flung Pacific Ocean trade which, though carried on in limited volume, was to involve China, Russian Alaska, the Sandwich Islands, California, Mexico, and South America. And lastly, the coastal trade gave renewed vision and greater zest to the Company as a whole. With foresight and imagination, with boldness and courage, with acumen and ruthlessness, the "honourable" gentlemen had completed successfully their march across a vast continent, and contributed greatly to the maritime interests of a nation devoted very largely to manufacture and trade.

---

[32] *McLoughlin's Fort Vancouver Letters*, first series, *passim*.

[33] *Ibid.*, p. 118. Simpson, on the other hand, disagreed with McLoughlin on the relative merits of ships and posts for the coastal trade. In 1841 he wrote the Governor and Committee at London that he regarded Forts McLoughlin, Stikine, and Taku as no longer necessary and that they could be abandoned "without any injury to the trade." The steamer *Beaver* could well do the work of the posts, he held. Differences on this issue mark the beginning of a deep rift between McLoughlin and Simpson, which eventually led to the Chief Factor's resignation. *Ibid.*, pp. xvi–xxi, xlviii.

[34] James Douglas to John McLeod, March 12, 1832, "Fort Vancouver Correspondence." MSS, Archives of British Columbia.

The "Beaver," First Steamer in the North Pacific

The Upper Cascades

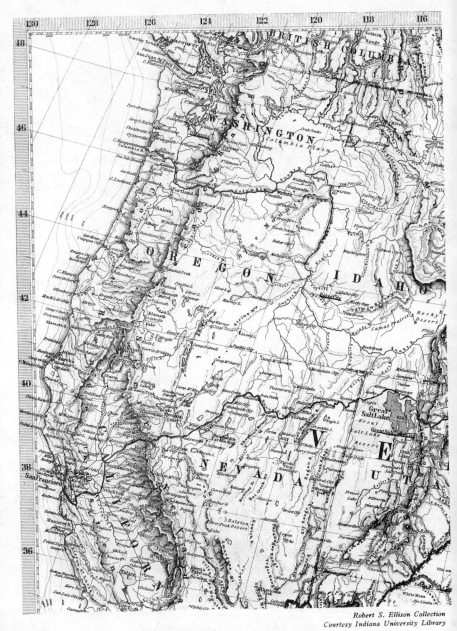

THE PACIFIC NORTHWEST (1879)

CHAPTER VI

THE HONOURABLE COMPANY'S LARDER

When Simpson and McLoughlin first entered the Oregon country their thoughts were not confined strictly to the fur trade; they had in mind stocking Columbia District's larder by means of utilizing many of the region's resources. Their writings betray a keen interest in the soil, in wild fruits and berries abounding there, in the green, lush grasses that blanketed the valleys west of the Cascades, in stately evergreens of "prodigious size" covering lofty mountains, and in fish that seemingly choked the clear, sparkling, greenish-blue streams rushing onward to the Pacific. To these two keen observers this wild hinterland with a "temperate regular and salubrious" climate had much to offer.[1]

To think in such terms was not original, for it was customary for some farming, gardening, and fishing to be done around trading posts, at least where Nature was friendly and where squaws were willing. Harmon, it is recalled, had a garden at Fort St. James in 1811, and thereby was the first white man to become a dirt farmer in British Columbia. At Fort Astoria, in the same year, men of the Pacific Fur Company planted a few wrinkly potatoes which grew and became the first white man's garden south of the Columbia River.[2] In years to come, other fur-trading posts became garden spots, some even became farms and ranches in an otherwise untilled country.

Later, while at Okanogan on his initial visit, the ever farsighted Simpson made this entry in his journal:

This Post is agreeably situated . . . . ; the Soil is much the same as at Spokane and produces the finest potatoes I have seen in the Country. Grain in any quantity might be raised here, but cultivation to any extent has never been attempted, indeed throughout the Columbia no pains have been taken to meet the demands of the trade in that way which was a great oversight . . . . .

Then as if to justify his eagerness to develop agriculture, he added: "It has been said that Farming is no branch of the Fur Trade but I consider that every pursuit tending to leighten the Expence of the Trade is a branch thereof . . . . ."[3] In a letter dated December 31, 1825, to the British Commissioner, Henry Addington, Governor Simpson even went so far as to declare that headquarters were in part being established at Belle Vue Point (Vancouver) rather than at Fort George, because he thought the country thereabouts "capable of producing large quantities of grain

---

[1] Merk, *Fur Trade and Empire*, pp. 105–6, 111.
[2] Clark, *Willamette Valley*, p. 199.
[3] Merk, *op. cit.*, p. 50.

of every kind"; and that "numerous herds of cattle" might be pastured there where the "nutritious roots are so abundant that almost any number of Hogs may be reared."[4]

To Chief Factor McLoughlin such diversified responsibilities were accepted with evident pleasure, and his future supervision of the projects was done with meticulous and painstaking care. During the very first season at Fort Vancouver clearings were made and some wheat was grown; during the second season, barley, Indian corn, peas, and potatoes were added to what was to become an imposing list of produce. On September 1, 1826, McLoughlin reported to the London office with reservations:

Our farming goes on as well as we could Expect; the pease yielded a hundred and fourteen Bushels the produce of nine and a half; the Barley yielded twenty seven the produce of two—we Expect to have ten Bushels Wheat from two—and six of Oats from One Sowen. This appears poor Returns But is owing to the seed being Greatly injured in coming here as the Wheat, Oats and Barley which Grew are the finest I ever saw in any Country.[5]

Though not sharing Simpson's optimism as to the productivity of the soil, the Chief Factor was confident that local requirements would be met within the next couple of years.

Reporting on progress in 1827 McLoughlin again stated that "Our farming comes on well Except the Indian corn and the pigs , ..." Peas, he believed, would provide an excellent substitute for corn. "Our wheat," he added, "Looks uncommonly fine," and of this and other grains he sent samples to the Governor and Committee in London.[6] Not, however, until 1832 did farming around Fort Vancouver reach near-maximum production. He then estimated the yield as follows: wheat, 3,000 bushels; oats, 1,500; peas, 2,000 to 3,000; corn, 800; barley, 2,000; buckwheat, 50; and potatoes, 6,000 bushels.[7]

As to the number of acres actually placed under cultivation, reports vary greatly. Dr. John Scouler, who visited the establishment in the year of its founding, estimated that no less than three hundred acres had already been turned by the plow.[8] In a letter written to the London office, October 31, 1837, McLoughlin seeks to correct mistaken notions held by the Governor and Committee on this matter of acreage, and it may be assumed he knew whereof he wrote.

In regard to the quality and extent of clear ground about Vancouver . . . . there is not Two Hundred acres which does not overflow in years of high water . . . . . There is a Plain about a Mile and a half behind the Fort, about a Hundred acres,

4 T. C. Elliott, ed., "George Simpson to H. W. Addington, December 31, 1825," *The Quarterly of the Oregon Historical Society*, XX (December 1919), 334.

5 *McLoughlin's Fort Vancouver Letters*, first series, p. 31.

6 *Ibid.*, p. 44.   7 *Ibid.*, p. 105.   8 Clark, *op. cit.*, p. 172.

also of dry miserable soil, and another of the same size and quality about a mile further; we have had Two Crops from each of these plains; . . . . There is also (which does not overflow) about a Hundred acres of sandy soil along the banks of the main Stream in the Lower Plain, in all, about Five and Six Hundred acres which does not overflow, but besides this, we have broken up and cultivated, about Four Hundred acres of the Plain which is apt to overflow.

McLoughlin cautioned that in case of flood or drought nearly all crops might be lost. This is the important part of his statement:

But let it be recollected, that during these Ten Years in which the Farm has been in operation, it has supplied all the Provisions required at this place, along the Coast, and for the Shipping in the country, which together generally amounts to about £2,000 annually . . . . .[9]

When Wilkes visited Fort Vancouver in 1841, the farms, so he reported, were nine miles square. Wilkes had arrived following a flood year, and therefore reported the loss of thousands of bushels of wheat.[10]

Impressive as the farms around Fort Vancouver had become, they scarcely overshadowed those at some of the subsidiary posts. On his first visit Simpson had left explicit instructions for farming to be done at designated places, one of which was Fort Colvile. In a letter dated April 16, 1825, to John Work, builder of that post, Simpson wrote: ". . . . you will be so good as to take care of . . . . seed *not ate* as next spring I expect that from 30 to 40 Bushels will be planted."[11]

The orders were scrupulously carried out and with each passing year more and more acres were put under cultivation at this eastern Washington post. Wrote Joshua Pilcher, an American fur trader who visited Fort Colvile in 1829:

About 60 or 70 acres of ground were under cultivation, and the crops were fine and abundant. Wheat, barley, oats, Indian corn, Irish potatoes, peas and garden vegetables of every description, grow well and were equal in the quality and in the product to any in this country.[12]

Farm products at Colvile soon increased in excess of local consumption, and surplus commodities were made available for outside use. Archibald McDonald, one of the men in charge of the fort, in 1837 described the farm as being then "on an extensive scale. . . . . upwards of 5000 bushels of grain . . . . 3000 of wheat, 1000 of corn and more than 1200 of other grain."[13] And visiting Fort Colvile in 1841, Lieutenant Robert E. Johnson of the Wilkes expedition estimated that the land then under culti-

[9] *McLoughlin's Fort Vancouver Letters*, first series, p. 205.

[10] Wilkes, *Narrative*, IV, 328, 334–36.

[11] William S. Lewis, "Information Concerning the Estab[l]ishment of Fort Colvile," *The Washington Historical Quarterly*, XVI (April 1925), 102–3.

[12] Oliphant, "Old Fort Colville," p. 38.

[13] *Ibid.*, pp. 40–43.

vation totaled about one hundred thirty acres and that the staples of wheat, oats, corn, beans, and potatoes were being raised somewhat to the exclusion of vegetables. He pointed out, though, that wild strawberries, wild cherries, and hawthorn berries were harvested from the countryside, and that the imported trees had not as yet succeeded.[14]

At Cowlitz and at Nisqually (about which more will be said later) similar farming operations were put in motion. From Cowlitz Farm Wilkes wrote in 1841:

They have here six or seven hundred acres enclosed, and under cultivation, with several large granaries, a large farm-house, and numerous out-buildings to accommodate the dairy, workmen, cattle, &c. The grounds appear well prepared, and were covered with a luxuriant crop of wheat. At the farther end of the prairie was to be seen a settlement, with its orchards, &c., and between the trees, the chapel and parsonage of the Catholic Mission gave an air of civilization to the whole.

Wilkes was reminded of the American frontier where Nature seemed ever "ready for the plough."[15]

Farther north was Fort Langley. There, too, gardening and limited farming activities were carried on under the direction of McMillan. Scattered through this chief trader's journal are found such references as these:

March 24, 1828: "All hands clearing and Preparing grounds for potatoes."
April 18: "Potatoes brought to Fort Langley aboard the 'Cadboro'."
September 1: "We had a trial of our potatoes and are finest I ever saw in the country. . . . ."
October 23: "Dry pleasant weather. 39 barrels of potatoes housed today. . . . . in all yielded 240 barrels—720 Bus."[16]

In addition to potatoes McMillan planted turnips, radishes, carrots, and red and white currants. Later he obtained glass which he used in devising a hotbed in which he seeded melons, cucumbers, pumpkins, gourds, and cabbages. Spring rains ruined his garden in 1830 but it was usually successful.[17] In 1842 there were harvested at Fort Langley 750 bushels of wheat, 500 bushels of oats, 250 bushels of barley, no less than 600 bushels of peas, and enough potatoes for local consumption. Moreover, quantities of beef, pork, and butter were among the items produced. It was from a larder such as this that Fort Langley and neighboring posts made shipments of grain, flour, salted beef, hams, and butter to the Russians in Alaska, and hence agriculture there became an important subsidiary business.

[14] Wilkes, *Narrative*, IV, 443, 445.
[15] *Ibid.*, IV, 315.
[16] "James McMillan Journal, 1828." Transcript, Archives of British Columbia.
[17] Sage, "Life at a Fur Trading Post," pp. 17–18.

At Fort George, New Caledonia, it was John McLean who first began farming operations in 1836. In that year a mere four acres were put under cultivation, but these subsequently increased. Seven years later this fertile Nechaco-Fraser River bottom land produced, in addition to assorted vegetables, 6,500 bushels of wheat. A mill was erected on the upper Fraser at which this wheat was ground into flour and subsequently distributed to other northern posts, such as Kamloops, Alexandria, and St. James.[18]

Elsewhere, too, at posts south of the Columbia River, and for that matter, at nearly all posts where crops would grow, gardening and farming was carried on for the chief purpose of lessening dependence on the outside world for essential food supplies.

Not nearly so important was horticulture, though here again it was the Hudson's Bay Company that gave this future key industry its initial boost. "The first fruit tree grown on the Columbia sprang from the seeds of an apple eaten at a dinner-party in London," wrote Bancroft. A lady had placed the seeds in Simpson's waistcoat pocket, so the story goes, and they were not discovered until the Governor again wore the coat at Fort Vancouver in 1827. Simpson thereupon gave the seeds to the gardener, who planted them. ". . . . and thence within the territory of Oregon," adds Bancroft, "began the growth of apple-trees."[19] When James Douglas transferred the District headquarters from Fort Vancouver to Fort Victoria, he brought apple trees with him and planted them, and thus their culture began on the big island.[20]

The correspondence between Chief Factor McLoughlin and Adolphe K. Etholine, the Russian governor at Sitka, shows that, try as they did, it was not easy for the Hudson's Bay Company to deliver to the Russians all the agricultural produce stipulated in their contract. For example, on June 26, 1842, Etholine wrote to McLoughlin: "Concerning the salt meat. I pray you Sir to have the goodness, to arrange so, that we could receive from you the next & future years exactly the quantity we want according to our contract." In a letter of September 1, 1843, the Russian governor complained of the poor quality and deficient weight of the wheat and butter. "I request to get from you, in 1844," he wrote, "five thousand

---

[18] J. B. Munro, "Agricultural Beginnings in the Interior of British Columbia." MS, Archives of British Columbia, p. 3.

[19] Bancroft, *Northwest Coast*, II, 441. There are several variations to this story. Another version is that McLoughlin planted the seed from which a tree grew. The yield was one apple which McLoughlin cut into seventeen pieces and served to guests. Narcissa Whitman was one of the guests. The next year there were twenty apples, and to this day the tree continues to bear. Others state that several trees grew from the seeds planted but that only one remains. See F. W. Laing, "A Few Notes on the Early History of Fruit Growing on the Pacific Coast." MS, Archives of British Columbia, pp. 2–5.

[20] *Ibid.*, p. 5.

fanegas of wheat, over and above our annual quantity,—the deficiency in our contract which you did not send us the first year."[21]

It was to help meet these demands, as well as to meet local needs, that the Hudson's Bay Company was prompted to begin agriculture and cattle raising on Vancouver Island, according to Chief Trader Roderick Finlayson.[22] Farming operations were accordingly begun around Fort Victoria in 1845. Indians were used to clear the land for what was first known as Fort Farm. The site of this farm corresponds with the present business section of the city of Victoria. Other farms in the vicinity of Fort Victoria during the 'fifties were Esquimalt, Craigflower (or Maple Point), Constance Cove, Viewpoint (or Viewfield), Beckley, North Dairy, and Uplands. Some of these were owned and operated by the Puget's Sound Agricultural Company, others were operated directly by the Hudson's Bay Company, and still others were managed and partly owned by men associated with the Hudson's Bay Company. It is estimated that by 1860 the Hudson's Bay Company and its subsidiaries owned about 15,000 acres of land on Vancouver Island, much of which was under cultivation. Anywhere from fourteen to thirty-five employees worked on each of these numerous farms, and a wide variety of crops and livestock was produced.[23] A census of Vancouver Island for 1855 records the island's production of wheat for the preceding year at 4,715 bushels; that of oats, 1,730 bushels; and that of peas, 1,567.[24]

In addition to its own farming operations the Hudson's Bay Company, by virtue of having received a royal grant to the island in 1849, was responsible for some general immigration from the United Kingdom. It was not, however, to the best interest of the Company to push developments of this kind.[25]

The introduction of peach culture has been associated with the name of Captain John Dominus, who is reported to have left some trees of this variety at the time of his departure from Oregon in 1830.[26] Little by little fruitgrowing developed and spread throughout the Pacific Northwest, until it reached the mammoth proportions of a leading industry.[27]

---

[21] *McLoughlin's Fort Vancouver Letters*, second series, pp. 327, 329–30.

[22] "Autobiography of Roderick Finlayson," p. 11.

[23] "The Census of Vancouver Island, 1855," *The British Columbia Historical Quarterly*, IV (January 1940), 51–58; F. W. Laing, "Early Agriculture in British Columbia." MS, 1926, Archives of British Columbia, pp. 2–3. Added information on each of these farms was secured with the help of Miss Madge Wolfenden, Archives of British Columbia.

[24] "The Census of Vancouver Island, 1855," p. 57; Matthew MacFie, *Vancouver Island and British Columbia* (London, 1865), p. 191.

[25] Leonard A. Wrinch, "Land Policy of the Colony of Vancouver Island, 1849–1866." Master of Arts Thesis, University of British Columbia, 1932, pp. 1 ff.

[26] Bancroft, *Northwest Coast*, II, 443.

[27] Laing, "Fruit Growing on the Pacific Coast," pp. 2–5.

To Dr. McLoughlin nothing seemed so important as his precious herds of cattle that grazed in plentiful pasture lands in the immediate vicinity of Fort Vancouver, and in the valleys of the Willamette and the Cowlitz. The doctor nursed his livestock most tenderly. He increased it and hoarded it, and years passed before he would permit anything but the most restricted slaughter.

Cattle, however, were not new on the American frontier. They are believed to have been brought first to the North American continent, to Mexico, by the Spaniards in 1521. They spread northward into Texas, into the Greater Southwest, into Alta California when that province was founded by Portolá and Father Serra in 1769, and finally in about 1790 they spread as far north as Nootka Sound.[28]

Not until 1814 were cattle known to have been taken to the mainland of the Oregon country. Two bulls and two heifers were then unloaded from the *Isaac Todd*, on which vessel they had been taken aboard at San Francisco.[29] When Peter Corney visited the post three years later he reported a threefold increase. Corney also noted the presence of pigs and goats around the place. He reported that predatory animals, wolves especially, had taken a sizable toll and that some of the domestic animals had increased rapidly.[30]

There were but twenty-seven cattle at Fort George when McLoughlin arrived to take charge. The Chief Factor presently added others brought in from the outside, and the combined herd was transferred to the pasture lands at Belle Vue Point where the headquarters were being erected. Until such a time when cattle would become plentiful it was McLoughlin's policy to increase and to preserve the herd. An occasional bull calf was killed for rennet used in cheese-making, but with this exception slaughter was strictly forbidden. McLoughlin's policy with respect to settlers was likewise restrictive. He would willingly loan to each family two cows, but under no circumstances would he sell cattle to the Americans. The care with which McLoughlin nursed his cattle bore abundant dividends. By 1828 the number at Fort Vancouver was about two hundred; and while Spanish cows were not champion milkers, the yield in dairy products by 1831 was in excess of local needs.[31]

While cattle were brought in from California from time to time, McLoughlin also imported some Durham bulls from England with the

---

[28] F. W. Laing, "Some Pioneers of the Cattle Industry," *British Columbia Historical Quarterly*, VI (October 1942), 257–58.

[29] C. S. Kingston, "Introduction of Cattle into the Pacific Northwest," *The Washington Historical Quarterly*, XIV (July 1923), 165.

[30] *Ibid.*; J. Orin Oliphant, "Winter Losses of Cattle in the Oregon Country," *The Washington Historical Quarterly*, XXIII (January 1932), 3–17.

[31] Kingston, *op. cit.*, pp. 167–68.

view toward improving the breed. Not until 1836, at which time the Columbia District's herd numbered 700, did the Chief Factor ease the restrictions on butchering, and then but slightly.[32] Thus the increase continued. When Wilkes was there in 1841, the number of cattle, according to him, was about 3,000. A large number of them continued to be milk cows which provided the whole establishment with "most excellent milk," reported Wilkes. The ones giving the best milk were those of a cross between the Spanish and the English varieties.[33]

At some of the outlying posts the story is the same as at headquarters. Fort Colvile, for example, received its start when two bulls and two cows were brought there from Fort Vancouver in 1825, and "from these have sprung," wrote Wilkes, "one hundred and ninety-six head of fine cattle." At Fort Langley cattle first arrived in 1829, and from this nucleus have come in part the thousands of cattle that are now raised in the province of British Columbia.[34]

These herds were not, as has been shown, a direct part of the Hudson's Bay Company trade, but, like the growing of grains, they helped to stock the Company's larder and thereby simplified immeasurably the problem of food supply. When one realizes, as the census of 1860 reveals, that there were 182,382 head of cattle in Oregon and the Territory of Washington alone (many, of course, having sprung from herds brought in directly by American settlers) one cannot ignore the great service which the Hudson's Bay Company rendered to the development of ranching, dairying, and the cattle trade in that region. And, in addition, as F. W. Laing has shown, large herds were driven to British Columbia, especially during and after 1859 when the gold rush brought thousands of prospectors into the Fraser, Cariboo, and Kamloops regions.[35]

Important and extensive as was this early cattle breeding in the Oregon country, it was by no means carried on to the exclusion of other phases of livestock raising. Horses, sheep, goats, and hogs (though less numerous than the cattle) were none the less important.

To the fur traders, the horse and the mule had proved indispensable both in the transportation of supplies and as a source of meat. Horses, as previously noted, had first been introduced to the Pacific Northwest Indians by their red brethren from east of the Rockies about 1734. They had multiplied considerably by the opening of the next century when additional numbers were brought in by the white fur traders, who were especially dependent upon pack animals wherever operations departed

---

[32] Kingston, *op. cit.*, pp. 168–69.   [33] Wilkes, *Narrative*, IV, 334.

[34] *Ibid.*, IV, 445; *McLoughlin's Fort Vancouver Letters*, first series, p. 207; Munro, "Agricultural Beginnings in the Interior of British Columbia," pp. 5–6.

[35] Laing, "Some Pioneers of the Cattle Industry," pp. 258 ff.

from the navigable streams.[36] Early traders, moreover, practically subsisted on horseflesh whenever wild game was not readily available. It was reported that during one winter alone no less than ninety horses were consumed at Fort Spokane; and in a three-year period no less than seven hundred horses were eaten for food at Fort Walla Walla.[37]

Hogs, as we have noted, were also among the earliest arrivals in the Oregon country, and though some difficulties were encountered in raising them, McLoughlin reported "upwards of 250 Pigs"[38] at the headquarters in 1831. With the passing of years pork greatly supplemented horseflesh as an item in diet.

Sheep raising also became an important part of the Hudson's Bay Company's ranching activities, and this concern contributed immeasurably to the future wool production in the region. Originally sheep, like cattle, may have been brought to Nootka Sound by the Spaniards. Just when sheep came to the mainland is not known for certain. It is known, though, that in 1829 the Hudson's Bay Company imported sheep directly from California. The American Captain John Dominus made the delivery. Then in 1834 Nathaniel Wyeth, another American, brought in an additional number of sheep from the Sandwich Islands, to which mid-ocean archipelago George Vancouver had transported sheep from California as early as 1792–1794.[39] The Company's interest in sheep was due partly to a desire to produce wool and tallow for export, and also to have mutton, always popular with Scots, on hand as an item of food.[40]

Growth of the flocks was reasonably fast. Mentioning his sheep in a letter to George Simpson in 1831, the Chief Factor gave as the number 15 rams, 361 ewes and wethers, and 142 lambs; ". . . . by bestowing upon them the necessary degree of care we may trust to a rapid increase, but wool is coarse and needs a cross to improve it." As a remedy for the coarseness of the wool he recommended the importation of such highly developed strains as the merino and Cheviot to be crossed with the California variety. McLoughlin saw in sheep great trading possibilities. "If we could succeed in covering the plains of the Columbia with flocks of sheep," he wrote Simpson, "we may provide a valuable succedaneum for Beaver, and open a much more extensive trade than the present."[41]

It was at Fort Nisqually and Cowlitz Farm, and upon the Vancouver Island farms, that sheep raising reached its fullest development under the auspices of the Hudson's Bay Company.[42]

---

[36] Morton, *Canadian West*, pp. 16 ff.

[37] *Ibid.*, pp. 718–19; Bancroft, *Northwest Coast*, II, 204.

[38] *McLoughlin's Fort Vancouver Letters*, first series, p. 259.

[39] Alfred L. Lomax, *Pioneer Woolen Mills in Oregon* (Portland, 1941), pp. 19–20, 25.

[40] *Ibid.*, p. 24.   [41] *McLoughlin's Fort Vancouver Letters*, first series, p. 285.

[42] "Returns, Columbia District and New Caledonia."

Was it the business of the Hudson's Bay Company solely to conduct the fur trade? Or was it to sidetrack the fur trade and devote itself very largely to agriculture and ranching? Was it not in violation of the Charter to develop ranching in the manner being done by McLoughlin? Did not the Charter speak exclusively of trading and fishing, saying nothing about farming? These and other questions were doubtless asked by officials of the Company as reports kept coming in about the steady increase both in agricultural production and in the size of the herds and flocks that now grazed in valleys of the old Oregon country. But the reports were optimistic; they augured well for the future trade and profits of the Columbia District, and the officials were therefore loath to apply the brakes.

A happy solution for this dilemma was found by none other than McLoughlin himself. When in London during 1838–1839, he proposed to the Committee meeting at Hudson's Bay House that there should be formed a separate concern devoted exclusively to agriculture. In a prospectus describing the plan, the concern would be styled Puget's Sound Agricultural Company; it would be capitalized at £200,000 and the stockholders of the Hudson's Bay Company would likewise become the stockholders of the new organization. John H. Pelly, Andrew W. Colvile, and George Simpson were to be the governing agents, but it would come under the direct management of McLoughlin at Fort Vancouver. Legally, therefore, the Puget's Sound Agricultural Company was to become what Simpson declared "an off-shoot of the Hudson's Bay Company." The prospectus specifically proposes that this new company was to be organized for ". . . . the raising of flocks and herds, with a view to the production of wool, hides and tallow, and also for the cultivation of other agricultural produce . . . . ."[43]

It was the object of the officers of this new concern, moreover, not only to raise and distribute livestock and agricultural produce within the Columbia District but, as Lieutenant Wilkes foresaw it, trade would be conducted with the Russians at Alaska; prospects were good for trade with the Sandwich Islands and possibly with California; and hides, horns, tallow, and wool would be exported to England, utilizing the available

[43] Prospectus of the Puget's Sound Agricultural Company (London, March 20, 1839). Also published with slightly different wording as "Puget's Sound Agricultural Company: Prospectus," The Quarterly of the Oregon Historical Society, XIX (December 1918), 345–49; Leonard A. Wrinch, "The Formation of the Puget's Sound Agricultural Company," The Washington Historical Quarterly, XXIV (January 1933), 3; Kingston, op. cit., p. 174; Walter N. Sage, Sir James Douglas and British Columbia (Toronto, 1930), p. 91. According to Sage, only £16,160 were ever paid in. It appears, though, that the financial affairs of the agricultural concern and the parent fur-trading company were closely connected, so much so that it was difficult to distinguish between the two. Evidence of this is the transfer, in 1842, of the fur-trading post, Fort Nisqually, to the agricultural firm. See also McLoughlin's Fort Vancouver Letters, first series, p. 137 n.

space in the Hudson's Bay Company supply ships returning to their home ports.[44] But whatever its objectives, official approval was given and by 1839 the Puget's Sound Agricultural Company was a going concern.

The region selected for operations lay between the headwaters of the Cowlitz River (an important tributary of the Columbia) and the southern tip of Puget Sound, an area subsequently claimed as being 167,040 acres in extent.[45] The choice of this baronial acreage was in many respects a happy one. The quality of the soil was especially acceptable for grazing purposes ;[46] the region was accessible to sea-borne and river-borne commerce ; and transecting the estate were important overland trails which connected Fort Vancouver headquarters with Puget Sound and many northern posts. There were also trails that ran in east-west directions and extended on across the Cascades to upper Columbia River posts. There was more than ample rainfall in this area and fresh-water streams, so essential for cattle raising, were abundant, as were thick evergreen forests that covered the surrounding hills and offered an unlimited supply of timber and wood to those who were about to undertake this large-scale venture.

There were to be two farm establishments, one near the Cowlitz River Landing and to be known as Cowlitz Farm, the other at or around the previously established Fort Nisqually, to be known as Nisqually Farm. The latter was to be headquarters for both establishments.[47]

Chosen to manage the Puget's Sound Agricultural Company under McLoughlin's general supervision was the capable, temperate, and engaging Scot, Dr. William Fraser Tolmie, M.D., University of Glasgow ; founder of and, at the time of his selection, the Chief Trader at Fort Nisqually. Dr. Tolmie had come to the Columbia District in 1833, the year after receiving his medical degree. He had come by way of Hawaii, from which he had brought dahlia seeds to be planted in a frame at Fort Vancouver. At first Dr. Tolmie served as surgeon at Fort Vancouver, but before the first summer was over he had been sent to his new and permanent assignment. He has been portrayed as having two dominant characteristics, namely, amiability and courage. To these might be added resourcefulness.[48] First hired to work for Dr. Tolmie at Nisqually were

---

[44] Wilkes, *Narrative*, IV, 308.

[45] H. H. Bancroft, *Washington, Idaho, and Montana* (San Francisco, 1890), p. 43.

[46] James Douglas, "Diary of a Trip to the Northwest Coast, April 22–October 2, 1840." MS, Archives of British Columbia. Douglas gives a description of the land, the soil, and the grasses.

[47] Wrinch, "The Formation of the Puget's Sound Agricultural Company," p. 6.

[48] Dorothy O. Johansen, "William Fraser Tolmie of the Hudson's Bay Company, 1833–1870," *The Beaver*, Outfit 268 (September 1937), pp. 29–32.

a ploughman, a carpenter, four herdsmen, and a desired number of ordinary Company servants. A "principal farmer" was soon selected to direct the work at Cowlitz Farm and he was given the immediate assistance of six ploughmen, three sheep herders, two "rough" carpenters, a blacksmith, and a half-score of servants. Some of the farm workers came directly from England, and the terms under which they came obliged them to be married, and to remain on the job for five years. Passage "out" was charged against the employees at the farms.

As for stocking the farms, the Hudson's Bay Company simply transferred to the account of the Puget's Sound Agricultural Company practically all of its livestock, consisting of horses, cattle, sheep, swine, and goats, and all farm implements. In short, the Hudson's Bay Company per se turned over to its new subsidiary, lock, stock, and barrel, all its farming business. In return the Puget's Sound Agricultural Company agreed not to engage in what was strictly speaking the fur trade.[49]

Under Dr. Tolmie's direction the new undertaking developed with efficiency and speed. Buildings of "well-hewn" logs were constructed, soon giving to Cowlitz Farm the appearance of a small village. Wilkes, who saw it in 1841, reported that the Company, though not without some difficulty, had met both its domestic obligations and the terms of its agreement to supply the Russians in Alaska with 15,000 bushels of grain and quantities of butter and cheese.[50] During the summer of 1842 the farms packed no less than 2,768 pounds of fine wool, 984 pounds of coarse wool, 72 pounds of black wool, 137 pounds of unclassified wool, and 78 pounds of Cheviot wool, all for exportation to England. In 1845 no less than 10,000 pounds of wool were sent to England. And to this were added hides, horns, and tallow.[51]

---

[49] Carey, *History of Oregon*, I, 250–51; Sage, *Sir James Douglas and British Columbia*, p. 91.
[50] Wilkes, *Narrative*, IV, 308, 315–16.

[51] Most revealing are the official reports and inventories of Cowlitz and Nisqually that give particular data on the Company's scope of operations. For the years 1845 and 1852 they are as follows:

Cattle on Hand

	Bulls	Cows	Oxen	Heifers	Bull Calves	Heifer Calves	Total
1845	107	775	406	269	340	383	2,280
1852	938	2,129	1,324	814	714	859	6,777

Sheep on Hand

	Rams	Ewes	Wedders	Do. under 2 years	Gimmers	Rams and Wedder Lambs	Ewe Lambs	Total
1845	107	1,652	765	920	959	688	781	5,872
1852	243	3,368	...	...	1,004	1,086	1,136	6,837

Horses on Hand

	Mules	Stallions	Geldings	Mares	Colts	Fillies	Total
1845	2	14	39	64	66	43	228
1852	2	10	100	57	34	65	268

The reports also give figures on sales, those transferred to other posts, and the number killed for use, and "killed or driven off by squatters"—the latter alone taking a toll of 1,500 head of cattle

Dr. Tolmie's "Journal of Occurrences," previously referred to, tells much about everyday life at the establishments; how he got his "Cattle, horses, and Pigs . . . . into order"; the ploughing for "our Kitchen garden"; how "We now have for our new field near the small river 2000 fence poles"; the arrival from Vancouver of "the Express from the east of the Mountains"; how his men were "employed thrashing the pease—one busy at harrowing the new plowed field," etc. These documents likewise allude to the repeated arrivals and departures of the Company's ships, the *Beaver*, the *Mary Dare*, and the *Cadboro*.[52]

The operations at Nisqually and Cowlitz proved to be highly successful. Profits from the sale of livestock and produce were good, at times exceeding £2,500, and seldom if at all did losses exceed the returns. Moreover, the Puget's Sound Agricultural Company continued to operate, as was its right under the treaty, long after political sovereignty over the Company's holdings passed definitely into the hands of the United States. The Americans, however, registered increasing protests against the concern; and as pressure for the liquidation of all Hudson's Bay Company property south of the forty-ninth parallel persistently increased, the Company gave way. In a settlement made between the American and British governments in 1869 the Hudson's Bay Company was awarded $650,000 for its holdings, $200,000 of which represented the value of the Puget's Sound Agricultural Company. During the following year Edward Huggins, the last of the clerks, and by then an American citizen, acquired his beloved Nisqually House as a homestead and lived there until his death in 1907. Huggins continued to make notes in his "Journal of Occurrences," much as Tolmie had done, and his entry for June 11, 1870, is a written testimonial that the older order had at last given way to the new. ". . . . Dr. Tolmie accompanied by myself (E. H.) and two eldest boys," he wrote tersely, "started for Olympia in Spring Waggon, to arrange with Land Office about Surrender of P. S. A. Cos. lands . . . . ."[53]

During the years that elapsed between the founding of Fort Vancouver and the passing of Nisqually from Company to private hands, the

in 1853. In this same year the Company transferred, killed for use, and sold in the open market no less than 1,007 head of cattle; but in 1854 this number was reduced to 562. No figures are available on the sale of sheep, but some are given relative to wool. An item for 1848–1849 indicates that sixty-eight bales of wool were "sold by order and for account of the Puget's Sound Agricultural Company by public auction at the Hall of Commerce—London," bringing a return of £474 19s. 5d. "Miscellaneous Papers" and "Journal of Occurrences," Nisqually, 1835 and after. MSS, Henry E. Huntington Library. See also Lomax, *Pioneer Woolen Mills in Oregon*, p. 38.

[52] "Journal of Occurrences," Nisqually, *passim*.

[53] "Journal of Occurrences at Nisqually in 1870," *The Washington Historical Quarterly*, XXV (January 1934), 63.

Hudson's Bay Company had contributed immeasurably to the future development of farming, ranching, and dairying in what is now the state of Washington. The concern cleared and improved hundreds of acres of land north of the Columbia River. It put crop raising beyond the experimental stage and made planting and sowing easy for the Americans who followed. Fruit trees were introduced; cattle, sheep, and hogs were raised, and new breeds, suitable to the area, were bred. By 1870 the Hudson's Bay Company gave reassurance to the 23,955 settlers then in Washington Territory that the region north of the Columbia was agriculturally rich.

That Pacific Northwest waters were at times teeming with huge, beautiful, and tasty red salmon was commonplace knowledge among the mountain men. Nor did the fact that giant spruce, firs, cedars, and pines awaited the sharp blade of the woodsman's axe escape the attention of even the least imaginative of fur men who roamed this country. Here, indeed, were rich resources that on some future day were to become principal sources of income for the area.

We have noted that Indians leaned very heavily on a fish diet, and that they also utilized available timber both for dwelling construction and for canoe construction. From the Indians Daniel Harmon and other Nor'westers learned how to dry and preserve salmon, although the natives appeared not to distinguish between good and bad fish. By 1823 Hudson's Bay men at Fort George began to experiment with salmon as a possible article of export, and two years later we find Simpson in favor of adding salmon to the fur cargoes destined for Canton. With regard to lumber Simpson believed, as indeed he wrote to Captain Aemilius Simpson in 1828, that ". . . . Timber Trade as a distinct branch of business would yield us large profits in proportion to the Tonnage employed therein."[54] McLoughlin likewise favored experimenting in the salmon and lumber business, particularly in the California and Sandwich Islands trade. With respect to the former he wrote to the home office in 1826: "We can purchase Salmon in the Columbia at an Averrage of 3½ to 5 d. Each with the advance of 70 p. Cent, and thirty of these fill a Barrel and I am given to understand it would sell well in New California."[55] And with respect to lumber, it was not long before the doctor planned the construction of a sawmill not far upstream from his Fort Vancouver headquarters.

The area thought best suited for catching and processing salmon was at or near Fort Langley. In 1827 the post's founder, McMillan, is known to have made his first large catch. As in the case of the fur trade, the

[54] Merk, *Fur Trade and Empire*, pp. 120, 121 n., 240, 298.
[55] *McLoughlin's Fort Vancouver Letters*, first series, p. 37.

natives were inveigled into doing the actual salmon fishing. For this purpose they used canoes, and boatloads of freshly caught salmon were taken to the beaches where still other Indians (usually the women) cut and cleaned the fish which were then ready for delivery at the fort. In payment the natives received the usual commodities familiar to the fur trade.[56]

So abundant were the salmon around Fort Langley that McMillan was prompted to boast that: "We could trade at the door of our fort, I suppose, a million of dried salmon, if we chose—enough to feed all the people of Rupert's Land."[57] This is perhaps an overstatement, but we nevertheless find Fort Langley in 1828 abundantly stocked with the red and pink fish. By then Archibald McDonald, who had assumed the functions of Chief Trader, reported that in his provisions shed were 3,000 dried salmon and 16 tiers of salted salmon; whereas all told probably 20,000 fish had been acquired. By 1829 the salmon trade got under way when McDonald exchanged 7,544 salmon for a paltry £13 17s. 2d.'s worth of trading truck. Each succeeding year witnessed a steady increase in this fishing business; 220 barrels of salmon were made ready for shipment in 1830 and nearly 300 the year thereafter.[58]

That the salmon trade was of no small importance, at least to Fort Langley, is clearly indicated in McLoughlin's letter to the Governor and Committee at London, November 15, 1836, in which he declared that "the expense of keeping up the Establishment at Fort Langley is in general paid by the Salmon Trade. . . . ."[59] The trend upward continued, and by 1846 the annual salmon export from Fort Langley, and by that time other Fraser River fisheries, is reported to have ranged between 1,000 and 2,000 barrels of salted and pickled salmon. In time this was supplemented by fishing done in the Columbia River where salmon was as equally abundant as in the Fraser River, but where the industry was not developed as rapidly. By the close of the period the demand for this commodity existed in many parts of the world, including the Sandwich Islands, China, the United States, and England. It was, however, in the Sandwich Islands that the best price for salted salmon was commanded.[60] Since then the salmon industry has enjoyed a remarkable history. Always salmon has provided northwesterners with an important item in their diet, and to outsiders the popularity of this delectable-looking fish has constantly increased.

---

[56] Dunn, *Oregon Territory*, p. 114; Sage, "Life at a Fur Trading Post," p. 18.

[57] Quotation taken from Sage, "Life at a Fur Trading Post," p. 18.

[58] Nelson, *Fort Langley*, p. 11; Sage, "Life at a Fur Trading Post," p. 19.

[59] *McLoughlin's Fort Vancouver Letters*, first series, p. 155.

[60] Clark, *Willamette Valley*, p. 202; Nelson, *Fort Langley*, p. 17.

Development of lumber trade hinged mostly on the California market, where 1,000 board feet brought from forty to fifty dollars. By 1828 McLoughlin had a small mill in operation about four to five miles above the Fort Vancouver headquarters.[61] Ten years later this mill was completely rebuilt, and its capacity was increased to where its twenty-eight operators could turn out 2,400 feet of lumber daily.[62] Writing the London office in 1838, James Douglas declared that no less than 60,000 feet of one-inch boards were shipped to the Sandwich Islands and at prices whereby a goodly return was made by the transaction.[63] At best the market for lumber remained limited and the output correspondingly small. And even at the Sandwich Islands where prospects were once good, American and New Zealand competition brought prices down to a point where the lumber trade, except when boards were exchanged for salt, became relatively negligible. At one time McLoughlin had taken steps toward the construction of a sawmill on the Willamette River, but the dismal foreign market caused him to abandon the project.[64]

The list of Hudson's Bay Company subsidiary activities could well be expanded to include at least milling and distilling, the former playing an important role in meeting local needs for flour. As for distilling, McLoughlin gave this up as a bad job after running off about three hundred gallons of spirits. ". . . . I began to Distil in '33," he wrote, "but '36, finding the bad effects it had on our affairs I gave it over, and would recommend if possible never to attempt it again . . . . ."[65] All told, the total investments in agriculture, lumber, and flour mills and other subsidiaries to the fur trade amounted to nearly £40,000. "It seems a conservative estimate," concluded R. C. Clark, "to place at least half the total investments of the Company to the account of industries and enterprises in no way essential to the fur-trade."[66] And to this one might append: these varied enterprises were in the long run of far greater importance to the growth and development of civilization in the Oregon country than the fur trade itself.

---

[61] *McLoughlin's Fort Vancouver Letters*, first series, p. lxxiii.

[62] *Ibid.*, pp. 259–60; Clark, *op. cit.*, pp. 201–2.

[63] *McLoughlin's Fort Vancouver Letters*, first series, p. 260.   [64] *Ibid.*, pp. xciii, cxvii.

[65] *Ibid.*, p. 208.   [66] Clark, *Willamette Valley*, p. 204.

CHAPTER VII

YANKEE INFILTRATION

The arrival at the wide, misty mouth of the Columbia River during May 1810, of the *Albatross* represents the first attempt on the part of Americans to establish a fur-trading post on Oregon soil. Captain of the *Albatross* was Nathan Winship, one of three remarkable brothers interested in this venture. The ship and crew had come from Boston. Belatedly Winship and his men had crossed the treacherous Columbia Bar, had sailed upstream about forty-five miles, and at an inviting meadow on the south bank they had lashed the *Albatross* to trees and had begun to build a two-story log fort and to plant a garden. Then came the inevitable flood; the river overflowed its banks, flooded the garden, and caused the men to seek a new location for their fort. No sooner had this been done than the threat of extermination by the Indians caused Captain Winship to seek still another location. Before this could be done the much more ambitious, but similiar, project of John Jacob Astor caused Winship to lose heart and give up his venture as a bad job.[1]

Even while the Winship expedition was en route around Cape Horn, perhaps long before, the famous New York merchant had his plans well laid. Astor had long had an interest in the fur business, and it had irked him greatly that such British firms as the North West Company and the Michilimackinac Company had powerful and strangling tentacles in his adopted United States. Astor knew that American furs flowed into Canada, and that at least 75 percent of the furs purchased in the United States came from the British-controlled province to the north. It was especially humiliating to this proud, calculating merchant prince to be obliged to buy his furs in Montreal at outlandish prices, and the time had now come, he thought, to give battle. He would organize powerful American companies that he hoped in five years would extend their control of the United States fur trade to the very shores of the Pacific Ocean.

Astor was a man of great vision, and he planned to do this job on a grand scale. New York, New Orleans, St. Louis, and, as plans unfolded, a post at the mouth of the Columbia River, would be important entrepôts connected by ocean, river, and overland trails of staggering lengths. He would have others share the risks, and thus it was that in 1808 Astor made known his plans to New York's Governor DeWitt Clinton, and in part to President Thomas Jefferson, with a view toward securing a char-

---

[1] Clark, *Willamette Valley*, p. 129; Morison, *Maritime History of Massachusetts*, p. 58.

ter. Jefferson approved Astor's plans (and, of course, they concerned the interests of the American government in the Oregon country) ; and with the blessings of the New York legislature and its chief executive, Astor secured his charter on April 6, 1808.

The Company was to be known as the American Fur Company; its capital stock was a million dollars ; and, with fortune on its side, it was destined to achieve success and prominence chiefly in the American Middle West. Moreover, it was largely as an outgrowth of this firm's activities that Astor's Pacific Fur Company was organized in New York June 23, 1810, the function of which was to operate in the Oregon country.

The articles of agreement of the Pacific Fur Company were numerous. Astor was to be the first partner, and associated with him were Alexander McKay, Donald McKenzie, Duncan McDougal, Wilson Price Hunt, David Stuart, Robert McLellan, John Clarke, and others. Funds advanced should not exceed $400,000; there would be a hundred shares, with Astor holding fifty which could, if Astor chose, be made over to the American Fur Company. Power generally was to rest with the founder, who in a step toward taking action on the northwestern coast, chose Hunt to reside as agent for the Pacific Fur Company on the Pacific Coast.[2]

Astor's plans called for the sending of two expeditions, one by sea and one by land, to the Columbia River region before the year 1810 was out, and once there to establish a post. McDougal, Stuart, and McKay joined those going by sea aboard the ill-starred ship, the *Tonquin*, commanded by the stern and irascible Captain Jonathan Thorn, veteran of United States naval operations in Algiers. Sailing from New York on September 8, and after a voyage filled with bickering and feuding between Captain Thorn, his crew, and his passengers, the *Tonquin* reached, by way of the Horn and Hawaii, the mouth of the Columbia River on March 22 of the following year (1811). A grim and tragic pall continued to hover over this ship.

In his effort to find a passable channel across the Columbia Bar at Cape Disappointment, Thorn had lowered a "jolly-boat" with First Mate Ebenezer D. Fox and four men aboard. The high winds were whipping the waves to ominous heights, and soon the men vanished from view forever. On the following morning one of three boats lowered capsized and three additional men (one a Sandwich Islander) were lost in what today is still a mariner's graveyard. In due time, though, the 290-ton *Tonquin* bounced and jogged its way through the treacherous channel to a safe and protected cove midway between Tongue Point and Point George on the

---

[2] For an account by Astor of his grand scheme for control of the American fur trade and its tie-up with the China trade, see letter, John Jacob Astor to James Madison, July 27, 1813. MS, William R. Coe Collection, Yale University Library, New Haven, Conn. See also Porter, *John Jacob Astor*, Vol. I, chap. 7.

south bank of the Columbia where passengers and supplies were unloaded, and where Fort Astoria was presently to emerge.[3]

Shortly after this precarious landing the unpredictable Captain Thorn
with twenty-two additional men aboard sailed northward. En route he
took aboard Lamayzie, an Indian interpreter. Thorn proceeded to Clayoquot Harbor (a few miles south of historic Nootka), Vancouver Island.
It was here in Templar Channel that Thorn made his ill-fated attempt
to begin the coasting trade with the Indians. "But the harsh and unbend-
ing manners of the captain," to use the words of Ross Cox, clerk and
historian for the Company, "were not calculated to win their [the Indians'] esteem." In any case, the events that were now to follow comprise one of the most lurid pages in the annals of the West. The following account is based very largely on what appears to be the most reliable
and the least embellished sources. This is what happened.

Scarcely had dealings begun when Thorn struck a chief with whom
he had been in disagreement concerning the value of furs. Smarting from
this "insult" the Indian planned to get vengeance by killing the crew and
gaining possession of the ship. Subsequently, when at least fifty of the
Indians had been permitted aboard ship, the slaughter began. Concealed
knives were suddenly flashed by the natives and caught Thorn and his
men unprepared to give battle. Lewis, a ship's clerk, was the first vic-
tim; then the notable Alexander McKay, whose battered body was
tossed overboard. Thorn's only weapon was a pocketknife with which
(so say some of the accounts) he ripped open the bellies of four assail-
ants before he too succumbed. Leaning in exhaustion over the tiller wheel
Thorn was given a blow from behind and his lifeless body followed
McKay's to the watery grave below.

Escaping attack for the moment were seven sailors who were in the
rigging above and who, fearing that their turn was imminent, made a
desperate effort to reach the cabin where guns and ammunition were
available. Two were killed in the attempt, and of the five who made it
one was severely wounded. Gunfire through the skylight and companion-
way now raked the deck, and the Indians fled. Accounts as to what then
happened vary. But sometime later four of the five sailors escaped from
the *Tonquin*. Not until the following morning, however, did the cautious
but eager savages return to the ship.

What next occurred was an explosion, and can best be told in the
words of Lamayzie, the Indian interpreter, who during the attack
jumped overboard and surrendered himself as a slave to Indian women
standing by in their canoes. "I was on the shore when the explosion

[3] Philip A. Rollins, ed., *The Discovery of the Oregon Trail: Robert Stuart's Narratives*
(London, New York, 1935), pp. 270–71. Hereafter referred to as *Robert Stuart's Narratives*.

took place," said the Indian, whose words Franchère admits having rendered into "civilized expression," and "saw the great volume of smoke burst forth in the spot where the ship had been, and high in the air above, arms, legs, heads and bodies, flying in every direction." About two hundred Indians were killed; many others were wounded. "I have told you the truth," concluded the Indian interpreter, "and hope you will acquit me of having in any way participated in that bloody affair."

It was the opinion of Ross Cox, who later wrote about the event, that the barricaded crewmen deliberately planned to take this "terrible revenge," and others were of the opinion that since only four escaped (Cox says three), the fifth, mortally wounded, decided to remain aboard to expend his life as dearly as possible by lighting the 9,000 pounds of powder in the ship's magazine. It will never be known for sure, for those who escaped the *Tonquin* were subsequently found on a near-by beach and were put to death by wrathful Indian survivors.[4]

The overland expedition, led by Wilson P. Hunt, had meanwhile been delayed and it was March 12, 1811, before they left St. Louis. They went up the Missouri to a point near the present North Dakota and South Dakota line, and then turned westward through present Wyoming until the Snake River was reached. From this point the course covered was not unlike that of the future Oregon Trail.[5] They had crossed barren and rugged stretches, had done some needless meandering, had starved, and had suffered tremendously. Not until January 1812, did the first contingent straggle into Astoria. The coming of these re-enforcements was welcomed by those already struggling against odds to erect a fort. The safe arrival in May 1812, of the supply ship *Beaver* with additional men and supplies gave further encouragement. Bit by bit initial obstacles were being overcome, and when Nor'westers' David Thompson, having come from Kettle Falls, paddled into view, completing an end-to-end coverage of the Columbia River, he found the American flag flying above the crude yet defiant Fort Astoria. Thompson had feared as much, and it was apparent that the Americans had now definitely tossed down before the British the competitive gauntlet and were making a bid for at least a share of Oregon's fur trade and perhaps for the ultimate control of the Oregon country itself.

---

[4] Gabriel Franchère, *Narrative of a Voyage to the Northwest Coast of America* (New York, 1854), pp. 180–86; Cox, *The Columbia River*, pp. 68–79, 88–95. See also Washington Irving, *Astoria* (Philadelphia, 1836), I, 118–20; F. W. Howay, "The Loss of the '*Tonquin*'," *The Washington Historical Quarterly*, XIII (April 1922), 83–92; Hiram Martin Chittenden, *The American Fur Trade of the Far West* (New York, 1902), I, 177–81. The first published account of this disaster appeared in the *Missouri Gazette*, May 15, 1813, and is reproduced in Chittenden, *op. cit.*, III, 909–11. This article states that there were 9,000 pounds of powder in the magazine and that about one hundred natives were blown to bits by the explosion.

[5] *Robert Stuart's Narratives*, p. lxv and map opposite.

In their pursuit of the inland trade the Astorians met with both successes and disappointments. They made a beginning at gardening, as fur traders invariably did, and at livestock raising. A small trading schooner, the *Dolly*, was built and launched. Partner Robert Stuart, and Donald McGillis, clerk, had begun trading operations by leading a party up the Willamette River in December 1811; they were followed during April of the next year by Donald McKenzie and William Matthews, who probably reached the swift, clear, and sparkling river that now bears McKenzie's name. These parties were in turn followed (late in 1812) by William Wallace and J. C. Halsey, clerks, who are believed to have tapped the very source of the Willamette River; and again in 1813 by clerks John Reed and Alfred Seton. With respect to the Willamette Valley the reports of these men were on the enthusiastic side, both with regard to the supply of beaver and to the abundance of elk and deer. No complete record of their accomplishments exists, but according to Franchère, whose duty it was to record the facts, Wallace and Halsey returned to Fort Astoria with seventeen packs of furs and thirty-two bales of dried venison.[6] Meanwhile, David Stuart, an uncle of Robert Stuart, had proceeded far up the Columbia to its tributary, the Okanogan, and there, deep in North West Company territory, established Fort Okanogan.

By March 1812, Robert Stuart and McGillis had returned from the Willamette, and perhaps, too, a short jaunt up the Cowlitz. New and important plans which Robert Stuart was to execute without delay were awaiting his return. Before the end of March he was seen heading a party of seventeen men paddling their way up the Columbia. Three of these men were to enter present-day Idaho in search of goods cached by Hunt's overlanders; a second party of six was to proceed to the East with messages for Astor. Robert Stuart and the seven remaining men would convey goods to Okanogan where David Stuart had established his fort during the preceding winter. An encounter with Indians, however, altered these plans, and the entire expedition continued in one body to Fort Okanogan, from where they then decided to return to Astoria with David Stuart's winter catch of furs. Counting also the furs brought in by Clarke and McKenzie, according to Franchère, there were 140 packs in all.

On June 29 Robert Stuart made a second leave-taking from Astoria. With six men, all veterans of Hunt's westward expedition, he now set his course directly toward the East. En route they went through South Pass and their entire course was so much like that followed by future thousands of Oregon-bound immigrants that Robert Stuart has been

[6] Fred S. Perrine, "Early Days on the Willamette," *The Quarterly of the Oregon Historical Society*, XXV (December 1924)), 301–6; Franchère, *op. cit.*, p. 170.

called, with much merit, the discoverer of the Oregon Trail. After considerable adventure, recounted in Robert Stuart's own *Narratives*, the party arrived at St. Louis April 30, 1813, and from there Stuart proceeded to New York to report to Astor,[7] whose only contact with his venture was through his representatives.

The list of achievements does not end here. In addition to Fort Okanogan (Americans' first structure built in the present state of Washington) there was the trading post of She Whaps at the junction of the branches of the Thompson River not far from Kamloops, British Columbia. In 1812 Fort Spokane was built by John Clarke, an Astorian. It was located near the North West Company's Spokane House, built two years before.[8]

Unfortunately, forces beyond the control of one man, even Astor, began to play havoc with a venture that was destined to fail. Before mid-year, 1812, the Americans were once again at war with Great Britain. To the far-off Astorians the problem henceforth was not competition with the Nor'westers, but it was how long would it be before the arrival of a British man-of-war. Astor did what he could to strengthen his Columbia outpost. He implored Secretary of State James Monroe to provide armed protection for his Astoria post, and appealed directly to President James Madison to dispatch a warship (frigate *Constitution* was suggested) to the mouth of the Columbia to forestall British interference. He even tried to have supplies sent to it from England, but this plan failed to work. In spite of the risk of capture he dispatched the supply ship, the *Lark*, but this ship was lost. Not only at sea, but also on land, the loss of life (ultimately sixty-five or more) was heavier than Astor could bear. "But alas!" as Chittenden viewed it, "there was not a could-have-been in the whole transaction that did not turn out adversely . . . . ."[9] Finally the difficulties involved were too numerous and too great.

News of the hostilities reached Fort Astoria early in 1813, at a time when Nor'westers had begun to make full use of their many advantages in their struggle with the American competitors. Now that war had come the British concern sought further to strengthen its position by securing what the Astorians feared most—naval support. The British Admiralty acceded to this request and took appropriate steps to protect British interests in the North Pacific waters. Though fully informed of the British intentions, neither Astor nor the government of the United States was

---

[7] *Robert Stuart's Narratives*, Foreword, *passim*.

[8] C. S. Kingston, "Spokane House State Park in Retrospect," *Pacific Northwest Quarterly*, XXXIX (April 1948), 185–88; Carey, *History of Oregon*, I, 207–8.

[9] John Jacob Astor to James Monroe, July (no day given) 1813. See also Astor to James Madison, July 13, 1813. MS, William R. Coe Collection, Yale University Library. See also Chittenden, *op. cit.*, I, 238.

in any position to checkmate such a move. At Astoria the mere news of
the outbreak of war was all that was required to convince the partners
that the post would have to be abandoned.

The time set for this abandonment was the summer of 1813. But as
this deadline approached, the partners postponed the date and proceeded
to make a bargain with the Nor'westers (by now low on supplies and
willing to negotiate) whereby the area would be divided between them.
This, however, proved to be merely a postponement of the evil day, for
when news reached the respective parties that a British fighting ship
might arrive in Oregon waters at any time, liquidation proceedings were
at once renewed. With the advantages now weighted heavily on the side
of the Nor'westers, the Astorians agreed to sell out lock, stock, and
barrel to their rivals. The latter, on the other hand, were eager to buy,
rather than await the actual arrival of the frigate, for fear that naval occupation of the fort might make of it a prize of war and as such would
deprive the British fur-trading company of becoming actual owners of
the deperately needed supplies stored behind the log palisades of Fort
Astoria.

By October 1813, an agreement was reached whereby the Pacific Fur
Company sold its various properties to the North West Company at
prices to be worked out largely on the basis of prime cost. The amount
finally paid the Pacific Fur Company was $58,291.02. With this trans-
action it may be said that the Pacific Fur Company had, for all practical
purposes, come to an end.

That the Pacific Fur Company suffered tremendous losses there is
no doubt; that it sold out to the British under partial duress (a fact that
gave the Astor interest a basis for subsequent claim) there is little room
for doubt. On November 30, 1813, there appeared at Astoria not the
Isaac Todd, as was expected, but the armed British sloop *Raccoon*. She
had been escorting the *Isaac Todd* (also assigned to the Columbia) and
had raced on ahead to take possession of Fort Astoria, which her commander did formally on the 13th of December.[10]

Chittenden has remarked that "It is no flight of fancy . . . . to say
that if the Astorian enterprise had succeeded, the course of empire on the
American continent would have been altogether different than it has
been." He thinks that had Astor succeeded, no part of the Oregon country
would today be British. The Astor experiment in any event must not be
thought of as entirely negative in its results. For one thing, not all was
lost to the Americans. Under the provisions of the Treaty of Ghent,
ownership of the property was recognized by Great Britain without

---

[10] Porter, *John Jacob Astor*, Vol. I, chap. 8.

reservation by 1818, and the whole adventure was to be one of many factors which established American rights to Oregon south of the Columbia River and strengthened American claims to Oregon south of the forty-ninth parallel. In other ways, too, Astor's venture in the Oregon fur trade led to positive results. Astor's men discovered the main outlines of a practical route from the States to Oregon, and they likewise formed the spearhead of advance, first of the fur trade, then of settlement in the rich Willamette Valley.[11]

Astor's West Coast adventure was followed by a fifteen-year lull so far as American trading in the Oregon country was concerned, except for an occasional upper Missouri River party, as for example those expeditions of William Ashley, which for good measure pushed west across the Divide. The importance of this inadvertent penetration of the trans-Rocky Mountain area should not be minimized, for it was activity of this kind that led to the discovery of suitable mountain passes, to the rounding out of the Oregon Trail, and to the conviction that good pelts were to be found abundantly in the valley of the Snake.[12] It was the lull that offered the British their golden opportunity to consolidate their strength. This freedom of operation was, however, suddenly and dramatically disturbed in the summer of 1828 by the appearance in the Oregon country of Jedediah Smith who was among the greatest of American mountain men.

Smith and his men had come for help, for a terrible calamity had occurred. What had happened was this. Smith, with a party of Rocky Mountain Fur Company traders, had entered California from the Great Basin in 1826; and in the following year he entered it again. On his latter visit to California, however, Mexican officials ordered him out of the province. With a party of nineteen men and about three hundred horses and mules Smith made his departure through the northern exit. The party had followed up the Sacramento River, trapping as it went, and upon coming to the upper reaches of the river turned westward through what are now Trinity, Humboldt, and Del Norte counties. Upon reaching the coast the expedition followed the shore as far north as the Umpqua River in Oregon. At this point Smith planned to turn inland, strike the Willamette Valley, and then make his way to Fort Vancouver. But while encamped at the mouth of the Rouge most of his men were unexpectedly attacked by Kelawatset Indians. Smith and three companions who had come to Fort Vancouver for help alone escaped the murderous assault,

---

[11] *Ibid.* See also Frederick V. Holman, "Some Important Results from the Expeditions of John Jacob Astor to, and from the Oregon Country," *The Quarterly of the Oregon Historical Society*, XII (September 1911), 217–19.

[12] John B. Wyeth, *Oregon; or a Short History of a Long Journey from the Atlantic Ocean to the Region of the Pacific, by Land* (Cambridge, 1833), pp. 26 ff.

and only after much privation had these men reached the Hudson's Bay Company headquarters.

Large quantities of furs, said to number 780 beaver, over 50 large otter, and others which had been in possession of the party, were taken by the Indians, but these the Hudson's Bay Company recovered by means of a punitive expedition led by Alexander R. McLeod. Moreover, this retaliatory raid resulted in the death of twenty-one Indians, the destruction of two villages, forty-six canoes, and much other Indian property. Smith spent the winter of 1828–1829 at the fort. He sold his furs to McLeod, and when spring came he moved eastward with two sizable checks from the doctor in his pocket.[13]

Smith's appearance in Oregon was at best an interlude, and it is doubtful that he ever planned to establish his company even semipermanently in the country. Not until the expedition of Captain Benjamin L. E. Bonneville, 1832–1835, does another American figure at all conspicuously in affairs pertaining to the fur trade.

The Bonneville party consisted, according to his own account, of 121 men, who with a wide assortment of goods packed in twenty wagons left Fort Osage for the West April 30, 1832. The leader, Captain Bonneville ("Old Bonny," as his friends called him) had recently received a leave from the Army "for the purpose of . . . . exploring the country to the Rocky Mountains and beyond." Just what the ulterior motive of the Bonneville expedition was is not known and may never be known. He may have sought to explore for its own sake; but perhaps, too, for the sake of the Army. Again, he may have had simply a yearning to carry on fur trade. At least it is in the capacity of a trader that he is considered here.

That Bonneville was to give thought to possible American occupation of the Oregon country is shown very clearly in a letter written to Adjutant General Roger Jones, July 29, 1833. "The information I have already obtained authorizes me to say this much"; wrote Captain Bonneville, "that if the Government ever intend taking possession of Oregon the sooner it shall be done, the better . . . . ." As for the Hudson's Bay Company, well, they are "too much exposed by their numerous small posts even to offer the least violence to the smallest force."[14]

To return to the story, by late summer of 1832 this adventurous band of Americans penetrated the Rockies, passed through Jackson's Hole and

---

[13] Maurice S. Sullivan, *Jedediah Smith* (New York, 1936), chaps. 13–15; Robert Glass Cleland, *Pathfinders* (Los Angeles, 1929), chap. 10. Amounts given vary concerning the sale of furs recovered. See also *Part of Dispatch From George Simpson Esq*, pp. 56–63.

[14] Anne H. Abel-Henderson and J. Neilson Barry, eds., "General B. L. E. Bonneville," *The Washington Historical Quarterly*, XVIII (July 1927), 210–11, 215; Chittenden, *American Fur Trade*, I, 400.

Pierre's Hole, crossed the Divide into Oregon Territory, and proceeded to a point three miles below the confluence of the Salmon River forks. There, on September 26, on the west bank of the Salmon, they began to erect their winter quarters, and their presence on the outer perimeter of the Oregon country constituted a renewed challenge to British interests which by now had become so thoroughly entrenched.

During the autumn months Bonneville's hunters established friendly intercourse with the Nez Percés, Flathead, and Pend d'Oreille Indians, and decidedly unfriendly contacts with the ever surly Blackfoot. The friendly tribes gladly assisted in the search for buffalo meat, which, reported Bonneville, the natives brought into camp in great quantities. The generous natives were not, however, adverse to being ravens at the feast, and they remained merrily in the Bonneville camp until all food donations had been devoured. Through the winter, in fact at all times, Bonneville found it necessary to have his well-armed hunters constantly at work.[15]

The party had come to this region, at least partly, for the purpose of trade, and through the spring and summer months of 1833 trappers and traders operated along the upper reaches of the Snake River. It was in this region that the surprised and disappointed Bonneville men met a rival American party led by Milton G. Sublette and J. B. Gervais of the Rocky Mountain Fur Company. Bonneville also met, on his way back East, Nathaniel Wyeth and a companion. All told, Bonneville spent three years in the mountains and he operated on both sides of the Divide. During the summer of 1834 he and his men achieved the farthest penetration into the Oregon country. On March 4 the Bonneville party reached the Hudson's Bay Company post at Fort Walla Walla, which was then managed by Chief Trader Pierre C. Pambrun.

The British trader received the Americans very cordially; he even traded a roll of tobacco and some dry goods for some furs (much to Dr. McLoughlin's regret) but Pambrun refused, in fact he did not have sufficient goods, to re-outfit his rivals. Pambrun was unduly maligned by Bonneville for this refusal, but unjustly so. Explaining the encounter Dr. McLoughlin wrote his home office that Pambrun had sold some goods to Bonneville at "Freemens prices," when they should have been sold at retail prices. Moreover, wrote McLoughlin: ". . . . our Stores were low," and the goods on the shelves were sorely needed for the Indian trade.[16] The thwarted Bonneville retraced his steps for a time, but the following July he and twenty-three of his men pushed across the Blue

---

[15] Chittenden, *ibid.*, I, 401–2; Washington Irving, *The Adventures of Captain Bonneville* (New York, 1883), pp. 72–74.

[16] *McLoughlin's Fort Vancouver Letters*, first series, pp. 195–96.

Mountains and reached the Columbia River, a distance of about fifty miles below Fort Walla Walla. En route he had met the American Wyeth party, and also one sent out by the Hudson's Bay Company. Bonneville had hoped to engage the Chinooks in trade, but found them loath to desert the Hudson's Bay Company for what was seemingly a fly-by-night affair. Reluctantly, therefore, he and his men turned back toward the Snake River Basin, spent the winter in the Bear River region of eastern Wyoming, and during the following spring returned to the States, where his expedition ended in August of 1835.

Captain Bonneville and his men had been gone, in fact lost to the outside world, for three years and four months. "Old Bonny" had been AWOL for more than a year. He had been given up for dead and his name had been stricken from the Army rolls. Not without the aid of Old Hickory was the supposed deceased taken back into active service. In 1852 Bonneville came to Oregon again. He was ordered there to lay out and take command of Fort Vancouver Barracks. It is interesting to note that Captain Bonneville should be in command of a military post near the crumbling palisades of the once-powerful Hudson's Bay Company post that less than a score of years before had thwarted the efforts of this enterprising American trader and explorer.

As a leader of men Bonneville was a great success, but in other respects he was a failure. Throughout, Bonneville showed himself to have been earnestly interested in the fur trade (more so than in exploration), but in this respect his expedition was another American failure that represented the loss of many thousands of dollars. His explorations, Washington Irving notwithstanding, were of little value, save perhaps the journey of his Lieutenant, Joseph R. Walker, who crossed the great interior basin and entered California. So from the standpoint of Bonneville's avowed purposes, as stated in his leave from the Army, the entire expedition has no other significance than to show a renewed American interest in the fur trade of the Far West; and, like Astor, the American party found British opposition too stiff for them to remain in the Oregon country for any appreciable length of time. For years all that reminded the Oregon citizens of the adventures of Captain Bonneville was a railroad station on the south side of the famous Columbia River Cascades. But at this site there is now located the giant and magnificent United States government dam bearing the explorer's name, an honor perhaps more generous than is deserved, yet one that is a lasting reminder of early American interest in Oregon.[17]

---

[17] Chittenden, *op. cit.*, I, 425–32; William S. Brackett, "Bonneville and Bridger," *Contributions to the Historical Society of Montana*, III (1900), 175 ff; Donald M. Major, "Benjamin Bonneville," *Journal of American History*, XXI (1927), 133–35.

Within two weeks following Captain Bonneville's departure from Fort Osage, another trading party, one led by the twenty-nine-year-old Nathaniel Wyeth of Cambridge, Massachusetts, left Independence for the Columbia River Valley. Wyeth, by profession an ice merchant, was totally without experience in the fur trade. But this in no wise deterred the man's unbounded determination and enthusiasm which had in part been fired by the imaginative pro-Oregon writings of Hall J. Kelley, who was then forming the Oregon Colonization Society. During the winter of 1831–1832 Wyeth organized a joint-stock company, its purposes: exploring, trading, trapping, and salmon fishing and processing in Oregon. Like Astor, Wyeth would dispatch a supply ship to the Columbia River by way of the Horn, and the main party would proceed overland to the same river valley where a trading post would be established.

During this winter the brig *Sultana*, laden with Wyeth's supplies, set sail for the Columbia, while the overlanders left Boston by mid-March 1832. The latter proceeded to Baltimore where four men were added to make the total number about twenty-five. From there the party traveled westward to St. Louis, thence to Independence, Missouri, where these easterners joined forces with a party then being formed by Captain William L. Sublette whose destination this year was the Rocky Mountain Fur Company's rendezvous at Pierre's Hole. The combined expeditions left Independence on May 12. The course westward was along the dreary, warm, muddy, and "foul" Platte River. The travelers suffered from the absence of good water and shortages of food within the very sight, to use the words of Wyeth's cousin, John, of "frightful droves" of buffalo. Along the trail no less than fourteen of Wyeth's men deserted. The rest of the combined parties reached Pierre's Hole the 8th of July.[18] From here on west through the country of the Blackfoot the Wyeth party accompanied the one led by Sublette; and after some savage encounters with Indians, managed to reach the Snake River, cross the Blue Mountains, and descend to the Columbia River at Fort Walla Walla, which place was reached on October 14. Wyeth was received with warmth by Chief Trader Pambrun, and after a five-day stay moved on to Fort Vancouver where he arrived on the 29th. It was probably there that he received the unhappy news that the *Sultana* had hit a reef along the coast of South America and had broken to pieces. To Wyeth this meant at least temporary disaster to his entire scheme, and on November 19 he granted his men their request to be allowed to shift for themselves. As for Wyeth, he was, as he wrote, " . . . . afloat on the great sea of

---

[18] Wyeth, *op. cit.*, pp. 26 ff; Chittenden, *op. cit.*, I, 434–41; Philip H. Overmeyer, "Members of First Wyeth Expedition," *The Oregon Historical Quarterly*, XXXVI (March 1935), 95.

life without stay or support."[19] He spent the winter as a guest of Dr. John McLoughlin, his would-be competitor, made a trip up the Willamette River, and laid plans to try again. During the spring of 1833 he accompanied a Hudson's Bay Company brigade eastward, meeting Bonneville en route, and on November 7 he reached his home at Cambridge.

Wyeth was not easily dismayed by his failure. He was eager to try again; he had, in fact, on his return home, made a definite contract with Sublette and Thomas Fitzpatrick, agreeing to deliver to them during the following year $3,000 worth of supplies. Thus, during the winter of 1833–1834, we find Wyeth once again making plans which in addition to fur trade called for salmon-fishing operations on the lower Columbia. And once again a supply ship, this time the *May Dacre*, was outfitted and in January 1834, set sail for the Horn. At Boston he organized what was called the Columbia River Fishing and Trading Company, the money for which came from Boston merchants. Seventy traders, hunters, trappers; two Philadelphia scientists named Thomas Nuttall and John K. Townsend; and, somewhat to Wyeth's disgust, the missionaries Jason and Daniel Lee, besides 250 horses, made up the second overland expedition which Wyeth led westward from Independence on the following April 28. The Green River rendezvous was reached June 19, at which spot they found a scene of wild disorder. There was "whooping, and howling, and quarrelling," wrote the scientist Townsend. Mounted Indians dashed to and fro "yelling like fiends" and the "barking and baying of savage wolf-dogs, and the incessant cracking of rifles and carbines, render our camp a perfect bedlam."[20] To the scientist and the missionaries this scene was revolting. To Wyeth, on the other hand, the rendezvous was simply an institution that was useful in the promotion of trade.

Fitzpatrick, however, broke his part of the bargain made during the previous summer; and Wyeth, left with a surplus of goods on hand, proceeded to build and man a trading post near the confluence of the Portneuf and Snake Rivers, and gave it the name of Fort Hall. At this post, afterwards to become famous, he placed his goods on sale and proceeded to his main objective, the mouth of the Willamette River, where he arrived on September 14, 1834, one day ahead of the *May Dacre*, which ship had survived excruciating hardships at sea.

---

[19] Chittenden, *op. cit.*, I, 444. Wyeth's Journal of 1832 appears in Archer Butler Hulbert, *The Call of the Columbia* (n.p., 1934), pp. 112–53. Frances Fuller Victor, "Flotsom and Jetsom of the Pacific—the Owyhee, the Sultana, and the May Dacre," *The Quarterly of the Oregon Historical Society*, II (March 1901), 42.

[20] John K. Townsend, "Narrative of a Journey Across the Rocky Mountains to the Columbia River," in Thwaites, *Early Western Travels*, XXI, 192–93.

At last Wyeth had his one big chance to fulfill his many plans with respect to the Oregon country, even though the *May Dacre* arrived too late in the season to play much of a part in the anticipated salmon trade. Instead, since part of the *May Dacre* cargo was lumber, she was sent out to trade it in the Sandwich Islands. On Wapato Island (now Sauvies Island) in the mouth of the Willamette River, Wyeth built his second post to which he gave the name Fort William. With Dr. McLoughlin he made a deal, so it appears, not to interfere with the Hudson's Bay Company trade, with the understanding that the English company would not interfere with Wyeth's fishing operations and horse trade. And " . . . . I believe," wrote McLoughlin on September 30, 1835, "Captain Wyeth has most honourably Kept his word."[21]

As was the custom, Wyeth began farming operations at or near the post. But again misfortunes befell the eager and industrious New Englander. Desertions followed, some goods were stolen, and his Fort Hall trader drank up his profits. Oregon rains seemingly disabled a third of the men, including Wyeth himself, and no less than seventeen of them died during the first winter. While the Hudson's Bay Company lived up to its part of the bargain with Wyeth, this concern did not encourage the American competition. By the very terms of the arrangement, McLoughlin wrote his home office,

. . . . I prevented his [Wyeth's] Interfering with Us in Any place where we had no previous opposition and I did this without Actually giving up any thing as though we did not Raise the price of Salmon We opposed him as much as was Necessary . . . . . We may be certain Wyeths Losses are Great . . . . .

Many other factors combined to defeat Wyeth's most strenuous and praiseworthy efforts, not least of which were sickness and death. "I have been very sick," he wrote his wife from the Columbia River, September 22, 1835, "but have got well, and shall be on my way to the mountains, to winter at Fort Hall, in about six days. I expect to be home about the first of November, 1836. . . . . We have lost by drowning, disease, and warfare seventeen persons up to this date, and fourteen now sick."[22]

Thus defeated at every turn, broken in spirit and in health, Wyeth beat a final retreat. Fort William was leased and Fort Hall was sold to the Hudson's Bay Company; debts were paid and with a moderate number of pelts Wyeth returned to Cambridge where he successfully reentered the ice business and lived, until his death in 1856, in the house where he had been born fifty-four years before.

---

[21] *McLoughlin's Fort Vancouver Letters*, first series, pp. 141, 166.

[22] *Ibid.*, pp. 165–66; John A. Wyeth, "Nathaniel J. Wyeth, and the Struggle for Oregon," *Harper's New Monthly Magazine*, LXXXV (November 1892), 846–47.

Wyeth's failure, like that of his American predecessors, was partly due to inexperience, partly due to his inability to compete with the more clever, resourceful, and better-entrenched British rivals. Moreover, the American government failed to support Wyeth, as it failed to support Winship, Astor, and Bonneville; whereas the British government stood ever ready to lend a helping hand to the Honourable Company.[23]

It would be unfair to Wyeth to dismiss him completely on this note of failure. Like Americans before him, and like many who followed, this son of a Harvard graduate, this Cambridge ice dealer, did much to advertise the country west of the Rocky Mountains. Fully a decade before Frémont was hailed as the great pathfinder, the man who marked the road to Oregon, Wyeth had traversed this already well-trodden trail four times. While self-effacing New Englanders scorned publicity, the experience thus gained was important to other emigrants who later went to the Willamette Valley. Moreover, some of Wyeth's men chose to remain in the valley of the Willamette, and unlike the Astorians who remained, several of them turned their efforts toward tilling the deep, rich, dark soil that was theirs for the taking. On such developments alone Wyeth subsequently based the contention, and with considerable merit, that he was Oregon's first successful colonizer; that he pointed the way, though inadvertently, to what Oregon was to become before many years passed.

---

[23] F. G. Young, ed., "The Correspondence and Journals of Captain Nathaniel J. Wyeth," *Sources of the History of Oregon* (Eugene, 1899); W. Clement Eaton, "Nathaniel Wyeth's Oregon Expeditions," *The Pacific Historical Review*, IV (June 1935), 101–13.

CHAPTER VIII

THE FUR COUNTRY IN TRANSITION

The success greeting American merchantmen engaged in the North Pacific fur trade stands out in bold contrast to the successive disappointments and failures attending the inland trade. In this there was an element of relative luck; but, in the main, bad management, insufficient resources, absence of United States government support, and lack of experience go far toward explaining (at least with the possible exception of the Astorians) the American failures in this inland trade. The remarkable British successes, on the other hand, may be in part explained by extension into the Oregon country of long-established, highly organized, and experienced fur-trading companies which operated as private monopolies under the strongly protective wing of the British government. With these many advantages at their disposal it would be erroneous to imply that the British traders, save perhaps the deal involving the purchase of Astoria by the North West Company, took unfair advantage of their American would-be competitors. No incidents or clashes, such as those involving two British companies on the Red River of the North, ever occurred. On the contrary, fur traders on both sides demonstrated an amazing reserve and usually displayed a willingness to reach an understanding relative to competitive practices.

To be sure, both Governor Simpson and Chief Factor McLoughlin regarded American trading efforts as annoyances. The sale of liquor to Indians of the region by American traders was disturbing to the Hudson's Bay Company. In a letter by William Smith, secretary of the Hudson's Bay Company, to William B. Astor, president of the American Fur Company, dated March 3, 1830, is found the proposal that American and British companies alike pledge themselves in the future not to give "ardent Spirits" to the natives within the Oregon region.[1] It has been noted with what hospitality and patience Chief Trader Pambrun at Fort Walla Walla greeted Wyeth and Bonneville, although the latter was none too gracious in his behavior toward Pambrun. Though Ogden was annoyed by the presence of Americans in the Snake River region, no embarrassing acts of violence occurred. A letter from Duncan Finlayson to McLoughlin, September 29, 1836, stated that "notwithstanding the vexatious annoyance given by the American Opposition" the proceeds "are nearly double those of last year." McLoughlin figured, and rightly so,

---

[1] Merk, *Fur Trade and Empire*, pp. 320–21.

that without well-established bases the Americans could not make a profit; and without a profit they would not remain too long in the fur business. In general he followed a policy of letting American fur traders hang themselves, and therefore did little more than supply the rope.[2] To McLoughlin it was a matter of great delight to outwit and outtrade his American competitors, though at times they did worry him. "At this moment I am informed," wrote McLoughlin to his London office, August 5, 1829, "the Americans give three Blankets of three points for two Skins, and so short are we of Goods that . . . . in consequence of the increased price we have been obliged to pay for Furs at Fort Langley that we had there only two hundred Blankets of two and a half point . . . . ."[3]

McLoughlin maintained this active competitive attitude toward the Americans until the end. "Wherever they attempt to establish a Post on shore, we should have a party to oppose them even at a loss," he wrote the Governor and Committee[4] as late as November 20, 1845.

It was the British hope that the final international boundary line through Oregon would be the Columbia, and working toward that end it was McLoughlin's unswerving policy to advise and urge Americans to operate or settle to the south of that river. In outmaneuvering or discouraging American fur trading (and salmon-fishing adventures) and in holding American settlers south of the Columbia River the British succeeded remarkably well. But in the long run these measures proved inadequate.

What had been begun by Americans as unconscious efforts in the direction of farming (antiquarians still argue about who was the first true settler in the Willamette Valley) was destined soon to become an agricultural boom. Settlers began drifting into the Willamette Valley in large numbers. The first were usually the former fur traders and trappers (both English and American) who entered the Willamette Valley and began farming and construction of homes for their families—most often Indian squaws and half-breed children.

The missionaries, Jason and Daniel Lee, who had accompanied Wyeth

---

[2] *McLoughlin's Fort Vancouver Letters*, first series, pp. 323, cxv.

[3] *Ibid.*, p. 77. Points refer to the standards of weight, size, and quality of wool used by the Hudson's Bay Company. The points are narrow, indigo blue lines (five and one-half inches long for a full point, and half this length for a half-point) placed by hand in one corner of the blankets. A blanket with one point on it is two feet eight inches wide, and eight feet long, and weighs three pounds and one ounce. A four-point blanket is the largest, and is six feet wide and fifteen feet long, and weighs twelve pounds. Within this range the gradation is by half-points. White blankets range from one to four points; colored from three to four. The point system was first referred to in 1779, and to this day a "Hudson's Bay 'Point' Blanket" is known throughout the world as a standardized product of superior quality. A. E. Dodman, "Hudson's Bay 'Point' Blankets," *The Beaver*, Outfit 257 (December 1926), 22–24.

[4] *McLoughlin's Fort Vancouver Letters*, third series, p. 127.

on his second trip, had remained to establish a Methodist mission about ten miles northwest of where Salem is now located. They established a second mission at The Dalles, a third near Fort Nisqually. While the Lees met with some success in their religious work with the natives, they could not, however, resist the attractions of farming the rich, productive soil, especially of the Willamette Valley. Consequently their mission near Salem became the nucleus of a future thriving agricultural community. Beginning in 1836 the American Board of Foreign Missions also sent missionaries to the Oregon country. The first to go were Dr. Marcus and Narcissa Whitman and Henry Harmon Spalding and his wife, Eliza. Others followed. Under their direction four missions were established in present Washington and Idaho: Waiilatpu on the Walla Walla River, Tshimakain on the Spokane, and Lapwai and Kamiah on the Clearwater. Into still a third area, namely what is now western Montana, ventured the Catholic Father Pierre Jean De Smet.

Taken in its entirety, the American missionary influence was a potent one, if not in the realm of the spirit, then certainly in the directing of American public attention to the rich agricultural potentialities of the Oregon country. Not only the Lees, but the other missionaries as well, engaged in farming, and they were most eager to have American settlers move in. Just how many settlers may have come to Oregon at the direct instigation of the missionaries is a moot question, but as a group they constituted one of the many elements which knowingly or unknowingly transformed the region south of the forty-ninth parallel from a fur empire to an agricultural frontier. Even as early as 1836 the astute McLoughlin saw the handwriting on the wall when he wrote to the Governor and Committee in London: "Every One Knows who is acquainted with the Fur trade that as the country becomes settled the Fur trade Must Diminish . . . . ."[5]

Mountain men, the missionaries, United States Senators and Congressmen, the Hall J. Kelleys, and the Dr. John Floyds were Oregon's first boosters, and their results were notable. In Oregon, not in California, was to be found the Promised Land where, as contemporary Amos Eaton phrased it, "plants and trees are in flower all winter; and the business of mowing grass can never be required there; it continuing fresh and green all the year. Vegetable growth is enormous, where rain falls, or rivers run."[6]

The coming to Oregon from across the plains of longer and more numerous caravans was an event that stirred even the most complacent.

[5] *McLoughlin's Fort Vancouver Letters*, first series, pp. 12–14, 173; Melvin C. Jacobs, *Winning Oregon* (Caldwell, Idaho, 1938), pp. 23–24, 31–33.

[6] Hulbert, *The Call of the Columbia*, p. 165.

To many of our countrymen it was Manifest Destiny on the march. "No power on earth, nor all the powers of the earth, can check the swelling tide . . . . ," wrote *Hunt's Merchants' Magazine* in May 1846. This, indeed, was "the irresistible progress of our people." Westward ho! Their plows will "turn its sods, their axes level its timber."[7] Not until the news of James Marshall's discovery of gold on the south fork of the American River in California, January 24, 1848, electrified the world did California become known to Americans generally as something more than a Spanish province somewhere to the south of Oregon.

It was not long before this high-pressure publicity extolling the virtues of Oregon's soil and climate began to affect the westward course of migration. What had been a trickle soon became a stream, and then almost a raging torrent. And what motivated most of these Willamette-bound Americans was not, one may be safe in assuming, the prospect of saving Oregon for the United States of America, but rather, it was the prospect of staking out for themselves a large piece of free land. Title to the country could afford to wait; land claims could not.

The tide of migration came in 1839 when Thomas J. Farnham and a fragment of the so-called "Peoria party" came to the Willamette Valley by way of the Oregon Trail. In 1840 came what was called the "Great Reenforcement," but in 1841 arrived the now famous Bidwell-Bartleson party which had made the initial (though not completely successful) attempt to reach the Willamette Valley by means of wagons. The expedition of the year 1842 marked a definite step forward in organization. A train comprising sixteen or eighteen covered wagons and 107 persons under the leadership of Dr. Elijah White set out for and reached Oregon. It had now been demonstrated that large parties could go through to the Willamette Valley, and for many years thereafter, with the coming of spring, covered-wagon caravans followed in the tracks of those who had broken the trail to Oregon.[8]

The caravans of 1843, which have become known as the Great Migration (although there were many greater), netted from 875 to 1,000 settlers who had brought their wagons through The Dalles on the Columbia River, albeit, as one of their party mildly phrased it, "over the roughest road I ever saw." From The Dalles the parties, as will be explained in detail later, were floated down the Columbia to the mouth of the Willamette Valley on Hudson's Bay Company bateaux or on self-improvised rafts. In that same year of 1843, a total of 700 head of cattle were driven over the trail alongside the caravans, and the safe ar-

---

[7] *Hunt's Merchants' Magazine*, XIV (May 1846), 436.

[8] Thomas J. Farnham, *Traveling in the Great Western Prairies, The Anahuac and Rocky Mountains, and the Oregon Territory.* A pamphlet, n.p., [1844]; W. J. Ghent, *The Road to Oregon* (New York, 1929), pp. 7–8, 58–67.

rival in Oregon of many of these was a clear sign to fur traders that the best trapping days were past, at least south of the Columbia. Each year had enlarged the size of the American population, estimated by Jason Lee to have been slightly more than one hundred in 1839, so that this migration of 1843 is believed to have raised the total population of the Willamette Valley (American except for about sixty-one Canadian families living in the vicinity of French Prairie) to about 1,500. The migration of 1843 inaugurated an entirely new era in Oregon history, and to settlers and fur men alike a transition was rapidly and unmistakably taking place.

There is little doubt that American migration to Oregon was stimulated by the final settlement of the boundary question in 1846, which in turn was followed by the organization of a territorial government and passage of the Donation Land Act in 1850, whereby an American settler would receive 320 acres of land (640 if married) in exchange for four years' residence. By 1845 the total population of the territory reached about 6,000. Thanks to the first census, taken in 1849 at the instigation of General Joseph Lane, first territorial governor, the count of that year is perhaps more accurate, and it revealed a total of 9,083. Of these, 8,785 were citizens of the United States and 298 were foreigners (most of the Hudson's Bay people having moved out); 5,410 were males, 3,673 were females. Even the prospect of the passage of the Donation Land Act is believed to have caused others to go to Oregon in 1850, and in that year a total of 13,294 was reached. The rate of acceleration was cut, however, by the exodus of many newly made Oregonians to the gold fields of California during and after 1848.[9] But even with these losses it was clear that in the Oregon country south of the forty-ninth parallel the mountain man had been pushed aside, and across the expanse of the Willamette Valley dirt farmers were sinking their plows in the soil. Manifest Destiny had reached flood tide. At last, as Timothy Flint envisaged it, the "tide of the advancing backwoodsmen" had "met the surge of the Pacific." What had been happening in Oregon was what George Tucker of Virginia once called the "unstoppable progress of our civilization to the West."

Neither England nor the United States had at first exclusive claims to the whole of the Oregon country. By the treaty of 1818, which was renewed in 1827, the two countries had agreed to occupation jointly. This meant that both countries should enjoy freedom of trade, but neither would establish exclusive political sovereignty over the region.[10] While

---

[9] Clark, *Willamette Valley*, pp. 434-35, 454; H. S. Lyman, "Reminiscences of F. X. Matthieu," *The Quarterly of the Oregon Historical Society*, I (March 1900), 91.

[10] Bailey, *Diplomatic History*, pp. 157-58, 230.

the respective governments adhered to this policy until a final settlement of the boundary was made in 1846, it was not surprising that the British-owned Hudson's Bay Company exercised considerable direct authority, particularly over its own employees and over the natives while in pursuit of its normal business operations.

As has been stated, it induced Americans to settle south and east of the Columbia River. But so long as the number of Americans in the Oregon country remained small, this persuasive influence of the Hudson's Bay Company as to place of settlement was not seriously challenged. The mere presence of a powerful organization with large-scale farming operations was in itself enough to induce Americans to remain on the left side of the river where it was generally conceded that the soil would ultimately become American. But with the arrival of huge American immigrant trains from across the plains, and with the choicest lands of the Willamette Valley being taken up in the form of claims, the provisional prerogatives of the Hudson's Bay Company could not long remain unchallenged. An ever increasing number of American settlers began casting about for lands more suitable than those remaining in the Willamette Valley, and their covetous eyes fell upon the Puget Sound area. It therefore became clear to the Hudson's Bay Company that the best days of fur trading were over in what is now the state of Washington. Bowing to the inevitable the Governor and Committee in London ordered the 1844 annual supply ship to proceed directly to the newly established Fort Victoria instead of going, as formerly, to Fort Vancouver. Although it was not until later that James Douglas, succeeding McLoughlin as Chief Factor, took up residence at the new post. The foregoing event was a clear indication that the focal point of the fur trade was retreating northward from the Columbia River to Vancouver Island.[11]

Among the very first American settlers, such as the missionary groups, there had emerged in typical American frontier fashion a semblance of self-rule. By 1841 this assumed a more definite form when, for example, steps were taken by the Willamette Valley settlers at Champoeg to consider the adoption of a code of laws. This step was occasioned by the death of Ewing Young, who, it was supposed, left no heirs to inherit his estate.

In February and March of 1843, there were held the so-called "Wolf Meetings" which, because of their accomplishments, have come to be credited with having laid the basis for a provisional government in Oregon which, however, assumed a more formal status as a result of a meet-

---

[11] Frederick Merk, "The Oregon Pioneers and the Boundary," *The American Historical Review,* XXIX (July 1924), 681–99; W. Kaye Lamb, "The Founding of Fort Victoria," *The British Columbia Historical Quarterly,* VII (April 1943), 90–91.

ing held at Champoeg, May 2, 1843, "to take into consideration the propriety for taking measures for civil and military protection of this colony." At this and later meetings held during this same summer, self-made governmental machinery was put into operation. With subsequent amendments this was to serve the settlers in Oregon for the duration of the boundary dispute and until March 3, 1849, when it was superseded by the regularly constituted territorial government.[12]

Meanwhile, a final settlement of the Oregon boundary question was reached on June 15, 1846. This treaty embodying the terms of agreement provided that the boundary between the United States and Canada should continue westward along the forty-ninth parallel to Juan de Fuca Strait, at which place it was to follow the middle channel to the Pacific Ocean, thus giving to the British all of Vancouver Island. It was further agreed that the channel would be open to navigation of both countries, and that the Hudson's Bay Company be allowed the free navigation of the Columbia River (and use of portages connected therewith) and possessory rights within the portion ceded to the United States.[13]

Settlement of the Oregon boundary at last cleared the path for the establishment of bona fide governments within the long-disputed area. In spite of sectional issues present in domestic politics, President Polk in 1847 recommended that the American share of the Oregon country be given territorial status. A bill to this effect was approved by Congress on August 13, 1848, and this measure received the President's signature on the following day.[14] Political subdivisions were later made, and finally there grew out of the region south of the forty-ninth parallel the previously named states of Oregon, Washington, Idaho, with the residue assigned to Montana and Wyoming.

Great Britain's share of the Oregon country continued for a time under Hudson's Bay Company management. The British government still feared American advances. In an effort to stem the tide, Great Britain, in 1849, declared Vancouver Island to be a British colony and assigned it, in the form of a temporary grant, to the Hudson's Bay Company. Then, as a result of the discovery of gold along the Fraser River, the mainland territory was likewise made into a colony in 1858 with the name British Columbia. So intertwined were the affairs of the two colonies, however, that in 1866 British Columbia was united with Vancouver Island under the same name. On November 16, 1869, the Hudson's Bay Company

    [12] Carey, *History of Oregon*, Vol. I, chap. 17; Marie Merriman Bradley, "Political Beginnings in Oregon," *Quarterly of the Oregon Historical Society*, IX (March 1908), 42–72; Frederick V. Holman, "A Brief History of the Oregon Provisional Government and What Caused Its Formation," *ibid.*, XIII (June 1912), 89–139.

    [13] [Department of State], *Treaties and Conventions* (Washington, D.C., 1873), pp. 375–76.
    [14] George W. Fuller, *A History of the Pacific Northwest* (New York, 1931), pp. 203–4.

surrendered its deed, and with this many of its rights, to the Dominion of Canada which had been created two years before and into which union British Columbia entered in 1871.[15]

Some independent farmers from the British Isles trickled into Vancouver Island following the boundary settlement, but most of the agricultural activities there continued directly or indirectly under the control of the Hudson's Bay Company. Fur trading north of the forty-ninth parallel, however, continued along the familiar pattern. While the trade continued to be profitable at several posts, the business as a whole had its troubles. Indians managed somehow to secure liquor, and increased dependence upon it brought indolence and demoralization in its wake. The substitution of silk for beaver in hats, begun in 1839, continued to depress the fur market.[16] And particularly burdensome grew the Company's operations on what became American soil. Here English-made supplies were subject to the payment of tariff; properties were subject to taxation; American settlers continued to encroach upon lands claimed by the Company; and costly litigation resulted. These, and many other factors, finally resulted in the complete liquidation of the Hudson's Bay Company holdings south of the international boundary.[17]

A discussion of the gold rush in British Columbia follows, but suffice it to say here that the effect of the inrush of miners upon the Hudson's Bay Company preserves was far reaching. Fur trade at and around the diggings came to a standstill, because the Indians found it more to their advantage to serve as carriers and to do odd jobs connected with the mining operations. White employees at the posts were restive; they wanted to go to the diggings. ". . . . all our men refused to work upon my refusing to give them the whole of their back allowance of Rum at one time," wrote Hamilton Moffatt, Chief Trader, from Fort Simpson, February 10, 1860. "The true cause of this is I fancy occasioned by the flaming accounts they have heard lately relative to the rich gold diggings in British Columbia."[18] On November 26 came this added pessimistic note: "our trade at present is very dull, the Indians being nearly all away and the few left in a continual state of intoxication." Moffatt explained

[15] F. W. Howay, *British Columbia* (Toronto, 1928), *passim*; [Hudson's Bay House], *Hudson's Bay Company*, p. 33.

[16] "Hudson's Bay Company Returns—New Caledonia, 1856," Archives of British Columbia; James Douglas to James Yale, March 23, 1848, Archives of British Columbia; W. H. McNeill to John Work, May 15, 1855, Archives of British Columbia.

[17] Clark, *Willamette Valley*, pp. 349–52; [Hudson's Bay House], *op. cit.*, pp. 34–38. Following prolonged negotiations, an agreement was reached in 1869 whereby the United States government paid $450,000 to the Hudson's Bay Company and $200,000 to the Puget's Sound Agricultural Company in extinguishment of the rights of the British company in the American portion of the Oregon country.

[18] "Fort Simpson Correspondence, 1859–1871," Archives of British Columbia.

that private traders were the ones who supplied the liquor for this continued debauch.[19] Most prophetic were the words of the English Naval Commander, R. C. Mayne, who visited British Columbia during the gold rush. He wrote:

It was not without regret that I missed seeing the Fur Brigade. It is one of those old institutions of this wild and beautiful country, which must give way before the approach of civilisation. The time will come—soon, perhaps—when such a sight . . . . will be unfamiliar as that of a canoe upon its rivers.[20]

As British fur men retreated northward they left precious little in their wake that betrayed their once feverish activities. Their posts were scattered far and wide in the forests and on the plains, and little besides foundation stones were to remain as landmarks of what had been a mighty fur empire in the old Oregon country. Remaining Company farms and gardens were but infinitesimal yellow-green blotches on a gigantic natural landscape. Before the retreat came, assiduous mountain men had, to be sure, reduced the fur-bearing animals to a point of extermination, but this was a matter scarcely observed by, or of little significance to, the onrushing settlers whose main interests lay in the soil.

How utterly different was to be the frontier of the farmer! Unlike the fur trader who came equipped with gun, hunting knife, and trap, and who traveled the routes offered him by Nature and the red man, the farmer arrived with his meager supply of tools and household goods, his wagon, and his oxen and plow. Soon the stillness of forest was broken by the resounding blows of the axe as the farmer began to make his clearings. Huge billowy smoke clouds rose as the pioneer applied the torch to the tree stumps and underbrush, and soon there emerged, in almost mushroom fashion, the first rude log or frame dwellings of the settlers. As far back as 1831 McLoughlin's successor, James Douglas, had sensed the changes about to come. Wrote he:

The interests of the [American] Colony, and the Fur Trade will never harmonize, the former can flourish, only, through the protection of equal laws, the influence of free trade, the accession of respectable inhabitants; in short by establishing a new order of things, while the fur Trade, must suffer by each innovation.[21]

Communities, villages, and towns began to emerge. At river landings, around the missions, and wherever crossroad traffic seemed to warrant the erection of a general store, the bases for future urban life had been

---

[19] "Fort Simpson Correspondence, 1859–1871," November 26, 1862; A. G. Morice, *The History of the Northern Interior of British Columbia*, (Toronto, 1904), p. 303. Morice points out that successful miners frequently turned to fur trading and competed with the Hudson's Bay Company. This was very much resented.

[20] Mayne, *Four Years in British Columbia and Vancouver Island*, p. 124.

[21] *McLoughlin's Fort Vancouver Letters*, first series, James Douglas to the Governor and Committee, March 16, 1831, p. 242.

laid, although this latter development remained somewhat stunted so long as good farms could be had, first for the taking, then on the extremely liberal terms of the Donation Land Law of 1850.

The region below the Willamette River Falls, an area where land was fair and transportation and trade were simplified, became an early favorite of American settlers. Moreover, it attracted prospective industrialists as favorite sites for sawmills, gristmills, and shipyards. This area, therefore, was the first to witness a lively urban growth. Oregon City, site of the falls, stole the march on its rivals. It served as the territorial capital beginning in 1849, and at mid-century could boast of a main street with three hotels, three dozen business establishments, four churches, five sawmills, two flour mills, and, by a liberal count of heads in or near the town, of 1,200 inhabitants. The townsite of Portland was surveyed in 1844–1845. Its initial growth was slow (there being but six houses there in 1848), but the boom had come two years later when no less than 150 houses were reported under construction.

The region above the falls (the vicinity of Lee's Methodist Mission) soon gained favor, and the town of Salem was to rise. When the best land in this area was snatched up, settlers pushed still farther backward into what are now Linn, Lane, and Benton counties, in which region the towns of Eugene City and Corvallis (originally Marysville) emerged. Then the construction of the South Road under the leadership of the Applegates facilitated settlement in the Umpqua and Rogue River valleys. In the former valley Umpqua City, Scottsburg, Elkton, and Winchester came into being; and the discovery of gold in 1851 in the Rogue River Valley brought about the boom town of Jacksonville. East of the Cascades, The Dalles (site of the famed immigrant landing and of a Methodist mission) began to achieve sufficient population to become incorporated in 1857, and subsequently Baker City, Umatilla, Wallula, and other small urban communities began dotting the map.[22]

Important as town life was in early Oregon, its dependence, with few exceptions, upon trade with rural communities cannot be overemphasized. Oregon at mid-century had become a farmer's frontier; her widely scattered settlers were devoting themselves to agriculture and to trade and transportation largely identified with a rural economy.

---

[22] Clark, *Willamette Valley*, chap. 12; Carey, *History of Oregon*, Vol. II, chap. 25; Lewis A. McArthur, *Oregon Geographic Names* (Portland, 1928), *passim.*

PART TWO

THE AGRICULTURAL FRONTIER

CHAPTER IX

IMMIGRANT TRAILS

To the pioneer settlers of the old Oregon country, trade and transportation were the major problems. How could better routes be located for the immigrant trains? How could water transportation as a means of marketing produce be improved? And how, as farms and towns were located away from water routes, could local roads be built to facilitate trade and communication with the outside world?[1]

To immigrants, fresh from the arduous and somewhat hazardous trek over the Oregon Trail, it seemed important that something be done to eliminate the dangerous last-leg stretch down the Columbia River.

At first the immigrants from across the plains came upon the Columbia River by way of the Whitman Mission and the Walla Walla River, but by 1844 most of the caravans chose to reach the Columbia at its confluence with the Umatilla River. From there they would follow a slow but passable road to The Dalles where for the remaining sixty miles of their 2,000-mile trek they were obliged to "take to water" if ever they hoped to reach the lower Willamette Valley.

The earliest immigrant parties were not infrequently met at one of the main landings by servants of the Hudson's Bay Company who escorted them downstream on bateaux as far as Fort Vancouver. W. H. Gray, an Oregon missionary, made such a trip from Fort Walla Walla to Fort Vancouver in 1836, and his account of it is not only vivid, but it describes what such a trip involved. The river, he recounted, flowed gently at first, from four to eight knots, save at the rapids where its velocity increased. "As to danger in such places," reflected Gray, "it is all folly to think of any; so on we go to repeat the same performance over and over till we reach the falls, at what is now called Celilo, where we find about twenty-five feet perpendicular fall."

Here boats were unloaded, carried over the portage by Indians, reloaded, and again the party "glided swiftly along." At The Dalles this was repeated. "We proceeded down the river for a few miles," continues Gray, "and met the Hudson's Bay Company's express canoe . . . . on its way to Lachine, going across the continent; stopped and exchanged greetings for a few minutes and passed on. . . . ." A third portage was required at the Cascades which was reached on the second morning.

---

[1] Some indication as to the importance of transportation in the minds of Oregon settlers may be gleaned from the official records. See archives of the Oregon Historical Society, Portland. See also M. P. Deady, comp., *Organic and Other General Laws of Oregon, 1845–1864* (Portland, 1866), chap. 47.

Here a storm held up travel for three days. After the storm, says this chronicler, "we were again on our way . . . . . next day we reached the saw-mill and camped early. All hands must wash up and get ready to reach the fort in the morning . . . . In coming round a bend of the upper end of the plain upon which the fort stands," concludes Gray, "we came in full view of two fine ships dressed in complete regalia from stem to stern, with the St. George cross waving gracefully from the staff in the fort."[2]

After the transfer of the Hudson's Bay Company headquarters from Fort Vancouver to Fort Victoria such conveniences of travel were no longer extended to the immigrants upon their arrival at the Columbia, and exhausted immigrants had to be, or at least they were, met at The Dalles by American relief parties from the Willamette Valley. While livestock could be driven overland along narrow Indian or trappers' trails on either side of the Columbia River, it became the custom, upon reaching The Dalles, for individual families or parties to build their own boats or flatboats. Upon these crudely and often poorly constructed bargelike creations were placed the women, children, the men not engaged in handling the livestock, the wagons, and what little supplies remained. When all had been put aboard, the voyage downstream was begun.

The tragedy was that such craft were extremely dangerous in the hands of unskilled Middlewestern farmers, whose only nautical experience thus far had been ferrying across the slow meandering streams encountered along the trail. And one of Oregon's first correspondents was quick to observe that the immigrants "experienced by far, more losses, hardships and sufferings in descending from the Dalles to the Willamette, than all the rest of the journey together; and almost in sight of the great object. . . . ."[3] Not infrequently the flimsily constructed rafts disintegrated in midstream, became engulfed in whirlpools, and broke up on snags as they moved swiftly downstream in a river that was already beginning to rise from autumn rains. At such times the chances of survival were slight, since attempts at rescue by other parties were only to invite still further disaster.

Many instances of misfortunes are recorded, but none has been more graphically recalled than one told by the son of Lindsay Applegate. There were three Applegate families which, along with others, were moving smoothly down the Columbia, apparently in boats, in the autumn of 1843. They had just come within view of Mount Hood. "Our boat,"

---

[2] James C. Bell, *Opening a Highway to the Pacific* (New York, 1921), 146 ff.; Ghent, *The Road to Oregon*, chap. 7; Bernard DeVoto, *The Year of Decision: 1846* (Boston, 1943, pp. 372–73; Irene D. Paden, *The Wake of the Prairie Schooner* (New York, 1943), *passim*; William H. Gray, *A History of Oregon, 1792–1849* (Portland, 1870), pp. 145–48.

[3] *Oregon Spectator*, January 21, 1847.

recalled the younger Jesse Applegate (son of Lindsay), "now was about twenty yards from the right hand shore, when looking across the river I saw . . . . Alexander McClellan, a man about seventy years old, William Parker, probably twenty-one, and William Doke, about the same age, and three boys: Elisha Applegate, aged about eleven, and Warren and Edward Applegate, each about nine years old." The boats, or rafts, had approached dangerous waters and "presently," this narrator recalls, "there was a wail of anguish, a shriek, and a scene of confusion in our boat that no language can describe. The boat we were watching disappeared and we saw the men and boys struggling in the water. Father and Uncle Jesse, seeing their children drowning, were seized with frenzy, and dropping their oars sprang up from their seats and were about to leap from the boat to make a desperate attempt to swim to them, when mother and Aunt Cynthia," he concludes, ". . . . brought them to a realization of our own perilous situation, and the madness of an attempt to reach the other side of the river by swimming." The command of one of the women: "Men, don't quit the oars," most certainly saved the lives of others, for the men returned to their oars, recalls Applegate, just in time to avoid, "by great exertion, a rock against which the current dashed with such fury that the foam and froth upon its apex was as white as milk."[4]

Not all parties experienced such tragedies as this, and by the use of extreme caution and careful piloting most boats and barges made their way safely, first to the Cascades where portaging was necessary, then on to Fort Vancouver. At the Fort the weary immigrants frequently encamped for a short while and then moved their separate ways. The following, an excerpt from a diary of 1844, certainly presents a much more prosaic account than the foregoing one:

Saturday, Nov. 16.—Started early and camped again below The Dalles near the boat landing. Here we find several emigrants . . . . .

Sunday, Nov. 17.—We got through yesterday and are resting, man and beast, a thing much to be desired. . . . .

Tuesday, Nov. 19.—The cattle were started and the day passed without much being done, as there was no wheat to be had until it was threshed. . . . .

Friday, Nov. 22.—We have been waiting for the boat . . . . . Late this evening the boat called *Lady of the Lake,* Captain Smith, commander, returned. They were wet and cold . . . . .

Sunday, Nov. 24.—Sailed early and by ten o'clock we landed at the Cascade Falls. We learned immediately of the arrival of a boat from below and made arrangements to have our goods transported around the portage to the foot of the riffle . . . . .

4 Jesse Applegate, *Recollections of My Boyhood* (Roseburg, Oregon, 1914), pp. 46–47. See also William D. Miner, "Jesse Applegate: Oregon Pioneer." M.A. Thesis, Indiana University Library, 1948, Bloomington, Indiana.

Friday, Nov. 29.—No rain last night. Made an early start and landed at Vancouver about sunrise. Here we laid in provisions, flour, salmon, etc. . . . . .

Saturday, Nov. 30—Made an early start and are now rowing up the Wallamette River. . . . . Landed at Linton this afternoon.

Sunday, December 1.—Rainy. This Lord's day spent in unloading the boat and securing our goods. . . . .

Wednesday, Dec. 11.—A rainy day. How thankful we feel that we have made our escape, and how glad that we have a shelter from the storm. . . . ."[5]

Wagon roads leading across the mountains were later mapped out, but even so there were some who preferred the dangers of the river current to the arduous and equally precarious labor of getting the wagons up over the mountain passes. Loren B. Hastings made the trip down the Columbia in 1847, and the following, taken from his diary, presents still a third account of the epic-making last-lap struggle to the Oregon country:

October 20. The next day we moved down the Columbia river and about noon arrived at the Methodist Mission, called The Dalles . . . . . We moved about nine miles below and camped and found a great many that we had started with building boats, etc., or contriving other ways to get down into the Willamette valley . . . . . We returned to camp and commenced our flat boat 13 feet by 47 feet long, whip sawing our lumber, etc. We were almost out of provisions. . . . . we did not finish our boat until about the 11th day of November. We put our cargo aboard, which consisted of 15 families and 18 wagons and luggage. Part of our men drove the cattle down the trail, "which is one of the trails we read of," going some of the time up the side of a mountain for four or five hundred feet like stairs, but only wide enough for one ox to walk . . . . .

More than a month passed and this group of settlers was still on the Columbia.

. . . . November 26, we again went aboard our boat, and five families that came in last, making in all 20 families. We took aboard a few wagons, boxes with their covers on to shelter us against the rain, leaving all of our wagons at the Portage. . . . . We passed a place called Cape Horn, which is the last perpendicular high spar of the Cascade mountains. This brought us to a country capable of settlement, with rich bottom land and heavy timber.[6]

Driving the livestock over the narrow mountain defiles from The Dalles to Willamette Valley was not an easy task. In view of the late arrival of many immigrant parties, some as late as November, the Mount Hood trails were not infrequently closed by snow. In such instances the animals, already worn and tired from their long journey across the plains, had to swim across the Columbia River at The Dalles and then had to

[5] Edward Evans Parrish, "Crossing the Plains in 1844," *Transactions of the Oregon Pioneer Association for 1888* (Portland, 1889), pp. 118–20.

[6] "Diary of Loren B. Hastings: A Pioneer of 1847," *Transactions of the Fifty-first Annual Reunion of the Oregon Pioneer Association* (Portland, 1926), pp. 24–25.

be driven to Fort Vancouver on the right side of the river where the altitude was lower. There was great danger in performing this feat and it generally cost the lives of half the livestock.[7] Thus it was that man and beast alike found the "Road to Oregon" long, dangerous, and difficult. Unlike the footpaths and the navigable Canadian streams used so successfully by fur traders as avenues of commerce, the Oregon Trail of the post-fur-trading era must be regarded primarily for what it was, an important immigrants' road to Oregon. Until 1832 there was not to be found so much as a cabin along its entire distance from Independence to Fort Walla Walla. Except for the construction of Forts Hall and Boise, this situation, by 1843, remained unchanged.[8]

It was in view of the precarious nature of the Columbia River voyage that in 1845 an effort was begun to locate an all-land wagon route from the vicinity of Fort Hall across the Cascade Mountains to the Willamette Valley. The prospects of success were not good, for as one phrased it: ". . . . the Cascades presented, to the eager eyes of the road hunter, no natural pass."[9] Among the first who nevertheless went in search of such a route was the veteran Dr. Elijah White. A month was spent by the White party exploring the upper regions of the Santiam River, but no suitable pass was found. "The failure of Dr. White's enterprise left the large emigration of 1845, to find their way into the Willamette valley by the usual means"; reflected a *Spectator* correspondent, "the supply of boats being wholly inadequate to their speedy conveyance down the Columbia, and the stock of provisions failing at the Dalles, famine, and a malignant disease at the same time raging amongst them, a scene of human misery ensued which scarcely has a parallel in history—the loss of life and property was enormous."[10]

Something had to be done. During December 1845, Provisional Governor George Abernethy, in a message to the provisional legislature, urgently recommended the building of a road into the Willamette Valley. In response to this appeal the legislature accordingly appointed an investigating committee and prepared a memorial to the Congress of the United States asking for necessary funds. Meanwhile, Thomas McKay was authorized by the legislature to construct a toll road from the present site of Albany to Fort Boise, crossing both the Cascade and the Blue mountains. This road was to be completed by August 1, 1846. McKay and seven men set out from Salem to find a suitable route, but failed in the attempt.

---

[7] *Oregon Spectator*, February 4, 1847.

[8] Oscar O. Winther, "Commercial Routes from 1792 to 1843 by Sea and Overland," *Oregon Historical Quarterly*, XLII (September 1941), 238.

[9] Walter Bailey, "The Barlow Road," *The Quarterly of the Oregon Historical Society*, XIII (September 1912), 287.   [10] *Oregon Spectator*, January 21, 1847.

Following up McKay's failure was that of Stephen H. L. Meek, brother of the illustrious Joe Meek, who made an unsuccessful attempt to secure a legislative charter for the purpose of locating a wagon road along the Hudson's Bay Company Trail over the Willamette Pass. Then in the spring of 1846 a veteran mountain man named Moses Harris and six followers set out to discover a pass supposedly used by Indians at one time, but this party, too, found the tangle of nature too much for them, and admitted defeat.

It was at this point that there came before the provisional legislature Captain Samuel Kimbrough Barlow, who, so it is said, defiantly expostulated that "God never made a mountain that he had not made a place for some man to go over it or under it. I am going to hunt for that place. . . . ." Barlow, who as head of a newly arrived immigrant party and one who with great difficulty had made his way across the Cascades south of Mount Hood, proposed the construction of a wagon route through the region over which he had just passed. With renewed hope the legislature authorized Barlow to proceed.[11]

On May 18, 1846, Barlow formed a partnership with Philip Foster, a fellow resident of Clackamas County, for purposes of construction and for operation of what was to be a toll road. The contract reads:

The said parties do agree to make and open a wagon road between Oregon City, to the foot of the Cascade Mountains on the east side, agreeable to an act of the legislature of Oregon . . . . and the said parties agree to bear an equal part in all expenses. . . . .[12]

As previously stated, Barlow already had acquaintanceship with the region he proposed to explore. He was captain of an Oregon party in 1845; and when this company reached the Deschutes (or The Dalles) region, Barlow, with a detachment of about nineteen persons, seven wagons, and livestock, left the main trail at The Dalles on September 24 in search of the very route he now proposed to create. Barlow's experiences are widely known and need no retelling here. Suffice it to say that the party did not reach the summit of the Cascade Mountains before the winter snows set in. At a place called Fort Deposit some goods were left to the lonely vigil of William Berry while the remainder of the company, using their oxen and horses as pack animals, moved ahead on foot. They arrived in the valley only after relief had been sent them by Dr. John McLoughlin of Fort Vancouver. It was Barlow's problem simply to find

---

[11] Mary S. Barlow, "History of the Barlow Road," *The Quarterly of the Oregon Historical Society*, III (March 1902), 72–79; Ghent, *The Road to Oregon*, pp. 84–85.

[12] Beulah Hurst, "History of Mountain Passes," MS, Files of the Oregon Writers' Project, Portland, Oregon.

a wagon road back from the Sandy River where the supplies were left. With the aid of about forty men, such a road was completed in 1846.

In its final form the road extended south from The Dalles to what was called Fifteen Mile Crossing (Dufur) and on to Tyghe Valley where it went northwestward, keeping to the north of the White River, a tributary of the Deschutes, to the summit of the Cascade Mountains at a point between Mount Hood and Mount Wilson; thence westward to the Sandy River, and finally to Oregon City and other points in the Willamette Valley. It become known as the Barlow Road—the first wagon road in Oregon. It was completed early enough in 1846 to capture some of the immigrant trade of that year. Over 145 wagons, 1,559 horses, mules, and cattle, and one drove of sheep passed over this road and through the toll gate before the first season closed.[13]

Until a railroad was constructed along the Columbia River, the Barlow Road remained a practical one. It was, concludes one of its historians:

an important asset to both immigrants and settlers [and it] enabled the former to divide their trains and avoid the overcrowded condition on the Columbia; it furnished the latter a means of communication and trade with the settlers east of the mountains. Large numbers of Willamette valley cattle were driven over it to be slaughtered in the mines and many a packer has paid toll at its gates.[14]

Until 1912 it continued to exist as a toll road.

Not only was the construction of the Barlow Road an important achievement in itself, but its existence meant that the bulk of immigrants in the succeeding years would in all likelihood move on into the Willamette Valley, rather than remain above The Dalles out of sheer fear of going down the Columbia River on flatboats, or, perhaps, thread their way across passes on the right bank leading into the Puget Sound region.

With each passing year that immigrant wagon trains arrived, the choicest farm lands of the Willamette Valley were claimed. By 1846 several families had settled near what was to be Eugene City (later just Eugene) at the southern end of the valley floor, and the upper limit of steamship navigation. Large numbers chose to make their homes among the foothills above this future townsite. Still others set their sights upon the less approachable Umpqua and Rogue River valleys that lay to the south.

In an effort to open southern Oregon to settlement, and also, in the event of war with Great Britain, to find another all-land route leading from Fort Hall into the Willamette Valley, there was formed, during

---

[13] *Oregon Spectator*, February 4, 1847; see also early maps in possession of Oregon Historical Society, Portland; Hurst, *op. cit.* Five dollars toll for each wagon; ten cents for each head of cattle and horses.

[14] Bailey, *Diplomatic History*, pp. 292, 295.

1846, a road-building company, the exploits of which are fully as memorable as those associated with the Barlow Road.

Participating in this great new venture were the familiar Jesse and Lindsay Applegate, Levi and John Scott of the 1843 immigration, Moses "Black" Harris, a veteran mountain man, and nine others. They formed what is known as the Old South Road Company. Each of the fifteen men equipped himself with a saddle horse and a pack horse, a rifle, as well as other essential supplies, and as a group they planned to go in search of the new route.

The general plan of the party, or the course to be followed, was clearly understood. The men were to proceed in a southeastwardly direction until the Humboldt section of the Fort Hall–California road had been reached; then they were to follow this well-worn trail to Fort Hall where Oregon-bound immigrants would be induced to proceed along the new course laid out for them. ". . . . we came to the conclusion," wrote Lindsay Applegate, "there must be a belt of country extending east towards the South Pass of the Rocky mountains, where there might be no lofty ranges of mountains to cross."

As finally organized, the party had gathered on the bank of La Creole (Rickreall), a spot near present Dallas. On June 22, 1846, it set forth. The Mary's River was reached on the first day and the men encamped near the site of present Corvallis. From there they moved south past Spencer's Butte (near Eugene City) to present Cottage Grove; thence to the north Umpqua River, across the divide to the south fork of the Umpqua and then moved on to the Rogue River. To this point the course followed was the old Hudson's Bay Company Trail. Up the Rogue they moved in a southeasterly direction until finally they reached the summit of the Cascade Mountains. On the Fourth of July, Applegate states, they crossed the summit of the Cascades and descended to Klamath Lake. Their eastward trek then carried them past Tule Lake and across rocky tablelands until they achieved the divide between the Pacific area and the Great Basin. From there they made their way eastward until, as they had fully hoped, they came upon the Humboldt River, the source of which they knew was not far from Fort Hall. On July 23, "The line of our road was now complete. We had succeeded in finding a route across the desert and on to the Oregon settlements, with camping places at suitable distances," wrote Applegate, "and . . . . we felt that our enterprise was already a success, and that immigrants would be able to reach Oregon late in the season with far less danger of being snowed in . . . . ."

All this was done with considerable peril. One man was killed through Indian treachery, and there were times when the absence of water nearly brought disaster to all. But none the less a new route to the Willamette

Valley had been opened, and during that very summer of 1846 no fewer than 150 wagons found the Willamette Valley over this course, called by the provisional legislature the "Southern Rout."[15]

This Applegate Cut-off, as some have called it, was not, however, without its critics, the severest of whom was J. Quinn Thornton. A member of the Oregon-bound caravan of 1846, Thornton and many of his fellow immigrants had been among those persuaded by Jesse Applegate to take his cut-off, on the grounds that it would save a distance of two hundred miles, would offer more water, better grass, and smoother going than would the road to The Dalles. But as it turned out, according to Thornton, "The difference, then, between 830 and 200 will afford a very good measure of the worth of Applegate's word, respecting the road . . . . ."[16]

The hardships encountered by the Thornton party were, at least according to him, great. "We had toiled on amidst great suffering . . . . ." he wrote. Where a spring had been promised "we found a desert as dry and blasted, as if it had just been heaved up from some infernal volcano,"[17] added the unforgiving Thornton. By the time the Siskiyous were reached, bread had given out among some of the immigrant families. It was October 19 before the Rogue River was crossed and by then "each day brought an increase of our cares, anxieties, and labors, and a diminution of our strength, in consequence of the scarcity of healthy food." What was most dreaded from then on was the approach of the heavy autumn rains that would impede, if not halt, their progress. Such were to come within the week and with them "new, and, if possible, more bitter denunciations of Applegate." November 4 found the party mired down in mud in the Umpqua region and "too weak, in consequence of want of food, to travel further." But after two weeks of recuperation we find Thornton and his wife proceeding toward the settlements, each exchanging rides on a hired riding horse. Finally, on November 29: "We arrived at Forest Grove . . . . . We were comparatively cheerful and happy also, for although we had lost upon our journey nearly every thing that we had owned, yet we did not permit the recollection of these losses to unfit us for the discharge of new duties . . . . ."[18]

Neither the hardships endured by the Thorntons and their comrades, nor the gratuitous venom poured on Jesse Applegate, could erase the fact

---

[15] Lindsay Applegate, "Notes and Reminiscences of Laying Out and Establishing the Old Emigrant Road into Southern Oregon in the Year 1846," *The Quarterly of the Oregon Historical Society*, XXII (March 1921), 14–37; Alice Applegate Sargent, "A Sketch of the Rogue River Valley and Southern Oregon History," *ibid.*, pp. 2–3; Buena Cobb Stone, "Southern Route into Oregon: Notes and a New Map," *Oregon Historical Quarterly*, XLVII (June 1948), 135–54.

[16] J. Quinn Thornton, *Oregon and California in 1848* (New York, 1855), I, 175.

[17] *Ibid.*, I, 187.   [18] *Ibid.*, I, 210–39, *passim.*

that a new route now linked the Willamette and southern valleys with the Oregon Trail. Later this route was to be a part of Lassen's Road leading through the Pit River country to the northern mines in California. At the instigation of the Oregon legislature, Captain Levi Scott was subsequently appointed to supervise work leading to a shortening and an improvement in the road. In time this route found favor with immigrants, especially those whose destination was the Umpqua and Rogue River valleys.[19] The discovery of a southern route in Oregon was a notable achievement. The group of stalwart men who located it had triumphed where one year before John C. Frémont had failed.

Migration was not always in the direction of the Pacific Northwest, and in 1843 there is the example of Lansford W. Hastings, who led fifty-three emigrants to California by way of the overland route. Of these only twenty-five were armed; the rest were women and children. The story of this party, "outward-bound for the second and last *paradise* of the west, California," is not without importance. The party left a rendezvous about twenty-five miles above the Willamette Falls on May 30 and moved expeditiously until it reached the Rouge River where it confronted the double problem of crossing the river and placating the natives at the same time. Hastings wrote:

In view of the peculiarity of our perilous situation, I directed twelve men to cross the river, in advance, in order to receive and guard the baggage, as it should be sent across. The residue of the men, remained, in order to protect the women and children, and to guard the horses and baggage, previous to their being sent across. During all the time, which was occupied in crossing the river, great numbers of Indians thronged around us, on each side of the river, frequently rushing upon us, in such manner, that it became necessary for us to draw our forces out, in battle array . . . . . Upon discharging a gun, they would, invariably, fall back, and flee in every direction, with the greatest confusion . . . . .[20]

It appears that the Indian strategy was to intermingle with the whites to such an extent that confusion would result and it would then be possible to steal, plunder, and perhaps even make a direct attack. The emigrants, however, managed to get across the river and move on in perfect safety, and nothing "worthy of remark" happened to them until, interestingly enough, they met a company of drovers, headed by J. P. Lease and John McClure, with cattle for the northern market and emigrants whose destination was Oregon. "We, of course, had nothing very favorable to say of Oregon . . . . nor had they much to say in favor of California," relates Hastings. Those from the south must have won the argument

---

[19] For a listing of early settlers in southern Oregon, see A. G. Walling, *History of Southern Oregon* (Portland, 1884), Appendix.

[20] Lansford W. Hastings, *The Emigrants' Guide, to Oregon and California* (Cincinnati, 1845), pp. 64–65.

which ensued, for at this point about one-third of the Hastings party decided that, delightful as the California climate must be, they would retrace their steps to the valley of the Willamette. Finally, after an Indian attack in the upper Sacramento Valley, the diminished Hastings party reached New Helvetia without serious difficulty save the temporary loss of two men.[21]

Similarly, in 1845, James Clyman led to California a portion of the 1844 arrivals after they had wintered on the Rickreall River. Clyman's diary likewise has much to say about the problems involved in following the overland route to the Sacramento Valley. Turning to the opening page of Clyman's Oregon-to-California diary one reads:

Sunday June the 8th
1845—Cloudy—
Made a finale start for california our company consisting of 35 men one woman and three children Left four men at camp hunting for a Lost Horse which ran away this morning in a fright
Passed over a fine undulating country handsomely and thickly clothed with grass some haveing the appeareance of rye and timothy. . . . .

For the days that immediately followed, Clyman seems to have been impressed with the wooded upper Willamette Valley as the small immigrant band gradually left the harmless Calapooya Indians and approached the danger zone of the Umpqua and Rogue River Valley Indians. At this place in the diary is inserted a loose leaf—"Directions," to wit:

Be carefull never to camp in the timber if it can be avoided. Be carefull to never Let any Indians come amongst you Never lit the Indian have any amunition on any account Keep careful watch both day and night Never neglect camp guard on any account
Never Fire a gun after (after) crossing the Umqua mountain untill you cross the siskiew mountain perhaps Five days travel. . . . .
[June] 18 arose early we now have to enter the continual war nations of Indians that inhabit the whole extent of country between here and California as so[o]n as packd we got on the trail and commenced assending the mountain by the way of following a dim trail up the steep bluffs and winding around decliveties of (of) the mountain after much fatiegue and labour we assended the tumbling mountain torrent untill branched into several smaller streams when we assended the Point of a mountain nearly perpendicular. . . . .[22]

By June 21 the Clyman party had reached the Rogue River and luckily they were ferried across this rock-bottomed stream by the Indians without encountering the harm which such a maneuver invited. By July 11, where this particular "Memorandum" ends, the party was deep in northern California and Clyman felt that "on account of our animals

---

[21] *Ibid.*, pp. 65–69; Clark, *Willamette Valley*, p. 359.
[22] "James Clyman Diary," MS, Henry E. Huntington Library.

we remain in our present camp to day to give them rest." He concludes on a gloomy note, saying : "many of our company are much discouraged at the report of the dullness of all kinds of Buisness as they Expected to find immediate employ at high wages [in California]."[23] Once within the vicinity of Sutter's Fort the party broke up, but once again it had been demonstrated that, treacherous and difficult though the trail had been, overland communication could and would be maintained between the Willamette Valley, Oregon, and California, the American ownership of which was not far off.

It was the discovery of gold in California on January 24, 1848, that led directly to the transformation of this now historic traders' trail into a wagon road. By August of 1848 the *Spectator* pointed out that "Quite a number of our fellow-citizens are leaving and preparing to leave for the gold mines of the Sacramento."[24] The first group traveled southward with the aid of pack trains, but by September a wagon company was organized that numbered 150 "robust, sober, and energetic men." Fifty ox-drawn wagons were assembled and loaded with mining equipment and provisions, and under the captaincy of Peter H. Burnett, California's future first governor, the caravan set forth. The train followed the Old South Road through the Umpqua and Rogue River valleys and went southeastward as far as Klamath Lake. Here it turned southward ; and having departed from the California trail in search of a route passable for wagons, the party shortly came upon a stretch of road newly laid out by Peter Lassen.

Serious difficulties were encountered as they continued their southward trek through the pine forests of the Sierra Nevada. Many desertions occurred, but this advance party was overtaken by a second party, this one from Puget Sound, and the combined force managed to blaze a roadway through to the Sacramento Valley where they arrived about November 1, just in time, reflects Bancroft, to avert "a tragedy like that of Donner Lake."[25] Wagons continued to pass over this route, but a full decade was to elapse before a passable all-year commercial wagon road was laid out and maintained between Oregon and her neighbor to the south.[26]

While Oregon's pioneer settlers were thus blazing new trails that would provide better communication with the outside world, steps were being taken to locate new routes for travel within the region itself. In this regard important work was done, not alone by the settlers, but by visiting explorers as well. To the Americans the region north of the

[23] "James Clyman Diary."   [24] *Oregon Spectator*, August 24, 1848.

[25] Bancroft, *History of Oregon*, II, 44–45, 45 n.

[26] Winther, "Commercial Routes," pp. 239–42.

Columbia remained somewhat of a mystery until after the withdrawal of the Hudson's Bay Company, although important information concerning the topography of the future state of Washington came directly from the *Narrative* of Lieutenant Charles Wilkes.

The commander brought two of his five ships into Puget Sound in the spring of 1841 and from there he ordered four land parties to set out; one under Lieutenant Henry Eld went down the Chehalis River to Gray's Harbor and from there to the Columbia; one under Lieutenant George Foster Emmons surveyed an area from the Columbia River to San Francisco; one under Lieutenant Robert E. Johnson explored the region around Okanogan, Colvile, Coeur d'Alene Lake, Lapwai, and Walla Walla; and lastly, Wilkes personally set out to visit Cowlitz, Astoria, Fort Vancouver, and the Willamette River settlements. Travel by these groups was negotiated by ships, canoes, horseback, and on foot, and as such represents the varying modes of travel within the territory. Moving down the Cowlitz by canoe, Wilkes reports having "met with many canoes passing up, loaded with salmon and trout, which had been taken at the Willamette Falls. . . . ."[27]

Also informative were the reports of John C. Frémont who, two years following the visit of Wilkes, explored the region east of the Cascades between the Dalles and Klamath Lake.[28]

---

[27] Wilkes, *Narrative*, IV, 291 ff.; V, 124 ff., 217 ff.

[28] John C. Frémont, *Narrative of the Exploring Expedition to the Rocky Mountains in the Year 1842, and to Oregon and North California in the Years 1843–44* (London, 1846).

CHAPTER X

OLD WAGON ROADS

Congress approved a bill creating Oregon Territory, August 13, 1848, and this measure received President Polk's signature on the following day. The Chief Executive then took immediate steps toward the appointment of officers for this westernmost possession. He announced the appointment of General Joseph Lane of Indiana as territorial governor. Lane had recently risen in distinction as the successful head of an Indiana regiment of volunteers in the war with Mexico. The President appointed as United States marshal none other than the energetic and persuasive mountain man, Joseph L. Meek, who at that very moment was present at the national capital as an official representative of Oregon's provisional legislature.

Scornful of an approaching winter, the two men decided to proceed at once to their posts. They first went to Fort Leavenworth where, with a military escort, they set out for Oregon via the southern Santa Fe route on September 10, 1848. All but one of the soldiers had vanished when Lane and Meek finally arrived at Oregon after what had proved to be a dangerous and trying journey of six months' duration. They reached their designated capital of Oregon City on March 2, 1849, and on the very next day Governor Lane officially proclaimed Oregon to be a territory of the United States.

In the decade from then until statehood in 1859 great attention was given to the problems of transportation and communication. The beginning of this ten-year period was, however, anything but auspicious, especially in view of the tremendous exodus of people to the California gold fields at the very time of the inauguration of the new government. To a certain degree this wild scramble for gold was counteracted by the passage, in 1850, of the Oregon Donation Land Law, the effects of which were particularly noticeable during the years 1851–1852. The ease with which land could be acquired under the provisions of this act appealed to the agrarian elements in particular, and when the gold fever subsided there remained hundreds who preferred a half-section of land in Oregon's Willamette Valley to doubtful fortunes in California's El Dorado.[1]

In any event, much work needed to be done by those remaining in the country, since the old settlers had done little more than meet the most

---

[1] "Joseph Lane Autobiography," MS, Bancroft Library, Berkeley, Calif.; Clark, *Willamette Valley*, chap. 14; Carey, *History of Oregon*, Vol. II, chap. 21; Bancroft, *History of Oregon*, Vol. II, chaps. 1–3.

basic requirements. New roads had to be built, and old ones had to be improved. For one thing, surfacing would be required for all-season use, and it was in this direction that much effort was expended during the 'fifties. Planking, or corduroy, was at first the most practical and most widely used method of surfacing roads, because timber was abundant and sawmills already were numerous. To this type of road construction newspaper references began to appear late in 1850. One notes, for instance, that the citizens of Salem and vicinity met to consider "the practicability of a Plank Road from Milwaukie up the valley to Albany," and after but a few minutes' consideration a committee resolved: "That, in our opinion, a Plank Road for general public use, is of far more utility to the people of a country, than rail roads." Further, plank roads would not be as monopolistic as railroads and would give every man, rich or poor, an opportunity to do his own trading.[2]

A much more pretentious project was advanced in January 1851, when a citizen asked the territorial legislature for a charter to construct a plank road between the mouth of the Columbia River and Yamhill County at an estimated cost of $800,000. It was to be part of a grandiose scheme to connect the Columbia River region with the Umpqua, "thence with the great National rail road to intersect the commerce of the world, and draw it across to the Pacific Coast . . . . ."[3] This road would, of course, be built with Oregon timber and the use of it would boost the rapidly growing lumber industry there.

Then the newspaper correspondent suggested that what Oregon needed was a horse-drawn railroad system. It would be made entirely of wood, and he gave three reasons why such a road would be superior to any other: first, the farmer could bring his own produce to market; second, he could haul six times as much with the same amount of horsepower; third, if and when the steam railroad should come to Oregon, it only remained to replace wooden rails with steel ones and substitute the locomotive for the horse.[4]

By the middle of 1851 plank roads received the blessing of the territorial legislature, a signal for nearly all cities and towns to jockey for advantage in the event such road projects might actually be realized. Thus, during August 1851, there was formed the Portland and Valley Plank Road Company, later known as the P. & V.P.R. Co., which actually began construction of a plank toll road from Portland over what is now the Canyon Road into Yamhill County. A month later one reads that the road had been "commenced with skill" and would be completed

[2] *Oregon Spectator*, December 26, 1850.

[3] *Ibid.*, January 9, 1851.

[4] *The Western Star*, January 23, June 5, 1851.

with "unflinching energy."[5] By September 27 enough grading had been done to permit inaugural ceremonies. Colonel William M. King of Portland, president and superintendent of the company, placed the first plank into position but not until the assembled group had listened to at least five fervidly patriotic orations. All were conscious of their pioneering venture in road building, for it was emphasized that this was to be the first plank road on the Pacific shores. The ladies lent their support by serving a barbecue dinner spread upon the newly laid planks.[6]

Construction contracts called for split planks or sawed slabs, split planks being regarded as superior to sawed ones, and cedar wood was preferred to the stately fir. Only a very short distance of the road was to be macadamized.[7]

The P. & V.P.R. Co. ran into financial snags and work was halted on the road after about ten miles had been built. The final upshot of the matter was that in 1855–1856 the Oregon legislature granted a charter to another company, the Tualatin Plains Plank Road Company, which completed the road, after a fashion, in the year 1856. It remained at best a very poor winter road.[8]

One serious drawback during at least the first five years of the decade was that such enterprises were left largely to private effort. The legislature did little more than direct the territorial road commissioners to indicate the general course of projected routes and to require from every male person between twenty-one and fifty years of age a day's work a year on roads.[9] Not until the middle of the decade, when $1,146 were set aside from public donation funds for improvement of the old wagon trail between the city of Portland and Linn City,[10] is there much evidence of public road construction. About that time one likewise notes renewed activity in the laying out of new roads, one project being the opening of a road between the coast and central Willamette Valley.[11]

The condition of Oregon's roads varied, of course, with the season. For the most part they were impassable during the rainy period, but by 1856 there are reports of fairly good roads during dry weather. In July of that year the Portland *Democratic Standard* said :

The Public will take Notice

THAT A GOOD WAGON ROAD is now open and in good repair between Portland, Multnomah county, and Salem, Marion county, by way of Gilbreth's Ferry on the

[5] *Oregon Weekly Times* (formerly *The Western Star*), July 24, August 7, September 11, 1851.

[6] *Ibid.*, October 2, November 15, November 22, 1851.   [7] *Ibid.*, November 22, 1851.

[8] Clark, *Willamette Valley*, p. 485.   [9] *Oregon Spectator*, August 26, 1853.

[10] *Oregon Weekly Times*, March 20, 1852; Clark, *op. cit.*, p. 487.

[11] *Oregon Statesman*, March 21, July 11, 1854.

Tualatin River, and Boon's Ferry on the Willamette. The distance from Portland to Gilbreth's Ferry is ten miles; from Gilbreth's Ferry to Boon's Ferry six miles, and from Boon's Ferry to Salem twenty-eight miles—making the entire distance between Portland and Salem on this route only forty-four miles.[12]

The condition of immigrant roads was never good, and in 1852 was such as to bring about the charge of "shameful imposition and fraud."[13]

It was not until Oregon became a state in 1859 that the first real boon to road building came. Then by an act of Congress the new commonwealth was required to use 5 percent of the net proceeds from public land sales for road building and other internal improvements.[14] During the first three decades of statehood the Oregon legislature lent an attentive ear to the popular demand for roads, while private road companies, reminiscent of earlier days, continued to function. In 1867 a road from Tualatin Plains to Springville was completed and not long thereafter Portlanders saw interest reviving in the Canyon Road project. Ferries, too, increased in number, and improvements were made in road surfacing.

During 1864 there was formed the Willamette Valley and Cascade Mountain Wagon Road Company. It had for its object the construction of a wagon road from the Willamette River in the vicinity of Corvallis, east across the Cascades, and on to the Deschutes River. This company sought and secured some federal aid for its project. Similarly, a second company known as the Oregon Central Military Road Company was organized during the same year. The purpose of this concern was to construct a wagon road from Eugene City along the middle fork of the Willamette River to Owyhee in the Snake River Valley. Later, however, an investigating committee found that these concerns had never carried out the work for which the federal grant had been made, and on this basis it was recommended that the proffer of aid in the form of public lands be rescinded. There followed a period of litigation and the filing of claims with the result that patents were issued to the Oregon Central Military Road Company, and the title of the Willamette Valley and Cascade Mountain Wagon Road Company was sustained.[15]

Down in southern Oregon there was formed, in 1858, under an act of the territorial legislature, the Siskiyou Wagon Road Company. Two hundred shares of stock were issued and these were divided equally between the brothers, Tobias and Michael Thomas. It was Michael's boast that he had built the road thus authorized, one which commenced "at or near the residence of Hugh Barron" (about eight miles from Ashland) in Jackson County, Oregon, and extended across the Siskiyou Mountains

---

[12] *Democratic Standard*, July 3, 1856. The distance here indicated is probably an underestimation.   [13] *Oregon Statesman*, August 28, 1852.

[14] Clark, *op. cit.*, p. 487.   [15] *Ibid.*, pp. 487–90.

for a distance of about seven miles. It became a toll road of considerable importance in southern Oregon.[16]

Throughout the whole period before 1890 there was a persistent effort to improve the lines of communication between Oregon and the States, especially by finding a better way to cross the Cascade barrier. A pass known as Walker's Road had by 1859 been cut through the mountains north of Mount Hood, but there appears to be some doubt as to whether it was usable. This was likewise the case with the McKenzie Pass and the Willamette Pass, which were not considered practical ones during the territorial period.[17]

Back of this vigorous road activity was, quite naturally, the general desire to relieve the isolation in which the Oregon pioneers found themselves. People needed to find better and quicker ways to reach the market; they wanted to move with more speed and facility from one place to another. The greater increase and spread of settlement that came with passing years accentuated, on the one hand, this problem of communication, and, on the other hand, helped to heighten the cry that was ultimately to bring some relief.

Not until 1844 did the American farmer frontier of settlement advance northward across the Columbia River into what is now the Commonwealth of Washington. The extension of the frontier would have come earlier had not Chief Factor John McLoughlin of the Hudson's Bay Company persuaded nearly all comers to stake out their claims either in the fertile valley of the Willamette or somewhere else south of the Columbia. But in 1844 the press of circumstances was such that McLoughlin could hold out no longer, and into the region came the first American contingent, which consisted of seven men, five of whom had families, and one of whom was a mulatto. At first this advance guard hovered closely about Fort Vancouver, but during the winter of 1844 and the following summer one of them, Michael T. Simmons, traveled by canoe, first up the Cowlitz and then with companions went overland to Puget Sound. On the southern extremity of the Sound Simmons founded Newmarket (now Tumwater), and so by mid-century American community life was forging ahead along the accustomed pattern.

Except for the retarding effects of the Whitman massacre in 1847 and the discovery of gold in California the year after, the population increased steadily until by the close of 1850 it had reached about one thousand.[18]

    [16] "Records of the Siskiyou Wagon Road Company," MSS, Courtesy of Robert E. Dodge, Ashland, Oregon.

    [17] *Pacific Christian Advocate*, May 28, 1859.

    [18] Thomas W. Prosch, "The Political Beginnings of Washington Territory," *The Quarterly of the Oregon Historical Society*, VI (June 1905), 147–50; George W. Fuller, *The Inland Empire of the Pacific Northwest: A History* (Spokane, Denver, 1928), II, 184–86.

By 1852 settlers arrived at Alki Point, and this led in the following year to the founding of Seattle; whereas the rapid growth of other scattered settlements early brought about the rise of the towns of Olympia, Steilacoom, and Port Townsend. By 1852 settlement had advanced north to Bellingham Bay and over to Whidbey Island.[19]

A census taken in 1853 revealed that 3,965 people then lived north of the Columbia River, and on March 4 of that same year President Millard Fillmore, in response to a demand of these people, signed a bill which separated them from Oregon into what was to be the Territory of Washington. The Columbia River was designated as its southern boundary from the point where the river intersects the forty-sixth parallel; from there the line was to run east to the summit of the Rockies, which mountains would form the eastern boundary. A treaty with England had already established the forty-ninth parallel as the northern limit.[20]

Why had these people of Washington Territory desired to separate from Oregon? The answer may in a large measure be explained, not on the basis of any marked economic or social differences, but upon the basis of transportation.

Prior to 1851, the year of the Cowlitz Convention, when steps were taken to form a separate government, the settlers were compelled to rely solely, as the Hudson's Bay Company had long relied, upon the streams and the trappers' trails as a means of travel. Lieutenant Charles Wilkes, whose extensive explorations of the country lying between Puget Sound and the Okanogan are so carefully reported in his published *Narrative,* relates how in 1841 the Company employees still relied upon their thirty-foot "clinker-built" boats, except at portages. While Wilkes' party did use horses, and on Indian trails at that, it was not without great encumbrance that the group did so. "The route lay, for several days, through forests of spruce," reported this American naval officer. And again:

The road or way, after passing the river, was over a succession of deep valleys and hills, so steep that it was difficult for a horse to get up over them with a load, and the fall of a horse became a common occurrence. They were all, however, recovered without injury, although one of them fell upwards of one hundred feet; yet in consequence of his fall having been repeatedly broken by the shrubs and trees, he reached the bottom without injury to himself, but with the loss of his load, consisting of their camp utensils, &c., which were swept off by the current of the river.[21]

It was into this kind of wilderness that the Americans came, and a decade after Wilkes' visit improvements in transportation were negligible. There was not even a wagon road between Tumwater and Cowlitz land-

---

[19] Bancroft, *History of Washington, Idaho, and Montana,* pp. 23–33.

[20] *Ibid.,* p. 62; Fuller, *op. cit.,* II, 188.

[21] Wilkes, *Narrative,* IV, 409 ff., 421.

ing, and communications between these points had to be negotiated either on foot or horseback.

The feeling with regard to such deplorable conditions was aptly expressed by *The Columbian* in 1852 as follows:

ROAD UP THE COWLITZ RIVER

We take the greatest pleasure in giving publicity to the fact—on the information of Mr. F. A. Clark, Cowlitz landing—that subscription papers are in circulation for the construction of a practicable wagon road up the Cowlitz river from a point opposite Monticello, to intersect at the landing, the road leading to the head of Puget Sound.—We learn that it is the determination of the citizens of Lewis county, to let no consideration deter or thwart them from a speedy completion of the project; and to which, in the name of the citizens of Thurston, we respond a hearty "AMEN" —God speed you in the highly necessary and laudable undertaking. There is not a resident of the "territory of Oregon" at all conversant with the present and ONLY means of communication between the northern and southern divisions thereof, but must be compelled at once to admit the absolute and indispensable necessity for the immediate construction of a good wagon road in the direction indicated.[22]

Futhermore, there were no inns along the trails to accommodate travelers.[23] It was no simple task, therefore, for the representatives of the people to attend the sessions of the Oregon legislature whether they were held at Oregon City or at Salem. When at the 1851 Fourth of July celebration at Olympia John B. Chapman launched a tirade in favor of a separate government, it is not at all surprising that his idea received hearty support and led to the calling of a convention at Cowlitz for August 29 of that year.[24]

The Cowlitz Convention was what Edmond S. Meany correctly called the inception of the Washington Territory. In a memorial sent to the Congress of the United States asking for a division of the Oregon Territory, the Convention set forth its reasons for such a separation. It is significant to note that every single paragraph contained in the section on reasons why separation should take place stresses either geographic isolation or inconvenience in travel. The following will illustrate:

. . . . That when ever any portion of That Community, from locality and Geographical position are left out of the existing rule . . . . It then becomes the duty of the Supreme power from which those rules of order emanates to reestablish those systems of protection and Government . . . . .

. . . . They maintain positively that it costs more for a citizen in the North of Oregon Territory to travel to a clerks office or to reach a District Judge than it does for a man to travel from S. Lewis, Missouri to Boston, Massachusetts and back; and, much longer;

---

[22] *The Columbian*, December 18, 1852; Bancroft, *History of Washington, Idaho, and Montana*, pp. 64–65.

[23] Prosch, *op. cit.*, pp. 151–52.   [24] Fuller, *op. cit.*, II, 185–86.

It is true that Judge [William] Strong, resides on the North Bank of the Columbia River, but in such a position . . . . he cannot be reached under any emergency under several days travel from the interior. . . . .

. . . . no Wagon Roads have yet been made from the Columbia or else where, to the interior of the Territory and hence wholy inaccessable except by water : and all the commerce of the North being monopolized by the Hudson Bay Co. there was no inducement for American Vessels, hence no means of conveyance as the Company Vessels were never allowed to carry an American Citizen. . . . .

. . . . That there is now about three thousand Souls North of the Columbia . . . . [yet] it is impossible for them to prosper in commerce, or advance one step in the improvement of Roads & highways. . . . .[25]

President Fillmore's term of office expired shortly after he signed the bill creating Washington Territory, so it remained for his successor, President Pierce, to appoint the first officers. Pierce appointed Major Isaac Ingall Stevens as Governor. The fact that the new Governor's first move was to plan a survey of the Cascade Range is evidence, not only that the demands of the Cowlitz Convention—and those of settlers everywhere—were not unheeded, but it is evidence that the federal government had, by 1853, embarked upon a new nationalist policy, namely, granting financial aid to a road-building program in the territories. It was Oregon's Governor Lane who had been the first to ask for and to secure, in 1853, a federal appropriation ($20,000) for two such road constructions. One of the proposed federal roads was to connect the Rogue and Umpqua River valleys in southern Oregon (discussed at end of chapter) ; the other was for building a road between Walla Walla and Steilacoom and over Naches Pass to enable immigrants to go directly to Puget Sound with their wagons. In making this initial appropriation Congress had in mind military contingencies (although the pleas of the settlers were also factors), and for this reason these and subsequently built roads in the territories were known as federal roads.[26]

No time was lost in initiating this federal road program in Washington Territory. Captain George B. McClellan was assigned by Secretary of War Jefferson Davis to work under the general directions of Governor Stevens. "The construction of the military road from Walla-Walla to Steilacomb, Puget's Sound . . . . is assigned to you." So read McClellan's instructions dated May 9, 1853. To continue :

It is important that this road should be opened in season for the fall emigration ; you will, therefore, use every exertion to do so.

Should it be found impossible to accomplish this, you will, at least, endeavor to

[25] Edmond S. Meany, "The Cowlitz Convention: Inception of Washington Territory," *The Washington Historical Quarterly*, XIII (January 1922), 6–8. Meany has here reproduced the manuscript memorial.

[26] Thomas W. Prosch, "The Military Roads of Washington Territory," *The Washington Historical Quarterly*, II (January 1908), 118–20.

fix the line of the road, especially through the Cascade mountains, and to perform such work on the most difficult portions as will enable the emigrants to render the route practicable by their own exertions, detaching a suitable person as guide and director to meet them at Walla-Walla. . . . .[27]

On May 9 the Governor's party left Washington, D.C., for the Washington in the wilderness. It was September 24 before Stevens crossed the summit of the Rockies and before he could proclaim the new government inaugurated. Leaving Captain McClellan in charge of the Cascade surveys and with 40 men and 173 horses and mules the Governor went by canoe down the Columbia and up the Cowlitz to his capital at Olympia where he arrived November 25.

While at Walla Walla Stevens had learned that the Washington settlers were anxious to bring as many as possible of the 1853 immigrants directly into Puget Sound and being too impatient to wait for McClellan, they had already begun work on the Steilacoom–Walla Walla road. That such was the case is evidenced by the following account in *The Olympia's Columbian*, Washington's first newspaper, dated June 18:

> The volunteer party from this vicinity, in search of a route across the Cascade mountains, have now been out two weeks, and it is ardently hoped their efforts have proved successful. If they have found or should find their way through, so that Capt. McClellan, by following them may meet the expedition from the States, under Gov. Stevens, we will have good reason to expect a large proportion of the immigration of this year. . . . . We have confidence that the road will be opened this season. . . . .[28]

McClellan, unfortunately, failed to perform his duty as a soldier. He believed the Naches Pass impracticable for winter travel and appeared at Fort Vancouver without having carried out the instructions given him by Secretary of War Davis.

In an almost desperate effort to offset McClellan's failure, there was organized, under the leadership of Edward J. Allen, Olympia, a group of settlers who were willing to contribute their money, equipment, and time in an effort to put the road in such shape that the autumn immigrants might still be directed to Puget Sound rather than to Oregon.[29] The course they had in mind was over the Snoqualmie, rather than Naches, Pass. On August 7 Allen reported to *The Columbian*: "We are going it like fire, making good time. . . . ." Judging from the editorial, *The Columbian* expressed great determination to see this road completed.[30]

---

[27] *Senate Documents*, 33 Cong., 1 sess., pt. 2, doc. 1, p. 67.

[28] *The Columbian*, June 18, 1853.

[29] *Washington Pioneer*, December 24, 1853; *The Columbian*, August 13, 1853; Fuller, *Inland Empire*, II, 157–58, 201–2; Prosch, "Military Roads," p. 120.

[30] *The Columbian*, August 13, 1853. Further progress is reported in *ibid.*, September 24, 1853.

By October 15 the victory was won and *The Columbian* could report with glee that "The Cascade, or Emigrant Road from Walla-walla over the mountains . . . . *is* FINISHED"[31]—a road, one might add, which for 234½ miles cut through virgin forests, wound its way over mountains which reached 5,000 feet in elevation, and crossed and recrossed the Naches River sixty-eight times.[32] The road was completed in time, and the reports indicate that scores of wagons passed over it even on the very heels of those who were doing the work.[33] The road, however, was not a popular one. After 1853 the population shifted rapidly toward Seattle, and there arose a demand for the construction of a road along one of the old Hudson's Bay Company trails which led southeastward from Seattle along Cedar Creek, over Snoqualmie Pass to Yakima, and then on to Walla Walla. Then, toward the end of the 'fifties, sentiment in legislative circles, as judged from memorials, appears to have favored the construction of still another immigrant road along the Columbia River. But in each case it was understood that the eastern terminus would be Walla Walla, to which point immigrants could come from the Oregon Trail; and if the Mullan Road were built between there and Fort Benton, Washington would likewise be able to tap the Montana-Idaho area which after 1860 was to enjoy a mushroom growth.[34] Then, too, the gold rush to Colville during 1855 occasioned much thought about connecting by road that place with established routes of travel. Anxious as the people seem to have been for the construction of immigrant roads, this interest had an immediate purpose, namely to get the immigrants into Washington. Once the rush was over the roads were allowed to fall into disrepair and, to use the words of a pioneer, were "soon overgrown by the lush, quick growth of the Northwest."[35]

The new government of Washington Territory was officially organized in February 1854. In his opening message to the first legislature Governor Stevens emphasized the urgent need for roads. That the territorial solons took road making seriously is indicated by the fact that the new government enacted into law at least ten road measures during the first session of the legislature. Such laws as these were passed: an act to locate a territorial road from Steilacoom to Seattle; an act to locate a

[31] *Ibid..* October 15, 1853.

[32] Prosch, "Military Roads," p. 122; *The Columbian*, September 24, 1853.

[33] *The Columbian*, October 1, 1853. Descriptive accounts of this road are found in Ezra Meeker, *Pioneer Reminiscences of Puget Sound* (Seattle, 1905), chaps. 11–19.

[34] Arthur A. Denny, *Pioneer Days on Puget Sound* (Seattle, 1908), p. 64; Prosch, "Military Roads," p. 122; Roberta Frye Watt, *The Story of Seattle* (Seattle, 1931), p. 150; *Statutes of the Territory of Washington*, 1855, third session (Olympia, 1856), pp. 51–52. For a description of the Snoqualmie route, see *The Columbian*, October 9, 1852; for a description of the Colville road, see *Democratic Standard*, August 9, 1855.

[35] Watt, *The Story of Seattle*, p. 151.

road from Steilacoom to Clark County; an act to locate a road from Seattle to Bellingham Bay; and similar acts to locate roads between Olympia and Shoalwater, Cathlamet and Thurston County, Shoalwater and Gray's Harbor, Olympia to the Columbia River, Seattle to the immigrant trail, etc.[36]

Each subsequent session of the legislature during the period under review passed a steadily increasing amount of legislation pertaining to transportation. Some of this provided for the location, establishment, and operation of ferries, although none of it seemingly refers to bridge construction. Still other enactments provided for authorization of private toll roads. A chart of all the roads and ferries provided for during the first six sessions of the legislature would reveal a concentration of construction between Seattle and the lower Cowlitz region with roads branching off to settlements in the Gray's Harbor region and to the immigrant trails.[37] Lastly, an examination of the legislative action of the territory reveals (and this applies to the Oregon legislature as well) an active appeal being made to the federal government in the form of memorials praying for appropriations to construct military roads within the territory. To quote from one of them:

> Your memorialists, the Legislative Assembly of the Territory of Washington, would respectfully represent, that there has been selected at Bellingham Bay, which is on the extreme northern verge of our Territory, a site for a military post: That there are no means of communication between Fort Steilacoom, at present the most northern military post in the Territory, and the said post . . . . except by water: . . . . That a military road connecting said posts, would, in a military point of view, be invaluable, to say nothing of the development of the resources of our Territory, and establishing communication between our people. . . . .
> Passed December 20, 1855. . . . .[38]

Roads in those early days in Washington were hardly worthy of the name. Some, like the immigrant road over Naches Pass, were laid out and then left to fall into disrepair. Still other roads, as Ezra Meeker said, "just growed" so that "one could scarcely say when the trail ceased to be simply a trail and when it could actually be called a road." Then, reflects Meeker, "And such mud holes! It became a standing joke after the road was opened that a team would stall with an empty wagon going down hill. . . . ."[39]

During the winter season the territorial newspapers not infrequently commented on the intolerable condition of the roads. Says the *Washington Pioneer* for December 1853:

---

[36] *Statutes of the Territory of Washington*, 1855, first session (Olympia, 1855), pp. 463–70.

[37] *Ibid.*, first to sixth sessions (Olympia, 1855–1859).

[38] *Ibid.*, third session, p. 63.   [39] Meeker, *Pioneer Reminiscences*, p. 159.

The miserable character of the road for about a mile from Olympia . . . . has been a matter for some time past of frequent discussion and earnest solicitation. . . . . That the business of this place has been seriously retarded this season, in consequence of the almost impassable state of the road . . . . both our business men and farmers are well aware, and the sad effect, in all branches of industry, has been seriously felt.[40]

In February 1854, the *Pioneer and Democrat* alluded to the "miserable condition" of roads and pointed out how this situation, together with the freezing over of the Cowlitz, made communication with Oregon "almost out of the question."[41]

Washington was to experience bitter Indian wars during the late 'fifties, wars which doubtless lost for the territory hundreds of would-be settlers. The slightly less than 4,000 souls there when it became a territory were widely spread throughout Puget Sound with a sprinkling in and around Walla Walla. A local historian has correctly referred to Olympia of 1853 as a "rain-drenched mudhole" and the future cities of Spokane, Seattle, Tacoma, Walla Walla, and Yakima as either nonexistent or as very tiny shacktowns.[42] In 1855 Mrs. Isaac Stevens came to the capital and her first impressions have been recorded as follows: "Below us, in the deep mud, were a few low, wooden houses, at the head of Puget Sound. My heart sank, for the first time in my life, at the prospect," continued the wife of the Governor. "After ploughing through the mud, we stopped at the principal hotel. . . . ."[43]

So long as the settlers lived along the edge of Puget Sound or along river banks, water transit remained at least a partial solution to their transportation problems. But when settlement moved inland there arose a greater dependence upon overland travel, as indicated by the growing emphasis on road building in the territory.

Throughout the territorial period and in the years that followed, the citizens of the Pacific Northwest never relaxed their effort to secure the aid of federal agencies.[44]

During the early 'forties the military took steps toward surveying the Oregon Trail, and it will be recalled that Lieutenant Frémont did some of this work on his first expedition to South Pass in 1842, and that subsequently he went in search of new routes that might connect with others mapped out by Wilkes along the Oregon coast.[45] In addition to the al-

---

[40] *Washington Pioneer*, December 17, 1853.

[41] *Pioneer and Democrat*, February 4, 1854.

[42] N. W. Durham, *History of the City of Spokane and Spokane Country* (Spokane, Chicago, Philadelphia, 1912), I, 167.

[43] *Ibid.*, p. 168.

[44] W. Turrentine Jackson, "Federal Road Building Grants For Early Oregon," *Oregon Historical Quarterly*, L (March 1949), 3-6.   [45] Fuller, *Pacific Northwest*, p. 184.

lotment of funds for Washington Territory, the Thirty-Second and Thirty-Third Congresses (1853–1855) appropriated funds amounting to about $50,000 for construction of three such military roads in Oregon Territory: Camp Stuart (near Jacksonville) to Myrtle Creek; Myrtle Creek to Scottsburg; and Salem to Astoria by way of the Tualatin Plains. Survey and construction of the first of these was under the direction of Major Benjamin Alvord, assisted by Jesse and Lindsay Applegate; the second was under Lieutenant John Withers. Between Grants Pass and Winchester these two roads (really two segments of one road) followed the general course of the old Oregon-California Trail. Survey and construction of the third road, Salem to Astoria, was at first directed by Lieutenant George H. Derby. Operations on these roads continued intermittently until statehood and the Civil War, and personalities associated with these first federal adventures in territorial road building changed with the years. In 1864 Congress worked out a partnership arrangement with the state of Oregon under which arrangements additional roads were either laid out or built: one, the Oregon Central Military Road (Eugene to eastern boundary of the state via Diamond Peak); in 1866, another from Corvallis to Yaquina Bay.[46]

During the next decade, substantial sums of money were appropriated by Congress for the survey of a road from Great Falls on the upper Missouri River west to intersect the military road previously mentioned as running between Walla Walla and Puget Sound. When completed this route became known as the Mullan Road, to which a chapter will be subsequently devoted.[47]

Roads, local or federal, were all essential to a healthy development of an agricultural economy. Attention is next directed to the varied aspects of frontier transportation and commerce for which road building—even though primitive—was so vitally essential.

---

[46] Jackson, "Federal Road Building Grants," *op. cit.*, pp. 6–29. Other military road developments, too numerous to discuss here, are treated in scholarly fashion by Professor Jackson.

[47] *House Executive Documents*, 34 Cong., 3 sess., vol. I, pt. 2, doc. 1, pp. 371–72; Prosch, "Military Roads," pp. 118–26.

CHAPTER XI

OVERLAND TRADE AND TRANSPORTATION ON THE OLD WEST COAST

The fur companies made some provision for the livelihood of their trappers and traders. But no company, no outside agency, assumed responsibility for the pioneer farmers whose very living had to be extracted largely from the soil. For this reason frontier agriculture was highly diversified; and yet as one early-day local historian said: "Wheat is the staple product of the Willamette Valley. Its suitableness has ever been recognized since the arts of agriculture began in the northwest, and the first rude attempts at cultivation were made."[1] In addition, quantities of oats, potatoes, hay for the livestock, poultry, eggs, and a variety of fruits such as apples, peaches, pears, and such vegetables as beans and peas were also produced. Families did most of their own processing. They dried their own fruit, pressed apples for cider, rendered lard, cured bacon and beef, salted the pork, dried and smoked fish, and made cheese. Wool was spun, woven, and made into garments, all in the home. The pioneer farmers, moreover, were adept at tanning hides, forging tools, tinkering, and building their own homes. In these and other respects pioneer life in Oregon was not unlike that experienced by numerous other American frontiers that had come and gone before the Pacific was reached.

Oregon pioneers, like other pioneers before them, were on the whole industrious, resourceful, and self-reliant, but not entirely self-sufficient. Many things were needed from the outside, articles that could best be secured by trade. The people were greatly in need of more and better farm machinery; they were anxious to increase by outside trade or purchase their small but growing numbers of horses, cattle, and sheep. Before boarding the covered wagons the pioneer mothers had sacrificed precious pieces of furniture in order that room might be made for seed, grain, and essential farm equipment. They now hoped to replace these articles in their new homes in the Far West.

In the final analysis the pioneers of the Oregon country, like those elsewhere, sought first to produce for immediate consumption, and then to produce for export and trade. Interest and activity in the field of transportation were means to these ends. Pioneers often had too much faith in the belief that good transportation facilities would bring them the

---

[1] H. O. Lang, ed., *History of the Willamette Valley . . . . with Personal Reminiscences of its Early Pioneers* (Portland, 1885), p. 547.

markets they desired. In this belief they were frequently mistaken, for at times the best of transportation facilities could not produce the desired market for their surplus wheat. The California and Inland Empire gold rushes produced a great demand for agricultural produce, but too often the outside market seemed anything but brisk.

It was toward Mexican California that the Oregon pioneer farmers first turned for trade—political, ethnological, and natural barriers notwithstanding. Fur traders had opened this southern door for them. In 1834 a new chapter in Oregon-California overland commerce began when Ewing Young, Hall J. Kelley, and others drove a band of horses from the Sacramento Valley to Oregon. Young had come to California in 1829 following a career in the Santa Fe trade. It was in California that he met Kelley who after failing to organize an emigrant expedition to Oregon in 1832 had likewise gone to the Far West by way of Mexico. According to Kelley's own story, the two had met in San Diego and there Kelley induced Young to go north, since, wrote the former, "like myself, he had an iron constitution. . . . ." The following is Kelley's own account of what took place :

With a party of nine men, on the 8th of July, we left the encampment, and arrived in the valley of the Wallamet on the 11th of Oct. 1834, having 120 valuable horses and mules which mostly belonged to Young. Some days after leaving the Bay of San Francisco, a band of *marauders* overtook and joined my party.[2]

The marauders turned out to be thieves, and as such placed the same stigma upon the seemingly honest American horse traders. Not until 1837 when Lieutenant William A. Slacum came to Oregon under orders from President Jackson were their names cleared in the minds of the settlers of the Willamette Valley.

Slacum saw the need for more horses and cattle in Oregon if American settlement there was to thrive. The bulk of the livestock (about five hundred head of horses and an equal number of cattle) were the possession of the Hudson's Bay Company, and any use made of them by Americans was by special sufferance of the Scottish doctor at Fort Vancouver. Slacum therefore encouraged Americans to purchase their own cattle, and to further this end offered free passage aboard his ship the *Loriot* to those who would go and buy cattle in California and drive them north to the Willamette Valley. "The advantage of being landed in California or Bodega free of expense, and the risk of the road, was very great," observed Slacum, who then recounted how in keeping with his offer, there was organized, in 1837, the Willamette Cattle Company. It was agreed that ten men should accompany Slacum south and that Young was to

---

[2] Fred Wilbur Powell, ed., *Hall J. Kelley on Oregon* (Princeton, 1932), p. 100.

head the party. Enough money was raised by private and by Hudson's Bay subscriptions to purchase at least five hundred head of cattle. With all the necessary arrangements apparently made, there was good prospect that the venture would succeed. "I certainly view this measure as one of the highest importance to the future growth and prosperity of this fine country," said Slacum, "even if no other object is attained by my visit to the Columbia."[3]

The Oregonians encountered some difficulty in getting permission from the Mexican government to take the cattle out of the country, but by June, thanks to the low price on livestock in California, they were ready to move homeward with eight hundred head of half-wild Mexican cattle and forty horses. Heavy losses, however, were incurred in the six-hundred-mile drive. Said an old Oregon pioneer:

Indeed, any one who has only known civilized life and tame herds can have little idea of those Mexican cattle, identical with the wide-horned, slim-flanked stock that inhabited Texas at the time of conquest. I had some experience with that herd, as I purchased an old cow fifteen years after, that bore the proper name of "Kicker."[4]

Philip L. Edwards, treasurer of the company and one of the drivers, has given us a glimpse of the hardships encountered, especially in the mountains which "appear every day to grow more difficult. 'Hills peep over hills and Alps on Alps.' The grass is so generally burned that our animals have become feeble . . . . . Our horses are so exhausted from the same causes that they are of more trouble than service."[5]

Troubles with cattle and Mexicans were slight compared with the trouble with the old "Rascals," the Rogue River Indians. One of the drivers unnecessarily shot one of the Indians and thereby revived the fighting spirit of this stubborn and treacherous tribe. The Americans were ambushed in a narrow ravine, one driver was wounded, and many of the cattle were killed. It was October before the goal was reached. Heavy though the losses were, 630 head were brought safely through to the Willamette Valley where they soon increased on the "nutritious grasses and equable climate."[6] Mrs. Jason Lee, in a letter to her brother October 26, 1837, aptly expressed what the arrival of these cattle meant to the American missionaries, so long dependent upon the Hudson's Bay Company for cattle: ". . . . the Company have just returned and . . . .

---

[3] "Memorial of William A. Slacum," *Senate Documents*, 25 Cong., 2 sess., vol. I, doc. 24, pp. 12–13; John W. Caughey, History of the Pacific Coast of North America (Los Angeles, 1933), pp. 230, 235.

[4] S. A. Clarke, *Pioneer Days of Oregon History* (Portland, 1905), I, 306–7.

[5] Douglas S. Watson, ed., *The Diary of Philip Leget Edwards: The Great Cattle Drive from California to Oregon in 1837* (San Francisco, 1932), p. 31.

[6] [Elwood Evans, comp.], *History of the Pacific Northwest* (Portland, 1889), I, 377; Bancroft, *History of Oregon*, I, 150.

we will have 80 head of cattle—we will have plenty of butter and milk in future I expect . . . . ."[7] The cattle experiment was tried again before the close of the period, but it was not until later that a route to California was clearly defined and that regular communication was established between the English- and the Spanish-speaking peoples of the Pacific Coast, but this great cattle drive clearly demonstrated the feasibility of such overland commerce. Therefore, the Applegate and California roads were opened up, and when the California Gold Rush of the 'fifties came, raising the price of beef to unheard-of heights, there already was known a very practical method of marketing cattle in a country where railroads were still a future dream. By then, one observes, cattle were being driven not only north from Los Angeles, but south from Oregon as well.[8]

Ordinary overland commerce, at least within the farming belt itself, was much less spectacular and much less exciting than the long drives. It was done by means of slow, lumbering Conestoga and other types of wagons that had been brought across the plains. Commercial wagon freighting, such as was so familiar to the Great Plains, never became extensive west of the Cascades. And it was in the Rogue River Valley, rather than in the Willamette Valley, that wagon freighting was greatest. There local farmers were unable to meet demands of the gold miners who stormed into the region during the early 1850's; and, since the Rogue River was not navigable for coastal vessels, great quantities of goods either had to be packed in or freighted in from outside sources.

Pack trains and lines of freight wagons converged on Jacksonville from both the Willamette Valley and from California. Crescent City, for instance, was 120 miles from Jacksonville; from this California seaport came not only local agricultural produce, but much other merchandise shipped there by water from San Francisco. "The road is mountainous," wrote the Portland *Oregonian* as late as 1868, "and every pound of freight hauled over it to Jacksonville costs three and a half cents."[9]

The distance from Portland to Jacksonville, on the other hand, was about 325 miles, but in spite of greater distance the future "rose city" found the Rogue Valley a ready market for its goods, especially merchandise.[10] During the 1870's, however, Rogue Valley farmers had begun producing for export such items as bacon, lard, butter, cheese, and hides. According to the *Ashland Tidings* (1876), "Our streets are daily crowded with freight teams loaded with Rogue River products for Fort Klamath,

    [7] Theressa Gay, *Life and Letters of Mrs. Jason Lee* (Portland, 1936), p. 163.

    [8] Robert G. Cleland, *The Cattle on a Thousand Hills* (San Marino, California, 1941), chap. 6; Evans, *History of the Pacific Northwest*, I, 337.

    [9] Leslie M. Scott, comp., *History of the Oregon Country*, by Harvey W. Scott (Cambridge, Massachusetts, 1924), III, 34–35.

    [10] Joseph Gaston, *Portland, Oregon* (Chicago, 1911), I, 235.

Lake County, and Northern California."[11] That Ashland was out to get its share of the freight trade is clearly revealed by the *Tidings'* statement that Ashland's merchants and millers had an "eye out" for several Modoc County, California, freight teams reported to have been traveling toward the future home of lithia water.[12]

Equally essential to the well-being of an agricultural society was some form of public conveyance. The sight of the first stagecoach in the Pacific Northwest was to most settlers like seeing an old friend once again. In the East, from whence most of the people in the Oregon country had come, stagecoaches had been in general use for nearly a century.[13] With road building (or at least what went by that name) initiated in Oregon during 1846, it is not surprising that the first mention of a commercial stage line on the Pacific Northwest appeared that same year. A notice in the *Oregon Spectator*, October 29, reads as follows:[14]

TELEGRAPH LINE
EIGHT OX POWER

The subscriber begs leave to announce to the public that he proposes to run an express—rain or no rain—mud or no mud—load or no load—*but not without pay*—from Oregon and Linn Cities to Tuality Plains during the ensuing season—leaving the two former places on Mondays and Thursday [*sic*], and the Plains on Wednesdays and Saturdays. The "cars" will be covered and every accommodation extended to passengers. For freight or passage, apply to the subscriber, proprietor and engineer, at Linn City.

Oct. 29, 1846.   S. H. L. MEEK

The concern described above does not appear to have existed long, and it was not until after the establishment of the territorial government in 1849 that stagecoach service in the Willamette Valley was begun on what appears to have been a permanent basis. By 1852 advertisements of stage companies in the Oregon City, and also in the Olympia, newspapers had become a regular feature, and by then the service had been extended to a large number of communities in the Cowlitz and Willamette River regions. The following is a typical example of a stagecoach advertisement for the early 'fifties:

NEW STAGE LINE!
THROUGH BY DAYLIGHT FROM CHAMPOEG
TO SALEM.

E. Depuis, has just established a line of Stages from Champoeg to Salem, which is well stocked with superior American horses. This being the daily line, the stages will leave Champoeg on the arrival of the Washington, and other steamers. . . . .[15]

---

[11] *Ashland Tidings*, July 20, 1876.   [12] *Ibid.*, June 24, 1876.
[13] Oscar Osburn Winther, "Transportation and Travel," *Dictionary of American History* (New York, 1940), V, 306.
[14] *Oregon Spectator*, October 29, 1846.   [15] *The Columbian*, October 2, 1852.

Another such line was the following which operated out of Portland:

Messrs. Scott and Abbott have established a line of stages between this city and Lafayette. The stage leaves Portland every Tuesday and Friday, and Lafayette every Monday and Thursday, at 6 o'clock, A.M. They have placed upon the road good carriages and horses under the charge of careful drivers. The enterprise should be well sustained as it has long been needed.[16]

By the middle of the decade stagecoach service was widespread. The Pioneer Line maintained a tri-weekly route between Oregon City and Corvallis. "The Stages are of Concord manufacture," is the assurance of this proprietor, "comfortable and safe. The horses are capable, and make good time, and the drivers are reliable."[17] Then during the following year B. and E. W. Davis pushed stagecoach transportation farther southward by establishing weekly service between Corvallis, Eugene City, and Winchester on the Umpqua. During the rainy season the roads between Eugene City and Winchester were such that the Davis concern had to convey the mails and passengers by horseback. Rates from Corvallis to Winchester were twelve dollars; from Eugene to Winchester, eight dollars.[18]

In 1864 a wagon road reached the Boise wagon trail and coinciding with this there was begun the wagon freight business, which reduced freight rates by fifty percent.[19]

By the close of the decade stagecoach routes were too numerous to mention here in complete form. George H. McQueen Company, Tracy and Company's Express, H. C. Riggs Company (later Riggs and Chase), the Oregon Stage Company's line, James Strang, and Benjamin Despain are among the firms advertising service in the Oregon newspapers when statehood came. Most of the companies operated in the Willamette Valley.

In each instance the best of service was assured the traveling public. The speed of the coaches operated by the Oregon Stage Company suggested to its owners a "head-swim" pace.[20] But not to be outdone, H. C. Riggs boasted thus:

. . . . The word "FAIL," has never been written or printed in his [Riggs'] "Lexicon"! "Live or Die, Sink or Swim, Survive or Perish," he is determined to keep up with the improvements of the day and age.—In the swift progress The Great American People are making in the direction of Universal Empire, should horse-flesh prove too tardy, he *may* avail himself of the breezes of heaven, as *indicated above,* and meet the wishes of a generous, go-aheaditive public.

N.B. This notice is merely "annunciatory." The *Horses will be hitched on* at the expiration of the twenty days.[21]

[16] *The Oregonian*, June 18, 1853.   [17] *Pacific Christian Advocate*, November 3, 1855.

[18] *Corvallis Occidental Messenger*, September 26, 1857.   [19] Bird, *Boise*, p. 105.

[20] *The People's Press*, November 19, 1859; *Corvallis Oregon Union*, April 2, 1859; *The Oregon Statesman*, June 14 and August 23, 1859; *Pacific Christian Advocate*, February 19, 1859.

[21] *Oregon Union*, April 2, 1859.

North of the Columbia River the development of the stagecoach business was similar and not unrelated to that of the Willamette Valley. The very first passenger service out of Olympia was in 1854, and it appears to have been offered in connection with wagon freighting. It was the custom for freighting concerns in Olympia to meet the Cowlitz River boats, and, with an eye for extra business, the freighters offered to transport passengers to and from the river landing. Regular stages, however, came as soon as business warranted the establishment of a line. The first regular stage vehicles used in Washington Territory were the mud-wagons, and the selection was an admirable one. Ezra Meeker, a prominent pioneer, recounted how the unhappy travelers in and out of Olympia were "conveyed . . . . over either the roughest corduroy or deepest mud, the one bruising the muscles the other straining the nerves in the anticipation of being dumped into the bottomless pit of mud."[22]

Hand in hand with stagecoach service was the question of mail transportation. Throughout the entire prestatehood period the mail service remained abominable. Complaints were constant, bitter, and many. "What has become of the Post-office agent for Oregon and California?"; "Oregon has been sadly neglected"; "Just think of it; the citizens of Oregon are required to pay *four* times the amount of postage, on all correspondence, that is exacted from Utah, Deseret, and Minnesota"; "Our suffering is intolerable!"; "We cannot account for the neglect. . . . ."; "From all parts of the Territory we receive loud complaint in regard to the mails . . . . "; these are some of the running comments on the United States mail service in Oregon before statehood.[23] "Job, who 'rests in Paradise,' is reported to have been a very patient man when upon the earth," to once again quote from the *Statesman*, "but we question whether he had enough of that amiable virtue to have enabled him to preserve his equanimity if he had been a 'sufferer' from the mail arrangements or *dis*-arrangements in Oregon."[24]

The complaints heard in Oregon were those heard in California where, in view of the extremely rapid rise in population, conditions were even worse. It was in part to meet these demands of the Far West that Congress, in 1851, reduced letter postage to three cents for a distance of less than 3,000 miles; ten cents if more remote. Beginning with 1854 the government modified this liberal law and required prepayment in the form of stamps on all letters, an act, incidentally, which greatly

---

[22] Meeker, *Pioneer Reminiscences*, p. 159; *Pioneer and Democrat*, December 30, 1854.

[23] *Oregon Spectator*, November 1, 1849, and February 21 and November 21, 1850; *The Oregon Statesman*, March 9, 1852.

[24] *The Oregon Statesman*, April 2, 1853.

affected the express businesses since a large volume of their business was letter carrying. Prepayment of postage occasioned complaints from Oregon, but not so much as did the 3,000-mile zoning rule for the reason that Oregon secured its mail by boat rather than by direct overland route, and therefore the rates were twice what they would have been had the Oregon mail come directly overland from Missouri. In short the *Oregon Argus* called it "Unjust Taxation of Oregon Letter Writers!"[25]

On the Washington side of the Columbia River the problem of mails was the same embarrassing one. Among the many memorials and resolutions passed by the first territorial legislature at Olympia was one asking the Congress of the United States for mail service between Puget Sound points and San Francisco, New Orleans, and New York.[26] Action on the part of the federal government toward establishing adequate mail service had always been slow in coming, at least in the minds of the people who made up such communities. During the 'forties Americans north of the Columbia River shared the position of those in the Willamette Valley; their nearest postoffice was at Weston, Missouri, and Weston was at least 2,000 miles away. If letters were to be sent to the States, one simply waited for someone who might be going east and would be willing to deposit the letter in a box upon reaching Missouri. Petitions of the kind sent by the first Washington legislature began, therefore, with the Oregon provisional government as far back as 1845. The need for a post road was stressed alongside the argument that the government should build immigrant and military roads in the region. In 1846 Congress, after inquiring into the establishment of a post road between Missouri and the Columbia,[27] actually appropriated $100,000 to provide bimonthly service between the States and Astoria via the Isthmus of Panama. Contract was let with the Pacific Mail Steamship Company, and in 1847 federal mail actually reached this distant outpost at the mouth of the Columbia.[28]

It was not until three years following the first delivery of United States mails at Astoria that the government, again after more memorials had been sent, established definite post roads in the Oregon Territory.

---

[25] *The Oregon Argus* (Oregon City), April 28, 1855.

[26] Bancroft, *Washington, Idaho, and Montana*, pp. 84 n., 85 n.

[27] *Senate Journal*, 29 Cong., 1 sess., pp. 57–58.

[28] John Haskell Kemble, *The Panama Route, 1848–1869* (Berkeley, 1943), pp. 12 ff. It was the recommendation of the Postmaster General that the most northern port of call be at the mouth of the Klamath River rather than at Astoria. Steamers would be allowed to terminate their voyages at San Francisco provided they would call at three ports south of that city and provided that mails were transshipped regularly in sailing vessels to the Klamath River for delivery in the Willamette Valley. See also F. N. Otis, *History of the Panama Railroad; and of the Pacific Mail Steamship Company* (New York, 1867), pp. 149–60; Clark, *Willamette Valley*, pp. 494–96.

Two of these post roads affected the region north of the Columbia. The first was from Astoria up the Columbia to the mouth of the Cowlitz; from there on up the Columbia to the Willamette, and southward to the Umpqua. The second was to run between the mouth of the Cowlitz River and Nisqually.[29] Mail up the Pacific Coast was to be carried by the Pacific Mail Steamship Company boats, and the service of this company left much to be desired. One of their ships, the S.S. *Caroline*, first sailed up the Columbia River with mail in 1850; the side-wheelers *Oregon*, *California*, *Sea Gull*, and *Panama* followed. Even so, it was not until the following year when the steamship *Columbia* was put in service on the Columbia River that anything resembling regularity existed.[30] Even then the postal service continued to be a sore spot with the people, particularly in the Puget Sound area. "The Mails! —the Mails!!" were the headlines of *The Columbian* in December 1852. It raged against "the provoking irregularity, and wanton disregard of the public accommodation" of the Pacific Mail Steamship Company and against its "reckless and almost ruthless manner in which the service is performed throughout the territory." This newspaper then enumerates specific violations of the mail contracts and concludes sarcastically with the remark that all this irregularity "should not be a matter of surprise, as the company receive from Uncle Sam, *only* $550,000 per annum, for carrying the mail from New York to Astoria, and consequently cannot *afford* to be very punctual."[31] High water in the winter created extenuating circumstances, even in the eyes of *The Columbian*, for at times boats could not ascend the Cowlitz River on that account.[32]

It does not appear that the establishment of a government at Olympia improved the postal service of the Pacific Mail Steamship Company. From *The Columbian* one reads:

ANOTHER GROSS OUTRAGE

. . . . Now, must we any longer submit to the serious consequences entailed by such culpable negligence? Are we to submit to such high-handed outrages? Must the entire population of Washington Territory be eternally tricked, fooled and swindled by that great enormity, the P.M.S.S. Co., and by its agents, officers and hirelings? There *is* a remedy for the evil, and we must apply it. We must petition Congress for the complete re-organization of the mail service for this Territory. We must ask that our mails be sent to PUGET SOUND DIRECT, BY OCEAN STEAMERS, STOPPING AT NO WAY PORTS WHATEVER. The Nicaragua Steamship Company are prepared to place a steamer on the route if they can get the carrying of the mails, and a suitable appropriation therefor. When this is accomplished, we may expect our mails regularly; but not till then. Let this petition be drawn, circulated, signed, and forwarded at once—the sooner the better. There is not the least necessity to

[29] Carey, *History of Oregon*, II, 736.   [30] Clark, *Willamette Valley*, pp. 495-96.
[31] *The Columbian*, December 25, 1852.   [32] *Ibid.*, January 15, 1853.

wait till we have a delegate. *Do it now.* "Put the ball in motion" and keep it rolling, until the desired object is attained.[33]

Two weeks following this journalistic attack on the mail system *The Columbian* further charged that not only was the service terrible but that there was actually "ROBBERY OF THE MAIL."[34] The *Washington Pioneer* newspaper was quick to support its rival's attack upon the Pacific Mail Steamship Company, and even proposed amendment of the mail contract rather than submit to the "gruff, discourteous, and sometimes cruel outrages" of "such a powerful, dangerous and soul-less monopoly."[35] Improvements were slow in their arrival. February 4, 1854, had come to Olympia and still the President's annual message to Congress in the previous December had not reached the Territory of Washington. It would be printed at Bombay and read by the subjects of the Czar (if they could read) as soon as by the people of Washington, was the contention of the press.[36]

However, an optimistic note in the press is observed during the late summer of 1854 at which time Commodore Cornelius Vanderbilt offered to carry the mails between New York and San Francisco at pay which was to be in proportion to the time involved.[37] Furthermore, it appears that press campaigns against the postal system of the territory brought some results as indicated in an open letter from the Rainier postal agent. The letter in part reads:

> The desired change in our mail arrangements has been effected. . . . . Mails leave Rainer [*sic*] every Wednesday at 6 A.M.; arrive at Steilacoom on Friday at 2 P.M. Leave Steilacoom every Saturday at 6 A.M.; arrive at Rainier next Monday at 2 P.M. . . . . and they will now be sent on without delay. . . . .

This having been achieved, the next campaign launched by the press was for direct steamer mail service between San Francisco and Puget Sound, not to mention an increase in the number of routes within Washington Territory.[38] On April 14, 1855, came the happy announcement that at length Congress had authorized the Postmaster General to contract for semimonthly mail service by sea from San Francisco to the head of Puget Sound, or at least to Port Townsend. With this announcement the newspaper correspondent showed his first signs (though not for long) of true enthusiasm when he wrote: "Daylight is now about to break upon this Territory. . . . ."[39]

The middle 1850's mark a definite change for the better so far as both

---

[33] *The Columbian*, November 12, 1853.
[34] *Ibid.*, November 26, 1853.
[35] *Washington Pioneer*, December 17, 1853.
[36] *Pioneer and Democrat*, February 4, 1854.
[37] *Ibid.*, August 5, 1854.
[38] *Ibid.*, August 19, 1854; January 27, 1855.
[39] *Ibid.*, April 14, 1855.

FRONT STREET, PORTLAND, IN 1852

The horse is tied in front of the Wells, Fargo and Company Express Office. Note the sailing ship anchored at the river bank.

JACKSONVILLE, ROGUE RIVER VALLEY, OREGON TERRITORY

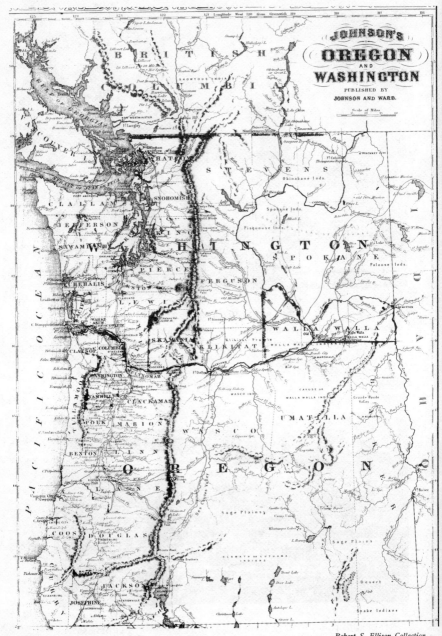

OREGON STATE AND WASHINGTON TERRITORY SHOWING WAGON ROADS (1866)

stagecoach and postal services were concerned. This is true not alone in the Pacific Northwest, but also throughout the entire American Far West. In 1854 there was organized the California Stage Company, destined to extend its services from Sacramento to Portland, and two years later steps were taken at the national capital to establish what became the historically famous Butterfield Overland Mail. Connections between these two lines were to bring the Oregon country into direct and relatively speedy communication with the Atlantic States. It was under the leadership of such prominent staging proprietors in California as James Birch, Frank S. Stevens, and Warren F. Hall that on January 1, 1854, a merger was officially announced to the public.[40] The capital stock was fixed at $1,000,000, and the assets of the company were represented to a large measure by material equipment which included 750 horses, and coaches, harness, and fixtures necessary to stock at least 450 miles of route.[41] Headquarters were established at the Orlean Hotel of Sacramento, that city's best hostelry, and the leading officers were: James Birch, president; Frank S. Stevens, vice-president; and Charles McLaughlin, general superintendent.[42]

With this organization and with ample equipment on hand, it was not long before this new company began to expand. Before the close of 1854, it advertised service over fourteen different routes with a grand total of 170 stations.[43] And on November 2, 1854, the *Sacramento Union* commented upon the "splendid Troy coaches" drawn by as "fine horses as we have ever seen driven upon stage routes in any portion of the Union."[44]

The California Stage Company made further developments in 1855. In order to assure a control over the staging business of the state, the fares were greatly reduced during this year,[45] and extensions were made to the company's routes in several sections of California and particularly in the direction of Oregon. From its original northern terminus at Shasta City, the firm "stocked the road to Yreka via the Pitt [*sic*] River," according to the reminiscences of H. C. Ward, "using an old immigrant road and avoiding Trinity & Scots Mountains." This chronicler adds, however, that in view of the fact that "Indians attack Stages killed stock tenders burnt stations and stole horses," it soon became necessary for the California Stage Company to substitute a

---

[40] Samuel Colville, comp., *City Directory of Sacramento for the Year 1854–55* (Sacramento, 1854), p. 106. Hereafter cited as *Sacramento Directory, 1854–55.*

[41] *Sacramento Daily Union,* October 23, 1865.

[42] *Sacramento Directory, 1854–55,* p. 106.   [43] *Ibid.,* p. 16.

[44] *Sacramento Daily Union,* November 2, 1854.

[45] *Ibid.,* February 15, 1855.

"saddle train" over certain parts of this route between French Gulch and Yreka.[46]

In spite of the difficulties alluded to, the California Stage Company was determined to push its line on to Oregon where a through road from Portland south to Jacksonville was likewise under construction.[47] To avoid the Indian menace the Company commenced on its own initiative the construction of a road over Trinity and Scott mountains in 1857. By 1861 this road was opened all the way to Jacksonville, Oregon,[48] to which point the Oregon road had been completed at least two years previously when the California Stage Company extended its lines to Portland.[49] With this feat accomplished, it was at last possible to drive a four- or six-horse stage through from Sacramento to Portland (a distance of about seven hundred miles) with comparative safety, comfort, and speed.

Meanwhile the California Stage Company had not ceased to expand. James Haworth succeeded Birch to the presidency of the firm in 1856, and under his leadership new lines were extended in every direction. In commenting upon this growth, a Marysville item published in the *Sacramento Union* remarked in September 1858, that there were few enterprises "equal in magnitude of operations, in amount of capital invested, or number of men employed." This same account stated that the company was then running twenty-eight daily lines of stages for which 1,000 horses, 184 agents, drivers, and hostlers were employed. The total length of the routes at that time was, according to this article, about 1,277 miles (more than 1,000,000 annual miles); and over more than 1,200 miles of this distance the company carried the United States mails.[50]

More important, at least so far as Oregon was concerned, were the developments made during 1859–1860. With only short gaps remaining in the road construction between Sacramento and Portland, the California Stage Company had its eyes upon a contract with the United States government to carry the mails between these two points. With this end in view Vice-President Frank S. Stevens went to Washington, D.C., where he urged the Post Office Department, as of course many others had done, to substitute a daily mail service for the rather intermittent services performed by the Pacific Mail Steamship Company.[51] Stevens' efforts were crowned with success. On June 21, 1860, Congress directed

[46] "Reminiscences of H. C. Ward," MS, Borel Collection, Stanford University Library, Stanford, California.

[47] Clark, *Willamette Valley*, p. 488.

[48] *Sacramento Daily Union*, May 22, 1860, and January 1, 1861.   [49] Clark, *op. cit.*, p. 498.

[50] *Sacramento Daily Union*, September 29, 1858. *The Marysville Express* article was reprinted in this paper.   [51] *Ibid.*, October 23, 1865.

the Postmaster General "to contract with the California Stage Company for daily service in stages, between Sacramento City, in California, and Portland, in Oregon, running through in seven days, from April 1 to December 1, and in twelve days the balance of the year, at $90,000 per annum."[52]

The new daily stagecoach service provided by the contract referred to above was formally inaugurated on September 15, 1860, under the order of the Postmaster General.[53] The estimated distance of the route was 710 miles. Stages left Portland and Sacramento every morning at six o'clock. The route, from the south to the north, was as follows: Sacramento to Nicolaus, Marysville, Oroville, Chico, Tehama, Red Bluff, Cottonwood, Shasta, French Gulch, Trinity Center, Calahan's Ranch, Scottsburg, Yreka, Jacksonville, Canyonville, Roseburg, Oakland, Eugene, Corvallis, Albany, Salem, Dutchtown, Oregon City, Portland. There were 60 stations along the route, 14 district agents, 75 hostlers, and 35 drivers. To stock the road it required 28 coaches, 30 stage wagons, and 500 head of horses. Although the contract time allowed for this run was seven days, the actual scheduled time was six days, seven hours.[54]

With the one exception of the Butterfield Overland Mail route established exactly one year earlier, it was the longest single route in the United States. It is not surprising, therefore, that considerable importance was placed upon this achievement of the California Stage Company. The enthusiasm with which the day of inauguration of service, September 15, 1860, was greeted, was well expressed by the *Sacramento Union*:

Today the trips of the Daily Overland Mail stage between Sacramento and Portland will commence from each terminus, at six o'clock, A.M., to continue daily . . . . This is an important era in the history of California staging, and indeed, of that of the whole country. We do not now recollect an instance of such a long continuous line of staging on a single mailing route—some seven hundred miles in extent—as one under notice. There are settlements for the whole distance, and the postal facilities which will be rendered to the people on the route is to them of the utmost importance, as they are most convenient to the citizens of Sacramento and Portland. No one need now subject himself to the delays of the uncertain ocean mail service, but can write daily, or when he pleases. A person, also, who has no desire to risk his life on the rough coast of Oregon, can take a quiet seat in the stage, pass through a most interesting section of country, and reach Portland at his leisure. . . . . Such an event as the starting of a Daily Mail stage to Portland should be announced by the firing of cannon and other indications of enthusiasm.[55]

The establishment of regular stage and mail, and, incidentally, express service,[56] between Sacramento and Portland very soon led to

[52] *Senate Executive Documents*, 36 Cong., 2 sess., vol. III, doc. 1, pp. 436–37.

[53] *Ibid.*, p. 436.

[54] *Sacramento Daily Union*, January 1, 1861.   [55] *Ibid.*, September 15, 1860.

[56] Company advertisements contained the notice: "Carries Wells, Fargo & Co's Express."

expansions into other regions. The same act of Congress which empowered the Postmaster General to make a contract for the above service, likewise directed him to organize a "six-times-a-week line, in steamboats and stages, between Portland, Oregon, and Olympia, in Washington Territory. . . . ."[57]

Coinciding with the development of the California Stagecoach Company system was the emergence of the Butterfield Overland Mail. The first of several feeble steps to establish overland communication was taken by the federal government when a contract to Absalom Woodward and George Chorpenning to carry mails monthly between Sacramento and Salt Lake City was confirmed on October 16, 1851.[58] Another attempt to extend this kind of service to the Pacific Coast came when in 1857, following a long dispute in Congress in which sectional interests manifested themselves, Postmaster General Aaron V. Brown at length determined to establish a temporary stage and mail line between San Antonio, Texas, and San Diego, California—a line which was too slow and too far south to help the Pacific Northwest in the slightest.[59]

Of much more importance to the West than the foregoing half-hearted measures was the passage by Congress on March 3, 1857, of the Post Office Appropriations Act providing funds for regular stagecoach passenger and postal service between St. Louis and San Francisco.[60] Bids were received up to June 1, 1857, with the understanding that the service was to "commence within twelve months after the date of such contract,"[61] which was awarded July 2, 1857, to John Butterfield, William G. Fargo, William B. Dinsmore, *et al.*

In accordance with the terms of the bid, and "after full and mature consideration," the Post Office Department selected a route about 2,700 miles long to start from St. Louis, Missouri, and Memphis, Tennessee, and to converge at Little Rock, Arkansas; "thence, *via* Preston, Texas, ... to Fort Yuma, California; thence, through the best passes . . . . to San Francisco." The service was to be semiweekly and the contractors were to receive $600,000 annually.[62]

Service over the Butterfield route began on September 15, 1858. The first trip from the East to the West was made in twenty-four days, eighteen hours, thirty-five minutes, and its successful completion was regarded everywhere with pride and approbation. So elated was President Buchanan when he heard that the first journey had been success-

[57] *Senate Executive Documents*, 36 Cong., 2 sess., vol. III, doc. 1, p. 436.

[58] *House Documents*, 32 Cong., 1 sess., vol. VIII, doc. 56, p. 398.

[59] William Banning and George H. Banning, *Six Horses* (New York, 1928), pp. 91–92.

[60] *House Documents*, 35 Cong., 1 sess., vol. II, pt. 3, p. 986.

[61] *Ibid.*, p. 987.   [62] *Ibid.*, p. 988 ff.

fully completed that he wired John Butterfield: "I cordially congratulate you upon the result. It is a glorious triumph for civilization and the Union."[63]

The inauguration of the Butterfield Overland Mail service between the East and California had an immediate effect upon the Pacific Northwest situation. It not only meant that the California Stage Company stages could connect with those of the Overland concern (which they did) but, as has been shown, within two more years this combined network of mail and postal service was pushed north to Portland. In 1860 passengers and mail could go from St. Louis to Portland, a distance of more than 3,400 miles via El Paso and over what must have seemed to the northwesterners a tremendous detour, in thirty-two days' time. Until the establishment of the Holladay system over the central route with branch lines extending into Idaho, Montana, Oregon, and Washington, the people of the Pacific Northwest continued to rely upon California as a major relay point in their greatly extended line of communication with the Atlantic states.

Also of great significance to the old Oregon country was the rise of fast express transportation. Until about the middle of the nineteenth century the methods of transporting freight were as inefficient as the proverbially tedious modes of passenger transportation. Freight, for the most part, was either moved aboard leisurely windjammers, in lumbering Conestogas, or on the backs of phlegmatic pack mules. The transmission of news and of the mails was fast only in relation to the snail's pace set by the freighters. If parcels were very valuable and there was need of extraordinary haste, either special messengers might be employed or delivery might be entrusted to a stage driver who as a special favor, or for a consideration, would personally transact such special business if it could be done along his prescribed route of travel. Not until about the 1830's did it occur to anyone that a profitable business, even great fortunes, might be made out of the speedy delivery of certain types of goods, namely small packages of high value, such as gold dust, bullion, jewelry, securities, and perishable commodities. The transportation of such items has come to be termed "express."[64]

Organized express companies first appeared on the Atlantic Coast, where stage drivers and shipping agents had, in a measure, fulfilled the

---

[63] Frederic L. Paxson, *History of the American Frontier* (New York, 1924), pp. 463–65. In 1859 the railroad had reached St. Joseph, Missouri, and thereafter this city became the point of departure for the Butterfield coaches. See also Lyle H. Wright and Josephine M. Bynum, eds., *The Butterfield Overland Mail*, by Waterman L. Ormsby (San Marino, California, 1942); Roscoe P. Conkling and Margaret B. Conkling, *The Butterfield Overland Mail, 1857–1869* (Glendale, California, 1947), 3 vols.

[64] See Oscar Osburn Winther, *Express and Stagecoach Days in California* (Stanford University, 1936), p. 16.

duties of expressmen for a long time.[65] Just who was the first expressman it is therefore difficult to tell, but a Boston-Providence express is
known to have been organized as early as 1834.[66]

It was in California that the express business first appeared on the
West Coast in anything like a permanent and well-organized business.
There scores of individual express operators began offering their services as postmen and pseudo bankers for the gold miners whose contacts
with the outside world were at best very restricted. One small express
operator after another began business until by 1860 there were nearly
three hundred such concerns in California, and many of them extended
their operations into Oregon. Alexander H. Todd, reputed to have been
the first expressman in California, was connected with Oregon in 1851.
Note the following :[67]

TODD & CO'S EXPRESS
For Oregon & California.

This company has been engaged for the last 18 months, running an Express
from San Francisco, via Stockton, to all parts of the Southern Mines, in connection
with the well known house of ADAMS & CO. to the States and Europe. Mr. Todd,
of the above firm, has been making arrangements, &c., through all the principal
cities in Oregon, and they are now prepared to transact any and all kinds of Express
Business, in any part of California and Oregon, through Adams & Co., to the
United States and Europe. . . . .

We respectfully solicit a portion of the patronage of the People of Oregon.

TODD & Co.

AGENTS IN OREGON—Abernethy & Clark, Oregon City; Hopkins & Donald,
Milwaukie; Capt. Samuel E. May, Portland; Sutler's Store, Vancouver; W. H.
Tappan, St. Helens [;] Hensil & Co., Astoria.

April 10, '51

Then came Newell and Company's Express which was successor to
Todd in California and which, according to its own advertisement, "will
continue our express as usual, to and from SAN FRANCISCO, and all parts
of the OREGON TERRITORY," retaining, like its predecessor, a connection
with Adams and Company.[68] Still another good example is Gregory and
Company, which house, incidentally, in 1851 had offices at Portland,
Oregon City, Astoria, and Salem in Oregon, and Olympia in Washing-

---

[65] Alvin F. Harlow, *Old Waybills: The Romance of the Express Companies* (New York,
1934), pp. 9–10; Malcolm Keir, *The March of Commerce* (New Haven, Connecticut, 1927), p.
157.

[66] Harlow, *op. cit.*, pp. 10–12.

[67] *Oregon Spectator*, May 15, 1851; *Oregon Weekly Times*, July 17, 1851; Winther, *Express
and Stagecoach Days*, pp. 18–33.

[68] *Oregon Weekly Times*, October 30, 1851; *Oregon Spectator*, November 25, 1851.

ton.[69] Then later came Cram, Rogers and Company,[70] and the Pacific Express Company.[71]

Cram, Rogers and Company had been formed at Shasta City in 1851, and moved into Oregon in 1853. It took over Dugan and Company's Oregon Express which had succeeded McClaine and Company as operators in the Umpqua-Rogue River region.[72] "The mines and community in general," reads the latter's notice, "can rest assured that all business appertaining to an Express Company will be attended to with promptness and dispatch, with due regard to safety."[73] In 1854 Cram, Rogers and Company expanded to the point where, as the following list shows, the firm had offices in nearly all the mining camps of the Siskiyous as well as other mining regions in the Pacific Northwest:

. . . . Yreka, Shasta, Althouse, Weaverville, Pittsburg, and Pitt River. Also, Trinity river, Scott river, Scott bar, Scott valley, Klamath river, Salmon river, Rogue river, Indian creek, Humbug creek, Belsville, Cherry creek, Cottonwood creek, Hungry creek, Humburg [*sic*], Deadwood creek, Greenhorn creek, Sailor diggings, Canonville, Crescent city, Winchester, Salem, Oregon City, and Portland, O.T.[74]

One must not conclude that all express companies in Oregon and Washington during the 'fifties originated in California. An exception, certainly, is W. G. T'Vault, in 1846 Oregon's first postmaster, and later editor of the *Spectator*. T'Vault combined express and postal service. His first system failed, but in 1852 this pioneer in Oregon transportation established T'Vault & Co.'s Oregon and Shasta Express, with offices at Oregon City, Winchester, Rogue River Indian Agency, Josephine Creek, Minersville on Humbug Creek, Humbug City, and Shasta City, California.[75]

A firm named Stuart's Express was in operation by 1854 and it too appears to have been strictly regional in character in that it operated between Portland and Olympia. Between these two places it forwarded and received express through Adams and Company. On August 12 of 1854 it boasted that, even with "stoppages" its messenger had covered the 180-mile distance between these two cities *within thirty-six hours!*" Then continuing: "This is a feat that we believe has never before been accomplished." Interesting is the fact that in order to set this record it was necessary for the messenger to avail himself of three modes of

[69] *Oregon Spectator*, July 3, 1851; *The Columbian*, September 11 and 18, 1852.

[70] *The Oregon Statesman*, January 1, 1853.

[71] *Democratic Standard*, August 30, 1855.

[72] *Oregon Weekly Times*, June 19, 1852; *The Oregon Statesman*, May 25 and July 10, 1852, and January 1, 1853.

[73] *The Oregon Statesman*, January 1, 1853.

[74] *Ibid.*, October 31, 1854.   [75] *Ibid.*, October 9, 1852.

transportation, namely, steamboat, canoe, and land travel.[76] When the gold rush to Colville took place in 1855 it appears that proprietor A. B. Stuart extended his services to that place. Adams then having failed, the Stuart firm switched its connections to that of Wells, Fargo and Company.[77] By 1856 Stuart extended regular stops to include St. Helens, Rainier, Monticello, Cowlitz Landing, Steilacoom, Seattle, Port Townsend, and Vancouver Island,[78] whereas in the year following his sphere of service extended southward to Champoeg, Salem, Albany, and Corvallis.[79] Toward the close of the decade Stuart's greatest competitor in Oregon appears to have been Tracy and Company. E. W. Tracy, proprietor, offered regular service to Fort Vancouver, Cascades, The Dalles, Walla Walla, Colville, Oregon City, Salem, Albany, Corvallis, Dayton, Butteville, Champoeg, and Eugene City.[80] Such places as Butteville, Fairfield, Independence, Boonville, Thurston, Dayton, Eugene City, and Lafayette were served by the firm of Levinson and Company's Express.[81]

It has been noted that the Washington side of the Columbia was served by express companies with head offices in Portland. With headquarters in Olympia, however, was the firm of Parker, Colter and Company's Express, founded in 1853, which forwarded parcels to and from Portland. It was later succeeded by Stuart's Express. Also at Olympia were Webber and Slater's Express, Johnson's Express, and Smith's Express—subsequently Lambert and Smith's Express, also organized in 1853 to carry on local package business between the capital and Alki Point on Puget Sound.[82]

These minor express companies performed many services, as has already been shown. Their very existence is sufficient evidence that they satisfied a great need by helping Oregon's territorial population to break down in a measure the isolated life in which it found itself. "Were our citizens dependent on the mails, as now managed on the coast, especially in Oregon," expostulated the *Pacific Christian Advocate* in 1856, ". . . . they would soon become veritable Rip Van Winkles, and bankrupt besides." The article then pointed out how the express service had saved the day.[83]

When express companies became numerous a tendency to consolidate and to compete for mastery in a given area became noticeable. By 1853

  [76] *Pioneer and Democrat,* August 12, 1854.   [77] *Democratic Standard,* October 4, 1855.

  [78] *Ibid.,* June 12, 1856.   [79] *The Oregon Statesman,* March 24, 1857.

  [80] *Portland Daily Advertiser,* October 13, 1859; *The People's Press,* October 1, 1859.

  [81] *The Democratic Crisis,* February 9, 1859.

  [82] *The Columbian,* September 11 and 18, 1852; *Washington Pioneer,* November 5 and December 3, 1853.

  [83] *Pacific Christian Advocate,* March 1, 1856.

two concerns, namely, Adams and Company and the Wells, Fargo and Company, were the leaders in California, and both extended their services into the North Pacific region.

Adams and Company bore the name of its founder, Alvin Adams (1804–1877), a native of Andover, Vermont. After a successful start in the East, Adams and Company, in 1849, joined the California parade and established a West Coast office in San Francisco.[84]

Daniel Hale Haskell, a highly esteemed clerk in the company's Boston office, became the "resident-partner" of Adams and Company. He first leased a shanty to serve him temporarily as an express office,[85] and on November 8, 1849, he was ready to do business. The volume of express handled by Adams and Company increased steadily, and between 1850 and 1852 connections were made with numerous smaller expresses reaching into the Pacific Northwest. Their chief Oregon connections were with Todd and Company and the Stuart Express, and an agreement with Colter's Express enabled Adams and Company to serve Olympia, Washington, and the Puget Sound region.[86]

The great success of Adams and Company was due to the dispatch with which it could collect and deliver mail and light freight. The *Pioneer and Democrat* of Olympia offers effective proof; wrote a special postal agent:

It might be a matter of interest to remark in this connection that since the establishment of STUART's Express between the Sound and Oregon Territory, connecting with Adams & Co., the receipts of the Post Office at this place, for stamps and postage for mail received, has fallen off at least one-fourth, and is quarterly on the decrease.

Not only do our mercantile and other business men avail themselves of the express, as the means of safe and speedy conveyance, but most of our farmers are transacting their business with Oregon and California through the same medium. Nor is this to be wondered at, when it is remembered that the express is not unfrequently not only *days,* but actually *weeks* in advance of the mails at this place. Was it not for the express, we should be in a sorry condition indeed.[87]

The Adams concern continued active in Oregon until 1855. It stressed the point that, if one shipped via the Isthmus through them, there would be no delay at Chagres when shipping to the East. Furthermore, reads the notice: "Parties may rest assured that although we do not keep it

---

[84] A. L. Stimson, *History of the Express Business; Including the Origin of the Railway System in America* (New York, 1881), chap. 3; Henry Wells, *Sketch of the Rise, Progress, and Present Conditions of the Express System* (Albany, 1864), p. 10.

[85] A. L. Stimson, *History of the Express Companies: and the Origin of American Railroads* (New York, 1858), p. 111.

[86] *Evening Picayune,* September 26, 1850; *Daily Alta California,* July 1 and November 29, 1851; Winther, *Express and Stagecoach Days,* pp. 34–46.

[87] *Pioneer and Democrat,* January 27, 1855.

continually before the public, we are never behind in the conveyance of news, treasure, etc. to and from the Atlantic states."[88] When the Adams Company failed, for reasons subsequently explained, it was superseded by the Pacific Express Company, which concern remained in the field, though less actively, until 1869 when it was taken over by Wells, Fargo and Company.[89]

The most important express concern of all was Wells, Fargo and Company, founded in New York in 1852 following varied and involved connections of the founders—William G. Fargo and Henry Wells. It was another Eastern firm which was destined to have a remarkable career on the Pacific Coast. As Wells pointed out in later years, it "demanded much courage and determination" to "establish another company in the face of the formidable opposition" offered by Adams and Company; but the move was nevertheless considered a practical one.[90] Thus, on March 18, 1852, a joint-stock company known as Wells, Fargo and Company was organized under the general incorporation laws of New York State.[91] It was capitalized at $300,000.[92] Among its principal backers were Henry Wells, William G. Fargo, Johnston Livingston, and E. B. Morgan, a prominent banker of Aurora, New York, and several other well-known men.[93]

The first step to organize the California operations was taken in early May, when Samuel P. Carter was appointed "for the purpose of establishing the Company there."[94] Carter, who had previously been connected with the American Express Company, was now charged with the specific duty of setting up the forwarding branch of the business in California. A second appointee, R. W. Washburn, because of his experience as a banker, was instructed to establish the banking department of Wells, Fargo and Company in San Francisco.[95] Carter arrived at San Francisco June 27, 1852;[96] four days later the public was notified that Wells, Fargo and Company was ready to transport express, and within a month the Western agents of Wells, Fargo and Company were able to give adequate service to the California miners.

While Wells, Fargo and Company was especially organized to do

[88] *The Oregon Statesman*, October 28, 1851.

[89] *Democratic Standard*, August 30 and December 20, 1855; Winther, *Express and Stagecoach Days*, pp. 125–27.

[90] Wells, *Express System*, pp. 15–16.

[91] J. S. Roberson, "History of Wells, Fargo & Co. and the Pony Express." MS, Stanford University Library, Stanford, California, p. 1.

[92] "Wells, Fargo and Company Records," Wells Fargo Museum, Wells Fargo Bank and Union Trust Company Building, San Francisco, p. 3.

[93] Wells, *op. cit.*, pp. 15–16; Stimson, *History of the Express Business*, p. 75.

[94] "Wells, Fargo and Company Records," p. 5.

[95] *New York Times*, May 20, 1852.   [96] *San Francisco Herald*, June 28, 1852.

business in California, it lost no time extending its organization to include the Oregon Territory. Company advertisements appeared in the Oregon papers as early as September 1852, to the effect that,

This company, having completed its organization . . . . is now ready to undertake a general Express Forwarding Agency and Commission Business; the purchase and sale of Gold Dust, Bullion and Bills of Exchange; the payments and collection of Notes, Bills and Accounts; the forwarding of Gold Dust, Bullion and Specie; also Packages, Parcels and Freight of all description. . . . .[97]

Throughout 1853 and 1854, Wells, Fargo and Company continued its policy of purchasing or otherwise gaining control of the leading regional express concerns in California and Oregon. The publication of what was entitled a "Statement of the Affairs of Wells, Fargo & Co. as per Books, San Francisco Office, February 23, 1855" listed assets amounting to $743,499.58; liabilities, $389,105.23. By this date the concern maintained Oregon offices at Portland, Oregon City, Prairie City, and Jacksonville exclusive of numerous connections with smaller and purely local operations north of the California line.[98]

Then on February 23, 1855, a panic began in the express and banking business on the Pacific Coast. To nearly all people, including the expressmen and bankers themselves, it came with terrific suddenness and seemingly without the presence of storm signals.

In any event, on the morning of Friday, February 23, 1855, the Adams and Company Bank did not open its doors; the firm had failed. The results of this day were so momentous and tragic to the people of the entire Pacific Coast that it has since been referred to as "Black Friday," a day of great misfortune.

Out of the ruins of Adams and Company emerged the Pacific Express Company, a new concern founded by a number of men previously associated with the bankrupt firm. By midyear of 1855 the Pacific Express Company began its operation in the Pacific Northwest, and an office was opened in Portland with S. J. McCormick as agent.[99] Though the Pacific Express Company never became as powerful as its predecessor, the new firm made several important business connections which enabled it to serve the entire Pacific Coast until 1869 when competition with Wells, Fargo and Company made disbandment necessary.[100]

The panic affected Wells, Fargo and Company very differently from Adams and Company. The Wells, Fargo banks everywhere, except in Sacramento, remained open on February 22, and the express business

[97] *The Columbian,* September 11, 1852.

[98] *Daily California Chronicle,* February 28, 1855.

[99] *Pioneer and Democrat,* June 8, 1855.

[100] Stimson, *History of the Express Business,* p. 260.

seems to have continued in full operation.[101] The crisis was apparently over by February 26, and on the following day banking operations were fully restored.[102] Like gold "seven times purified," *The California Farmer* stated, it comes "from the fiery ordeal with increased lustre," and sends "abroad a name and fame that will endure."[103]

In spite of a deficit on December 31, 1855, Wells, Fargo and Company was apparently well assured of a profitable future. The company had developed its organization satisfactorily; it had expanded its territory; and it was at last ready to face the future with renewed vigor, unchallenged as the leader in the express business in the Far American West. Its subsequent role as a monopoly is to be related in a later chapter.

---

[101] *Sacramento Daily Union*, February 24, 1855.

[102] *California Chronicle*, February 27, 1855.

[103] *The California Farmer*, March 1, 1855.

CHAPTER XII

THE COMING OF THE PADDLE WHEELS

Life at Fort Vancouver was often dull. Through the long winter months little happened that broke the monotonous routine of everyday living. But on the afternoon of April 10, 1836, there was great stir and excitement. The steamship *Beaver* rounded Parting Point. Two shots boomed out from the ship's deck as she "came to, abreast of Ft. Vancouver." She had come rigged as a brigantine in order to make the long voyage from England. For McLoughlin and other servants of the Hudson's Bay Company who had waited anxiously for this ship's arrival, the event marked the coming of the first steamship ever to ply the Pacific Coast waters of the New World.[1]

It had been with great reluctance that the strong-willed McLoughlin had agreed to the construction of a steamer for service in his department. It was a new and as yet untried invention. It was very expensive. But finally at Governor Simpson's insistence the Chief Factor acquiesced.

The order for the *Beaver's* hull was placed with a reliable English shipbuilding firm at Blackwall on the Thames. She was strongly built. Her keel was of elm; the rest of her structure was made of sturdy British oak and African teakwood. Great oak spikes and copper bolts held fast huge timbers that made up her hull. When completed she measured one hundred feet nine inches long; her width was twenty feet; and the depth of her hold was eleven feet. She was of 109 tons' burden.

Installed in the *Beaver's* hull were two thirty-five horsepower Bolton and Watt steam engines, the best that money could buy, and these were capable of attaining a speed of nine and three-quarters miles per hour. As a steamer she carried a complement of thirty-one men.

After a trial run in the English Channel her paddle wheels were temporarily removed, and she became rigged technically as a brigantine. With Captain David Home at the helm, and a crew of twelve men, the *Beaver* left Gravesend, England, on August 29, 1835, in the company of the bark *Columbia*. The voyage across the Atlantic, around the Horn, across the Pacific to Hawaii, and finally from Honolulu to the Columbia River, occupied 225 days.[2]

---

[1] W. Kaye Lamb, "The Advent of the 'Beaver'," *The British Columbia Historical Quarterly*, II (July 1938), 171; Sir Charles Piers, "Pioneer Ships on Pacific Coast," *The Beaver*, Outfit 258 (June 1927), pp. 24–25.

[2] Lamb, *op. cit.*, p. 168; Norman R. Hacking, "Paddle Wheels and British Oak on the North Pacific," *The Beaver*, Outfit 265 (March 1935), pp. 25–26; C. H. French, "H. B. C. Pioneer Steamer Ruled West Coast Trade 20 Years," *The Beaver* [no outfit or volume number], (February 1921), pp. 2–4.

At Fort Vancouver there was work to be done. The paddle wheels had to be installed, the machinery examined, the fire started. Then, to quote from a remnant transcript of the ship's log for May 17, 1836: "At daylight unmoored ship and got the steam up. . . . . At 1:30 took the *Columbia* in tow up to the sawmill. At 6 returned and anchored off Fort Vancouver in 5 fathoms." Thus twenty-eight years after Robert Fulton's *Claremont* first chugged up the Delaware, the first puffing steamboat began operations on the great "River of the West."[3]

The "Old Steamer *Beaver*," as pioneers fondly came to call her, had a long and varied life. No Hudson's Bay Company post within reach failed to transact business with this ship. She proved highly satisfactory in the conduct of the Russian-Alaskan trade. Fur and a countless variety of supplies were hauled by her crew.[4] She had four brass cannons mounted on her deck; and with muskets, cutlasses, and hand grenades within easy reach, the *Beaver* greatly facilitated the maintenance of order among the coastal Indians.[5] For exploratory work in and out of the hundreds of northwest coast inlets this faithful little steamship proved indispensable. The Fraser River gold rush placed new demands upon the *Beaver*. During 1858–1859 she transported hundreds of gold seekers from Victoria to the mouth of the Fraser River. In 1863, and for seven years thereafter, this first West Coast steamship was taken over by the British government for hydrographical survey work. By this time the *Beaver's* usefulness to the Hudson's Bay Company had dwindled. Upon regaining possession of the vessel, the Company converted the steamship into a tug and sold her in 1874 to a grocer in Victoria. Her timbers, wrote a Victoria newspaper, were still "as sound as they were the day she was launched." For another fourteen years she did service on the coast, towing log booms, ships, and the like. Finally on July 26, 1888, the S.S. *Beaver* reached her journey's end when she ran aground at Prospect Point at the entrance to the Vancouver, B.C., Harbor. The engines were removed and found still good. Other relics were salvaged. Some of her timbers were cut into small pieces and sold as souvenirs. A plan was on foot to salvage what was left of her for purposes of exhibit at the 1892 World's Columbian Exposition in Chicago. But before this was done the hulk of the beloved "Old Steamer *Beaver*" rose slightly from the swell caused by a passing ship and then slid gently below the surface of the water into Burrard Inlet.[6]

[3] E. W. Wright, ed., *Lewis & Dryden's Marine History of the Pacific Northwest* (Portland, 1895), pp. 14–18. Hereafter cited as *Lewis & Dryden's Marine History*. Ronald Todd, "The Steamer 'Beaver'," *The Pacific Northwest Quarterly*, XXVII (October 1936), 367–68.

[4] "Steamer Beaver Fur Trade Journal," MS, Archives of British Columbia.

[5] Hacking, *op. cit.*, p. 26.

[6] *Lewis & Dryden's Marine History*, pp. 14–18; Todd, "The Steamer 'Beaver'," pp. 367–68; "S. S. Beaver," *The Beaver*, Outfit 260 (June 1929), pp. 207–8.

The *Beaver* was not the only steamship operated by the Hudson's Bay Company, although it was not until 1853 that a second one made its appearance in the Columbia District. This ship was the 220-ton *Otter*. She was of the latest design, which included the newly invented screw propeller. By then Victoria was the Company's headquarters and it was there that the *Otter* first docked. One of her first assignments was to go to San Francisco, a trip which was made in four days down and five back. Like the *Beaver,* the *Otter* saw active service in the Fraser River gold rush, and served the Company in many other useful ways.[7] Still other steamships, namely the *Enterprise* and the *Labouchere,* served the Hudson's Bay Company in Pacific Northwest waters. The first of these saw long and active service as a passenger ship, into which business the Company entered actively, but the unfortunate *Labouchere* ran onto a reef in 1866 and sank.[8]

In this manner did the Hudson's Bay Company introduce steamship operations in the old Oregon country. Not until mid-century did the Americans in Oregon emerge from the flatboat era and turn their attention to steamship transportation. By then the river towns had mushroomed into existence, especially along the Willamette River, and their presence had laid the basis for what was a boom era in the paddle-ship trade.[9]

In its early stages steamship building became identified with municipal pride. One group of promoters, wishing to outdo another, began to stress the importance of steamship building as a way of bringing trade to their own towns. Into this pattern fell colorful Lot Whitcomb, who was part-proprietor of the Milwaukie townsite, the Milwaukie sawmill, and the sole owner of the newspaper *Western Star*. Go-getting Whitcomb wanted to build a ship larger and better than the one being built by the Astorians and, with some financial aid, succeeded in his effort. On Christmas Day, 1850, to the tunes of "Yankee Doodle," "The Star Spangled Banner," and "Hail Columbia," was launched the beautiful steamer that bore the builder's name. The *Lot Whitcomb* had a length of 160 feet and a beam that measured 24 feet and the depth of the hold was 5 feet 8 inches.[10]

Service by this steamer was first offered between Milwaukie and

---

[7] French, "H. B. C. Pioneer Steamer," p. 4.

[8] Hacking, "Paddle Wheels and British Oak," pp. 27–28.

[9] Howard McKinley Corning, *Willamette Landings* (Portland, 1947), pp. 13–34, also *passim.*

[10] The first regular paddle-wheel service was offered by the *Columbia* between Astoria and Portland in 1850. The ship, a ninety-foot side-wheeler, was launched by Astoria businessmen. Scott, *Oregon Country,* I, 338; Randall V. Mills, *Stern-Wheelers Up Columbia* (Palo Alto, 1947), pp. 15–17; *The Western Star,* December 26, 1850; *Oregon Spectator,* January 2, 1851; *Lewis & Dryden's Marine History,* pp. 28–30.

the long-since-forgotten Pacific City (now Ilwaco). Her master was
John C. Ainsworth, who was later regarded as one of the West's most
skilled river-boat captains and steamship entrepreneurs. By 1853 the
Lot Whitcomb offered service between the new and booming town of
Portland and Astoria. In addition to hauling passengers and freight,
she offered to tow vessels up or down the river.[11] Not long after the
inauguration of the river service the Lot Whitcomb grounded near
Milwaukie and a hole was torn in her hull. She was nevertheless repaired and for some time used as a towboat. In 1854 she was purchased
by the California Steam Navigation Company, a concern which by this
time monopolized the California river trade. Taken to San Francisco
the Lot Whitcomb was put into service on the Sacramento River, where,
with the changed name of Annie Abernethy, she did service for several
years.[12]

Meanwhile the trade of the Willamette Valley continued to grow.
During 1851 and 1852 at least a half-dozen steamships were launched to
serve on the Willamette River and its navigable tributary, the Yamhill.
For a brief period Oregon's territorial capital (Oregon City), located at
the Falls, became the center of considerable maritime activity. From
the high bluffs overlooking the town, people could have looked down
upon this steadily growing number of steam-propelled vessels churning in
and out of their slips. Nestled as the settlers were among the wooded
hills surrounding the town, they must have been sensitive to the loud
blasts of the steam whistles, the slow chugging sound of the engines, the
splash of huge wheel propellers, and the cries of "All Aboard for Portland, Vancouver, Cowlitz Landing." The steamboat had come in earnest.
A new era had dawned.

One of these ships was the Wallamet, "calculated to afford greater
facilities for freight and passage than have ever before been offered."[13]
Another was the Hoosier, the first to operate above the Falls, and the
Washington.[14] Still another was the 108-foot Multnomah which on August 18, 1851, made its first trip to Salem.[15] By August 26, 1853, no less
than four steamboats were then operating on the Willamette River above
the Falls, and two more were only awaiting the higher waters of autumn
to join in this now brisk trade.[16] Between 1850 and 1857 Willamette

---

[11] The Columbian, October 1, 1853; Washington Pioneer, December 10, 1853.

[12] Lewis & Dryden's Marine History, pp. 30–31.

[13] Oregon Spectator, August 26, 1853.

[14] Lewis & Dryden's Marine History, p. 33. According to James O'Mera, pioneer editor,
it was 1855 when the first stern-wheeler was built on the upper Willamette. See James O'Mera,
"An Early Steamboating Era on the Willamette," Oregon Historical Quarterly, XLIV (June
1943), 140–41.

[15] Oregon Spectator, August 19, 1851.

[16] Ibid., August 26, 1853.

Courtesy Wells Fargo Bank and Union Trust Company

A WAGON BEING FERRIED ACROSS A RIVER

Courtesy Donald Bates

THE "LOT WHITCOMB"

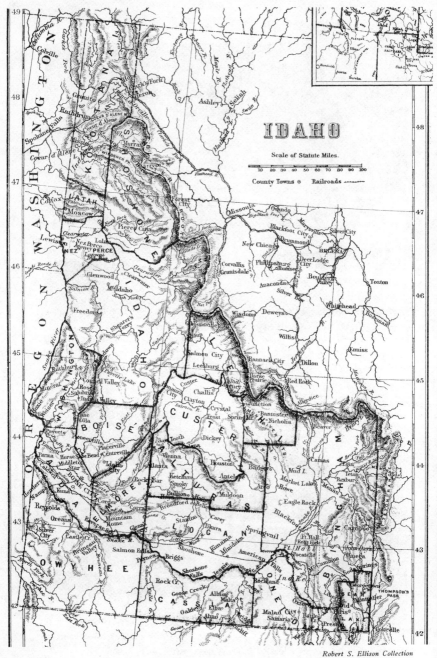

MAP OF IDAHO (1890)

River service was extended as far up as Eugene City, a development which might possibly be explained by the appearance, during the last half of the 'fifties, of a new type of steamer. This was the keelboat, or flat-bottomed stern-wheeler, which drew less water than any other steam-propelled vessel. It could skim across the many shallow rapids of the river, avoid many of the snags that lurked treacherously below the surface of the water, and due to its low water line operate far into the dry season of the year.

The question asked in a steamship advertisement was:

Is the Willamette river navigable above the mouth of the Yam Hill? The new Keel Boat SALEM CLIPPER!! will answer that question by informing the public, that she has successfully navigated this "frightful" river during the summer, as far as Salem. . . . .[17]

During the early 'fifties at least four or five steamers operated on the Willamette below the Falls; an equal number operated above and called at Salem, Albany, Marysville (Corvallis), and less frequently at Eugene City.[18]

As for the tributaries, it appears that the tiny *Hoosier,* at first put into service on the Yamhill (and South Yamhill), tributaries of the Willamette, was especially well adapted for shallow water, and for that reason monopolized the Yamhill commerce during the dry season of the year. The *Yamhill, Washington, Wallamet, Canemah* (a mail boat), *Enterprise, Fenix, James Clinton,* and others at one time or another during the 'fifties carried freight and passengers on the Yamhill and the upper Willamette rivers. It was to the many upriver ports, most important of which was Dayton, that farmers brought their wagons—scores of them—loaded with grain or flour for transshipment. For their produce the farmers were paid in gold, which according to one local chronicler was carried upstream by the skippers who (and this gives some indication of the volume of trade) sometimes paid out as much as $50,000 worth of gold in a single day. Likewise much lumber was shipped on the Yamhill.[19]

By the close of the decade the Yamhill farmers organized what was called the Yamhill Steamboat Company with a capital of $12,000. This company was responsible for several new additions to this already active Yamhill service. Among the new ships added were the *Enterprise, St.*

---

[17] *Ibid.*, March 6, 1851.

[18] Mills, *Stern-Wheelers Up Columbia,* p. 53.

[19] Beulah Hurst, "Water Transportation," MS, Files of the Oregon Writers' Project; *Oregon Spectator,* October 14, 1851; Ruth Rydell, "Tributaries of the Willamette: Yamhill, Santiam, Calapooya," *Oregon Historical Quarterly,* XLIV (June 1943), 147–56.

Claire (later to achieve the distinction for being the first ship to navigate the Cascades), the *James Clinton* (a ship which also ran to Eugene City), the *Yamhill* (placed in operation on the Tualatin River), and finally, the *Union*. The *Enterprise* was regarded as the most active on the upper Willamette until 1858 when this stern-wheeler joined the Fraser River trade.[20]

Steam navigation in the Oregon country during the 'fifties was by no means concentrated on the Willamette River; as early as 1850 steps were taken by F. A. Chenoweth on the Washington side to pave the way for steamboat operations above the Cascades on the Columbia River by establishing horse-drawn tramcars there. As yet there were no ships operating regularly above the Rapids, but during the following summer there went into service the sixty-foot side-wheeler *Jas. P. Flint*. This "little gypsy," as one pioneer affectionately dubbed her, had been built a hundred miles above Fort Vancouver (above the Cascades), and her machinery had been brought in by means of rowboats for final installation. This, according to local historians, was "the first steam propelled vessel to traverse the Columbia above the Cascades." The ship's captain, J. O. Van Bergen, began to make regular runs in August 1851, between the Cascades and The Dalles, and made a special effort to offer services to the immigrants who, tired and weary from their long overland trek, could scarcely have wished for more. To them, wrote a grateful pioneer, the *Jas. P. Flint* was "an oasis at the *end* of the desert. It has saved many a fainting female the necessity of making the toilsome passage of the Cascade Mountains. . . . ."[21]

Much more leisurely was the service offered over the stretch between the Cascades and Portland. It was at first confined to an unseaworthy sailing vessel named the *Henry* and owned by F. A. Chenoweth. Freight charges were twenty dollars per ton. Early in 1852 the *Jas. P. Flint* was brought below the Cascades and was put into service there until later in the year when it went on the rocks.[22] Captain Van Bergen, however, succeeded in salvaging and rebuilding his ship, and again put it into operation, this time along with another steamer named *Fashion*. Moreover, in April of 1853, Van Bergen began the construction of still another side-wheeler to be used between the Cascades and The Dalles which

---

[20] Clark, *Willamette Valley*, pp. 468–69; O'Mera, *op. cit.*, pp. 142–43; Mills, *op. cit.*, p. 53.

[21] *Oregon Weekly Times*, November 29, 1851; Scott, *Oregon Country*, III, 190.

[22] Frank B. Gill, "An Unfinished History of Transportation in Oregon and Washington," MS, Northwest Collection, University of Washington Library, Seattle, Washington, pp. 13–14, 31, 37. Hereafter cited as "History of Transportation." Copy in Robert S. Ellison Collection, Indiana University Library. This manuscript history is in no sense a digest or an analysis of transportation. It is essentially a compilation of data regarding steamships operating in the region for the period 1850–1855.

would make direct connections with the *Fashion* below the Cascades. On August 6 of that year appeared this newspaper announcement:

Accommodation Line
Through to Dalles
The well known Steamer
"Fashion"
J. O. Van Bergen, Master.

Will ply regularly the balance of the season between Portland and the Cascades, touching at all intermediate landings and connecting with Boats on the Upper Columbia. Leaving Portland every Monday, Wednesday and Friday. Returning leave Cascades every Tuesday, Thursday and Saturday. Freight and passage at the lowest rates—for the same apply to Captain on Board, or to Agents, L. A. Anderson & Co. Portland, Bradford & Co., Cascades.[23]

For a short time toward the end of the summer the *Multnomah* was also put into service between the Cascades and points below, whereas the "iron steamer" *Allan,* belonging to Allan, McKinley & Co., formerly Hudson's Bay men, was added to the service above the historic Columbia River Rapids. During the next year still another pair of steamers, the *Belle* and the *Mary,* offered service between Portland, Monticello, the Cascades, and The Dalles. They carried ordinary freight between Portland and The Dalles for $30 per ton, but horses cost $6 apiece. Then in August of 1855 Captain M. F. Farlane launched a seventy-foot steamer named *Wasco* for The Dalles–Cascades service which connected with the *Fashion.* Thus by the middle 'fifties there were two competing lines engaged in the upper Columbia trade, and for public convenience it was so arranged that the *Fashion-Wasco* Line and the *Belle-Mary* Line ran on alternate days.[24]

Hardly had this seemingly well-systematized service been established when serious Indian outbreaks disrupted it. Early in 1856 a band of red men composed of Yakimas, Klikitats, and Cascades planned a mass attack, not only upon the white settlers living near the Cascades, but upon the river steamers as well. Waiting for the opportune moment when steamers from both below and above the Rapids were at the Chenoweth portage, there was launched a concerted attack upon both settlers and the ships. Fortunately all did not go well for the Indians; for one thing, they failed to capture the steamships. One of these, the *Mary,* had a sufficiently large number of armed men on board to stave off the marauders long enough to get up steam and make an escape. One white man drowned during the encounter, and two were wounded. The other ship at the scene of the attack was the *Wasco,* and it too escaped, fortunately with all of its crew aboard.

---

[23] *Ibid.*, pp. 37–38. [24] *Ibid.*, pp. 38–40.

The escape of these vessels was of utmost importance in that they spread the news of the attack and brought help to the besieged settlers left at the Cascades. Help came from Lieutenant Philip H. Sheridan and forty dragoons stationed at Fort Vancouver, who, rather than ride to the scene of war, arrived there aboard the steamer *Belle*. After the dragoons disembarked, the *Belle* hastened downstream for additional reinforcements. The timely arrival of Sheridan and his men prevented a wholesale massacre and brought about a restoration of the normal navigation on the river.[25] In 1857 the *Mary* was joined by another steamer, the *Señorita*, on the Cascades-Portland run.[26]

Not until February 1, 1859, did a steamship appear on the Columbia above The Dalles. During the previous year there was launched the stern-wheeler *Colonel Wright*, of fifty tons burden, which had been built at the mouth of the Deschutes River by L. W. Coe and R. R. Thompson, and was put in operation between the Falls of Celilo and Fort Walla Walla on the strength of a government contract for hauling freight to the latter place. Then came the discovery of gold in the Clearwater River, and business for the *Colonel Wright* boomed. By April the ship was employed by the government to go up the Snake River and did go as far as the mouth of the Palouse, at which point direct overland connections could be made with Fort Colvile.[27]

Beginning in 1844, Americans began to settle north of the Columbia River in spite of McLoughlin's admonitions not to do so. The number of settlers increased slowly. Nearly all of them, save those connected with the mission establishment east of the mountains, settled first near the lower tip of Puget Sound where the towns of Tumwater and Olympia emerged, and then at Alki Point and Elliott Bay, which today are part of Seattle. In 1853 Congress deemed this nucleus sufficiently important to warrant the creation of Washington Territory. In that same year a road was opened between Walla Walla and Olympia which enabled immigrants to enter the Puget Sound country without first sailing down the Columbia, and this marked the beginning of an ever increasing number of settlers in western Washington.[28]

Foremost in the thoughts of these settlers was the establishment of communication with their American brothers in the Willamette Valley. The Hudson's Bay Company had long ago hewn out an ox-cart trail

---

[25] Fuller, *Inland Empire*, II, 240–47; Philip Henry Sheridan, *Personal Memoirs* (New York, 1888), I, 70–84.

[26] *Lewis & Dryden's Marine History*, p. 51.

[27] Lulu Donnell Crandall, "The 'Colonel Wright'," *The Washington Historical Quarterly*, VII (April 1916), 126–29.

[28] Oscar O. Winther, "Inland Transportation and Communication in Washington, 1844–1859," *The Pacific Northwest Quarterly*, XXX (October 1939), 371–77.

between Fort Nisqually (near which Olympia emerged) and the Cowlitz River. It remained only to improve this road and to establish boat connections between Cowlitz Landing and the Willamette River ports. In February 1851, the *Lot Whitcomb* became the first steamer to offer this service.[29]

Meanwhile two men, Edward D. Warbass and Alfred Townsend, in an announcement from Monticello dated April 10, 1852, offered bateau and canoe service on Cowlitz River, and were prepared to portage passengers and freight between Cowlitz Landing and Puget Sound. At Monticello Warbass and Townsend offered to carry passengers and cargo to the Oregon side via Columbia River steamers, the first of which was the *Jas. P. Flint* mentioned above.[30] Not long after these arrangements were made the *Jas. P. Flint*, it will be recalled, went on the rocks and service was at least temporarily disrupted. In an announcement dated March 19, 1853, it is noted that the *Fashion* would ply between Oregon City, Portland, the Cascades, and Townsend's Landing on the Cowlitz. At Townsend's Landing connections would be made with a mail boat,[31] probably one operated by F. A. Clarke, who in the *Columbian* ran the following announcement:[32]

COWLITZ NAVIGATION!

The undersigned is prepared, at all times, to transport passengers and freight up and down the Cowlitz river.

The mail canoe leaves the Cowlitz Landing every Thursday morning, at 7 o'clock, for Rainier and leaves Rainier every Tuesday morning at 6 o'clock for the Landing.

For freight or passage at Monticello or Rainier, apply to R. C. Smith.

F. A. CLARKE.
Cowlitz Landing, July 2, 1853.

In order to stimulate further Cowlitz River navigation, the first territorial legislature of Washington passed an act authorizing the formation of a company to carry on steamship operations on the river. Accordingly, on September 17, 1854, a public meeting was held at Cowlitz Landing where it was reported that the river would be navigable even at low water, and where $10,000 was subscribed for the construction of a steamer for the purpose of navigating the river. "The advantages that would arise to this portion of the country by a successful carrying

---

[29] Gill, "History of Transportation," p. 6.

[30] *Ibid.*, p. 31. This dated announcement still appeared in *The Columbian*, March 19, 1853.

[31] Gill, "History of Transportation," p. 37; *Pioneer and Democrat*, April 8, 1854; *The Columbian*, March 19, 1853.

[32] *The Columbian*, September 10, 1853.

out of the project," said the local press, "is well understood by our citizens, and all who we have heard make mention of the subject join in hopes of its speedy accomplishment."[33]

In 1854 still other developments in the Washington trade came when the owners of the steamer *Wallamet* secured a government contract for carrying mails between Astoria and Portland by way of Fort Vancouver. Service was begun August 10, and the owners, "being desirous of promoting the Exportation and Transportation business of Oregon and Washington," announced new and reduced rates.[34]

If the American settlers at Tumwater and Olympia were disturbed about their isolation from the larger and thriving settlements in the Willamette Valley, their plight was as nothing when compared with the suffering of the courageous American pioneers who settled at the present site of Seattle.

Rarely, during the first critical stages, did these families have contact with the outside world. "In early times," reminisced pioneer Arthur Denny, "we occasionally saw the Hudson Bay steamers, 'Beaver' and 'Otter', passing to and from the station at Nisqually . . . . ."[35] The Americans in the Puget Sound area, however, maintained very little contact with the Hudson's Bay Company, and for this reason they were at first compelled to rely upon the lazily inclined Indians and their canoes as a means of communicating with the settlements at the lower tip of the Sound.[36]

The rapid growth and spread of American settlement in the Puget Sound area was such that it soon attracted the attention of enterprising steamship men who made an effort to capitalize upon new and promising markets in the Pacific Northwest. During January 1853, came the first announcement of service. Captain Warren Gove of the bark *Sarah Warren* had made arrangements in San Francisco for the purchase of a steamer "of sufficient size, strength, and power to run between the head of Puget Sound and Whidby's Island, Port Townsend &c."[37] Gove kept his promise and by the next October he arrived at Olympia with a small side-wheeler (of which A. B. David was co-owner) on the deck of his own ship. He had given to the steamer the name *Fairy*. "Captain Gove," wrote *The Columbian* gleefully, "deserves great credit for his enterprize in placing the pioneer on Puget Sound."[38] Then on November 12, 1853, appeared the following advertisement[39] by its skipper:

[33] *Pioneer and Democrat*, January 27, 1855.

[34] Gill, "History of Transportation," p. 51.

[35] Denny, *Pioneer Days on Puget Sound*, p. 69.

[36] *The Columbian*, September 25, 1852; Eva G. Anderson, *Chief Seattle* (Caldwell, Idaho, 1943), pp. 186–87.

[37] *The Columbian*, January 15, 1853.

[38] *Ibid.*, October 29, 1853.   [39] *Ibid.*, November 12, 1853.

REGULAR PACKET!

The splendid steamer FAIRY,

Capt. W. Gove, will ply regularly between Olympia, Steilacoom, Alki and Seattle; leaving Olympia every Monday and Wednesday at 10 o'clock, a.m.; returning will leave Steilacoom every Tuesday and Thursday at 9 o'clock, A.M.

The Fairy will make one trip each week to Alki and Seattle, leaving Olympia every Friday morning at 9 o'clock.

Fare to Steilacoom $5; to Alki and Seattle $10. For freight or passage apply to Jos. Cushman, at Kendall Co.'s store, Olympia; Philip Keach, Steilacoom; C. C. Terry, Alki; A. A. Denny, Seattle, or to the Captain on board.

Nov. 12, '53.

It was the opinion of Denny that the *Fairy* was inadequate,[40] although in later years some of the old-timers reminisced fondly about her. "Her cabin was just the size of a feather bed," wrote one, who relates how "Grandmother Denny," when making a trip on the *Fairy*, "put her feather bed on the floor of the cabin, and the whole family piled in."[41] This steamer was "small and slow," comments *Lewis & Dryden's Marine History,* "and cut no great figure in Puget Sound navigation."[42] She finally ended her days with a boiler explosion in 1857. Except for tramp ships and ships offering very intermittent local service, the settlers on Puget Sound normally had to content themselves with sloops, scows, and Indian canoes.[43]

It is little wonder that Olympia's newspaper, *Pioneer and Democrat,* hailed as an outstanding event in the territory the coming of the *Major Tompkins* in the autumn of 1854. This ship's fame preceded her, for she had previously seen service in the recent war with Mexico, at New Orleans, and on the Sacramento River. Now she had come to Puget Sound "to accomodate the merchant, farmer and business man, in the transmission of mail matter, freight and passage to the various ports in the Sound."[44]

By September the *Major Tompkins* ("Pumpkins" to some) was ready for actual service, and it was announced that at first it would ply regularly between Olympia and Victoria and intermediate places, Seattle being one of them. Her maiden voyage was one of rejoicing. When on the morning of the sixteenth she first hove into Port Townsend the news of the day reports: "There being no artillery at that place with which to answer the gun of the steamer, small arms were called into requisition, and quite a salute was got up with 'Colts' revolvers!" At Bellingham Bay she merely took on coal (discovered there in 1852) and moved on to Victoria, where three vessels in the harbor gave her a gun salute;

[40] Denny, *Pioneer Days on Puget Sound,* p. 69.

[41] Watt, *The Story of Seattle,* pp. 144–45.   [42] *Lewis & Dryden's Marine History,* p. 45.

[43] *Pioneer and Democrat,* June 17, 1854. For a brief period the steamers *Columbia* and *Fremont* extended their trips from the Columbia River to Puget Sound.

[44] *Ibid.,* September 16, 1854.

then she went back to Seattle "where the citizens were out en masse, and received her approach with the booming of cannon."[45] Due to the absence of artillery at Fort Steilacoom it appears that the "patriotic joy" of the people "manifested itself by the blowing up of stumps, which they used to fire as a salute." From there she returned to Olympia. "Success to the 'Major Tompkins,'" exclaims the *Pioneer and Democrat*, "and may all interested in her, succeed as they so well *deserve.*"

On September 25 she began her regular weekly passenger service and distribution of the mail and express, touching at Olympia, Steilacoom, Alki Point, Seattle, Port Gamble, Port Ludlow, Port Townsend, Penn's Cove, Bellingham Bay, and Victoria.

That this ship subsequently came to grief in February 1855, when she went on the rocks during a squall in Juan de Fuca Strait, was one of the major disasters of early Puget Sound marine history.[46] The *Major Tompkins* was replaced later in the year 1855 by the "iron propeller *Traveler*" which came from San Francisco. She was launched at Port Gamble and for three years operated on a mail route which touched Olympia, Steilacoom, and Seattle. At irregular intervals this little steamer also called at Port Townsend, and at Victoria, British Columbia, and she deserves the distinction of being the first steamer to navigate the Duwamish, White, Snohomish, and Nootsack rivers. But three years later the *Traveler* likewise was wrecked in a severe storm off Foulwater Bluff.[47] To offer a stopgap the former owners of the *Major Tompkins* put into service a small and flimsy side-wheeler called the *Water Lily*.[48] But, say Lewis and Dryden, she "was so slow and frail that she seldom wandered from Steilacoom and Olympia. . . . ."[49] It was becoming very apparent that the good citizens of Puget Sound, many of whom were practically stranded on out-of-the-way islands, were suffering badly in comparison with their fellow Americans who chose for their home the Willamette Valley.

This deplorable situation was not one to escape the transportation-minded politicians of the new government at Olympia. In an effort to alleviate the situation in which the people found themselves, the Washington territorial legislature instigated (in 1855) the formation of the Puget Sound Navigation Company. The concern thus created was charged with the responsibility of promoting navigation by steam within "the waters of Puget Sound, Hood's Canal, Admiralty Inlet, the Strait of Juan de Fuca, and the northern waters of the Territory of Washington."[50] Even

[45] *Pioneer and Democrat*, September 23, 1854.

[46] *Ibid.*, September 23, 1854 and March 3, 1855.

[47] *Lewis & Dryden's Marine History*, p. 55.   [48] *Pioneer and Democrat*, March 24, 1855.

[49] *Lewis & Dryden's Marine History*, p. 56.

[50] *Statutes of the Territory of Washington, 1854* (Olympia, 1855), pp. 64–65; Clarence B. Bagley, *History of Seattle* (Chicago, 1916), I, 114–15.

so, progress was slow and the decade of the 'fifties ended as it had begun; the earnest, hard-working settlers of Puget Sound were still without the essential means of transportation. Not until the next decade did any real relief come.

Of utmost importance to all who lived in the Pacific Northwest was the problem of contact with the outside world. There were the slow but reasonably sure overland routes, yet these were inadequate for trade and they were much too slow. As indicated in chapter xi, the Pacific Mail Steamship Company had been awarded a mail contract to connect Astoria with coast-to-coast service (1847) but it will be recalled how unsatisfactory this service was. In view of unforeseen events, namely discovery of gold in California, Oregon became a mere sideshow to this concern, and a forgotten one at that. Yet the fact remains that the Pacific Mail Steamship Company did much to augment somewhat regular commercial relations between Oregon, California, and eastern states.

Meanwhile, irregular commercial contacts by means of sailing vessels, especially newer and faster clipper ships, continued to be made. As in the fur-trading era, now in the gold rush era, these vessels entered the Columbia and lower Willamette rivers in search of foodstuffs and other commodities for the California market; some even operated a regular packet service between Portland and San Francisco.[51] Oregon was fast becoming what the *Oregon Spectator* in 1851 called "the New England of the Pacific," which as such would reap "much of the benefit of the California treasures, in exchange for its lumber, its wheat, potatoes, and other fruits of the earth and of the orchard."[52]

Lumber led the list of exportable commodities; flour was second in importance. One mill alone, the Standard Mills at Milwaukie, completed at the close of the 'fifties, produced over 250 barrels of flour daily. The salmon industry continued to increase over its humble beginning during the Hudson's Bay Company days, although the export of canned salmon did not begin until 1871. A woolen mill was erected in 1856 to take care of the local wool, which according to the accounts for 1860 had reached 200,000 pounds. Upon the basis of these scattered figures H. H. Bancroft makes this statement with reference to actual exports and imports for Oregon:

In 1857 Oregon had 60,000 inhabitants, and shipped 60,000 barrels of flour, 3,000,000 pounds of bacon and pork, 250,000 pounds of butter, 25,000 bushels of apples, $40,000 worth of chickens and eggs, $200,000 worth of lumber, $75,000 worth of fruit-trees, $20,000 worth of garden-stuff, and 52,000 head of cattle, the total value of which was $3,200,000.[53]

[51] Bancroft, *Washington, Idaho, and Montana*, chap. 6; Henry B. Williams, "Pacific Mail Steamship Co.," MS, Bancroft Library; Corning, *Willamette Landings*, pp. 25–27.

[52] *Oregon Spectator*, June 12, 1851.

[53] Bancroft, *History of Oregon*, II, 727–44.

The trade with foreign countries was as yet very small. In return Oregon imported liquors, glass, iron, tin; such foodstuffs as rice, sugar, molasses; and other items such as ore and hides.[54]

According to Bancroft, the first American steamship to enter Puget Sound was in 1840 (before Americans had ventured north of the Columbia River), but by the middle 'fifties the number of itinerant trading vessels, many of them clipper ships, was greatly increased.[55] Some of these ships limited their run to the Pacific Coast trade, while others were tramp ships engaged in world-wide trade. Examples of the former were Saywards Line, Merritt and Coves Lines, and B. P. Barstow's Line, which operated packets between Puget Sound and San Francisco.[56] Even as early as 1853 *The Columbian* carried an advertisement such as this:[57]

BALCH & PALMER
MERCHANT & SHIPPING AGENTS
Steilacoom, Puget Sound, and
San Francisco, California

Cargoes of piles, hewed timber, ship spars, sawed lumber, shingles, cord wood, salmon, whale oil, potatoes, grain and Oregon produce generally, furnished at the shortest notice and at the most reasonable rates. The attention of ship owners is respectfully solicited. . . . .

For particulars apply to the Masters on board, or to

LAFAYETTE BALCH
Steilacoom, Puget Sound.
CYRUS PALMER,
California street Wharf, San Francisco.

This already thriving ocean commerce was greatly augmented in 1857 by the discovery of gold in the upper Fraser River country. Not only did the shipping interests profit from this passenger service, but they profited from the shipment of supplies as well.[58]

In spite of disasters and reverses the shipping business of the Pacific Northwest (mostly of the steamship variety rather than sailing) emerged from the 'fifties upon a firm footing. It was meeting very definite needs which, with the absence of railroads, could hardly have been met any other way. One can scarcely escape the conclusion that the many services offered by the shipping interests, chiefly the transportation of passengers, freight, express, and mail, hastened the growth of civilization in the Oregon country and thereby paved the way for the coming of the iron horse.

---

[54] Bancroft, *History of Oregon*, II, 745; *Ninth Census* (Washington, D.C., 1872), III, 231 *passim*.

[55] Bancroft, *History of Oregon*, II, 15 n.–18 n.; Iva Luella Buchanan, "An Economic History of Kitsap County, Washington," Ph.D. Dissertation 1930, University of Washington Library.

[56] *The Columbian*, September 10, 1853; *Pioneer and Democrat*, February 11 and April 29, 1854.

[57] *The Columbian*, October 8, 1853.   [58] Fuller, *Inland Empire*, III, 61–62.

PART THREE

THE MINERAL EMPIRE

CHAPTER XIII

THE PACK TRAIN ERA

To here discussion has been focused, for the most part, on the region lying west of the Cascade Mountains. At this point the spotlight shifts east of the Cascades to the Inland Empire and up the Fraser River in British Columbia where gold discoveries during the decades of the 'fifties and 'sixties brought an influx of fortune seekers. The pattern was not unlike the one witnessed in California.

To be sure, the place first to report gold discovery in the Northwest was not inland, but on the coast, at Waldo, Oregon. This was in 1851. And for a while southwestern Oregon, especially Jacksonville, was host to an overflow mining population from its neighbor to the south. Other western areas, such as Coos Bay and the Santiam regions, also experienced slight flurries of excitement, but it is in the Inland Empire—roughly defined as southern British Columbia, eastern Oregon and Washington, Idaho, and western Montana—that the most sustained and significant mineral development occurred.

It was in 1855 around old Fort Colvile, the region between the Spokane and Pend d'Oreille rivers, that the first important gold discovery was made in this region, and to it gold seekers rushed during the autumn of that year. Grave difficulties soon presented themselves. Gold was not abundant, the region was rather hard to reach, the Indians caused trouble, and absence of adequate transportation facilities restricted the flow of supplies to the miners.[1]

It was, however, not until the turn of the 'sixties that a series of rich gold discoveries were made in what are now the states of Idaho, Oregon, and Montana. In Idaho these discoveries were made on the tributaries of the Snake River—on Oro Fino Creek, a branch of the Clearwater which in turn empties into the Snake River at Lewiston. A small party of prospectors led by "Captain" E. D. Pierce made the first find, and news of Pierce's success soon spread. During the winter of 1860–1861 the diggings on the Oro Fino became extensive. In 1861 deposits were also found on the south fork of the Clearwater in what is known as the Elk City district, and this in turn was followed by rich discoveries in the Salmon River and the Boise River country in 1862. Lewiston, Florence, Pierce City, and Oro Fino City came into being in this Clearwater-

---

[1] Glenn C. Quiett, *Pay Dirt* (New York, 1936), pp. 165–70; William J. Trimble, *The Mining Advance into the Inland Empire* (Madison, 1914), Part I. Hereafter cited as Trimble, *The Mining Advance*. See also Bancroft, *Washington, Idaho, and Montana*, chaps. 4–5.

Salmon River region. Then in 1864, far to the south, the entire Boise Valley became the scene of great mining activity. In this area Boise City, Idaho City, Centreville, Placerville, Eagle City, Pioneer City, and other towns emerged. Farther to the southwest, in what is called the Owyhee district, mining activity likewise boomed, and there the towns of Ruby City and Silver City grew up. Still later gold discoveries were made in the Coeur d'Alene Mountains, well up in the Idaho panhandle, and such towns as Coeur d'Alene, Beaver City, and Murray arose to accommodate the people who concentrated there.[2] As each new discovery occurred there was a stampede, not alone for a mining claim, but for the most favored townsites as well. But when the miners moved on to greener pastures what had once been booming urban centers now became ghost towns, whose deserted, wobbly, board sidewalks and empty buildings were to be silent reminders of a once-bustling past. Throughout the 'sixties and 'seventies gold mining nevertheless remained active; and with the introduction of machine methods of mining, silver and copper gained the ascendancy.[3]

In Montana, gold was first found in 1852.[4] But not until the arrival of the James and Granville Stuart party in 1858 was prospecting taken seriously.[5] Gradually excitement and interest spread until between 1862–1864 fever height was reached with the development of extremely rich placer and quartz mines at Bannack (Montana's first mining town), Gold Creek (especially Grasshopper Diggings), Alder Gulch (served by Virginia City), Confederate Gulch, Deer Lodge, Last Chance Gulch (Helena), and many other places. The population growth of the individual mining towns was tremendous. In 1863 Bannack's inhabitants had reached, according to some estimates, 2,000 to 3,000; Virginia City had a population of 10,000. These numbers, however, shifted constantly. Most of these people were in the southwestern part of present Montana, literally hundreds of miles away from the source of supplies, and goods of all kinds had to come in from the outside.[6] Bannack and Virginia City, for instance, lay 400 miles from Salt Lake, 1,400 from Omaha, 1,000 from Portland, 600 from navigation on the Columbia River, and 200 miles from Fort Benton.[7]

---

[2] Bancroft, *op. cit.*, chap. 7; Harold E. Briggs, *Frontiers of the Northwest* (New York, 1940), pp. 8–22.

[3] M. D. Beal, *A History of Southeastern Idaho* (Caldwell, Idaho, 1942), p. 235.

[4] Merrill G. Burlingame, *The Montana Frontier* (Helena, Montana, 1942), p. 79.

[5] Paul C. Phillips, ed., *Forty Years on the Frontier as Seen in the Journals and Reminiscences of Granville Stuart* (Cleveland, 1925), I, 133–40. Hereafter cited as *Journals of Granville Stuart.*

[6] Robert E. Albright, "The Relations of Montana with the Federal Government, 1864–1889," Ph.D. dissertation, Stanford University, 1933, pp. 26–27.

[7] Bancroft, *Washington, Idaho, and Montana*, p. 629.

Eastern Oregon also had its gold stampede, but it was small. Immigrants who passed through Meek's Cut-off in 1845 are known to have found some gold in present Malheur County. But not until 1861 were gold seekers in that region adequately rewarded. The Malheur, John Day, and Powder rivers then became the scene of panning activities, and individual finds of from $20 to $50 per day were common (one man took out $6,000 in four days); stamp mills were subsequently erected, and the town of Baker City owes its founding to this eastern Oregon rush.[8] In this general picture belongs also the British Columbia scene. It was during the spring of 1858 that the Hudson's Bay Company's steamer, the *Otter*, tied up at the San Francisco docks. Among her cargo was some gold dug along the banks of the far-off Fraser River, and reports of a new gold field traveled fast. As on other frontiers, gold had been found north of the forty-ninth parallel at earlier dates (some had been found on Queen Charlotte's Islands in 1851) but not until 1858 did news, such as was conveyed by the *Otter*, of substantial discoveries come to the attention of a transient American mining population anxious to find some new El Dorado.

Leaving at once for the Canadian mines were hundreds of Californians. To the host of hardened and experienced Argonauts one "might add," wrote the Britisher Alfred Waddington, "a good stock of gamblers, pickpockets, swindlers, ... thieves, drunkards, and jail birds, let loose by the governors of California for the benefit of all mankind besides the halt, lame, blind and mad."[9] At San Francisco on June 4, 1858, John Domer, another Britisher wrote: "From California the exodus of miners continues. Some thousands have left by sea, and great numbers are going overland, ... travelling through Oregon to the new El Dorado."[10] Oregonians were likewise stirred by this news. Dr. Carl Friesach, writing about Portland in August 1858, reported "the whole population in the greatest state of excitement on account of the news of the discovery of gold fields on the Fraser River; it was the only topic of conversation in the whole town." In the Puget Sound area large numbers of the settlers, ships' crews, soldiers stationed at Forts Steilacoom, Townsend, and Bellingham, cast duty and responsibility to the winds and headed north to the diggings.[11]

The sudden inrush of these tough and hardened California miners upon the once quiet and peaceful fur-trading post of Victoria was overawing. James Douglas, who had by this time become governor of Van-

---

[8] Quiett, *Pay Dirt*, pp. 170–71.

[9] Alfred Waddington, *The Fraser Mines Vindicated* (Victoria, B.C., 1858), pp. 9–10, 18.

[10] John Domer, *A Guide to British Columbia and Vancouver Island* (London, [1858]), p. 31.

[11] Howay, Sage, and Angus, *British Columbia and the United States*, p. 140.

couver Island, sought to regulate the stampede since stopping it would be impossible, but such restrictions failed to discourage the gold seekers who were eager to get to the new diggings. In June 1858, no less than 7,147 left San Francisco for Canada, while still others poured in from Oregon, and, indeed, from Great Britain as well.[12]

The open seaport of Victoria became the unquestioned entrepôt for the Fraser River diggings. "Victoria," wrote a Britisher, "appeared to have leapt at once from the site of a promising settlement into a full-grown town."[13] The story of how the miners moved on from Victoria, across the ninety miles of treacherous Sound to Fort Langley at the mouth of the Fraser, and how they managed to reach the many upstream bars, among them Forts Hope and Yale and Lytton, will be told in the following chapter. Suffice it to say here that in British Columbia the mining population ran true to form—forever on the go. The total number of this population certainly did not exceed 30,000, and the figure might well have been lower. Some bars proved to be very productive: $25 for a man's hard-day's labor was not uncommon. Some men made $150, and some as low as $2.50.[14]

In time some of the more adventuresome miners managed to surmount the physical obstacle offered by the Fraser River Canyon (a feat of no small magnitude), and drifted northward into a wildly wooded and mountainous district known as the Cariboo. Here gold was found in added abundance, and by 1863 no less than 4,000 had reached the distant British Columbia hinterland, and the shacktowns of Barkerville and Cariboo sprang up as a result. Later there came news of a rich discovery at Kootenai followed in 1865 by discoveries in the upper Columbia River region between Cariboo and Kootenai.[15] Taken as a whole, the British Columbia gold rush of the late 'fifties and early 'sixties was extremely spectacular, but like those in southern Oregon the mines proved to be rather short-lived. Several mines which were developed two to three decades later, for example those in the Rossland district, proved more lasting.[16]

The history of events in nearly all of these mining camps seems to follow a given pattern. First there would be the discovery of precious ore, announcement of which was usually followed by a mad rush to the new diggings. Close upon the heels of the gold seekers were such groups as the merchants, traders, hostlers, gamblers, barkeepers, and the "hurdy-

[12] Sage, *Sir James Douglas and British Columbia*, pp. 203–14; Quiett, *op. cit.*, pp. 192–94.

[13] Mayne, *Four Years in British Columbia and Vancouver Island*, p. 44.

[14] Sage, *op. cit.*, pp. 222–26.

[15] Alexander Begg, *History of British Columbia* (Toronto, 1894), pp. 267–68.

[16] Quiett, *Pay Dirt*, pp. 209–11.

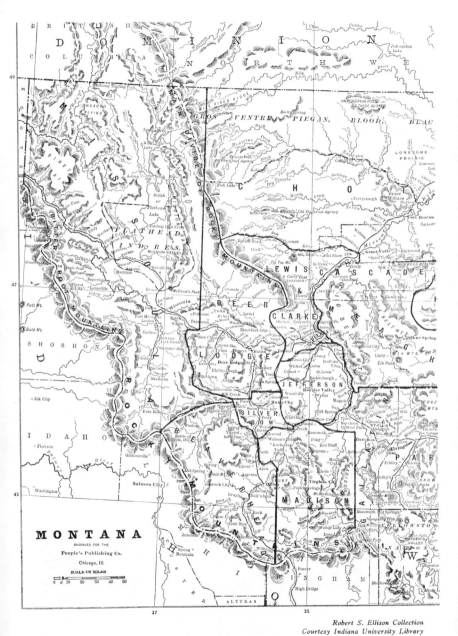

MAP OF WESTERN MONTANA

YALE, B.C., 1858

VICTORIA, B.C., DURING GOLD-RUSH EXCITEMENT

gurdy" girls, whose object it was to exploit the business possibilities associated with a new "strike."

It was relatively easy for people to get to a new gold field, but the bonanza towns created by a gold rush presented unique problems of supply. An individual miner could and did carry with him certain essential mining equipment and foodstuff to see him through the first few days, or, at most, weeks. Beyond that time he was obliged to rely upon the merchant and the transport operation for the replenishment of his larder. In the more remote mining camps the task of bringing supplies proved to be as enormous as it was hazardous. One transportation system used was the pack train.

Like water transportation, pack-animal transportation is nearly as old as civilization itself. It was certainly the most representative of the transportation systems of New Spain where for more than three centuries the mules had trudged faithfully over its winding mountain trails.[17] Pack mules had enabled the Spaniards to push northward into Mexico and ultimately into Alta California. Those beasts of burden also served in the Santa Fe trade, in Western fur trade, and in practically every gold rush connected with the history of the West. Scarcely had the mining frontier moved into the Oregon country when one could have witnessed those familiar strings of lazy, slow, lumbering, yet dependable pack animals winding their way across the Siskiyou Mountains, first into southern Oregon and then into the Inland Empire.

Almost without exception the animals used in the packing business were the Mexican burros, or as the Northwesterners called them, just plain "Mexican mules."[18] Their usefulness has been well attested to by Hinton R. Helper, author of the famed *Impending Crisis*, who had carefully observed how extensively pack animals were used in California during the Gold Rush:

These hybrids, unamiable as is their appearance, are truly valuable for this purpose; they carry ponderous burdens, walk with ease upon the brink of a precipice, and can be kept in good serviceable condition by provender on which a horse would starve. After making a few trips they become very tractable, and it requires only four or five men to manage fifty or sixty of them. The packers have but little trouble with them, after strapping the loads on their back and starting them off.[19]

Others, too, wrote in praise of this primitive but none-the-less practical mode of transportation to the diggings whether in California or in

---

[17] Eleanor Lawrence, "Mule Trains and Muleteers on Early California Roads," *Touring Topics*, XXIV (July 1932), 16–17.

[18] There were instances when, instead of the burros, horses, cayuses, donkeys, true hybrid mules and hinnies, and even camels were used. The commonly used term "mule" here means burro.

[19] Hinton R. Helper, *The Land of Gold: Reality Versus Fiction* (Baltimore, 1855), p. 138.

the Pacific Northwest. Shut out as the miners were from cities and plains, "packing to them," to use the words of *Hutchings' California Magazine*, "has become an indispensable necessity; and is not only the means of obtaining their supplies, but . . . . a kind of connecting link between the vallies and the mountains."[20]

The care and management of these pack animals was, regardless of ownership, left to the Mexican muleteers, or *arrieros*, whose experience with them was long standing. Caring for the mules was a job that required both patience and skill, and the *arriero* seemed to possess a native skill conducive to the happiness of this beast. For generations he and his kind had become inured to the wandering life for which his work called, and he learned how to cater to the mule's idiosyncracies and whims. Muleteering was one profession not as a rule sought by *Americanos*, and it was one in which they would be admittedly inept. Says one writer:

The Mexican muleteers had elevated packing and driving to a science. Their knowledge of mule nature and their skill in the nice balancing of packs, learned through long association and practice, gave their lowly occupation a luster and dignity that never failed to bring forth comment from those who saw them at their work.[21]

Driving mules was obviously no task for amateurs whose clumsiness the animals would not be long in detecting—and exploiting. Mules have their mischievous and their stubborn side, and if they choose to exercise it, there is no use arguing, not even cursing. Rather than yield to indecorous motivation, they would prefer to fall, to roll their cargo into the ditch or creek, or start out on a lusty, rampaging stampede.[22]

Mules, then as now, had to be well looked after if satisfactory service was to be expected from them. Care had to be exercised to prevent galling, and the best insurance against that was to keep the animal fairly fat. ". . . . let your mules once get thin, from over-driving, over-loading," admonishes a contemporary named Lord, ". . . . and all the care and skill the most practised hands are able to adopt will not prevent the occurrence of galled backs and chafed ribs." To judge a pack animal was no easy matter. A first-class mule should be, according to Lord, five to seven years old, "short upon the legs, strong and rather arched along the back, thick in the shoulders and muscular about the loins. The hoofs," he adds, "should be small and black, and the hocks straight and fine, without any tendency to bend inwards, or what is technically designated 'cowhocked.' He should have bright full eyes, sharp teeth, a good long swishy tail, and a sound skin."[23]

The money value of a mule was always changing with the fortunes

[20] *Hutchings' Illustrated California Magazine*, I (December 1856), 241.
[21] Lawrence, *op. cit.*, p. 17.　　　　[22] *Ibid.*
[23] John Keast Lord, *At Home in the Wilderness* (London, 1876), pp. 14–15.

of the miners, although an average price in Oregon for one well-broken animal appears to have been from $120 to $150. Unbroken Texan mules could be had for less, as could mules secured from individual miners whose luck had failed them. During flush times in the Inland Empire, on the contrary, prices on mules even reached $400.[24]

Tough and strong as were the Mexican mules, difficulties were experienced with them in the Pacific Northwest where climatic conditions were so unlike those of Mexico and the Southwest. Many mules died during the cold and rainy seasons. In order to shelter the animals, muleteers were obliged to build sheds. In the Fraser River country, where the snowfalls were frequently heavy, the problem of forage, solved in warmer climates by simply turning the animals loose to graze, had to be dealt with. In the early stages of the gold digging very little hay was available and the hungry mules were often obliged to subsist on dried foliage. Unless precautions were taken the starved beasts would devour poison horsetail rush (*Equisetum*) which grew high under trees and near the swamps. "As soon as the mules began to eat it," Lord relates, "they were seized with a disease precisely resembling Asiatic cholera; the most violent purging came on, accompanied with cramp, rigors, utter prostration, and speedy death."[25] It was reported that once at two camps on the Fraser River over five hundred mules died in less than a month. Later precautions were taken and prairie grasses were cut during the summer months and stacked for winter use.[26]

Similarly, in Idaho and Montana there is evidence that pack animals suffered severely during the cold seasons. The *Montana Post* relates how in the vicinity of Lake Pend d'Oreille these beasts were "perishing in great numbers, from want of feed and extreme cold combined."[27]

In addition to the large-scale use of pack animals, then as now individual miners or prospectors used the burro to carry personal belongings, such as blankets, tools (including a shovel, pick, axe, gold pan, mortar and pestle), a canteen filled with water, cooking utensils, food, and tobacco. It was advisable never to overload or push a pack animal; at least a proverb reads: "Never crowd a burro if you are in a hurry!" A book dealing with mining in the Southwest describes this servant of the prospector thus:

Burros resemble human beings: some of them can be allowed to roam at will during the night and are easily caught in the morning; others have to be hobbled. . . . .

[24] *Ibid.*, p. 16; William S. Lewis, ed., "Experiences of a Packer in Washington Territory Mining Camps During the Sixties," by James W. Watt, *The Washington Historical Quarterly*, XIX (October 1928), 286. Hereafter cited as Watt, "Experiences of a Packer."

[25] Lord, *op. cit.*, pp. 17–18.

[26] *Ibid.*, pp. 18–19.   [27] *Montana Post*, December 30, 1865.

A bond of friendship exists between a prospector and his burro that is not understood by one who has never followed their paths. In barren country they are dependent upon each other for their very existence, although elsewhere the burro could dispense with his master and lose far less in the deal.[28]

It was upon the backs of these tough-skinned animals that the freight was carried. There were numerous methods used for placing the packs on the backs of the mules, determined somewhat by the shape, size, and weight of the freight. One method recommended for use in the Pacific Northwest, according to the experienced Lieutenant John Mullan, builder of the Mullan Road, was the "cross-tree packsaddle" with crupper, breeching, and thick pads. This saddle was held on the animal by means of a bellyband drawn tight with a lash rope. A double blanket was used under each saddle and the load was equally balanced on the two sides of the animal.

By far the most widely used packsaddle was the Spanish aparejo. It was made of leather and stuffed either with moss, dry hay, grass, or any other soft substance which would protect the back of the animal, and one cost thirty-five to sixty dollars. With each aparejo there was usually a *caronie*, or fancy embroidered Spanish blanket, which was placed in between the "sweat blanket," next to the mule's back, and the saddle. Each mule had his own saddle and *caronie*, on which appeared a special design or flower for purposes of identification. Each animal likewise carried the same pack (often weighing four hundred pounds) for the duration of the trip. When in camp the equipment with its pack was systematically arranged in open squares or circles.[29] A canvas covered each pack. Each animal had its picket rope (about thirty-five to forty feet long) for use when staked out at night. When a string of animals was engaged, it was necessary to have a "bell animal" and a gray mare was preferred, says Mullan. The animals should be shod, at least on the forefeet. Mules should never be maltreated, advises Mullan, "but govern them as you would a woman, with kindness, affection, and caresses, and you will be repaid by their docility and easy management."[30]

The size of the mule trains varied, but the usual number of animals in one string was from thirty to fifty. A string of this size was cared for by four or five muleteers, although this number of men could easily handle more. Apparently a very definite routine or system was followed by the packers when on the trail. The men were up long before daybreak, usually about two or three in the morning. While certain ones prepared

[28] Philip A. Bailey, *Golden Mirages* (New York, 1940), pp. 5, 8.

[29] Watt, "Experiences of a Packer," *op. cit.*, XX (January 1929), 45–46.

[30] Captain John Mullan, *Miners and Travelers' Guide to Oregon, Washington, Idaho, Montana, Wyoming, and Colorado* (New York, 1865), pp. 8–9.

breakfast and broke up camp, others went out in search of the bell mare. Upon finding her, the bell would be rung, and the mules from all around "would answer by bawling out, and starting towards the bell mare." When all the mules were assembled, a muleteer would mount the bell mare and ride back into camp, usually at a trot.

Once in camp the mules were herded into their respective places next to their packs, and with heads facing into the square or circle they were rigged together with rope and "hackamores" (headstalls). This done, the muleteers breakfasted, and thereafter the aparejos and packs were put upon the backs of the animals while the cook cleaned up camp and packed his equipment. It required from one and a half to two minutes for two expert muleteers, one called "near" and the other "off," to pack a mule with its odd assortment of goods such as kegs of whiskey, barrels of flour, chairs, cartwheels, iron bars, assorted spices, and on one occasion, at least, a pool table.[31]

The start of the day's march was not without its picturesque aspect. Still at a very early hour, usually about six, the signal was given. The cook mounted his gray bell mare and rode off. The mules followed at their own volition. The packers then mounted and, if the road was wide enough, rode at the side of the mules which moved along in single file. At the rear rode the "Boss." A distance of about fifteen miles was covered during the day with nothing but pauses for drink. Sometime between noon and two o'clock, depending upon the ease with which a suitable place could be found, the train halted for its next encampment.

The life of the muleteer was never one to be envied. It called for endurance, patience, and courage. He worked hard and also drove his animals hard. His job necessitated rising long before dawn; it required long tedious miles of walking or riding (usually on horseback); it also involved considerable heavy work in the loading and unloading of freight. "In the first days of my packing," reminisced Watt, "we averaged only 15 mules to the man, later this was increased to 18 or 20 mules, and at last it was customary to give two men 36 to 40 mules to handle. It was some work, I'll tell you."[32]

During the cold seasons the packers suffered much, and especially if caught in a winter storm. According to a *Montana Post* reporter:

To be out in the [Montana] mountains, unsheltered, with the thermometer ranging from zero to thirty below, is certainly to endure great suffering, if not to take desperate chances between life and death. . . . . We are prepared, at any minute, to hear of loss of limbs, and, perhaps, lives, among these bold and enterprising freighters.[33]

---

[31] Watt, "Experiences of a Packer," *op. cit.*, XX (January 1929), 46–47.
[32] *Ibid.*, p. 47.   [33] *Montana Post*, December 30, 1865.

There appear many contemporary references to holdups in connection with packing. To forestall them as much as possible each man, including the cook whose other duty it was to ride the "bell mare," was armed either with a shotgun or a rifle. Some, and particularly the muleteers, also carried a revolver. *The Idaho World* tells of a case in which mules were stolen at a point on the Snake River from a man named Douthitt who followed the thieves' tracks all the way to the Malheur River where he found the mules in the hands of a party of Indians.[34] The same newspaper also relates the case of E. W. Sigsbee of Umatilla who sold his pack train for $75 per mule and was robbed of his money shortly thereafter.[35] There is further the story about the packer John Welch who was held up at Grass Valley. Upon turning over a considerable quantity of gold dust to the robber, Welch burst out: "I'll see you again."

"No you won't," the robber replied, and promptly blew off Welch's head with a double-barreled shotgun.[36]

Within the Oregon country pack animals were, of course, used by the Hudson's Bay Company and by private fur traders who ventured into the region, as well as by prospectors and explorers. Important as were these first uses of pack animals, it remained for the United States Army and the gold miners to accord the lowly mule an envied role in the transportation system of the Pacific Northwest. It was during the gold rush and Rogue River Indian trouble in southern Oregon during the middle 'fifties that packing operations first began on a fairly large, regular, and, at least so far as the civilian life was concerned, competitive basis. In the absence of practical, all-season wagon roads pack trains were first organized to transport goods from such northern California supply depots as Shasta City, Crescent City, and Humboldt Bay across the narrow and winding mountain trails into Rogue River Valley, to which placer miners and settlers alike came during and after 1850.

During 1851 it is reported that one hundred mules left Union (Humboldt Bay) weekly for the north California mines, carrying $4,000 to $5,000 worth of goods, and when news of the influx of settlers into southern Oregon reached this north California coastal area, many of these packers opened up trade between the two districts. The chief seat of this Oregon trade was Jacksonville, but Illinois Valley, Sailor Diggings, New Orleans Bar, Applegate Creek, and many other places were among those served by the Crescent City entrepôt.[37] The distance from Crescent City to Jacksonville was 120 miles, and it usually took packers ten days to

---

[34] *The Idaho World*, May 27, 1865.   [35] *Ibid.*, September 9, 1865.

[36] Watt, "Experiences of a Packer," *op. cit.*, XIX (October 1928), 286–87.

[37] *Hutchings' Illustrated California Magazine*, I, 246; Owen C. Coy, *The Humboldt Bay Region, 1850–1875* (Los Angeles, 1929), pp. 67–71.

cover this stretch. For a vividly descriptive account of this trade we must turn to the pages of contemporary *Hutchings' California Magazine.* It reads:

There are about one thousand five hundred mules in the packing trade at these points. It is no uncommon circumstance, to meet between twenty and thirty trains, with from twenty to seventy-five animals in each train, and all heavily laden, on your way from Jacksonville to Crescent City. The loud "hippah," "mulah," of the Mexican muleteers, sounds strangely to the ear, in the deep, and almost unbroken stillness of the forest.[38]

The early residents of southern Oregon felt singularly isolated from the settlers in the Willamette Valley, and practically their only contacts with the outside world were those established by means of mule trains with northern California and occasional wagon and mule trains from the Willamette Valley. The importance which the southern Oregon people placed upon the arrival of pack trains from California is clearly indicated in the diary of Mrs. Ashmun J. Butler who, with her husband, reached the Rogue River Valley from Yreka by means of horseback in 1852. The following are random excerpts from the Butler diary:

Tuesday, May 24, 1853. . . . . Quite a number of packtrains this week for Wyre[ka].
Tuesday, June 7, 1853. Another very large pack train yesterday loaded mostly with flower . . . .
Tuesday, June 14, 1853. This morning a large pack train passes of fifty mules leaving one with us that was crippled   In the afternoon another one passed of ten or fifteen mules . . . .
Saturday, July 2, 1853. A packtrain today. . . . .
Monday, August 8, 1853 . . . . a pack train passed this morning; reports much loss of hay and other property below by the Indians also one man killed in the Cannion
Thursday, September 1, 1853. Business seems to be reviving for here comes five pack trains from Oregon a greater number than passed all last month
Sunday, October 9, 1853 . . . . Two pack trains camp close to us this evening.
Wednesday, October 19, 1853. Pack trains passing quite briskly . . . . .[39]

From the Willamette Valley, and particularly from Portland and Scottsburg, either by pack train or by wagon freight, there came to Jacksonville much-needed supplies;[40] and especially was this the case when the military forces were brought in to fight the Rogue River Indians. During the winter of 1855–1856, for instance, we find one of Jacksonville's businessmen, B. F. Dowell, serving as "packer" in the First Regi-

---

[38] *Hutchings' Illustrated California Magazine,* I, 246.

[39] "Diary of Mrs. Ashmun J. Butler," MS, G. S. Butler, Ashland, Oregon. See also Oscar Osburn Winther and Rosa Dodge Galey, eds., "Mrs. Butler's 1853 Diary of Rogue River Valley," *The Oregon Historical Quarterly,* XLI (December 1940), 337–66.

[40] Gaston, *Portland,* I, 235; Walling, *History of Southern Oregon,* p. 338.

ment of Oregon Volunteers. And thereby hangs a tale. Dated January 17, 1856, a document found among the Dowell papers reads:

> I hereby appoint Lewis Ward pack Master in my absence, of pack train No. 1., and he is instructed to pack supplies to any place the commanding officer may direct . . . . but he is strictly prohibited from letting anyone ride the pack mules according to my contract.[41]

Another document, a letter from Ward to Dowell, reveals how well the newly appointed fared, and it helps to explain why it was that Americans had no great fancy for becoming muleteers either in or out of the Army. Here is the letter[42] in full:

Wild Horse Creek
Feb 26 1856

B F Dowell Esq
 Dear Sir

with mutch trubble I write to you to inform you of our difficulty and misfortune on the night of the 25 Insant [*sic*] the Indians stampeeded the muls and took them from us the gard raseed [*sic*] the allurm and we all sprang to our guns and run out and fired on them but without mutch affect they took them all we persude them as farr as we could that night beeing afoot we could not keep in hearing of them so we had to give it up for the night we persude them next morning early and found one of the Biglo muls and too two [*sic*] horses and found Puss & Darkus & Babcock lanced [*sic*] in the left Side the Babcock mule was killed ded and the other two I think will die the Indians went in the direction of the Calumbra rive [*sic*] I am now on wild horse cree [*sic*] wating for relief and horses to pack the flower to Hedquarters I would like for you to come up and see what is to bee done I think I shal quit the service as soon as you cum or join some Company and seek reveng I shal take cear [*sic*] of what there is left untill you come I think I shal have the riging & blankets appraised and turn them over to goverment we are a lonesome and a discontented set

yours respetfully [*sic*]
Lewis Ward

In a third document, dated February 12, 1867, finis is written to this episode. We may infer that Dowell sought government indemnity for his losses, and after eleven long years the Commissioner of Indian Affairs in the Department of Interior regretfully informed Dowell "that upon thorough examination of the files and records of this office" with respect to the loss of one mule in the Indian war of 1856, "there is not found any evidence that . . . . proof [of the death of the mule] was ever received here."[43]

The thousands of Argonauts who in 1858 rushed madly to the British

---

[41] B. F. Dowell Collection, MSS, Henry E. Huntington Library. Letter from B. G. [*sic*] Dowell, packer, to Hd. Qts., 1st. Reg., Ore. Vol. Jan. 17, 1856.

[42] *Ibid.*

[43] Commissioner of Indian Affairs, Department of Interior, Washington, D.C., to B. F. Dowell, February 12, 1867. MS, Dowell Collection.

Columbia diggings, the region between Hope and the Thompson junction on the Fraser River, faced transportation problems never before encountered. Had they read the records of the intrepid Alexander Mackenzie and Simon Fraser who first penetrated the wilds of that country, they might, perhaps, have paused to consider the dangers and privations that lay before them. But the miners as a rule were little schooled in the history of the United States, much less in that of Canada. So with reckless abandon they moved into this forbidding terrain in large numbers and with insufficient supplies.

All who approached the Fraser River and Cariboo diggings by sea and who (as was the common practice) landed at Victoria had three difficult stretches of travel before them. The first lap of this journey, a distance of ninety miles, was from Victoria to Fort Langley near the mouth of the Fraser across the Strait of Georgia. It was a channel that was extremely swift and capricious. For this dangerous jaunt crafts ranging from canoes and rowboats to steamers and sailing vessels were employed. Even old California steamers had been imported and put into service on the strait. At best it was a voyage "fraught with peril," related Commander Mayne, especially to those "too impatient or too poor to wait until they could take passage in the ordinary steamer or sailing-vessel." The number who lost their lives attempting to cross the strait in inferior craft was believed by Mayne to have been far, far greater than the number of those who met their fate under different circumstances in this first wild rush.[44] In good ships, however, this initial lap of the journey to the Fraser diggings was perfectly safe. Moreover, sturdy ships with as much as eighteen to twenty feet draught could (once they were across the strait) navigate up the Fraser as far as Hope.

Most vessels, however, stopped at Fort Langley, and the next lap of this journey was from this point to where the diggings began in earnest. This was a distance of thirty miles. Over this stretch river steamers could navigate, though not without difficulty, and regular service was early offered by the *Enterprise, Surprise*, and *Umatilla*.[45] Because of the shallowness of the water above Fort Langley, specially built flat-bottomed stern-wheelers were later to prove most successful.

Above Hope the swiftness of the river and protruding rocks made navigation extremely difficult, although Yale (fourteen miles above Hope) was, at times of high water, reached with steamers. In some cases this stretch was made in a small canoe, usually with the assistance of an Indian or two who would do the paddling.

All this was by way of introduction to the final lap, which was the

[44] Mayne, *Four Years in British Columbia and Vancouver Island*, p. 49.

[45] Howay, *British Columbia*, p. 122; Mayne, *op. cit.*, pp. 86, 90–95.

region above Hope. Into this rugged country the miners fanned out in many directions, and there commercial river transportation ceased and overland packing began. During 1858–1859 they worked the bars as far up the Fraser as Lillooet, about two hundred miles above the mouth of that stream. Soon thereafter the rush to the Cariboo began, which brought still other thousands into a region four hundred to five hundred miles above the mouth of the Fraser. Travelers above Yale were advised to follow the foot and pack-mule trails, dangerous though they were, which had been marked out into the heart of the Cariboo country.[46] There were three such trails, and they were known as the mule trail, the lower, and the upper canyon trails. The mule trail was closed from seven to eight months of the year on account of snow. It hugged the riverbank when possible but, as was the case above Yale, it often drew away from the river in order to follow a more suitable course. The lower trail could be used only when the water was low enough to expose a ledge of boulder at the bottom of the cliffs. Mayne said that the upper trail often passed along from ledge to ledge, at a height ranging from fifty to eight hundred feet above the river.

"The mode of rounding these cliffs, which literally overhang the river, is peculiar," relates this early-day visitor, "and makes one's nerves twitch a little at first." Slides, too, were frequent, and several people were known to have lost their lives because of them. One of the worst passes was Jackass Mountain, so named because a mule and his driver plunged to their death from one of its tortuous bends. The roughness and rocky barrenness of the trail continued all the way to Lytton, but from there to Kamloops it passed through grassy and timbered valleys.[47] John Damon, also one of the first to write about this operation, commented on the toughness of this trail, which "after crossing Yale creek ascends a rugged precipitous hill, a distance of 2½ miles," then after a leveling off "4 mile house" is reached, "from which place to the river a distance of ¾ of a mile is very difficult steep and precipitous. . . . . From this point we continued the river course, over one of the most rough & rugged roads that it ever fell to my lot to travel. Sometimes for a while," wrote Damon at the end of his day's activities, "we were leaping from point to point on huge boulders of slate & granite with here and there some pretty specimens of limestone & marble" that might at any moment "fall & crush the traveler; . . . . one slipping foot would open the gates of eternity."

[46] E. O. S. Scholefield and R. E. Gosnell, *A History of British Columbia* (Vancouver and Victoria, 1913), I, 176–77; John F. Damon, "Journal, Victoria, 1859," MS, Henry E. Huntington Library.

[47] Mayne, *op. cit.*, pp. 104–12.

Packing into this treacherous hinterland proved to be challenging and instantly profitable. It was done both by man and beast, usually though by means of the mule. The Bishop of Columbia who in 1860 entered the mining region, for example, wrote in his diary, July 10 of that year: "Packing is one of the most lucrative employments. A train of twelve or eighteen horses and mules very soon pays the expense of the first cost, and then great profits are made." The Bishop also stated that Mexicans did most of the packing but that many Americans were engaged in the work.[48]

At first gold seekers to Cariboo found the old Fraser River, or Hope, Trail (the one used by the Hudson's Bay Company) extremely difficult. It was not long, though, before interested persons found what might be thought of as a great detour around the more impassable mountain barriers that blocked the mid-Fraser gorge. It became known as the Harrison and Lillooet route, or Douglas and Lillooet route.

This famous trail left the Fraser River at its confluence with the Harrison River. The trail then followed the Harrison River to Harrison Lake, a distance of about sixty-five miles. Boats traversed the forty-five mile length of this lake to Port Douglas, at which place a segment of trail went as far as the Little Lillooet Lake. This, in turn, was connected by a one-fourth mile portage with the Big Lillooet Lake. Steamers operated over these lakes and goods were by this means carried north to Pemberton where another portage trail (this one, twenty-four miles long) led to the town of Anderson at the lower end of Anderson Lake. The final stretch was along this lake by boat, across a one and one-half mile portage to Lake Seton, and then again by boat to the town of Lillooet which sat snugly between Seton Lake and the Fraser River. The total distance of this route was 111½ miles. From Lillooet the trail followed the upper Fraser all the way into Barkerville and Cariboo. Its great inconvenience was in its many portages, but it was, on the other hand, a fairly safe route.[49]

By 1862 the original all-Fraser River route, or Hope Trail, was greatly improved by the Royal Engineers. Above Yale it zigzagged northward over Jackass Mountain to Lytton, ninety-six miles from Hope, and at the confluence of the Thompson and Fraser rivers. From there it went to Foster's Bar and on north to Lillooet where it was joined by the Harrison and Lillooet route described above. When the great rush to the Cariboo country began in 1863, competition between the two

---

[48] William Carew Hazlitt, *The Great Gold Fields of Cariboo with an Authentic Description, Brought Down to the Latest Period, of British Columbia and Vancouver Island* (London, 1862), p. 163; Damon, *op. cit.*

[49] Norman Hacking, "Early Marine History of British Columbia," MS, Archives of British Columbia, p. 49.

routes arose and continued unabated until the completion of the Cariboo
Wagon Road two years thereafter.[50] It was not uncommon, as one finds
similarly in certain places today, to see a signboard or an advertisement
reading: "Experience has proved that the Douglas and Lillooet Route
is the Shortest, Best, and Most Economical One to the Cariboo Mines!"
Then, just to remind people of the hazards of the alternate route:
"TRAVELER, REMEMBER! That there are no Yawning Gulfs, no 'Riffles',
no Sunken Steamers, no Explosions, no Tricks on Travelers, on the
Douglas-Lillooet Route!"[51]

Proponents of the Hope Trail had its staunch advocates, too. In an
advertisement headed "FACTS FOR THE PUBLIC," one reads:

LOOK AT THE MAP OF B.C. AND examine the line of the Yale and Lytton route
and the line of the Douglas-Lillooet route and see for yourselves. Then consider
that you have nearly a dozen different fares to pay to different individuals, over
different lakes, portages, &c in the short distance of 109½ miles on the Douglas
route, and compare these with the fact that there is uninterrupted steam travel to
Yale, and but one fare to pay. You can walk from Yale to Lytton in two days, and
when there you will find that you have saved in traveling expenses nearly sufficient
to carry you to Quesnelle River.[52]

One of the most graphic accounts of the packing trade to and from
the Cariboo is that given by W. Champness, another Britisher, who in
the spring of 1862 sailed from Southampton for these far-distant diggings.
At Victoria this British traveler rested for a few days and then crossed
the strait to New Westminster where, like the boom town Victoria, he
found its dwellings "mostly of wood, but with many temporary tents
interspersed." At New Westminster a river boat carried him up the
Fraser to Harrison, up the Harrison River and across Harrison Lake
to the town of Douglas, his jumping-off place for the overland part of
the trip to Cariboo.

At Douglas Champness followed the customary procedure of attach-
ing himself to a group of other Cariboo-bound emigrants in order that
the journey over the trail might not have to be made alone. Indications
are that the party packed some of their own goods from Douglas to
Lillooet, a three days' hike, and then at the latter place made final preparations for a 250-mile march over the most rugged part of the trail into
Cariboo. There were now twenty in the party and these formed a company and hired a California packer with seven animals to haul their

[50] *Ibid.* A table of distances appears in the *British Colonist* (Victoria, B.C.), February 2,
1860. From Lytton a new trail was opened in 1860 by way of Hat and Bonaparte rivers and
on north to Fort Alexandria, which was near the future town of Cariboo. The distance from
Hope to Alexandria by this route was about 350 miles. See *British Colonist*, January 24, 1860.

[51] *Victoria Daily Chronicle,* May 4, 1864.

[52] *British Colonist,* April 30, 1862.

supplies over this final stretch. For these services the company paid thirty cents per pound. Regarding this phase of the trip Champness made the following remarks:

The operation of packing a team of horses or mules with baggage requires great skill, and is a long and tedious affair. The average burden put on each horse is three hundred pounds weight. Besides provisions, our cooking utensils (obtained at Lilooett [*sic*]) were thus carried. Altogether we found our expenses here much greater than we had anticipated; and this is universally the experience of those who come to British Columbia.

The trip from Lillooet to William's Lake through "wild and awful ravines" and "along the most frightful precipices" required sixteen days. "Fortunately for ourselves," related Champness, "we escaped any serious accidents amid these wild scenes." No more than five to six miles were covered on certain days. He continues:

The backs of several of our poor beasts became very sore. This, again, caused delays, and the utmost care in packing and adjusting the burdens. Not unfrequently our horses stumbled and fell. Our packer several times beat them harshly, attributing it all to their temper; and we had to interpose, to prevent cruelty. . . . .

British Columbia is truly a horse-killing country. At other times we dragged our burdens heavily up steep and forested mountains. Then, again, we met frequently with rapid and deep streams. . . . . Repeated practice, however, enabled us to perform feats of climbing, leaping, and crawling which formerly would have seemed utterly impossible to us. We now remarked to one another our belief that, if St. Paul's Cathedral were in British Columbia, we could safely walk round the steep side of its lofty dome, provided there was a trail of a foot wide on it.

From one such hair-raising experience to another this Britisher continues the story of his long march to Cariboo:

Having resumed our journey, with numbers thus diminished, we soon reached a rude log bridge across a torrent in a ravine. Here one of our horses fell over into the water. Our packer, by means of a rope, hoisted it up, and, nearly drowned as it was, beat it savagely to make it move on; but the plunge and the blows, after so much slavery of exertion, were too much, and the wretched beast died close to the bridge where it had slipped. And thus miserably perish hundreds of horses and mules along this weary track. Often we had to hurry past their offensive carcases, left by the side of our narrow ways.[53]

There were those who did use canoes for transporting themselves and their supplies to the diggings above Hope, but it is believed that about one-fourth of those who tried it lost their lives.[54]

At best, packing into Cariboo was hazardous. One engineer present at the time relates how "Cariboo is closely packed with mountains of

[53] [W. Champness], "To Cariboo and Back," *The Leisure Hour*, Nos. 692–96 (April 1865), pp. 203 *passim*.

[54] Howay, *British Columbia*, pp. 137–40.

considerable altitude, singularly tumbled and irregular in character, and presenting steep and thickly wooded slopes. Here and there," he continued, "tremendous masses, whose summits are from 6000 to 7000 feet above the sea, tower above the general level, and form centres of radiation of subordinate ranges."[55] But difficult as was this route, there exist the written words of Governor Douglas to the Colonial Secretary on July 16, 1861, to the effect that no less than "1200 transport horses and mules" were then engaged in the business of keeping Cariboo alone supplied with food.[56]

Some evidence as to the Cariboo packing trade may be had from advertisements such as the following:[57]

SMITH & CO.,
PACKERS

Over the Douglas & Lillooet Route
Are still Packing and Forwarding Goods to

LILLOOET.

And are Prepared to Forward 250 Tons per Month,
At Moderate Rates.

All Goods marked in our Care will be received and forwarded without delay.

P. SMITH & Co.,
Packers, Douglas and Lillooet, B.C.

Put figures into pounds, rather than tons, and compare with the competing Q. E. T. Doge and Company, which boasted of handling "One Hundred Thousand Pounds of Freight per Month. . . . ."[58]

It was the opinion of the Governor that "The great commercial thoroughfares, leading into the interior of the country, from Hope, Yale, and Douglas, are in rapid progress, and now exercise a most beneficial effect on the internal commerce of the colony."[59]

To Easterners and Middlewesterners, both American and Canadian, who wanted to go to the Cariboo diggings (and many of them did in 1862), there was available to them the old fur-traders' trail which, it will be recalled, ran from Montreal west across the Canadian plains past Forts Ellice, Carlton, Pitt, Edmonton, thence to Catholic St. Albert's

[55] Trimble, *The Mining Advance*, pp. 46–47.
[56] Hazlitt, *The Great Gold Fields of Cariboo*, pp. 116, 122.
[57] *British Colonist*, October 10, 1861.   [58] *Ibid.*, September 18, 1861.
[59] Hazlitt, *op. cit.*, pp. 116, 122.

Mission, across the Rockies (and here there was a choice of passes), and finally into Cariboo.[60]

During the winter of 1858 residents of the Puget Sound area sought to blaze an all-land trail directly from Whatcom (Bellingham) Bay to Yale in order that those interested in going to the British Columbia mines could avoid the water detour via Victoria. Such a trail would be 120 miles in length. It would have to cross snow-covered mountains and other natural barriers. It appears, though, that this trail-making party tired of its job, and was called by one contemporary "the greatest humbug of the season."

The failure to complete this trail proved a disappointment to residents of Puget Sound and California alike. When the spring of 1859 came, hundreds of Californians gathered at Whatcom Bay hoping to use this trail.[61] Their only recourse was to await passage by boat to Victoria, and then recross inland waters to the mainland.

Those who were at Fort Colvile and other upper Columbia River diggings likewise sought some more direct overland route to the Fraser than had been used in earlier years by the fur traders. A satisfactory trail was worked out, and it is interesting to note that among the first pack mules to arrive on the Fraser were five hundred from Walla Walla. They had been driven over the Colville–Fraser River Trail and before the 1858 season ended stood ready to carry supplies from boat landings to the mines.[62]

Some of the hardships endured in reaching Cariboo from Victoria have been graphically told by Alexander Allan in the following reminiscent statement made about twenty years after the event:

Upon reaching Victoria there was 200 miles of river travel before them with no steamers then in use. . . . . At Yale commenced their greatest troubles. From this to a distance of 400 miles it was with many a poor fellow a fight for life. Houses were scattered at very long distances apart, so they were obliged to carry provisions for one, two or three days according to the distance intervening between the supply stations. Instead of it being a level road, they had a rough mountain trail to follow if it could even be called a trail, up precipitous sides, and over morasses; when a high bluff was reached they were obliged to ascend and pass over it, and even take their animals over it. This was very difficult as the road was so steep that a mule or horse could scarcely secure a footing. . . . . Pack trains came from the Sandwich Islands, Mexico and elsewhere, and when these pack-animals from warmer countries reached the cold streams . . . . the exposure resulted in the death of many of their horses. Provisions, with which these animals were laden, were obliged to be abandoned in consequence. From the Mouth of the Quesnel to the old town

[60] Margaret McNaughton, *Overland to Cariboo* (Toronto, 1896), chaps. 2–5; Agnes C. Laut, *The Cariboo Trail* (Toronto, 1916), pp. 58–67.

[61] Waddington, *The Fraser Mines Vindicated*, p. 9; Howay, *British Columbia*, pp. 121–22.

[62] Howay, *op. cit.*, p. 137.

of Vanwinkle was so bad that a large portion of the animals were mired and died standing there with the packs on their backs, with no feed to keep them from starvation. The men waded through as best they could. From Vanwinkle to William's Creek all provisions had to be carried on the backs of men over a large tract of snow, which if crossed while there was a crust upon it was passable, but after the crust had melted was a fearful journey.[63]

After enduring these first harrowing experiences in getting to the diggings, there still remained, as has been shown, the problem of shipping supplies into the hinterland. "Until '61," Allan relates, "mule trains, were the only mode of conveyance"[64] to the Cariboo. During and after 1861 steps were taken to construct, with revenues from Cariboo, wagon toll roads which, connecting with the lakes and the navigable parts of the Fraser, would make wagon freighting and steamshipping possible in connection with the Cariboo rush. So long as the miners (approximately 4,000 of them) depended upon pack animals as the sole means of bringing in supplies, the cost of living remained very high, even for mining camps. In August of 1862 flour cost $1.50 per pound; beans, $1.50 per pound; beef, 50 to 55 cents per pound; picks and shovels, $10 each. That the packers and traders made tremendous profits out of the Cariboo trade may be shown by the example of one trader alone who in 1862 bought $15,000 worth of goods in Victoria and sold them in Cariboo for $70,000. In 1863 the charges for transporting freight from San Francisco to Cariboo were, according to a calculation of the London *Times,* $1,628 per ton, $1,440 of which was for land transport. These prices, however, tumbled far when in 1864 traffic over the wagon road from Yale to Cariboo became heavy. The advantages of this were short-lived since one year later the Cariboo rush went into decline. Some gold continued to come from these upper regions, and both wagon and river transportation facilities remained available until the railroad era. Captains William Irving and John R. Fleming remained leading figures on the Fraser; an array of transportation personalities came and went on other parts of the British Columbia system.[65]

The transportation problem in the Kootenai and upper Columbia River mines within British Columbia was different in that physiographically these regions were more a part of the Inland Empire, and all

[63] Alexander Allan, "Cariboo and the Miners of British Columbia, Victoria, 1878," MS, Bancroft Library, pp. 17–19.

[64] *Ibid.*, pp. 6–7.

[65] Trimble, *The Mining Advance,* pp. 53–55, 119–20. In 1860 the British government sought to impose what was called a "five dollar mule-load tax," in other words, a flat five-dollar tax on each mule load going to the mines. This would have greatly increased the cost of living, and it was vigorously opposed by the press. See *British Colonist,* February 9, 1860; Norman R. Hacking, "British Columbia Steamboat Days, 1870–1883," *The British Columbia Historical Quarterly,* XI, (April 1947), 69–111.

Courtesy Archives of British Columbia

EXPRESS STATION ON THE CARIBOO ROAD, BRITISH COLUMBIA

Courtesy Archives of British Columbia

WAGON FREIGHTING ON THE CARIBOO ROAD, 1870

BRITISH COLUMBIA AND VANCOUVER ISLAND (1862)
From William C. Hazlitt, *The Great Gold Fields*

British efforts to establish communication with these regions from Victoria failed. The ports of Victoria and Hope, on the Fraser River, were about 500 miles away from the Kootenai mines; whereas Lewiston, Idaho, was only 342 miles and Walla Walla 408 miles from Kootenai. Practically all trade with these mines therefore was tied in with the American Inland Empire packing, freighting, and steamship trade.[66]

Although not so inaccessible as the Cariboo district, the mining camps of the Inland Empire were faced with serious transportation problems. Great distances separated them from St. Louis, Salt Lake City, Portland, San Francisco, and other depots from which supplies might come. The Missouri, Snake, and Columbia river systems, to be sure, provided ready-made routes of travel for the miners and settlers, but in too many instances the mining camps were not within easy reach of the navigable parts of these great waterways, and other forms of transportation had to be improvised.

Fortunately for Montana, the completion of the Mullan Road (the subject of the ensuing chapter), and the opening of the upper Missouri River to steamboat traffic as far as Fort Benton unwittingly came in time to provide the Montana camps with much needed avenues of commerce. Wagon roads were later constructed, and the relatively dry, open country of the Inland Empire provided very satisfactory conditions for packers whose experiences in California and the Cariboo country had been much more hazardous.

The Colville gold rush of 1855–1856 sounded the advance of fortune seekers into the Inland Empire, but since these particular diggings were within easy reach of the Columbia River, the miners experienced relatively little difficulty in securing supplies during the brief time that circumstances permitted them to remain there. It was in Montana and Idaho that the packing business in this interior part of the Oregon country experienced its greatest growth. Before wagon freight lines could be organized to operate between Fort Benton and Virginia City and other Montana camps, pack animals were put into use. Since the western end of the Mullan Road did not prove very suitable for wagon traffic, the muleteers very early established a thriving business carrying supplies over long stretches of the 624 miles of winding, mountainous, and wooded course that by 1860 Captain John Mullan had blazed between Walla Walla and Fort Benton in an effort to connect the Missouri and the Columbia river systems.[67]

---

[66] Trimble, *op. cit.*, pp. 58, 126–27.

[67] Captain John Mullan, U.S.A., "Report on the Construction of a Military Road from Fort Walla-Walla to Fort Benton," *Senate Documents*, 37 Cong., 3 sess., doc. 43. Hereafter cited as Mullan, "Report."

References to this Montana packing trade are numerous. For example, in the *Journals* of Granville Stuart, for May 5, 1863, appears this notation:[68]

Two pack trains arrived from Walla Walla. Bought from them the following:

52	lbs.	Tobacco	@	$4.00	$208.00
168	lbs.	Bacon	@	.40	67.20
241	lbs.	Sugar	@	.60	144.60
17½	lbs.	Soap	@	.50	8.75

$428.55

These Inland Empire pack trains varied in size but most frequently there were about twenty animals in a train.[69] The arrival and departure of such trains was usually referred to in the local press in much the following manner: "LARGE TRAIN.—A large pack train of forty-four animals, belonging to Messrs. B. F. Flathers and L. A. Choate, arrived in town on Saturday evening, loaded with goods for different merchants in the city." The account goes on to say that the train had left Wallula October 23, and had traveled every day. "From Cabinet Landing to Helena they were much troubled by snow, the roads being very bad. The freight charged from Wallula was thirty cents per pound."[70]

In a memorial to Congress sent by the Washington territorial legislature one reads that from January 1 to November 15, 1866, no less than "6,000 mules have left Walla Walla and the Columbia river loaded with freight for Montana," which gives some indication as to the volume of the packing business over this particular route.[71] And similarly, the *Montana Post* estimated in 1866 that from 8,000 to 10,000 pack animals would be operating in the Montana freight trade during the season which was then beginning.[72] The *Helena* (Montana) *Weekly Herald*, December 12, 1867, relates, however, that the employment of steamships on Pend d'Oreille Lake and on Clark's Fork from Thompson Falls to the town of Pend d'Oreille at the southern point of the lake bearing this name had slashed five days of the worst travel from the Mullan route and thus forced the pack animal in part to give way to water-borne means of transportation.[73]

We thus early in the season experienced the benefit of having a communication with the outside; by means of which we can receive goods from one to two months

[68] *Journals of Granville Stuart*, I, 239.

[69] Hiram T. French, *History of Idaho* (Chicago, New York, 1914), I, 404.

[70] *Helena* (Montana) *Weekly Herald*, December 5, 1867.

[71] Henry L. Talkington, "Mullan Road," *The Washington Historical Quarterly*, VII (October 1916), 306; Helen F. Sanders, *A History of Montana* (Chicago, 1913), I, 281.

[72] *Montana Post*, March 17, 1866.

[73] *Helena Weekly Herald*, December 12, 1867.

in advance of the river route, and though the present rates of freight from Oregon here are about three times as great as from St. Louis, yet the price of many descriptions of goods will be materially cheapened by the arrival of these trains, even at freight ranging from 20 to 25 cents in gold, and the difference in prices caused thereby will be for the benefit of the people. As the season advances freight by pack trains will be reduced, but we are of the opinion that except early in the season, when our market is nearly bare of everything it will not pay to ship goods from Oregon here, and that in ordinary seasons it will be impossible to compete with goods from the States shipped by river. We notice the arrival of between one and two hundred animals thus far, loaded with dry goods, clothing, groceries, etc., and other trains will soon be in, amply supplying our market with the goods which are scarce, and which have been commanding an unusually high price. We can now look for a gradual descending scale of prices in such articles till the arrival of large stocks from below when the level will be reached.[74]

Throughout the gold rush period Portland remained the leading supply depot in Oregon for the entire Inland Empire. Goods were usually carried by steamship to upriver landings and from there were transshipped to all points inland by means of pack trains and wagon freight. There is little evidence of many pack animals being used between Portland and the upriver landings although a pack trail was prepared during 1862–1863 under the direction of such leading Portland citizens as A. C. R. Shaw and L. Quimby.[75] Still others in the Willamette Valley urged the use of a trail from Eugene City to The Dalles by way of McKenzie Pass. Supporters of this route contended that packers could cover it in eight days, whereas it would take at least ten days to drive a pack of mules from Portland to The Dalles.[76] Several droves of cattle are known to have been driven to the Boise Valley over the McKenzie Pass route.[77]

With the exception of these sporadic efforts to use the Willamette Valley as a place of departure for Inland Empire diggings, it was really such prominent river towns and landings as Umatilla, Wallula, Walla Walla, and The Dalles that became early day gateways to the Idaho and Montana mines. John Hailey, a pioneer Idaho transportation man and local historian, relates how in the early spring of 1863 when the Boise Basin mines "started in earnest," not only miners and packers, but merchants, ranchers, sportsmen, lawyers, and even preachers were assembled at Umatilla awaiting such improvements in the weather as would permit their proceeding to the interior. At Wallula, twenty-two miles up the river, the situation was similar. "Some brought saddle horses and a few pack animals," wrote Hailey, "but the majority were without animals. . . . ." Frequently a few of the prospectors would club together

[74] *Montana Post*, May 2, 1868.   [75] *Ibid.*

[76] H. H. Bancroft, *Scraps: Oregon Miscellany*, Bancroft Library, II, 409.

[77] *Ibid.; Idaho World*, May 27, 1864.

and purchase a pack animal as a way of transporting their equipment to the Basin. Often, too, the owner of a number of animals would provide individuals with a horse and saddle in order that they might ride to their destination. "This kind of traveling," says Hailey, "came under the name of 'saddle trains.'" Fifty dollars was the fare charged from Umatilla to Boise.[78]

In addition to the transportation of arrivals there grew up the regular freighting business—the packing of freight from Columbia River points to a population which in Boise alone has been estimated at from 15,000 to 20,000 people[79] in 1863. At first everything had to be packed into the Boise Basin, except for a small quantity hauled in from Salt Lake City. It took hundreds of pack animals to handle this work, for in addition to taking care of immediate needs it was necessary for the merchants and miners to store up supplies for the winter months when travel virtually ceased. "Packing was quite a good business," relates the veteran Hailey, "freight ranging from sixteen to twenty-five cents per pound." In 1863–1864 Idaho City, Centreville (or Centerville), Placerville, Pioneer City, and Granite Creek were among the other places served by the packers.[80]

Keeping the animals alive during the winter months was not as difficult in Idaho as it was in the Cariboo region, but it was costly. A kind of swamp grass, cut from the bottoms during the summer, was used for hay. Grain had to be imported from Oregon and cost forty to fifty cents per pound. Hay, too, sold by the pound and brought twenty-five to forty cents per pound.[81] Hailey relates that on one occasion he and another person arrived in Idaho City in December 1863, on two saddle mules. They left their animals at a feed yard while the men ate their meal at a restaurant. In an hour the men returned to the feed barn where they were presented with a bill amounting to $13.60. The stable man said he had fed the two mules thirty-four pounds of hay at forty cents per pound.[82]

Equally enlightening are the reminiscences of James W. Watt, in later years a resident of Cheney, Washington, whose gold-seeking exploits took him into Oro Fino mining camps in July 1861. Watt first attests to the lively character of Oro Fino at the time of his arrival, and estimates that 12,000 people were then in that district. Hard-working miners were making $20 to $60 per day, whereas $6 to $10 were regarded as very poor returns. Then in October 1861, there occurred an important rush to Florence, about eighty-five miles from Oro Fino, and it is in connec-

[78] John Hailey, *The History of Idaho* (Boise, 1910), pp. 61–62.

[79] *Ibid.*, p. 62; Bird, *Boise*, p. 107. Based on Report of Mining Commission, 1867.

[80] Hailey, *op. cit.*, pp. 62–63.   [81] *Ibid.*   [82] *Ibid.*, pp. 63–64.

tion with Florence that Watt discusses the transportation problem. At once, when news of the Florence strike came, a string of no less than eighty-five mules was outfitted at Lewiston and set out for Florence, whereas a second one of thirty-five animals headed for the new diggings from Oro Fino. Watt accompanied the latter train and he relates that six days were involved in covering the eighty-five-mile stretch. Over two hundred people arrived ahead of the Oro Fino train and, hastened by unexpected early snow, were already experiencing privations. Flour sold quickly at $100 to $125 per hundred, and other goods brought proportionate returns.[83]

The winter of 1861–1862 was very cold in the Inland Empire and much livestock perished for want of fodder and water. This made the Idaho people even more dependent upon outside food supplies and thereby greatly complicated the transportation problems. In 1862 Lewiston was added to the list of important river points then reached by steamer and from which goods were packed in to mining camps, but Umatilla and Walla Walla were the more important transshipment points. It was over these trails that Watt developed his packing business which lasted about ten years. The distance from Umatilla to Boise he placed at around three hundred miles and states that at the very first freight rates ranged from forty to eighty cents per pound. Other interesting information about this pioneer form of transportation is best told in Watt's own words which follow:

> On these packing trips we seldom carried food for the mules that were employed in packing, but depended upon the grass produced by the regions through which we passed. This native forage usually kept the animals in fine condition. The average pack mule sold for $250. A very good mule would bring $400.00. The wages of the packers varied from $100 to $125 a month, in addition to board. The train master would frequently receive as much as $150 a month. Gold dust was then the only legal tender used; . . . . Freight and wages were thus always paid in gold and as a result many of the pack trains carried quite an amount of gold dust and they were frequently held up and robbed by road agents.[84]

Watt confirms other contemporaries in the statement that mules were most widely and most profitably used, but he does add that cayuses, or Indian horses, were employed in the Boise trade. On one occasion the Indians stampeded a cayuse train in which four hundred to five hundred horses were involved.[85] There were occasions, recalls this interesting pioneer, when in place of transshipping goods from one train to a boat and back again to pack trains the loaded animals would be transported by steamer along navigable stretches of the rivers. Such was the case,

[83] Watt, "Experiences of a Packer," *op. cit.*, XIX (July 1928), 206–11.

[84] *Ibid., op. cit.*, XIX (October 1928), 286.   [85] *Ibid.*, pp. 286–87.

for example, along the Mullan Road after the *Mary Moody* was launched on Lake Pend d'Oreille. This boat could accommodate sixty mules and their packs.[86]

The routes for wagon travel between the main towns were well marked but those leading off to the various bars could scarcely deserve to be designated as roads, "principally," says Watt, because "there weren't any; leastwise a tenderfoot would have gotten lost a dozen times a day just trying to follow some of them. We penetrated into the most remote and inaccessible places; over all kinds of country and in all kinds of weather conditions."[87]

Pack trains likewise reached Idaho directly from the Sacramento Valley but the greatest volume of freight, largely because of passable routes from California, was carried by means of freight wagons.[88]

Packing rates varied not only in accordance with distance, but from year to year. Rates were determined in part by the competition offered by St. Louis river-shipping concerns and with the wagon freighters from California and Oregon. In 1865, for example, the steamer freight rate from St. Louis to Fort Benton was from fifteen to twenty cents per pound with an additional charge of five cents to freight goods from this river port to the Montana mining towns. Portland to Montana pack train rates were in that year about fifteen cents per pound, whereas those between San Francisco and Montana were fifteen to twenty cents per pound.[89] In places where the packers encountered direct competition with wagon freight, the former were obliged to reduce their rates still more, as for example over the Columbia River–Boise route where transportation charges were reduced to about six and eight cents per pound.[90]

An interesting but relatively unimportant aspect of the packing business in the Pacific Northwest was the use of camels. These animals had been brought into the Southwest by the United States Army during the middle of the nineteenth century, very largely at the instigation of Secretary of War Jefferson Davis, with the belief that they could be used on the American deserts of southern California, Arizona, and New Mexico very much as they had been used traditionally in Africa, Asia, and other parts of the world, as valuable and efficient pack animals. On March 3, 1855, Congress appropriated $30,000 for the purchase of camels, and on May 14, 1856, the first shipment of thirty-four of these hunchbacked animals arrived at Indianola, Texas, after a stormy three-month voyage from North Africa. Naval Lieutenant Edward Fitzgerald Beale, Superin-

[86] Watt, "Experiences of a Packer," *op. cit.*, XX (January 1929), 36–37.

[87] *Ibid.*, p. 51.   [88] *Chico Weekly Courant*, April 28, 1866.

[89] H. H. Bancroft, *Scraps: Montana Miscellany*, Bancroft Library, pp. 93–94.

[90] French, *History of Idaho*, I, 406.

tendent of Indian Affairs in California and Nevada, and one of the staunch camel advocates, declared one camel worth four good mules ; and so well were these first arrivals thought of that an additional forty-four were brought to the United States the following year.[91] During the fall of 1857 the War Department, then headed by John B. Floyd, ordered a survey of a wagon road from Fort Defiance, New Mexico, to the Colorado River. Appointed to head this road-finding expedition was Lieutenant Beale, at whose disposal a detachment of the camels was now put. The Beale expedition made its way west and even went as far as Los Angeles where on January 8, 1858, the *Los Angeles Star* commented upon the presence of fourteen "huge ungainly awkward but docile animals" that had given their streets an "Oriental aspect."[92] Beale made further use of the animals, but when his survey work was finished a herd of twenty-eight camels was turned over to the quartermaster in California.[93]

The Army's experience with camels aroused private interests and in 1859 there had been formed the California and Utah Camel Association which imported an additional herd from Asia with less favorable results. After an unsuccessful effort to sell the camels at auction at a minimum price of $1,200, they were sold separately. Some ultimately found their way into Nevada for use in the mines, others to Arizona, while a few escaped into the desert.

At the instigation of Joseph Trutch, associated with the building of the Cariboo Wagon Road, twenty-two camels were purchased at San Francisco and in 1862 were shipped north to Victoria, B.C., and eventually were placed in service between Douglas and Lillooet where, according to Lewis Lesley, the authority on this subject, "For over a year the camels were thus employed, but with the usual confusion—horses and mules were frightened, and frequent accidents ensued. The train was finally disbanded, and the camels were soon wandering through the region."[94] Private operators had made one grievous mistake, namely, they had employed old-fashioned Western "mule skinners," rather than skilled Arabs, as camel drivers, and apparently there was a decided difference in their respective techniques. As one writer reflects, "the dislike between the camels and their new drivers was immediate and mutual," and

[91] Lewis Burt Lesley, ed., *Uncle Sam's Camels: The Journal of May Humphreys Stacey, Supplemented by the Report of Edward Fitzgerald Beale (1857–1858)* (Cambridge, 1929), pp. 3–11. See also Joseph W. Fabens, *The Uses of the Camel: Considered with a View to His Introduction into Our Western States and Territories* (New York, 1865), pp. 25–32; J. Marvin Hunter, *Old Camp Verde: The Home of the Camels* (Bandera, Texas, 1936). See also "Prospectus of the Overland Camel Company," Robert S. Ellison Collection, Indiana University Library.

[92] Lesley, *op. cit.*, p. 121.

[93] *Ibid.*, p. 124.

[94] *Ibid.*, pp. 124–29.

when put to it the "mild, slow moving camels, aroused by ill treatment, could kick and bite to surpass the most ornery army mule."[95]

What finally became of all the camels once employed in the Cariboo country is not clear. A few of them were subsequently employed on the Fort Hope–upper Columbia River trail but there, too, the experiment failed. The story is told that a French Canadian named Gill Brehaut bought one of the camels and continued to use it for a while and then turned it loose on the Kootenai River. In 1870 this sole survivor in the upper Columbia was with permission killed by a quarter-breed Indian and eaten. Unlike others who tried to eat camel meat, the quarter-breed declared it made tasty fried steaks.

Two camel trains also made trips over the Umatilla-Boise-Bannack City trail but here too they caused a freight outfit to stampede. Still another train of about six camels was used over the Mullan route, but it appears that one by one they disappeared. One was shot for a moose; still another drowned. There are those who even doubt that camels were used in the Montana trade, but repeated references to them in contemporary sources seem to verify their existence. In any event, their use was limited and they were never regarded as successful in the mining camps of the Pacific Northwest.[96]

The packing business as a whole was much more closely associated with the mining than with the agricultural frontier. Farmers settled near navigable streams and used them for the transportation of their crops, but the miners usually went to the mountainous and relatively inaccessible parts where diggings emerged. Hastily improvised methods of transportation were necessitated, and the old and familiar use of pack animals was instantly and successfully adopted in southern Oregon, in British Columbia, and in the Inland Empire.

Before stage lines were established, saddle trains were common in mining communities, some connecting with river steamboats. These "horseback passenger lines" provided horses or mules, furnished supplies and equipment for the trip, and allowed each passenger a small amount of personal luggage. Dagmar Mariager, a pioneer woman of the railroad era, says the trains were "comparatively safe, being well supplied with blankets and buffalo robes" for the comfort of the passengers.[97]

The appearance of bridges, ferries, and passable roads soon brought into competition with the muleteers the "bullwhackers" and "mule skin-

[95] William S. Lewis, "The Camel Pack Trains in the Mining Camps of the West," *The Washington Historical Quarterly*, XIX (October 1928), 275.

[96] *Ibid.*, pp. 278–84.

[97] Watt, "Experiences of a Packer," *op. cit.*, XIX (October 1928), 292; Dagmar Mariager, "Nomadic Experiences of a Frontierswoman," *The Overland Monthly*, Second Series, X (September 1887), 316–26.

ners"; and since wagons could haul bigger loads, make better time, and operate at a lower per unit cost, the wagon freighter was soon to replace the packer in such regions where the heavy vehicles could be employed.

However, without the rugged packers and their faithful animals, the exploitation of the fabulous resources from California to the Cariboo and the Inland Empire would have been impossible. To every gulch and digging, to every camp and placer where enterprising merchants catered to the miners and the necessary and questionable hangers-on, the essentials of life and a few comforts—at a price—were packed by the sure-footed mules. In all seasons, wherever footing could be found, pack trains pushed through. Even today in isolated regions of the West one may see a grizzled packer and his train of heavily burdened burros plodding across the desert or crashing down a trailless mountainside.

CHAPTER XIV

THE MULLAN ROAD

When in 1853 Isaac I. Stevens came west to assume the office of territorial governor of Washington, he brought with him no less than 243 officers and men, some of whom were scientists and artists. Stevens proposed to explore the northern Rockies, Cascades, and intervening mountain ranges in the hope that a practical northern railroad route to the Pacific might be found. One of the officers assisting with this survey was Lieutenant John Mullan. Upon arrival in the Oregon country Stevens left Lieutenant Mullan with thirteen men at Fort Owen, an outpost in the upper reaches of Clark's Fork and the Coeur d'Alene Mountains, in which general region he was to collect data on winter weather. Not since the Lewis and Clark Expedition had there been any formal or official exploration of that country, and so the young lieutenant made the most of his opportunities. During the winter he crossed and recrossed the Continental Divide six times and traveled an aggregate distance of 1,000 miles. And in addition to making personal observations, Mullan and his men learned much from the Indians and from the Catholic Fathers who were carrying on missionary work in that area.[1]

The purpose of the general survey was, as stated, to find a suitable railroad route, but it is clear that from the outset Lieutenant Mullan sensed the more immediate prospect of constructing over the mountains a wagon road which would join together the two great river basins of the Columbia and the Missouri. To Mullan the prospect of such a road was foremost in his mind even though a tangled network of mountains had thus far defied wagons to pass over them. Mullan's belief that a road could be cut through the mountains was greatly supported by information received from Gabrielle Prudhomme, a half-breed *voyageur* who had previously gone through that region with the missionary, Father Pierre Jean De Smet.[2] "From what I saw of Clarke's Fork and the neighboring country," wrote Mullan in his official report, "I concluded that a wagon route could be easily and ceonomically [*sic*] constructed from Hell's Gate Ronde to the east end of the lake . . . . . I concluded a construction at this point could only be made at a heavy outlay . . . . ."[3] Then in 1854 Lieutenant Mullan returned East only to find that Congress had appro-

---

[1] Mullan, "Report," *passim.*

[2] "Bradley Manuscript—Book II," *Contributions to the Historical Society of Montana*, VIII (1917), 162–63.

[3] Mullan, "Report," p. 5.

priated $30,000 for the survey of a military road to run between Fort Benton, the head of navigation on the Missouri, and Wallula (the site of Old Fort Walla Walla) on the Columbia River—a route very similar to what Mullan had in mind—and that he was asked to take charge of the work.[4]

It will be recalled that from Wallula emigrant roads leading over the Cascades to Puget Sound had already been built, and from this river point it was possible to sail down the Columbia River into many parts of the Oregon country. Thus the successful construction of this proposed road would enable emigrants, or other people for that matter, to go from St. Louis up the Missouri to Fort Benton and from there to travel directly overland into the Pacific Northwest.

Official negligence, Army red tape, sectional jealousies, and finally the "Mormon War" of 1857 all conspired to postpone operations, and it was March 1858, before the much-disappointed Army officer was permitted to begin his work. Even then came interruptions, for hardly had Mullan come to Oregon and assembled his crew when ominous news came that the Palouse Indians were on the warpath, that Lieutenant Colonel E. J. Steptoe had been defeated, and that these blood-hungry Indians were seeking to destroy Mullan and his men. "The news," to use Mullan's own words, "though much exaggerated, as is usual on the frontier, was such as to cause me to halt at this point till I could confer by letter with Colonel Steptoe." What he actually did was to make a nine-day march to Walla Walla with two messengers, three employees, and an Indian boy, there to join the forces of Colonel George Wright who with his United States regulars dealt a revengeful blow to the recalcitrant Palouse.[5]

Congress, meanwhile, showed a renewed interest and generosity with regard to the proposed road, and in March 1859, appropriated an additional $100,000 not only for the survey but also for the actual construction of the Fort Benton–Wallula road.[6] "This sum," reported the *Oregon Union* gleefully, "with an unexpended balance of some twenty thousand dollars . . . . will be ample to build an excellent road. . . . . This will open up a direct communication between the valley of the Mississippi and Oregon." Furthermore, the *Union* believed that the construction of such a road would bring about an "immense immigration pouring into the Flathead country from Minnesota, Missouri, Iowa, and other western States. We have a promising future before us."[7]

---

[4] *Pacific Christian Advocate*, April 23, 1859.

[5] Mullan, "Report," pp. 8–9; Pal Clark, ed., *Journal From Fort Dalles O. T. to Fort Wallah Wallah W. T. July 1858*, by Lieutenant John Mullan (Missoula, 1932), pp. 3–10.

[6] *Pacific Christian Advocate*, April 23, 1859.

[7] *Oregon Union*, May 7, 1859.

With the restoration of peace in the Palouse country, Mullan, who meanwhile had gone to Washington for new instructions, reorganized his construction gang and on June 4, 1859, is reported to have arrived at the mouth of the Palouse River with an escort of one hundred artillerymen and with the news that other workers were en route.[8] By June 27, so reads a report, Mullan's survey and grading work had reached the mouth of the Toukahnon River, the point chosen for crossing the Snake. It appears that Mullan did his work with more than the usual care exercised in pioneer road construction, although the forces of nature were quick to play havoc with it. Some bridges were built, places and distances were indicated on signposts, all of which were branded "M. R." (military road). Thus one would note signs such as these: "To Dry Creek, 9 miles"; "To Touchet, 21 miles"; "To Fort Taylor, Snake river, 50 miles." Interestingly enough, one such inscription may still be seen at Fourth of July Summit in Idaho at a place where United States Highway 10 follows the course of the old Mullan Road.[9] It reads: "M. R. Fourth of July 1861."

Week by week work on what was to be known as the Mullan Road progressed. "The general character of the country from Walla-Walla to the mouth of the Palouse," wrote Mullan, "is an easily rolling prairie; road excellent; camps good, with fine water and most abundant grass."[10] By October The Dalles *Journal* wrote:

We have advices from Lieut. Mullan, in charge of the Fort Benton Wagon Road Expedition, to the 12th ult. At that date he was camped twenty-six miles east of Coeur d'Alene Mission, and the work was being vigorously pushed forward.

The camp was about ten miles from the summit of the Bitter Root Mountain, and Lieut. Mullan writes that he hoped to reach the foot of the Mountains by the 18th of September. . . . .

An emigrant train is reported *en route*, and some of the settlers think of locating in the Bitter Root country, where it is said great inducements are offered for settlement.

Lieut. Mullan, notwithstanding the apprehension of others, is still confidant of reaching the Bitter Root country in time to winter.[11]

For a more complete account of the construction of this road one must turn to the Army engineer's own official report. In plain, direct statements he told of the problems and the progress associated with the work. Thus for July 14–15 he wrote:

Our route of this date skirts the lake from which Colonel Steptoe retreated the day of his noted defeat . . . . Leaving the Nedlwhuald, the road, for three miles,

---

[8] *Pacific Christian Advocate*, June 4, 1859.

[9] A roadside historic marker, as well as a marble statue of John Mullan, indicates where the inscription may be found.

[10] Mullan, "Report," pp. 12–13.   [11] Reprinted in *Oregonian*, October 8, 1859.

passes over gently swelling hills . . . . . After halting to improve the road, we journeyed on through an open prairie basin for seven miles to some wells, where, being provided with wood in our wagons, we made camp for the night. This portion of the route may be termed a natural wagon road, needing but very slight improvement.[12]

From where the road crossed the Snake, it followed a northeasterly course until on August 5, 1859, it reached the Coeur d'Alene Lake and from there it followed up the left bank of the river bearing the same name until Coeur d'Alene Mission was reached on August 16. Mullan constantly kept his eye on possible economic developments which his new road might bring. He commented on the "abundance of timber," the indications of gold, and on the presence of game. He spoke of the "fine tracts of land for settlement," about the "most excellent grazing," and mentioned mill sites on tributary streams.

It was at Coeur d'Alene Mission that the construction party encountered its first serious test in mountain road building, and about this Mullan wrote: "That this proved a difficult task to handle our three years' labor abundantly proves."[13]

From Mission Coeur d'Alene the road continued to follow the Coeur d'Alene River to Sohon Pass in the Bitterroot Mountain Divide. On the east side of the Divide the route entered the beautiful St. Regis Borgia River country, which in turn joined the Bitter Root River along which the road was to go until it reached scenic, if not spectacular, Hell Gate. From this point it entered the rugged country of the Hell Gate River Valley, wound its way southeastward until it reached the famous Deer Lodge Valley, thence northeast through the mountains along the Little Blackfoot River until it ascended the summit of the Great Rocky Mountain Divide. Finally it came into the vicinity of the Missouri, and at this junction the road followed the west side of this river until Fort Benton was finally reached after a distance of 624 miles.[14] In general, Mullan followed the course of an old and familiar Indian trail, but this does not detract from the fact that he was able to mark out a course over which hundreds of white men were later to pass.[15] The construction of the road had involved the cutting of a swath through heavy virgin timber 120 miles in length and 25 feet in breadth, 30 miles of excavation of from 15 to 20 feet in width, the building of hundreds of bridges and many ferry-

---

[12] Mullan, "Report," pp. 14–15.

[13] *Ibid.*, p. 17.

[14] "War Department Map of Military Road From Fort Walla Walla on the Columbia to Fort Benton on the Missouri Made under Direction of Topl. Bureau by Captain John Mullan, U.S. Army," Senate Documents, 37 Cong., 3 sess., doc. 43, n. p.

[15] T. C. Elliott, "The Mullan Road: Its Local History and Significance," *The Washington Historical Quarterly*, XIV, (July 1923), 207.

boats, and then further construction of open prairie road until a total length of 624 miles was reached.[16]

It will be possible here to recount only an occasional detail relative to the construction of this road. The party reached the St. Regis Borgia Valley on December 4, 1859, where camp was made. Here winter in all its fury overtook the men. Lieutenant Mullan wrote that he had pushed his stock "to the last point of endurance, dreading to be caught in a mountain gorge to battle out the winter, or to contend with the high water of the coming spring."[17] Enfeebled as were the cattle, it was found necessary, since no pasturage existed there, to drive them another hundred miles ahead over slippery and difficult mountain trails. Great losses were incurred. "I took the precaution," said Mullan, "to have the beef cattle driven to camp and slaughtered and the beef frozen, in which condition it kept until the month of March."[18]

This winter and others were spent gauging snowfalls, surveying, building boats and ferries. Since no animals were available, all packing had to be done by men. During this first winter of 1859–1860 the men built six bateaux and one large flatboat. One man was dispatched to Washington, D.C., to ask for additional men and supplies, and during the following spring 300 recruits were sent to Mullan directly from St. Louis. Supplies were brought in from Fort Benton, but not without the help of friendly Flathead Indians who furnished men and horses for the task. "Such nobleness of character as is found among some of the Flatheads is seldom seen among Indians," reflected Mullan. Communication was also established between Mullan and Salt Lake City by his expressman Ned Williamson who though "caught in the mountains by deep snows, ... lost his horses, made snowshoes from his saddle rigging, and, though snow-blind for several days, made the greater portion of the five hundred miles on foot . . . . ." He succeeded in reaching Camp Floyd and returning within fifty days.

The work during the spring of 1860 was hazardous and strenuous. For six weeks 150 men were employed cutting a six-mile stretch through mountains in the vicinity of present Missoula. By June 28, however, the work to Hell Gate was completed, and when making his report in 1863 Mullan said: "The 90 miles from the Bitter Root ferry to the Hell's Gate ronde affords a good road, with camp grounds at convenient points, with an abundance of wood, water, and grass. Many beautifully situated agricultural tracts are found through this region." On July 1 they reached Blackfoot River, and from there regular communication with Fort Ben-

---

[16] "Bradley Manuscript—Book II," p. 168.   [17] Mullan, "Report," p. 18.

[18] *Ibid.*, pp. 18–19. See also "Military Road From Fort Benton to Fort Walla-Walla, *House Executive Documents*, 36 Cong., 2 sess., doc. 44.

ton was established. On July 22 work on the Medicine Rock section was completed—"by far the most difficult of any point along the entire line, from Hell's Gate to Fort Benton . . . . ."—and on July 28 they reached Sun River where work ceased, for as Mullan said, "the remaining distance of fifty-five miles to Fort Benton was over an easy and almost level prairie road, with no running streams."[19] Thus on August 5, 1860, the job, so at least it appeared to Lieutenant Mullan at the time, was done, and he and a contingent of his men retraced their steps to Walla Walla 624 miles away. And scarcely had these road makers left Fort Benton on the Missouri when Major Blake initiated the new route by dispatching troops over it, a feat which was accomplished in fifty-seven days.

It must be remembered here that what passed for a road in those early days would scarcely be graced with the name today. What Lieutenant Mullan had in reality done was to provide a route over which it might be possible to convey vehicles during the dry seasons of the year. But even this proved questionable since the builder had not reckoned the full damage which can be inflicted by the heavy spring rains of that region. It was found necessary for Mullan to remain in the field until May 23, 1862, during which time improvements on the road were constantly made. At that time the road which by then was generally known as the Mullan Road represented seven years of effort on the part of its maker, less time for scores of other men, and a total expenditure of $230,000. The Mullan Road was ostensibly designed for military purposes, but it was hoped by those who originally petitioned Congress for it that immigrants might make extensive use of it. Mullan personally anticipated this and made provision for supplies for the immigrants and left memoranda at given places along the route regarding suitable camp sites.[20]

The Mullan Road was, as stated, first thought of as a military road connecting the Missouri and Columbia rivers. By the time of its completion in 1862 the military urgency of the road was greatly diminished in view of what appeared to be a marked quiescent state among the Oregon Indians. More important, therefore, from the point of view of meeting immediate needs, was that Montana, already enjoying a fur trade, was on the verge of what was destined to be a great and historic gold rush. And in no small measure the eastern portion of the Mullan Road was to play a very significant role in the early history of Montana, first as an important route of commerce, and second as an avenue for immigration.

In 1822 there was organized the western department of the Ameri-

---

[19] *Ibid.*, pp. 20-26. For early construction work see *House Executive Documents*, 36 Cong., 2 sess., vol. VIII, no. 44.

[20] Mullan, "Report," pp. 33, 36.

can Fur Company with headquarters in St. Louis. Immediately this concern began penetrating the upper reaches of the Missouri River and it was not long before the American Fur Company built several posts in Montana, namely, Fort Union, near the mouth of the Yellowstone, Forts Piegan and McKenzie on the Marias, Fort Cass near the mouth of the Big Horn, and, among others, the previously referred to Fort Benton which was located not far below the Great Falls and as such was destined to become the head of steam navigation on the Missouri River. Near Thompson Falls and on the banks of Flathead Lake the rival Hudson's Bay Company had its two only posts in Montana, but out from Fort Colvile in what is now northeastern Washington came many traders who penetrated into the Montana country.[21]

In addition to the fur traders there were the missionaries, but not until the general rush of population to California and the coming of Governor Isaac Stevens and his party to this country in 1853 in search for a railroad route to the Pacific did the Montana region attract the attention of people who might wish to settle permanently there. Among the first to settle were retired mountain men, and these appear to have gone into the little valleys of the Bitter Root Mountains which now separate Montana from Idaho. Mullan made reference to such people as being there when his road was being built. Added to these was Major John Owen who as early as 1850 came as a sutler and had purchased the St. Mary's Mission in the Bitter Root country, and developed a trade that embraced the whole area spanned by the future Mullan Road. Then, finally, between 1857–1865 came what gave Montana its first great impetus and what on May 26, 1864, made her a separate territory—the development of gold diggings.

These were the factors which gave importance to the Mullan Road. Steamers had for a long time plied the waters of the Missouri, but never before 1859 had such vessels ascended this great stream from its mouth to near the Great Falls. But on November 1, 1859, Charles P. Chouteau wrote to Secretary of War John B. Floyd:

I have the honor to submit the following report of my journey by steamboat from St. Louis to Fort Benton on the Upper Missouri. I left St. Louis on the 28th of May last, taking two boats, the "Spread Eagle" of 550 tons measurement, and the "Chippewa" a stern wheeler, 165 feet long, 30 feet beam and 350 tons capacity.

Leaving the first of his ships at Fort Pierre, Chouteau moved on up the river to Fort Union where he recorded in his log:

By my present experience I have arrived at the conclusion that with suitable boats and the removal of boulders here and there obstructing the channel and form-

---

[21] Albright, "The Relations of Montana with the Federal Government, 1864–1889," pp. 26–27.

ing the rapids, that the navigation of the Upper Missouri can be made just as safe and easy and [*sic*] the Upper Mississippi or Ohio rivers, and I have no hesitation in affirming that the trip from Saint Louis to Fort Benton can be easily accomplished within thirty-five days.[22]

That this feat was practical is demonstrated by subsequent arrivals of steamboats at Fort Benton, the number of which coincided with the rush of population to western Montana and the completion of the Mullan Road. Up until 1864 no more than four steamers arrived in any one season, but in 1865 eight came; in 1866, thirty-one; in 1867, thirty-nine; in 1868, thirty-five; in 1869, twenty-four; etc.[23] Hiram Chittenden adds, furthermore, that as many as seven steamers could be seen loading and unloading cargoes at one time.[24]

The opening of this Missouri River freighter service at a time coinciding with the completion of the Mullan Road was not accomplished without having far-reaching effect. Not only was there opened up an entirely new transcontinental line of communication via Montana, but there emerged immediately a keen awareness of competition between St. Louis, Missouri, and Portland, Oregon, for the Montana trade. To put it another way, there was competition between steamboat transportation and mule packing, for it must be emphasized here that very few wagons ever passed over the Mullan Road. Nearly all freight transported over this route was carried on the backs of mules. At first there was a ratio of fifteen to thirteen cents per pound on rates over the two routes, with Portland offering the lower figure, but in later years St. Louis gained a very decided margin. Freight rates from Oregon to Montana, wrote the *Montana Post* in 1868, "are about three times as great as from St. Louis, yet the price of many descriptions of goods will be materially cheapened by the arrival of these trains, even at freight ranging from 20 to 25 cents in gold. . . . ."[25] Regardless of rates each region had certain necessities to offer Montana, for example, food from the West and merchandise and mining equipment from the East, and as a result a vigorous trade was maintained over both routes for several years. Salt Lake City and San Francisco were not unaware of the profits made in this Montana trade, and in time exerted much effort to share in it.

Traffic over the Mullan Road was frequently confined to the eastern section of it, and during the first year or two of the Montana gold rush this was particularly true. As early as 1861 the pioneer miner, Granville

[22] "Early Navigation of the Upper Missouri River," *Contributions to the Historical Society of Montana*, VII (1910), 253–56.

[23] "Steamboat Arrivals at Fort Benton, Montana, and Vicinity," *ibid.*, I (1876), 317–25.

[24] Hiram M. Chittenden, "The Ancient Town of Fort Benton in Montana," *Magazine of American History*, XXIV (December 1890), 422.

[25] *Montana Post*, May 2, 1868; Albright, *op. cit.*, p. 41.

Stuart, made many references in his diary to goods taken over the Mullan route to Hell Gate and vicinity. Note the following for July 11, 1861, and random notes thereafter:

> The American Fur Company's steamboat [*Chippewa*] burned and blew up at the mouth of Milk river. Cargo total loss, no lives lost. [Christopher P.] Higgins and [Frank L.] Worden of Hell Gate lost a big stock of goods . . . . the fire was caused by a deckhand who went down into the hold to steal some alcohol . . . . . The d—— fool had a lighted candle . . . . .
>
> September 7. . . . . Robert Pelky and party of three wagons arrived from the states en route to Bitter Root valley and passed here in the afternoon.
>
> September 9. . . . . Last night Jack Collins and Ned Williamson arrived from Hell Gate en route for Fort Benton with whiskey for Indian trade.
>
> October 14. . . . . Put handles in the picks and sharpened the shovels and got ready to dig on our mining ditch. These tools were brought up for us from Walla Walla by Worden and Higgin's pack train.

Then in 1862, writing in Deer Lodge Valley, Stuart again refers to the Montana–Walla Walla traffic.

> July 13. Many emigrants arriving some going back to the states and some adventurous spirits are going to Salmon river, others to Walla Walla. . . . .
>
> July 20. Worden and Higgins's wagon arrived from Fort Benton loaded with merchandise from their store at Hell Gate.[26]

Similar and repeated references appear for the year 1862, chief of which relate the coming of the Captain James Fisk immigrant party from St. Paul, Minnesota, and of how this officer was "inspecting Captain John Mullan's military wagon road from Fort Benton to Walla Walla." Then with the coming of thousands of immigrants to Montana in 1863 Stuart was quick to recognize the Mullan Road for what in the final analysis it was—a pack trail.[27]

The discovery of gold on the Little Blackfoot River and its tributaries in 1865 brought additional thousands to Montana, and to use the words of one of Montana's pioneers: "Nearly all of this restless, shifting crowd came over the Coeur d'Alene mountains by way of the Mullan road and through the old Hell Gate Ronde." During the whole of the summer and the fall of 1865, it was reported that the road was packed with men and beasts en route to the "new El Dorado."[28]

Evidence indicates that the western portion of the Mullan Road was never much used. More preferred was the Old Nez Percé Trail which began at Lewiston, crossed the Camas and Nez Percé prairies, and went on to the south fork of the Clearwater. Continuing eastward this trail reached the divide of the Clearwater and Salmon rivers, crossed the

---

[26] *Journals of Granville Stuart*, I, 181–89, 213–14.

[27] *Ibid.*, I, 224, 239.   [28] Sanders, *A History of Montana*, I, 280–81.

Magruder Mountains, crossed Nez Percè Pass, thence down the west fork of the Bitterroot River to Darby, Montana.[29]

As to the status of the Mullan Road with respect to commerce between the Columbia River region, on the one hand, and the Montana-Idaho area on the other, there is no more revealing document than a letter written by Philip Ritz, at one time a prominent figure in Washington Territory. The letter was addressed to and published in the *Walla Walla Statesman,* September 14, 1866, and reads in part:[30]

> Having just returned [to Walla Walla] from a tour to Montana, perhaps a few items in regard to the country and the different routes may be of interest to you.
>
> The route by the Mullan road is certainly one of the most beautiful, healthful and pleasant mountain roads on this coast to travel over at this season of the year. . . . .

It is, however, clear that no through wagon freight passed over this western end. It is Ritz's opinion that improvements should be made to provide for such traffic. If this had been done, says Ritz, "Walla Walla flour would have entirely driven the Salt Lake and St. Louis flour out of the market." Moreover, he argues that "hundreds of persons and small families would like to make a visit to the Atlantic States," and if the Mullan Road were open for vehicles then such persons could drive East in light wagons for a small amount of money.

That this western end of the Mullan Road could be made a practical wagon route is further emphasized by a California correspondent who in a letter published in a San Francisco paper, November 1866, wrote:

> Wagons have passed over the road the present season, and with little trouble, and the idea of its requiring an immense sum to make it a good, practical wagon road is fallacious in the extreme . . . . to make it a perfectly good road in low water, will not require a sum in excess of three thousand dollars . . . . would cost $18,000 to repair bridges.[31]

In a memorial to Congress for 1866, which asks that the road be repaired, one finds this important statistical account of the volume of business on this road:

> From January 1 to November 15, 1866, 1,500 head of horses have been purchased by individual miners at Walla Walla horse markets, 2,000 miners have outfitted at Walla Walla, 5,000 head of cattle were driven from Walla Walla to Montana, 6,000 mules have left Walla Walla and the Columbia river loaded with freight for Montana . . . . .[32]

---

[29] Based on the researches of R. G. Bailey and information kindly provided the author by C. S. Kingston.

[30] *Walla Walla Statesman*, September 14, 1866. This copy was made available to the author in manuscript form by C. S. Kingston.

[31] *Daily Alta California*, November 7, 1866. [32] Talkington, "Mullan Road," p. 306.

Toward the close of the 'sixties two things occurred which bring to a close this particular episode in Montana history. First, the gold rush had spent its force, with the result that those who remained in Montana turned to the business of raising their own food supplies and hence they became less dependent upon the outside world for such commodities. Second, the first transcontinental railroad was completed in 1869, and while this road did not pass directly through Montana it was not long before connections of different types and over varying routes were made with it. In any event, the emergence of community life elsewhere brought in other and better roads as well as the further expansion of steamship navigation in regions where use of the Mullan Road would be at least modified. But as T. C. Elliott has said: "There always has been, and still is a steady use of the Mullan Road. . . ."[33]

In retrospect the Mullan Road, nevertheless, was of great commercial and military importance to the early history of the Far West in general and of Montana in particular. To refer again to the memorial of the Washington Territory:

The opening of this road is of the greatest, most vital importance to the people of Washington, Idaho and that portion of Montana lying West of the Rocky Mountains. There is a constant stream of population flowing into the region of country lying along and adjacent to this so-called Mullan road. . . . . Mining towns are springing into existence in all parts of the newly settled region. Branch roads leading from this main trunk (Mullan road) to the different mining camps are being made by individual enterprises. . . . .[34]

For a time this remarkable road was even a challenge to the Oregon Trail, particularly in its early stages when thousands of men were rushing into the Montana gold fields.[35] Many easterners, and particularly those living in the north central area, regarded the Mullan Road, and not the Oregon Trail, as the most desirable route to the Montana diggings and the Pacific slope.[36]

In addition to its usefulness in the mineral advance of the Inland Empire, Mullan's achievement also served as a military road, the purpose for which it was originally intended. It brought the Army to Walla Walla only fifty-seven days out of Fort Benton, and during the Civil War it was regarded as having strategic importance.[37] When the war was over and the railroad came to the Pacific Northwest it followed very closely the original Stevens-Mullan survey.

---

[33] Elliott, "Mullan Road," p. 209.

[34] Talkington, *op. cit.*, p. 305.

[35] Samuel Flagg Bemis, "Captain John Mullan and the Engineers' Frontier," *Washington Historical Quarterly*, XIV (July 1923), 203.

[36] E. W. Carpenter, "A Glimpse of Montana," *The Overland Monthly*, II (April 1869), 383.

[37] Bemis, *op. cit.*, p. 204.

Finally, the Mullan Road, such as it was, must be thought of as a monument to Lieutenant John Mullan who at this early date first had the vision and the courage even to conceive, let alone build, a road through 624 miles of rugged wilderness, over the precipitous passes of the Coeur d'Alene Mountains, and finally over the Great Continental Divide. Today a broad paved highway (U.S. No. 10) winds its way along much of Mullan's original route, through beautiful and scenic Idaho and western Montana; and the existence of this road is in itself a monument and a tribute to the man who first mapped its course. Once in after years Mullan reflected how

Night after night I have laid out in the unbeaten forests, or on the pathless prairies with no bed but a few pine leaves (needles), with no pillow but my saddle, and in my imagination heard the whistle of the engine, the whirr of the machinery, the paddle of the steamboat wheels, as they plowed the waters of the sound. In my enthusiasm I saw the country thickly populated, thousands pouring over the borders to make homes in this far western land.

For John Mullan all these dreams came true.[38]

---

[38] Addison Howard, "Captain John Mullan," *Washington Historical Quarterly*, XXV (July 1934), 188.

CHAPTER XV

LONG HAULS TO THE HINTERLAND

In regions where something answering the description of roads appeared, pack trains were largely displaced by commercial wagon freighting, a form of transportation which had its Oregon beginnings (see chapter xi in the Willamette and Rogue River valleys. Wagon freighting (important as it was to the short-lived gold rush in southern Oregon) had its fullest development and longest life on the mining frontiers of British Columbia and the Inland Empire.

Attention is here directed to the upper Fraser River and Cariboo areas where in 1863 construction began on a wagon road between Yale (which succeeded Hope as the upper limit of river navigation on the Fraser) and Cariboo. By constructing such a road it was the aim of Governor James Douglas of British Columbia to secure, as he wrote, "the whole trade of the colony for Fraser's River" and defeat "all attempts at competition from Oregon."[1]

This thoroughfare became known as the Cariboo Wagon Road, and from the point of view of sheer daring and human ingenuity it was a signal achievement in frontier road making. From Yale the road wound through great mountain defiles to Lillooet, thence to Soda Creek, and finally to Barkerville in the heart of the Cariboo district. A charter was accordingly drawn up and work soon began at several points along the proposed route by a firm known as Oppenheimer, Moberly and Lewis. Plans, however, called for having the respective sections of the route put under simultaneous construction by several contractors. The story of the building of this road comes largely from the pen of Walter Moberly whose personal job it was to locate the road and supervise the general construction.

The difficulties were many, according to Moberly, who recounts how,

When we arrived at Yale a large number of men seeking employment on our work could not get beyond that point, as they were without money, food, clothing and boots, and as they had to walk from Yale to Lytton along the pack trail were obliged to make them advances of all those articles. I had already paid the fares of a large number of men from New Westminster to Yale, which cost me between $2,000 and $3,000.

The regular packers boycotted the road makers who threatened the muleteers' very existence, and, finally, it was necessary to employ Chi-

---

[1] Scholefield and Gosnell, *British Columbia*, I, 175; Begg, *British Columbia*, p. 336. Begg estimates that from 1858–1893 no less than $54,014,854 worth of gold was taken out of British Columbia, although the highest yearly earning per man was $1,222 in 1875.

nese (who worked "most industriously and faithfully") and Indians to pack supplies into the construction camps. Even the government failed in some of its financial obligations. In spite of these obstacles the road was completed into the center of Cariboo by the end of 1864, a distance of about four hundred miles,[2] at a cost of about $1,000,000.

The important places and landmarks along the road were 6-Mile Post, Suspension Bridge, Alexandria, Boston Bar, Lytton, Cook's Ferry, 93-Mile Post, Lillooet, Clinton, Soda Creek, Quesnelle, Cottonwood, and finally Barkerville. In addition to building the main wagon road to Cariboo, Moberly was also employed to locate a road from Fort Alexandria to Richfield. He recalled:

I constructed a temporary sleigh road from Fort Alexandria to Quesnelle mouth, and another from Cottonwood River to Richfield via Lightning Creek. I also located a line for a wagon road from Cottonwood River via Willow River as far as Richfield, and I supervised the construction of a branch road into the valley of the Horse Fly River, then known as "Captain Mitchell's Road." I also explored a line for a proposed branch wagon road into the valley of William's Lake.[3]

But of all these many roads, none was so vital or so famous as the main one leading to Cariboo. Over this road a motley procession was not long in coming: pack trains, men walking with packs on their backs, freight wagons, stagecoaches,[4] and, to the consternation of the public, camels, and what was known as Thompson's Patent Road Steamers used in the conveyance of freight.[5]

To meet what for that time was a very high cost of construction of this road, Governor Douglas placed a one-shilling toll on every fifty pounds of freight traveling over the road.[6] This tariff the freighters accepted without too much complaint and people generally were, says Howay,

loud in their expressions of surprise at the daring conception and skilful execution of the work. In the most dangerous and awe-inspiring section, from Yale to Spence's Bridge, it was sometimes supported by piling, sometimes by immense dry-work "fills," and sometimes by gigantic crib-work. Clinging closely to the course of the rivers, it was now at water level and now raised to giddy elevations.[7]

Beautiful and awe-inspiring as was the Fraser River scenery it can scarcely be said that people traveled over the Cariboo Road for personal enjoyment. For one thing the climate of Cariboo was, in the opinion of

[2] Walter Moberly, "History of Cariboo Wagon Road," *Art, Historical and Scientific Association*, Session 1907–08, pp. 25–39; Howay, *British Columbia*, pp. 139–41; Noel Robinson, *Blazing the Trail Through the Rockies* (n.p., n.d.), p. 41.

[3] Scholefield and Gosnell, *op. cit.*, p. 177; Robinson, *op cit.*, pp. 53–54.

[4] Scholefield and Gosnell, *op. cit.*, p. 141.

[5] *British Colonist*, March 12, 1871. The Thompson Road Steamers did not prove successful.

[6] Howay, *British Columbia*, p. 138.   [7] *Ibid.*, p. 141.

British Lieutenant H. S. Palmer, "anything but an enviable residence, owing to the rains and the steaming mists." He wrote that eleven months out of the year the country had a "gloomy, cheerless aspect."[8]

This same Britisher was, however, impressed by the "400 miles of excellent waggon-roads" which led from Yale to Cariboo, and pointed out how one could, in 1864, cover the entire stretch from New Westminster at the mouth of the Fraser to Cariboo in from six to seven days.[9]

E. O. S. Scholefield, at one time the British Columbia provincial librarian, says of this piece of pioneer road construction:

The building of the Yale-Cariboo wagon road was a magnificent engineering feat of which any community might justly be proud, but when it is remembered that this gigantic enterprise was undertaken by less than 12,000 settlers in a virgin wilderness, some idea is gained of the faith these men had in the future of their country.[10]

And in the opinion of B. A. McKelvie the Cariboo Road was "one of the greatest pieces of road-engineering on the continent. So well was the work done," says this writer, "that even to this day sections of it through the canyons may be travelled over in safety."[11]

With the completion of the Cariboo Road, wagon freighting became heavy and continued unabated over its full length until the coming of the Canadian Pacific Railroad.[12]

Similar developments occurred in the Inland Empire where, however, road building was left almost solely to private initiative. In an effort to connect the Boise Basin with the Sacramento Valley there was organized on February 6, 1864, the Idaho and California Wagon-Road Company with a capital of $50,000. Beginning at the Snake River Ferry near old Fort Boise, this concern proceeded to lay out a road southward to Ruby City (Owyhee district) through the Pit River Valley, Goose Lake, Malheur Valley, and finally coming out at Red Bluff, California.[13] By May 1 of the same year a passable route had been marked out and the first train of eighteen wagons left Scott Valley and Yreka, California, with goods consigned to Boise. Other wagon trains soon followed, although depredations from the notoriously hostile Pit River Indians resulted in heavy loss to this pioneer enterprise.

---

[8] H. S. Palmer, R.E., "The Geography of British Columbia and the Condition of the Cariboo Gold District," *Excerpt from Royal Geographical Society Proceedings* (1864), VIII, 89.

[9] *Ibid.*, p. 90.   [10] Scholefield and Gosnell, *op. cit.*, p. 177.

[11] B. A. McKelvie, *Early History of the Province of British Columbia* (Toronto, London, 1926), p. 94.

[12] *Ibid.;* General Joel Palmer, MSS, Bancroft Library, and Robert S. Ellison Collection, Indiana University Library.

[13] Frank T. Gilbert, *Historic Sketches of Walla Walla, Whitman, Columbia and Garfield Counties, Washington Territory* (Portland, 1882), p. 230.

It was not long before other California groups became interested in the Boise trade, and in 1865 a second road was marked out which connected the Sacramento and Boise valleys by cutting through the northern passes of the Sierra Nevada into Susanville (a distance of about one hundred miles), to Summit Lake, there turning northward past Buffalo Springs, White Horse Meadow, and on north to Boise Valley. Red Bluff likewise made use of this route,[14] as did also Chico and other northern Sacramento Valley communities interested in the Idaho trade. That goods were actually taken over this Chico route as early as 1865 is apparent from the following comment published in the *Idaho World*, August 26:

Mr. —— Hornback arrived here a few days ago from Chico with six teams, loaded with freight for Messrs. Miller & Berstiel. One wagon was loaded with 8,600 pounds of freight, another with 6,600, and four with 4,000. They came through from Chico in about ninety days, traveling about two hundred miles out of the straight road in order to avoid a portion of the road undergoing repairs. Mr. Hornback expects to make the return trip with empty wagons in three weeks. The road is reported by him to be a fine natural highway nearly the entire distance—the worst portion of it being that between Boise Oity [*sic*] and Idaho City.[15]

The distance between Chico and Ruby City, estimated by the *Chico Courant*, was 401 miles, and from Chico to Virginia City, Montana, 801 miles.[16]

Still a third practical route available to the Californians who sought to establish commercial contact with Idaho was to follow the old and familiar Sacramento–Fort Hall immigrant route. This latter route was, however, soon to be displaced as construction of the Central Pacific Railroad advanced eastward. By 1866 the Central Pacific had already reached Colfax, California, and from this terminus wagon freighters, having goods shipped by rail to that point, proceeded eastward through Truckee Pass and then either followed the Humboldt or went directly northward to connect with the Chico and Red Bluff route referred to above. As work on the Central Pacific Railroad proceeded eastward it naturally remained the practice of the freighters to have their goods brought as far as possible by rail, thus reducing the time involved in transporting their cargoes to Idaho. The following excerpt taken originally from the *Sacramento Union* illustrates how this plan worked:

On Monday ten 10-mule teams, belonging to W. Prichard and Charles Kaiser, left this city [Sacramento] for Colfax, for the purpose of loading at that point with freight for Silver City, Idaho. These teams will take out 75,000 pounds of freight and will take the Truckee river and Humboldt route. . . . .[17]

---

[14] Bancroft, *Washington, Idaho, and Montana*, pp. 425–26, 439–40.

[15] *The Idaho World*, August 26, 1865; *Chico Weekly Courant*, April 28, **1866.**

[16] *Chico Weekly Courant*, March 3, 1866.   [17] *Idaho Weekly Statesman*, May 13, 1866.

A letter dated March 28, 1866, and also published in the *Idaho States-man* further illustrates how freighters were making use of the Central Pacific Railroad then under construction:

About the 1st of April twenty-five loaded teams will start from the end of the railroad, bound for Ruby City with goods, and be followed by others hauling freight, now at Colfax waiting transportation. . . . .[18]

The *Idaho Statesman* even went so far as to predict that when the Central Pacific Railroad would reach Truckee there would be "no use for any other route to try to compete with it for the travel and trade between Idaho and California. . . . ."[19]

Freight rates between the Sacramento and Boise valleys appear to have ranged from eight to twelve and a half cents per pound,[20] and about thirty to forty days' time was involved in transit, although in 1866 John Mullan, who by then was operating a stagecoach line between Idaho and California, offered to cut drastically the time factor.[21]

It appears that Ruby City was very early regarded as the destination of most of the California freighters. From there goods were redistributed throughout the Owyhee mining district. From there, too, they were forwarded to Boise City, an important distributing point for the Central Idaho area.

This importation of goods from California did much to relieve the food shortage in Idaho which at times had been acute. Even so, during the unusually severe winter of 1864–1865—following the first season of the California trade—the shortage of food essentials was such as to cause serious privation as evidenced by the fact that in the more isolated Idaho settlements flour is said to have sold as high as $5 per pound and potatoes at 45 cents a pound. The resumption of wagon freighting in the spring very soon restored prices to a more reasonable figure.[22]

Meanwhile, Oregon freighting interests did not stand idly by. The Oregon-Idaho freighting business, unlike the California trade, was intricately combined with water transit concerns, and in particular the Oregon Steam Navigation Company. Just as the pack trains had previously served as connecting links between the intermittent river steamship routes, the laying out of passable wagon roads enabled the freight companies to take over this service. The realization of this prompted the Oregon Steam Navigation Company (about which more will be said later) to offer through-freight service of its own between Portland, Ore-

---

[18] *Idaho Weekly Statesman*, May 6, 1866.

[19] *Ibid.*, May 20, 1866.　　　[20] *The Idaho World*, August 26 and September 9, 1865.

[21] *Chico Weekly Courant*, May 12, 1866.

[22] Briggs, *Frontiers of the Northwest*, pp. 66–67.

gon, and Inland Empire points.[23] Goods to be shipped from the Willamette Valley and Puget Sound areas were not unlike those from California in that they consisted of the basic necessities of life. In fact, many of the commodities were California goods which had been sent by water to Portland and there transshipped to mining regions of the Inland Empire.[24]

In view of the steamship–pack train arrangement first established between Portland and the interior, it was not until 1867 that serious attention was given to new road building between these points. In June of that year a new and more level road connecting Oregon, Washington, and Idaho was built. This wagon road began at the old and familiar Columbia River landing at The Dalles, passed through Umatilla, and ended at Walla Walla. It meant a reduction of fifty-five miles over previous routes. At Walla Walla this road connected with an existing wagon route leading to Lapwai and Lewiston.

Connecting with The Dalles–Walla Walla Road was the old Oregon Trail which in places had been altered and improved, and it was now also used in the Oregon-Idaho trade.[25] Maps of the late 'sixties show no less than four wagon trails extending from the Columbia River through the Blue Mountains to the Boise Valley. As to which was the most practical route, a certain David C. Kelley of La Grande, in a letter published in the Portland *Oregonian*, leaves little doubt. The Meacham Road running from Umatilla to La Grande was, according to Kelley, "*the only road* that can be traveled over the Blue Mountains in the winter and spring with any certainty." Kelley further explains that the Meacham brothers expended "a large amount" to improve this road. In contrast with this Kelley explained that the Walla Walla Road running through the Blue Mountains was relatively impassable; in fact, wrote he: "two men . . . . were frozen to death in attempting to cross the mountains" on the latter route. ". . . . *these are the facts*," concludes Kelley; "and I make the statement in truth and not from any personal interests. . . . ."[26]

It was, of course, possible for wagons to proceed the entire distance from the Willamette Valley to Idaho by following the Barlow Road between Oregon City and The Dalles, but the relative cheapness of river freight service between these two points meant that the Barlow Road had ceased to be as popular as in earlier days when immigrant caravans found it so welcome.

The routes just described refer only to those leading into southern

---

[23] Bancroft, *Washington, Idaho, and Montana*, pp. 425–26; Gilbert, *Historic Sketches*, pp. 230–31.

[24] Bancroft, *op. cit.*, pp. 425–26, 439–40; *Oregonian*, December 5, 1866.

[25] *Oregonian*, June 12, 1867.   [26] *Ibid.*, January 17, 1865.

Idaho. To reach by wagon the northern mines at Fort Colvile and Kootenai, roads were laid out extending northward from Walla Walla or
Lewiston to Palouse City where the Columbia River was crossed by
ferry, and then on north for about another fifty miles at which point the
road forked. The left branch extended to Fort Colvile, the right one
wound onward in the direction of Lake Coeur d'Alene and Pend d'Oreille
into the Kootenai district.[27]

Wagon freighting over these various Oregon-Idaho routes was confined to the summer season,[28] the months of July, August, and September,
when the volume of freight was very heavy.

It is practically impossible to divorce Idaho freighting from that of
Montana. The mineral developments in the two regions were simultaneous, and even though separated by the Bitter Root Mountains, Idaho
and Montana were none the less bound together by many common lines
of communication with the outside world.

The Oregon-Montana freighters reached their destination by following the same roads used in the Idaho trade as far inland as Boise. From
Boise they followed the Oregon Trail, which connected with Fort Hall.
At this key point a road ran northward to serve Virginia City, Bannack
City, Deer Lodge, and numerous other Montana mining towns. The distance from the Umatilla landing to Virginia City, Montana, was estimated at from 850 to 900 miles.

Montana was also served by the Californians, and one important
avenue was that previously described which connected northern California with Boise. From Boise, Montana-bound Californians followed
the route via Fort Hall that was also taken by their Oregon competitors.

The distance between upper Sacramento River points and the Montana mining districts (eight hundred miles) was just twice as far as
between the former and the Boise Valley. But that there was wagon
freighting engaged in by Californians is well illustrated by the following

---

[27] The following, for example, is a table of distances between Lewiston and Kootenai published in the *Golden Age* and reprinted in the *Oregonian* April 16, 1864:

From Lewiston to	MILES
Palouse Crossing	40
Pine Creek	10
Lottow	7
Forks of Trail	2
Willow Prairie	5
Rock Creek	10
Antoine Plante's Ferry of Spokane	15
Soltesa's	6
Pend d'Oreille Slough	23
Pend d'Oreille Crossing	24
East to big bend of lake	15
Northeast, to Chelumta Crossing of Kootenai	50
A little East of North, along the divide between the waters of the Kootenai and a North Fork of the Columbia, to Elk Creek, about	120

[28] *Idaho Weekly Statesman*, April 29, 1866.

excerpt from the Virginia City (Nevada) *Enterprise,* reprinted in the Virginia City *Montana Post:*

There, yesterday, arrived in Carson City, a train of forty-five wagons, bound for Montana. The wagons are loaded with general merchandise—a little of everything except hardware, and a good deal of that, in the shape of whisky. This is the train that for three days past has been wallowing through the snow about the summit of the Sierras, and getting in the way of and delaying the coaches of the Pioneer stage line.[29]

This same issue of the *Montana Post* published another excerpt regarding the California trade, this one a reprint of the *Sacramento Union.* It stated that most of the Montana-bound freight from California was then (1866) traveling by way of the Truckee Pass and across the Humboldt Sink in the direction of Fort Hall. At the same time the newspaper had urged the drivers to wear veils as protection from the gnats which infest the region of the Sink.[30]

While the northern California towns were the ones most vitally interested in the Inland Empire trade, by 1866 San Francisco appears to have given it some special attention. Pointing out how much of the Montana gold was flowing eastward, San Francisco's *Alta California* urged its merchants "to go to a few hundred dollars expense" to open an all-year road to the Montana mines.[31] For the benefit of the local merchants, the San Francisco Chamber of Commerce in 1866 published the following information[32] which gives some index to the all-important question of freight routes of commerce in relation to freight rates:[33]

From San Francisco, by way of Owyhee and Snake river, to Helena, 1,190 miles, costs per ton... $345
From San Francisco by way of Portland and Snake river to Lewiston, thence by land to Helena, 1,338 miles, costs per ton................. 320
From San Francisco, by way of Portland to Wallula, thence by land to Helena, 1,283 miles costs per ton................................. 275
From San Francisco, by way way [*sic*] of Portland to White Bluffs, thence by land to Helena, 1,370 miles, costs per ton....................... 270

Similarly, a San Francisco Chamber of Commerce member, charged with the duty of studying the volume and flow of goods to the Montana mines, reported that no less than one hundred pack trains of about fifty animals each, and each carrying about three hundred pounds, making an aggregate of 750 tons, were sent from Columbia River points to the Montana mines in the 1865 season. This alone involved a freighting cost of $240,000 which places the total value of the goods laid down in Helena at about $1,440,000.

[29] *Montana Post,* May 12, 1866.   [30] *Ibid.,* May 12, 1866.
[31] *Daily Alta California,* February 5, 1866; *Chico Weekly Courant,* February 24, 1866.
[32] Gilbert, *Historic Sketches,* pp. 237–38.   [33] *Ibid.*

From the vital junction of Fort Hall a road extended southward, through Utah's famous freighting town of Corinne, to Salt Lake City. Here was the terminus of still another wagon road to Los Angeles by way of the San Bernardino Desert. To many the latter road was known as the Mormon Trail over which the well-remembered "Reese Train" of twenty-four wagons and more than eighty animals passed during the winter of 1853–1854. Among the first to cover the entire distance from Los Angeles to Montana was Remi Nadeau, whose corral opposite the present Pershing Square in Los Angeles is reported to have had sixty-five mule teams engaged in these freighting operations.[34] Other important roads led into Salt Lake City and Corinne, and it may be presumed that goods from other areas found their way by wagon freight into Montana.

From Fort Benton westward to Helena (a distance of 135 miles), and to the lower Montana mining camps (about two hundred miles), the Mullan Road was a satisfactory route for wagon travel and as such enabled the wagon freighters to participate in the St. Louis–upper Missouri River trade.[35] St. Louis steamboat companies engaging in the upper Missouri trade usually established wagon-freighting connections at Fort Benton to assure their Eastern and Midwestern customers safe delivery "to all points in the mines." The time involved in such a transaction was thirty-five to sixty days from St. Louis to Fort Benton by steamer (2,300 miles), then ten to fifteen days by wagon freight from the dock to the camps. The grasses around Fort Benton were good the year round, which proved a great boon to the bullwhackers to whom feed for the animals was a constant problem.[36] Helena, more than any other Montana city, was the beneficiary of this Missouri River trade. By 1866 many changes and improvements had been made on the road between that city and Fort Benton, and freight wagons were able to cover this distance in about one week. Helena, largely because of her relative nearness to Fort Benton, regarded herself as a distributing center for the northern Montana mines.[37] Handling of much of this freight was done by the Fort Benton and Montana Transportation Company, the Diamond "R" Transportation Company, E. G. Maclay & Company, and many others. Competition among the freighters was, to say the least, frantic.[38]

---

[34] Maurice H. and Marco R. Newmark, eds., *Sixty Years in Southern California, 1853–1913; Containing the Reminiscences of Harris Newmark* (Boston, 1930), pp. 187, 304; John S. McGroarty, *Los Angeles from the Mountains to the Sea* (Chicago, 1921), III, 518; James M. Guinn, *A History of California and an Extended History of Los Angeles and Environs* (Los Angeles, 1915), I, 215; William B. Rice, ed., "Early Freighting on the Salt Lake–San Bernardino Trail," *The Pacific Historical Review*, XI (March 1942), 73–75.

[35] *Montana Post*, February 3, 1866; *Oregonian*, May 10, 1866.

[36] [J. L.] *Campbell's Western Guide* (Chicago [1866]), pp. 8, 15, 74.

[37] *Montana Post*, February 3, 1866.   [38] *Ibid.*, April 29, 1865.

Distance, it has been shown, was no deterrent to enterprising traders in the East, in California, and in Oregon, who sought to exploit the early mining communities of the Inland Empire. Whether by steamboat, by pack train, or by wagon freight, ways and means were found to supply Montana and Idaho with the essentials of life. The costs involved were great but none the less profitable. St. Louis (the gateway to the Missouri), the upper Sacramento Valley towns, and Portland, Oregon, were the three great depots from which the bulk of goods at first converged upon the Inland Empire, and competition between these three places was at all times keen.

From the outset Portland took an aggressive lead in this competition, particularly for the Idaho trade. Out of Portland the powerful Oregon Steam Navigation Company had the advantage over the Missouri River shipping companies, at least so far as Idaho was concerned, in that it could usually operate twelve months of the year. The Missouri River concerns, on the other hand, were compelled to confine their trade to the spring and summer months. During this period St. Louis, however, was able to underbid its competitors, at least so far as the Montana trade was concerned. Even the *Oregonian* in 1865 admitted that the "goods now in the Montana market, have for the most part, been brought from St. Louis."[39] The Portland shippers, of course, encountered difficulties in moving goods by wagon during the winter months, but pack trains could be substituted for wagons so that goods could be transported except during the most inclement weather. The Californians, while enjoying a good, all-year travel season, encountered more obstacles from Indians than those shipping from other places.

Figures as to the volume of the Inland Empire trade are scarce, but it has been estimated, for example, that the amount of freight carried from Fort Benton to the Montana mining camps in 1866 alone amounted to 6,000 tons, was valued at $6,000,000, and that 3,000 teams and 20,000 oxen and mules were required to convey this amount of freight from the river landing to its destination.[40] The volume of goods shipped up the Missouri River to Montana increased steadily, and by 1868, judging from the following contemporary correspondent for the *Overland Monthly*, the St. Louis shippers appear to have frozen out their Pacific Coast competitors:

. . . . the trade of Montana with the Pacific coast, which was quite extensive three years ago, has now dwindled to insignificant proportions, and in place of the long trains of pack animals, loaded with clothing, saddlery, and merchandise of every

[39] *Oregonian*, December 28, 1865.
[40] Bancroft, *Washington, Idaho, and Montana*, pp. 729–30 n.

description, which once reached the [Montana] Territory from the "other side," there is now received almost nothing save a few sacks of flour and boxes of apples.[41]

This change may be attributed to "the very rapid and extraordinary" reduction of freight rates on the Missouri River, no doubt brought on by the entrance of the new Union Pacific Railroad into this competitive field.

The volume of the upper Missouri River freight was also increased by the completion in April 1868, of an unbroken railroad line from Chicago to Sioux City, Iowa, which offered Eastern shippers direct connections with Fort Benton bound Missouri River steamers at a point farther upstream than St. Louis. The volume of this freight to Montana was placed by the *Helena Weekly Herald* at $8,000,000 annually. Furthermore, says the *Herald:* ". . . . it is plain that Chicago has the inside track for this trade hereafter."[42] In any event, it was the opinion of the *Helena Herald* in 1868 that "five-sixths of the mining products of Montana reach the east by way of the Missouri river." As it turned out, 1868 was the peak year. In 1869 the river level fell drastically, and so too did shipping. Anyway, completion of the Union Pacific–Central Pacific Railroad made it most economical to ship goods by rail either from the East or the West Coast to Corinne, Utah, where transshipments to Montana were made by wagon freighters.[43]

And as for the California-Montana route, it was the opinion of the *Overland Monthly* correspondent that the Californians (charging as they did fifteen to twenty cents per pound for freight) would never be able to compete favorably with the Missouri River people unless the cargo be fruits, wines, or Oriental goods. He admitted, however, that during the season when the Missouri River was frozen the Pacific Coast region did have a definite advantage in disposing of blankets, saddlery, flour, and other goods produced in that part of the country.[44]

Then with completion of the Union and Central Pacific railroads in 1869 the Utah Saints achieved a new advantage in that goods from both the East and the West were shipped by rail either to the Utah capital, or to other convenient points in that area, for transshipment by wagon freight over the Corinne Road to Fort Hall and points in either Idaho or Montana. The following account of this trade has been left by a contemporary:

Both freight wagons and passenger stages were sent over the [Corinne] road. The former cumbrous outfits traveled only about twelve miles a day. . . . . They were

---

[41] Carpenter, "A Glimpse of Montana," p. 383.

[42] *Helena Weekly Herald*, May 28, 1868.

[43] *Ibid.*, March 12, 1868. For other ramifications of this subject, see Alton B. Oviatt, "Steamboat Traffic on the Upper Missouri River, 1859–1869," *Pacific Northwest Quarterly*, XL (April 1949), 93–105.   [44] Carpenter, *op. cit.*, pp. 383–84.

FREIGHT WAGON ON THE CARIBOO ROAD. TAVERN,
59 MILE HOUSE, IN BACKGROUND

OX-DRAWN FREIGHTER ON THE CARIBOO ROAD

Courtesy Donald Bates

SIMEON G. REED

Courtesy Donald Bates

JOHN C. AINSWORTH

Courtesy Donald Bates

R. R. THOMPSON

LEADERS IN COLUMBIA RIVER STEAMSHIP NAVIGATION

drawn by from four to six horses, that were changed every twelve or fifteen miles. They were usually accompanied by an armed messenger who rode beside the driver.[45]

In the case of Idaho, the volume of West Coast imports continued to increase. More and more California goods were being shipped by water to Portland, and from there they reached the Idaho region over the established routes. "Every steamer from San Francisco," wrote the *Oregonian* in 1866, "comes laden to her utmost capacity" with goods destined for Idaho.[46]

"These freighter wagons remained a familiar sight in Idaho until the coming of the auto truck," remarked a Boise historian. "Two or three wagons, joined together by very short tongues, were loaded high with provisions and supplies of all kinds and then covered with a large tarpaulin to keep out the fine alkali dust which seemed to penetrate every crevice."[47] These well-braked wagons were pulled by from four to fourteen horses, mules, or oxen with the driver either mounted on the lead horse or seated on the front wagon. If in the wagon seat, he drove by means of a single jerk line attached to the lead horse, an operation aided by a whip and a box of pebbles at the driver's side. The advantage in these enormous wagons and large teams was that fewer teamsters were required. Equipping a freighting concern was a major business enterprise.[48] Powerful mules cost $350 each and some of the finest brought $1,400 a span; the wagon cost from $900 to $1,100, harness $300 to $600. James M. Hutchings, a contemporary, declared that this type of wagon, which was used by immigrants and freighters alike, would average 25,000 pounds a trip. Because of their great carrying capacity they were known as "prairie schooners."

Those who stayed with the work became accomplished in the art, and fabulous tales have been told about the skill of teamsters at handling their animals, at dealing with smug stage drivers as they hurried past a freight train, at modifying the King's English, and most of all, at wielding the whip. Teamsters were not known for their modesty and often gave added support to stories which extolled a mule skinner's or bullwhacker's accomplishments. There was at least one general agreement among all of the class: one never admitted hauling less freight for the size of his wagon and the number of draft animals than any competitor.[49]

[45] Jennie Broughton Brown, *Fort Hall on the Oregon Trail* (Caldwell, Idaho, 1932), p. 354.

[46] *Oregonian*, December 5, 1866; Bancroft, *Washington, Idaho, and Montana*, pp. 425–26, 439–40.

[47] Bird, *Boise*, p. 105.

[48] *Ibid.*, pp. 105–6; James M. Hutchings, *In the Heart of the Sierras: The Yo Semite Valley Both Historical and Descriptive* . . . . (Oakland, 1888), p. 209.

[49] J. A. Filcher, *Untold Tales of California* (n.p., 1903), p. 122.

A teamster established a remarkable rapport with his animals. Toward nightfall, the simple command "gee" meant camp to the lead bull or ox team which at this sound swung around to the right in a circle forming a corral. A log chain extended from the hind wheel of each wagon to the fore wheel of the next, making a solid barrier, except for a wide gap through which the animals could be driven. The force required included the wagon master and assistant, the teamsters, someone to look after the extra animals, and two or three reserve men for emergencies, though there were few. The average salary was a dollar a day and expenses.[50] Skill had to be exercised to prevent the bulls from running for water before being unyoked, and harsh words were required to maintain control. During the night the animals were either turned out to graze or were fed and "bedded down," while the men took turns maintaining a sharp watch over the valuable cargo. At dawn the animals were run into camp and yoked or harnessed while the men gulped down strong coffee, heated by a fire of buffalo chips, and the prosaic bread and bacon. Little fuss was made over the noonday meal. While the teams rested, a wagon endgate might be lowered from which a bit of bread and more coffee were consumed.[51]

In his *Memoirs*, Alexander Majors, one of the great wagon freighters of the plains from 1848–1866, describes the organization of an overland train. About twenty-five large wagons, each drawn by six yokes or pairs, and containing upwards of three tons, made up an outfit. It was wise to drive twenty or thirty extra head in case of accident or lameness of some of the animals.

Oxen proved cheapest and most reliable for long trips where grass was the only feed.

At first, mules were used altogether for traveling, but they would either die or become useless from the bite of a rattlesnake, and the men would sometimes be sent ahead of the caravan with whips to frighten the snakes out of the pathway, but later on, the ox-teamsters, with their large whips, destroyed them so fast that they ceased to trouble them to any great extent.[52]

While little is known about volume of business in the Pacific Northwest, a few figures are recorded for freighting on the plains, some of which went to Montana and Idaho. In the spring of 1858 Russell, Majors and Waddell obtained a government contract to carry freight. Sixteen

[50] Prentiss Ingraham, ed., *Seventy Years on the Frontier: Alexander Majors' Memoirs of a Lifetime on the Border* (Chicago, 1893), p. 105. Hereafter cited as Majors, *Seventy Years*. See also Raymond W. Settle and Mary Lund Settle, *Empire on Wheels* (Stanford, California, 1949), chap. 4.

[51] William F. Hooker, *The Bullwhacker: Adventures of a Frontier Freighter* (New York, 1924), pp. 24–41.

[52] *Ibid.*, pp. 71–77, 103–5.

million pounds were transported that year. This company, which had previously owned 300 to 400 wagons and teams, at "topnotch" expanded to 6,250 wagons requiring 75,000 oxen and over 4,000 men and 1,000 mules.[53]

An idea of how ox-wagon freighting was conducted comes from Alexander Toponce:

We travelled in wagon trains with a wagon boss in charge and we were always instructed to camp on high ground. That meant that we had to carry all the water for the camp in kegs from the river up the hill to where we camped.[54]

Wagon freighting, wherever it was done, was hard, dirty, tedious, and dangerous business. It was work which tried men's patience and only the toughest of the tough ever made bullwhacking or mule skinning his life's work.

Over good roads and bad annually were freighted millions of tons of supplies representing more millions of dollars' investment. Connections were early made with water routes and later with the railroads. An immense part in the building of the West was played by the wagon freighter —the link between the pioneer era and the agricultural and mineral development spurred by the coming of the Iron Horse.

[53] Majors, *Seventy Years*, pp. 143–49; William L. Visscher, *A Thrilling and Truthful History of the Pony Express; or Blazing the Westward Way with Other Sketches and Incidents of Those Stirring Times* (Chicago, 1908), pp. 18–19; Settle and Settle, *Empire on Wheels*, chaps. 2–3.

[54] *Reminiscences of Alexander Toponce: Pioneer, 1839–1923* (Ogden, Utah, 1923), p. 24.

PART FOUR

THE MONOPOLY ERA

CHAPTER XVI

STEAMSHIP MONOPOLY

The steamship business had its troubles in the late 'fifties. There was overexpansion, and even though the volume of river freight increased, there was not enough business to go around. There were too many operators, and the competition among them became fierce and ruthless. Toward the close of the decade, therefore, the trend was toward mergers. Out of these combinations evolved the powerful Oregon Steam Navigation Company which soon achieved dominance over Columbia River transportation. The Oregon Steam Navigation Company outstripped all other early transportation enterprises in the Pacific Northwest in size and capital investments, and its profits laid the basis for some of the largest personal fortunes in the region.

The history of the Oregon Steam Navigation Company is highly complex. Not unlike other successful business enterprises, it was the product of brains, capital, and machines. In short, it is the re-enactment in youthful Oregon of the mad scramble for business on a big scale and for wealth and power which technological advances had earlier made possible in older sections of the United States.

One personality contributing much toward the creating of this new Western business giant was Captain John C. Ainsworth who throughout life retained a vital interest in river steamship transportation. He had been born in Warren County, Ohio, June 6, 1822, and it was there that he first felt in his veins the call of the floating palaces which churned the muddy waters of the Ohio and Mississippi rivers.

Then came the discovery of gold in California, and Ainsworth joined the great, mad rush into the Western diggings. He was certainly not one to stay put, and before long the youthful Ohioan moved north to Oregon where a position awaited him as captain of the steamer *Lot Whitcomb*. Ainsworth was very daring, and on at least one occasion performed the remarkable feat of navigating a steamer safely over the Columbia River Cascades.[1]

In Oregon, Ainsworth found his niche. From the time of his arrival there until the end of his life he was identified with Columbia River navigation. In 1859 Ainsworth formed a partnership with Jacob Kamm, very well known in Oregon steamship circles, and with William S. Ladd whose financial influence in Portland was becoming considerable. To-

---

[1] "John C. Ainsworth Statement," MS, Bancroft Library, pp. 1 ff.

gether these men launched the steamboat *Carrie Ladd* which won esteem as the leading ship of its kind in the Pacific Northwest. But faced with unrelenting cutthroat competition, the owners of this ship proposed and secured a sort of loose merger with Beujamin Stark and associates, which group owned the Columbia River Steam Navigation Company. This concern operated steamers between Portland and the Cascades, and it worked in close harmony with Bradford and Company, operators of a portage tramway on the north side of the Cascades.[2]

Continuing efforts to merge all important steamship interests of the Columbia River region, promoters took steps to join forces with Colonel Joseph S. Ruckel and Harrison Olmstead of the Oregon Transportation Line who operated some steamers between the Cascades and The Dalles, as well as the important tramway portage on the south side of the Cascades.[3]

Out of this series of loose connections, or working arrangements, came what was known as the Union Transportation Company, which business combination, it might be said, controlled the lower Columbia and Willamette River steamship trade as far up the latter stream as Eugene City.[4]

Factionalism nevertheless continued within and without the Union Transportation Company, and to the tireless Captain Ainsworth the goal of consolidation of all major Columbia River shipping concerns remained far from achieved. Efforts in this direction persisted, however, and in 1860 an invitation to join the collaborators was extended to R. R. Thompson and L. W. Coe who operated the *Colonel Wright* on the Columbia between the Cascades and The Dalles. This business was small but lucrative, and only on very generous terms did these "up-river gentlemen" join with the Portland, or lower-river, crowd. The addition of Thompson and Coe was considered very important in that the road was at last cleared for the final act, namely, the reorganization into one power-

---

[2] Irene Lincoln Poppleton, "Oregon's First Monopoly—The O. S. N. Co.," *The Quarterly of the Oregon Historical Society*, IX (September 1908), 279–80. A wooden tramway on the north side of the Cascades had first been built in 1851 by Justin Chenoweth. The road had been purchased by Daniel Bradford in 1854. Dorothy O. Johansen, "Capitalism on the Far-Western Frontier: The Oregon Steam Navigation Company," Ph.D. dissertation, University of Washington, 1941, p. 71.

[3] In competition with Bradford, W. R. Kilborn had completed a portage wagon road on the south bank in 1855. It is assumed that Joseph S. Ruckel and associates bought the road, for in 1858, after lease of John Chipman's claim, there began construction of the Oregon Portage Railroad. It was Oregon's first railroad. Wooden rails were used in the beginning, but these were later reinforced with iron strips. At first mules pulled the tramcars, but in 1862 were replaced by a diminutive locomotive, the "Oregon Pony." By 1857 Harrison Olmstead had joined the Ruckel interests in what was by then known as the Oregon Transportation Line. See Frank B. Gill, "Oregon's First Railway," *The Quarterly of the Oregon Historical Society*, XXV (September 1924), 178–88.

[4] For data on Union Transportation Company, including statements on profits, see the Donald H. Bates Collection, Board of Trade Building, Portland, Oregon.

ful monopolistic concern of what up to 1860 had been but a loosely knit business organization.[5]

On May 12, 1860, final terms were agreed upon and articles of incorporation were drawn up and signed. On December 19 of that year the company received a grant from Washington Territory which empowered the new concern—termed a corporation and named the Oregon Steam Navigation Company—"to purchase and receive in all lawful ways, own and possess, boats, vessels, lands, goods, chattels and effects of every kind." On December 29 organizational details were worked out at a meeting held at Vancouver, Washington Territory, a constitution was adopted, and the way was cleared for operations. Under the terms of incorporation and general agreement, shares, each valued at $500, were allocated to members of the company. The respective number of shares allotted varied with the individual, depending upon the valuation placed upon his ships and other property that went into the new company. Highest shareholders were: Daniel F. Bradford, $36,875; R. R. Thompson, $30,000; Harrison Olmstead, $26,000; and L. W. Coe, $15,000. Among the other shareholders appear the names of Simeon G. Reed, J. C. Ainsworth, T. W. Lyles, Beujamin Stark, A. H. Barker, Josiah Myrick, Jacob Kamm, J. S. Ruckel, and others whose names are familiarly associated with the maritime history of the Pacific Northwest. In all, the total value of the shares[6] was placed at $172,500.

On October 18, 1862, new articles of incorporation were drawn up and filed with the Oregon territorial government, the territory having by then passed appropriate legislation. These articles placed the capitalization at $2,000,000 and modestly declared the purpose of the corporation to be:

. . . . the navigation by steam and otherwise of the Columbia River from its mouth to the 49th parallel of North Latitude, and the Snake River from its mouth to Fort Boise, and the Willamette River from its mouth to Eugene City, and the Pacific and other oceans, together with the construction and use of all necessary rail or plank or clay roads and bridges at any of the Portages of the said Columbia, Snake, and Willamette Rivers, or to purchase, own, and use any such roads that may be constructed . . . . and to collect such tolls, fare, or freight on all roads, boats or vessels that may be owned, chartered or controlled . . . . and to purchase, and own all lands, lots, wharves, boats and vessels, and all real and personal property of every name and nature, that may be deemed necessary to the interests of said incorporation. . . . .[7]

---

[5] *Lewis & Dryden's Marine History*, p. 91.

[6] "Minutes of the Oregon Steam Navigation Company," MS, Northern Pacific Railroad Company, Portland, Oregon, pp. 1–12. Hereafter cited as "Minutes of O. S. N. Co."

[7] A printed copy of the "Articles of Incorporation of the Oregon Steam Navigation Company" with handwritten additions is in the Leo J. Hanley Collection, Economics Records Library, Reed College, Portland, Oregon. See also Poppleton, "Oregon's First Monopoly," pp. 285–87; Bancroft, *Oregon*, II, 480 n.

This provided plenty of room in which to operate. It now remained to be seen what the management of this new company could accomplish in actual operations.

On December 29, 1860, the first election of directors had been held. Positions on the board were accorded to those representing different interests: J. C. Ainsworth, J. S. Ruckel, L. W. Coe, S. G. Reed, and D. F. Bradford. At another meeting held December 31, 1860, officers were elected. Chosen as president of the new company was Captain J. C. Ainsworth, who probably more than any other person had encouraged this organization, although others were not modest when it came to a statement of their respective roles in bringing the company to life. Bradford, the former portage tramway operator, was elected vice-president, and George W. Murray, a business associate of Bradford's, was chosen as secretary.[8]

Such was the organization of the Oregon Steam Navigation Company as seen in its initial stages. As time passed, there were shifts in personal influence within the ranks of the company. All the changes in the alignment of officeholders and directors are too numerous to mention, but most notable was the rise to prominence of Simeon G. Reed whose part in the early stages of the merger had been a negligible one. Reed had been born in Plymouth County, Massachusetts, but like Ainsworth had gone to Oregon in 1852 by way of the California diggings. During the winter and spring of 1853–1854 he established and operated a store on the south side of the Columbia River opposite the mouth of the Cowlitz. In a statement made in later life to H. H. Bancroft, Reed immodestly claimed sole credit for having been the originator of the great consolidation. Wrote Reed:

Having in mind the success the California Steam Navigation Co. had in controlling the navigation of the waters of the State of California, it occurred to me that if the consolidation of these different interests could be brought about on suitable terms and proper management, that all the different interests would be better protected and we could grow up with the business of the country. . . . .[9]

Space, however, does not permit a detailed exposition of the inner workings of the company. Suffice it to say that by 1862 the organization was sufficiently stabilized to assure successful and expanding operation.

Bradford had at first retained personal control over the north-side Cascades portage tramway, but in May 1862, this was relinquished to the

---

[8] "Minutes of O. S. N. Co.," pp. 9, 13; P. W. Gillette, "A Brief History of the Oregon Steam Navigation Company," *The Quarterly of the Oregon Historical Society,* V (June 1904), 124–25; *Lewis & Dryden's Marine History,* p. 91. The figures vary somewhat, and, of course, the number of shares held by each individual changed with each passing year.

[9] "Simeon G. Reed Statement," MS, Bancroft Library, pp. 1–4.

Oregon Steam Navigation Company for $28,000. The company also acquired The Dalles-to-Celilo portage railroad, and steps were hastily taken to modernize the railroad equipment on all of the portages. With control of The Dalles-Celilo portage, steamers could now be placed upon the Columbia River above this point and on the navigable tributaries leading into the upper stretches of this great stream.[10]

When in 1860 the Oregon Steam Navigation Company was formed, the business outlook of the Pacific Northwest was not bright. The nation as a whole was torn in a sectional dispute that already had thwarted the Westerners' hopes for internal improvements and pointed ominously toward open civil strife. Furthermore, while Oregon had been happily admitted into the Union the year before, the new state and its neighboring territories were confronted not only with serious factional disputes but with active Indian hostilities that threatened the lives and property of the people.[11]

Brushing aside these difficulties, the founders of the Oregon Steam Navigation Company proposed to capitalize on the increasing troop movements and immigrant arrivals along the Columbia River and upon the ever widening agricultural activities which by 1860 had more than recovered from the reverses occasioned by the California Gold Rush a decade before.

Little did the officials anticipate that within a year after the merger thousands of Idaho-bound miners would be gathering on the Portland docks clamoring for passage upstream. And little did these men realize that presently the holds of their ships would be laden with cargo destined for the many mining camps of the Inland Empire. But such was to be the case, and within two years the Oregon Steam Navigation Company found itself doing a record business. "Well," recalled Reed, "we occupied the position of a monopoly."[12] So they did, and the profits rolled in. During 1862 the rush to Florence, Idaho, began, and at Portland the volume of freight to the docks was so enormous that wagons had to stand in line to take their turn in delivering goods. Lines of trucks were said to have been unbroken day and night for weeks on end.[13]

During its first full year of operation, 10,500 passengers and over 6,000 tons of freight were hauled. Four years later no less han 36,000 passengers and 21,000 tons of freight were transported.[14] Over the facilities of the Oregon Steam Navigation Company was also shipped

---

[10] *Ibid.*, pp. 5–6.

[11] Carey, *History of Oregon*, Vol. II, chap. 24.

[12] "Reed Statement," pp. 6–7.

[13] Gillette, *op. cit.*, p. 128.

[14] H. H. Bancroft, *Scraps: Washington Miscellany* (Bancroft Library, n.d.) p. 53.

much of the gold taken from the Idaho, Montana, and eastern Oregon mines. The Wells, Fargo and Company usually handled these shipments, but the express firm paid high rates to the steamship company for the gold transport. Exact figures on gold shipments are absent, but starting with a few thousand dollars at the opening of 1861, they exceeded $8,000,000 four years later.[15]

From the very outset freight rates were all the traffic would bear. From Portland to The Dalles, a distance of one hundred miles, the freight rate was $40 per ton, and a ton was figured at forty cubic feet of space. To transport freight over The Dalles portage, a distance of fifteen miles, cost $15 per ton; from The Dalles to Wallula, $55 per ton; straight through from Portland to Lewiston the cost was $120 per ton.[16]

Passenger rates were in line with freight rates. A single fare from Portland to Lewiston cost $60, meals and bed one dollar each. With a full complement of passengers, it was not uncommon for the company to net $6,000 per trip over this run. On one up trip alone, namely, that of the *Tenino* between Celilo and Lewiston on May 13, 1862, the receipts were $10,945. And on another single trip that same month this vessel grossed $18,000 for freight, fares, meals, and berths. High as were the rates at this time, they represented a reduction over those of the previous decade.[17] Moreover, the goods and passengers were transported with much greater speed and efficiency than was ever before known to the people of the Pacific Northwest. On the steamers of this company only two to three days were involved in traveling from Portland to Lewiston, a distance of 280 miles. Only one day was required for the return voyage. This represented much faster service than had even been possible during the 'fifties, and the comfort of the passengers had been immeasurably improved.[18]

The profits of the Oregon Steam Navigation Company were immediate and great. At the end of its first six months of existence, the organization could have declared a 20 percent dividend. Its officials did not do this, however, but instead increased capitalization $690,000 and issued four certificates for every original share held by the stockholders. The gross earnings for the period of January 1, 1862, to September 30, 1865, were, according to one record sheet available, no less than

[15] Johansen, "Capitalism on the Far-Western Frontier," p. 83; Poppleton, "Oregon's First Monopoly," p. 290.

[16] Gillette, "A Brief History of the Oregon Steam Navigation Company," p. 126.

[17] *Ibid.*; William Dennison Lyman, *History of Yakima Valley, Washington* (n.p., 1919), p. 332; *Lewis & Dryden's Marine History*, p. 107; *Oregonian*, December 11, 1867; *Vancouver Telegraph*, February 8, 1862.

[18] Lyman, *Yakima Valley*, p. 332.

$4,486,054.03. Expenses charged against this figure amounted to $2,146,613.79. Within a twelve-month period a return of no less than 48 percent had been made on the original investment.[19] In other words, $240 were made on shares that had cost $500 a year before.[20] The company as a whole made a net earning of $2,339,440.24 from January 1, 1862, to September 30, 1865, which was the period of its greatest prosperity.[21]

Ready use was found for the company's increased capital resources. New real estate had to be purchased, machine shops built, docks repaired, and new ones added. But of all these important needs, none was so important as the need for additional ships. Officials hastened to order the construction of new steamers and went on the buying market for old ones in good repair.

By 1865 the Oregon Steam Navigation Company operated on the Columbia River no less than twenty-nine passenger steamships, thirteen schooners, and four barges. These vessels were to be found running on all sections of the great river, although more than half of them were concentrated below the Cascades. A good appraisal of the company's operations was made by Samuel Bowles,[22] of Massachusetts, editor of the *Springfield Republican*, after his visit to the Columbia Valley in July 1865:

> The navigation of the Columbia River is now in the hands of a strong and energetic company, that not only have the capacity to improve all its present opportunities, but the foresight to seek out and create new ones. They are, indeed, making new paths in the wilderness, and show more comprehension of the situation and purpose to develop it than any set of men I have met on the Pacific Coast.

Developments, however, did not end here. During three years following 1865, for example, important and most profitable extensions were made on the upper Columbia. By 1868 the Oregon Steam Navigation Company operated over stretches of the Columbia River that crossed the boundary into Canada, over tributaries eastward to within 125 miles of the Missouri River in Montana, and southward to within 150 of Salt Lake City.

By 1868 the capitalization of the Oregon Steam Navigation Company amounted to $5,000,000, with which generous resources and with capable management there came into being an integrated transportation network such as exceeded the fondest hopes of the founders. Where river steamers

---

[19] Johansen, "Capitalism on the Far-Western Frontier," pp. 91–92.

[20] *Ibid.*, p. 92.

[21] "Minutes of O. S. N. Co.," June 24, 1861, and after; "A Record of Achievement by an Oregon Monopoly," MS, Donald H. Bates Collection.

[22] Samuel Bowles, *Across the Continent* (Springfield, Massachusetts, 1866), pp. 193–94; Johansen, *op. cit.*, pp. 94–95; *Washington Statesman*, March 26, 1864.

could not go, stagecoaches, wagon freighters, and mule trains could. They were all tied up together into one elaborate whole.[23]

The Oregon Steam Navigation Company was highly conscious of competition with California and St. Louis for the Montana trade, and for this reason the Company stretched out its operation as much as possible in order to bring Oregon and Washington within a relatively easy reach of those distant markets.[24] In 1867, thanks to the marine facilities established, it was possible for a person to ship goods from Portland to Helena, Montana, in seven days. This record of speed was envied by St. Louis and California freighters to Montana. Excessive handling of freight at the portages, however, boosted transportation costs on the Columbia River route to a point where Portland merchants could never hope to monopolize any trading markets east of the Rocky Mountains; but until the completion of the Central Pacific Railroad in 1869, the Oregon Steam Navigation Company at least made a strong bid for the carrying trade as far east as Helena and Salt Lake City.[25]

To the Pacific Northwest it looked very much as if the age of business tycoons and staggering business ventures had come, and as if transportation developments had at last come into stride with those of California, the Great Plains, and other parts of the country. Here at last was an organization that far outdistanced and overshadowed the small, individualistic, competitive operations of the preceding decade. In its conception and scope of operations, the Oregon Steam Navigation Company was a business venture that compared favorably with those of the Central

---

[23] Bancroft, *Scraps: Washington*, pp. 53–54. According to data furnished by J. C. Ainsworth, the distances along parts of the Columbia River system on which the Oregon Steam Navigation Company operated ships or portage trams, or otherwise arranged for service, in the year 1867, were as follows:

1. *Columbia River*   Distances
   Astoria to Cascades 160
   Cascades Portage Railroads 6
   Cascades to The Dalles 50
   The Dalles-Celilo Portage Railroad 14
   Celilo to Priest's Rapids (navigable part of the time) 185
   Priest's Rapids to Colville Portage 100
   Colville to British Columbia Terminal 250

2. *Snake*
   Walla Walla to Lewiston 160
   Portage Road above Lewiston (river not navigable) 150
   Navigation above this point 150

3. *Clark-Pend d'Oreille*
   Columbia to Pend d'Oreille Lake Road 160
   Foot of Lake Pend d'Oreille to Jako 225
   Navigation had been conducted previously on the Clark River, but no boats were on it in 1867.

4. *Willamette*
   Mouth to Eugene with portage at Willamette Falls (Oregon City) 120

Total number of miles over which river-land transportation service was offered 1,730

[24] *Lewis & Dryden's Marine History*, p. 145.

[25] Carpenter, "A Glimpse of Montana," pp. 383–84; *Oregonian*, December 28, 1865.

Pacific and Union Pacific railroads then seeking to extend a railroad line to the West Coast.

Powerful, extensive, resourceful, and ruthless as was the Oregon Steam Navigation Company, it nevertheless fell short of its goal to crush all opposition on the Columbia River. Many of the smaller concerns held on and challenged the giant. When rates of the big company were exorbitant, the smaller ones took heart; when rates were cut to the bone, on the other hand, many of the small operators went under. One fairly successful opposition concern, the People's Transportation Company, or People's Line, was formed in 1862 under the direction of A. A. McCully and D. D. McCully, leaders in Willamette River transportation. Around this concern other companies aligned themselves. The Peoples' Line, however, had no control over the Cascades portages, without which no concern could ever hope to outdistance the "O.S.N. Co." Later the People's Line was purchased by Ben Holladay for $200,000 only to have it fall into the hands of the Oregon Steam Navigation Company at a time when the Stagecoach King, hard pressed for funds, was forced to sell.[26]

Such processes repeated themselves. Captain Alexander P. Ankeny operated steamers between the Cascades and The Dalles and managed to hold on in spite of efforts to drive him out. A so-called Merchants' Transportation Line emerged to combine with others in forming the Independent Line. Even the foreign-owned British Columbia Steam Navigation Company put a ship, the *Maria*, on the Columbia. In this instance the United States government came to the rescue of the would-be monopoly by forbidding ships of foreign registry to operate exclusively on inland waters.[27]

Also thwarting the Oregon Steam Navigation Company in her efforts to rid the river of opposition were political developments and a rising tide of public criticism. One thing the people of the Washington side of the river felt was that their Oregon compatriots were receiving more advantages than they from the steamship trade. Accordingly, the Washington territorial legislature sought to remedy this situation by issuing charters freely to prospective railroad and steamship companies which might compete with the Oregon Steam Navigation Company and which might bring improved service to the Washingtonians. Examples of these were the Columbia Transportation Company and the Washington Transportation Company. The Washington territorial legislature, moreover, realigned counties in such a way that the north-side Cascades portage might be more easily brought under their political control.

---

[26] *Lewis & Dryden's Marine History*, pp. 108–9; Mills, *Stern-wheelers Up Columbia*, pp. 56–60.

[27] Johansen, "Capitalism on the Far-Western Frontier," pp. 116–19.

In the face of what to the Oregon Steam Navigation Company was unwarranted interference with free business enterprise, Simeon G. Reed sought help from the national government. Reed personally went to Washington, D.C., where he lobbied for and in 1867 secured passage of legislation designed to safeguard the vested interests of the Oregon Steam Navigation Company.[28]

While the American people disliked governmental restrictions on business enterprise, they nevertheless expostulated against the abuses of monopolies. On the one hand people in the West expressed admiration of such big concerns as the California State Company, the Pacific Mail Steamship Company, Wells, Fargo and Company, and the Oregon Steam Navigation Company; on the other hand, there was public indignation over their excessive rates, inadequate service, and ruthless competitive practices. The Oregon Steam Navigation Company endured much public scorn from the people of Oregon and Washington, but in the face of it the organization carried on with remarkable success.

Shifts were continually made in the organization structure,[29] though externally the operations continued in good order. John C. Ainsworth continued to be active in the company's affairs, but after the panic of 1873 the influence and power of Robert R. Thompson, William S. Ladd, and Simeon Reed began to equal, and in the case of Reed exceed, that of Ainsworth. "Reed was a striking contrast to the personalities of his associates," writes Dorothy O. Johansen. "Where they were restrained and impersonal in their relations with people, Reed was genial, good-natured, and an easy mixer with every class and type of person."[30] In spite of some internal dissensions, the Oregon Steam Navigation Company was a remarkably smooth-working organization. Large profits were an ever present motive for close co-operation, and the concern held together until May 23, 1879, when Henry Villard of the Northern Pacific Railroad Company purchased the Oregon Steam Navigation Company for $5,000,000. Out of his total holdings in the Pacific Northwest, Villard organized and became president of the Oregon Railroad and Navigation Company.[31]

Puget Sound suffered tragically by comparison with the Columbia River when it came to steamship operations. During the great Columbia River boom of the 'sixties, the people of Washington had to content them-

[28] Johansen, "Capitalism on the Far-Western Frontier," pp. 134–43; Dorothy O. Johansen, "The Oregon Steam Navigation Company: An Example of Capitalism on the Frontier," *Pacific Historical Review*, X (June 1941), 185.

[29] "Minutes of the O. S. N. Co.," *passim*.

[30] Johansen, "Capitalism on the Far-Western Frontier," pp. 163, 214–65.

[31] "Minutes of the Oregon Railway and Navigation Company," MS, Office of the Northern Pacific Railroad Company, Portland, Oregon.

A STEAMER ON THE FRASER RIVER

STEAMER CONNECTIONS AT YALE, B.C., 1882

THE STEAMER "CARRIE LADD"

THE STEAMER "W. S. LADD"

selves with extremely limited regular service and with the occasional calls by tramp steamers and sailing ships. For the most part, the *Eliza Anderson*, first launched at Portland in 1858, "was almost alone in her glory" in Puget Sound. Mail from San Francisco, reminisced an early Seattle postmaster, was usually one hundred days old before it reached the Sound.[32]

Slight signs of new life became apparent in 1863 when two new steamers, the *J. B. Libby* and the *Mary Woodruff*, began operations in the Sound and, together with the *Eliza Anderson*, became welcome household words among the settlers who were very dependent upon water transportation. G. A. Meiggs, William Renton, Henry Yesler, and other pioneer lumbermen of Puget Sound were certainly among those whose business life was absolutely dependent upon the existence of vessels to carry their lumber to markets.

It was not, however, until 1869 when L. M. and E. A. Starr of Portland focused their attention on the less populous regions of the north that the people of Washington had reason for optimism. In 1871, at the instigation of the Starr brothers, there was incorporated the Puget Sound Navigation Company with a capital of a half-million dollars.[33] Throughout the 'seventies these erstwhile Portland industrialists contributed much to the modernization of Puget Sound navigation. In 1879 they built in Seattle the beautiful *George E. Starr*, and they became owners of the equally attractive *North Pacific*. Both served on the Seattle-Victoria run.

The Starrs may be credited with the establishment of good, regular service between Seattle and Victoria. But it remained for the Pacific Coast Steamship Company, organized in 1877, to give a semblance of regular steamship connections between certain Puget Sound ports and ports along the Pacific Coast. This company controlled and operated seventeen ships, and competition with other operators in the area became fierce.[34]

The 'eighties were marked with the completion of two transcontinental railroads to the Pacific Northwest, the Northern Pacific and the Canadian Pacific. A prelude to such giant achievement was the gradual absorption of much of the steamship business by the railroad companies. In keeping with the inevitable trend the Starr interests, in 1881, sold out

[32] William O. Thorniley, "Famous Pioneer Steamboats of Puget Sound," *Marine Digest*, XXII (April 22, 1944), 2; *Lewis & Dryden's Marine History*, p. 110; Edward Huggins, "Puget Sound Pioneer Vessels," *The Washington Historian*, I (July 1900), 197.

[33] Huggins, *op. cit.*, p. 254. The Starr brothers are believed to have had some connection with the Oregon Steam Navigation Company. See Buchanan, "Economic History of Kitsap County."

[34] *Lewis & Dryden's Marine History*, pp. 253–57; *Seattle Post*, April 19, 1879.

to the Oregon Railway and Navigation Company for $600,000. The most important event in Puget Sound navigation during the period came at the close of the 'eighties. This was the establishment of the Puget Sound and Alaska Steamship Company. Its steamers were attractive and numerous, and a prosperous future business was in store.[35]

Steamship navigation in Puget Sound was slow in coming, but once in stride its growth was remarkable. Since 1835 no less than one thousand steamers have, at one time or another, operated in those magnificent inland waters.

To some old Willamette Valley settler who in the middle 'fifties might have been a passenger on a luxurious Columbia River steamer, it must have seemed that at long last the painful pioneer days were over. Such comfort! Such service! Such punctuality!

Little, perhaps, was the old settler aware that not far to the north, in the British part of Old Oregon, the means of transportation still remained somewhat primitive, simple, and haphazard. There the Hudson's Bay Company was still dominant, and everyday life was much as pioneers had known it to be around old Fort Vancouver a full decade before. In and out of Fort Victoria Harbor the ships of the Hudson's Bay Company plied at random. There was no schedule, no turmoil, no seeming haste.

But then came the British Columbia gold rush, and overnight this situation altered. Only the steamers *Beaver* and *Otter* were permanently available to carry the crushing mob of miners from Victoria to the Fraser River, and these two vessels were incapable of going up the Fraser River above Fort Langley.

Eager to profit from the mining trade, Chief Factor Douglas did what probably hurt him most, namely, made arrangements with the American Pacific Mail Steamship Company to handle traffic between Victoria and the falls on the Fraser River.[36] Accordingly, five American steamers entered this service which began in June 1858. The steamer *Surprise* made the pioneer run from Fort Langley to Hope, and later the steamer *Umatilla* penetrated the more treacherous waters above Hope to reach Yale, which was the head of navigation on the Fraser.[37]

The Pacific Mail Steamship Company encountered many difficulties in its Canadian venture. The ships drew too much water, and extraordinary skill was required to pilot a steamer either up or down the

---

[35] *Lewis & Dryden's Marine History*, pp. 284, 363.

[36] Douglas drove a hard bargain. The American concern was obliged to collect for the Hudson's Bay Company a $5 mining fee from each prospective miner, give the H.B.C. $2 for each passenger carried to the mining ports, and carry only H.B.C. goods. Such a contract was later declared illegal by the British Government. See Howay and Scholefield, *British Columbia*, II, 28–30.

[37] *Ibid.*, II, 29–32.

Fraser, although the going down was the more dangerous. Declared Commander Mayne:

Going up against the current, ... the steamer can afford to disregard the snags; for if she strikes on one, it is easy to shut off the steam and drift back from it. But spinning down the current, it is a very serious matter for one of these large unwieldy boats to become transfixed upon a well-rooted, obstinate snag. . . . . The perseverance of the Yankee skipper in overcoming these difficulties is certainly remarkable.

He recounts how passengers might have to be landed in order to pass "Umatilla Snag," and how, on occasions, the patient skipper worked two hours with his ship in order to progress a few hundred yards.[38] Not until the coming of the indomitable flat-bottomed stern-wheelers, already famous on the Sacramento and the Willamette rivers, did steam navigation prosper on the Fraser River. Such a vessel was the steamer *Enterprise*, and her record on the treacherous Fraser was an enviable one.[39]

Given time to marshall their resources, British interests sought to resume control of what they rightfully regarded as their business domain. Entering the field were ships of British registry which belonged to the Yale Steam Navigation Company, the British Columbia and Victoria Steam Navigation Company, and to several other independent British operators. Best known among the pioneer British operations men was William Irving Scott, and to many he is remembered as the father of steam navigation in British Columbia.[40]

Meanwhile, Americans gradually withdrew from the Fraser trade and confined their operations to the coast and to Puget Sound. Between 1859–1870 the familiar American-owned *Eliza Anderson* maintained what was termed a one-ship monopoly between Victoria and points on the Sound. In a less vigorous role this venerable old ship continued to be seen in Puget Sound waters until 1889 when she was finally tied up in the Snohomish slough and allowed to rot.[41]

Aside from the regular Fraser River service up to Hope and Yale, there were the involved land-water operations over the so-called Lillooet route. Those who at first found the Fraser Trail too rugged (before the completion of the Cariboo Wagon Road) took the circuitous detour around the Fraser Canyon. This route has already been described in con-

---

[38] Mayne, *Four Years in British Columbia and Vancouver Island*, pp. 90–92.

[39] Richard Byron Johnson, *Very Far West Indeed: A Few Rough Experiences on the North-West Pacific Coast* (London, 1872), p. 56; Hacking, "Marine History of British Columbia," pp. 57–58. See also Norman R. Hacking, "Steamboat 'Round the Bend," *The British Columbia Historical Quarterly*, VIII (October 1944), 255–80.

[40] Hacking, "Marine History of British Columbia," p. 63; *British Colonist*, February 28, 1860.

[41] Hacking, "Marine History of British Columbia," p. 61.

nection with staging, but it should be noted here that steamers operated forty-five miles up the Harrison River and Lake, a tributary of the Fraser, to Port Douglas, and small steamers were placed on each of the many elongated lakes along the hundred-mile Lillooet route. Until 1863 this route was almost a monopoly, but with the completion of the Cariboo Wagon Road, the Lillooet route, because of its many portages, almost ceased to exist. A general decline in the gold output of the Cariboo, moreover, brought with it an over-all slackening of the upriver trade.[42]

Then came, however, a renewed spirit in the mining when, during the middle 'sixties, gold discoveries were made in the Big Bend of the Columbia. This area could be reached over American territory by traveling up the Columbia River, and it could also be reached over British territory by way of the Fraser and Thompson rivers. Steamboat navigation on the Thompson was something new, but it was found feasible by the Hudson's Bay Company which in 1866 placed its steamer *Marten* on a 120-mile run up the Thompson River from its confluence with the Fraser. From the end of navigation, newly worked-out overland trails and some lake-canoe stretches wound their way eventually to what were called the Wild Horse Creek or Kootenai diggings.[43] The competition between the two routes, namely, the American and the British, was terrific; but the eager miners naturally favored the route which lay within closest grasp. Anyway, the bubble broke in 1866, and the Big Bend gold rush became another thing to talk about around a pot-bellied stove on a winter's day at some trading post or general store.[44] Even the steamer *Marten* did not pay for itself, and for a decade there was little steam navigation on the Thompson. By the middle 'seventies settlers began entering the valley and once again (this time on a permanent basis) steamboat transportation revived and a number of new steamers appeared, both on the Fraser and Thompson rivers.

The coming of the Canadian Pacific Railroad into the region in 1885 gave added zest to settlement; but, unfortunately for the steamers, it meant that the peak was past.[45]

Later gold flurries in upper British Columbia registered renewed steamboat activity on the Fraser. A sizable fleet of such vessels was in operation by 1880, and the Hudson's Bay Company continued to hold its own in the business. Until 1883, no one company, not even the Hud-

---

[42] Hacking, "Marine History of British Columbia," p. 49; *British Colonist*, April 21, 1860, and March 26, 1862. See also Hacking, "British Columbia Steamboat Days, 1870-1883," pp. 69-111.

[43] Howay and Scholefield, *British Columbia*, II, 231-33.   [44] *Ibid.*, II, 241-42.

[45] Howay, *British Columbia*, pp. 219-20; Hacking, "Marine History of British Columbia," pp. 106-10. The last spike on the Canadian Pacific Railroad was driven November 7, 1885, at a place called Craigellachie. Not until 1887 was the road completed to Vancouver, B.C. See also *British Colonist*, November 13, 1878.

son's Bay Company, may be said to have controlled the shipping interests in British Columbia. But in that year a bid was made by John Irving— a pioneer and for years a successful operator in the region—who organized the Canadian Pacific Navigation Company. It was capitalized at $500,000 and is reported to have been comparable in power to the Oregon Steam Navigation Company. Business on the Fraser River at this time could not have been better, for most of the supplies needed for the Canadian Pacific Railroad construction work at the western end were being transported by steamer.

The completion of the Canadian Pacific Railroad into Vancouver in 1887 left the great steamship company either at loose ends, or, it may be said, with marvelous new opportunities to extend its transportation facilities over numerous available water routes, not only in immediate waters, but across the vast Pacific to the Orient.

In many local areas the railroad replaced the steamers; but elsewhere, such as in Puget Sound and across to Victoria, steamers would continue in use. Rivalry between the railroad company and the Irving interests remained keen, but finally in 1901 Captain Irving sold out to the Canadian Pacific Railroad Company. Meanwhile, many other smaller operators had faced the inevitable and had either gone out of business or had sold out to the big company.[46] But the "little fellow" in British Columbia held out for a much longer time than was the case in Oregon where monopolistic control had come about nearly four decades before. As the period closed, a great new era in navigation was in store for British Columbia. A number of supermodern ocean steamships known as the "Empress liners" were being built by the Canadian Pacific Railroad for service that would connect Vancouver and Victoria with all parts of the world.

---

[46] Hacking, "Marine History of British Columbia," p. 124.

CHAPTER XVII

FULL STEAM AHEAD

"Puff! Puff! . . . . How exquisitely pleasant, how cozy and delightful, our little steamer seemed." In this manner did Brigadier General Rusling respond to his voyage down the Columbia River on the little steamer *Nez Perce Chief*. Her staterooms were clean and tidy, her meals well cooked and excellent. Steaming downstream "without thought or care" was like being on "summer seas."

Scenery on either side and along the full length of the Columbia River gorge was, and is, changing, golden, fresh, and beautiful. Scenery-loving passengers escaped the monotony that so frequently beset those who voyaged down the long, winding distance of the Missouri and the Mississippi. The river jaunt through the Cascade Mountains was to this widely traveled general of the United States Army a notable one, and surpassed everything in the way of wild and picturesque river scenery "that he had ever witnessed."[1] "The navigation of the Columbia . . . ." wrote another traveler, "is a never ceasing wonder, full of interest to the traveler and the lover of nature. For beauty and grandeur of scenery," he boasted, "the portion of country lying between the mouth of the Willamette and the Dalles cannot be surpassed on this continent."[2]

Even for the more callous it was almost impossible to escape a feeling of freshness and restfulness aboard ship that those traveling by stage-coach over dusty, dirty, or bumpy corduroy roads did not experience.

Oregon-bound stagecoach travelers from across the Oregon Trail, or parts connecting with it, usually boarded steamers of the Oregon Steam Navigation Company at The Dalles. From there to the Cascades was one uninterrupted run; but at this point a railway portage was necessary before again boarding a different ship for the final lap into Portland. Varying connections, as has previously been shown, would carry the passengers to almost any desired point. By the late 'fifties connections would take them to Astoria, up the Cowlitz or for a short distance up the Willamette. The prevailing type of steamers, either stern-wheelers or side-wheelers, were of the flat-bottomed variety and to the average traveler such a voyage must have seemed smooth, though leisurely.[3]

---

[1] James F. Rusling, *Across America: or, The Great West and the Pacific Coast* (New York, 1874), p. 252.

[2] Bancroft, *Scraps: Oregon*, I, 275.

[3] Randall H. Hewitt, *Across the Plains and Over the Divide; A Mule Train Journey from East to West in 1862, and Incidents Connected Therewith* (New York, 1906), p. 470.

A traveler who had been on almost any one of the scores of river steamers would have felt very much at home on successive trips. The steamers were all very much alike except that some had their paddle wheels starboard and port, others aft.

Almost on a level with the main deck slightly fore, and in plain sight, were the boilers, fed by coal, wood, pitch, or resin fires. Anything that would burn fast and hot would do as fuel, although wood, which was most plentiful in the Pacific Northwest, was generally used. Good, dry, pitchy fir made a roaring red fire if only the fireman would keep tossing in the pieces. But tending furnaces was no lazy man's job when, as in some instances, a cord of wood was consumed for each hour of operation.

Pipes conducted the steam to the cylinders in the engines. On some of the steamers, especially on stern-wheelers, these steampipes ran along the surface of the main deck, and thereby made it unpleasantly hot for the "Indians, Chinamen and 'niggers' " who were unceremoniously relegated to this portion of the ship. The engine rooms were astern on these ships; there the steam-powered cylinders operated the massive cranks and connecting rods used to manipulate the paddle wheels which usually drew about eighteen inches of water.[4] The power units were known as walking-beam engines. They were of very simple construction. An engine consisted largely of a cylinder, valve gear, beam, crank, and a few minor accessories. Because of iron boilers the earlier engines were of a low-pressure type. Sometimes as little as ten pounds of pressure were used, but even so explosions occurred that took a heavy toll of life.

Above the main deck was the saloon deck where passengers were provided with the best accommodations the ship could afford, and on some ships that was nothing to boast about. Normally there were available a few staterooms, while in addition practically all passenger steamers had or were provided with saloons or dining rooms. The quality of the furnishings and service depended on how expensively and luxuriously the ship's officials could afford to make them. On some steamers these were very simple; again, others were richly furnished and appointed, though probably never reaching the plushy elegance of the floating palaces on the Mississippi River of that age.

The quality and quantity of food aboard ship varied with the individual shipping lines. On the upper Fraser foodstuffs were hard to get; on the Columbia they were plentiful. Many travelers mentioned their satisfactory meals. On the other hand one English passenger en route to Yale aboard a Fraser River steamer was not a little taken aback by the

---

[4] Johnson, *Very Far West Indeed*, pp. 56–57; Hacking, "Marine History of British Columbia," p. 44; Jerry MacMullen, *Paddle-Wheel Days in California* (Stanford University, 1944), pp. 76–77.

uncouth table manners of the passengers. "When dinner was spread in the saloon, everybody made a simultaneous rush for places, knocking over on their way one or two nigger stewards bearing savoury dishes, and appearing to think that the first man there would certainly eat up everything and leave none for the rest."[5]

On the very top at the extreme fore of every river steamer was the pilot house. Here was the ship's wheel, connected by chains to the rudder, which in turn determined the direction of travel. At the wheel was a responsible officer, either the captain, a first or second mate, or a pilot. Ships' captains were usually of a rough and ready sort. It has been said of them that their chief qualifications were to have a strong arm, to be able to make quick decisions, have a fluent swearing vocabulary, and a capacity for strong drink.[6] But these captains and pilots, according to one old local chronicler, were "as fine a set of men as ever turned a wheel." They were "bold, bluff, genial, hearty, and obliging," although given to an occasional "outburst of expletives" which was accompanied by "voluminous repertoires of 'cusswords'."[7]

As to the rest of a ship's personnel, there were aboard every steamer worthy of the name at least one engineer and one fireman. The number of deck hands varied with the size of the vessel, as well as the amount of cargo stowed away in the hold and on the main deck. Lastly, for the convenience of both crew and passengers there were aboard ship stewards, cabin boys, cooks, and waiters.

There were times when steamboating on the Columbia River was anything but pleasant, and especially was this true during the height of the Inland Empire gold rush. Then "two ounces for the privilege of lying on the upper deck" were paid. During such boom times when there was more business than could be handled, the guiding principle was to charge everything that the traffic would bear, and to load aboard all human creatures the steamer would hold.

For outsiders wishing to enter Oregon by steamer there was always the dangerous Columbia River Bar with which to contend. Most people who experienced this difficult stretch of navigation were in agreement with the captain who expressed it simply: "We have reason to congratulate ourselves . . . . ."[8] To this very day the Columbia River Bar remains a constant threat and a curse to all navigators in Pacific waters. Because of the large number of ships that during the years have come

---

[5] Johnson, *op. cit.*, p. 60.   [6] *Ibid.*, pp. 59, 63.

[7] Lyman, *Yakima Valley*, pp. 332–33; Robert M. Graham, "Memoir," MS, Yakima, Washington, Library.

[8] Gustavus Hines, *Life on the Plains of the Pacific. Oregon: Its History, Condition and Prospects* . . . . (Buffalo, 1851), p. 86.

to grief there, this Bar has won for itself the onerous title of "Grave-yard."[9]

Steamboating on the Fraser River had a flair and flavor all of its own. In some ways, however, it was like the Willamette, only worse. Snags, rapids, bends, a swift flowing current, whirlpools, sharp rocky banks, and abrupt changes in water levels were all part and parcel of the Fraser River's make-up. It all contributed toward giving character to this historic stream and especial thrills to those who ventured upon her. "There is something very exciting about it, certainly . . . . ,"[10] wrote the British Commander Mayne.

There were risks both going up and coming down. Going up, the greatest of all dangers was a boiler explosion: too much steam pressure on a cast-iron boiler. But "tearing down the current at some twelve or fourteen knots an hour, bumping over shoals, sticking against snags, and shooting rapids," says Mayne, "is far more animated work."[11]

A snag was something earnestly to avoid. A snag is ordinarily under-stood to be a large tree with the thick end of its trunk embedded in the mud, sand, or gravel at some shallows, and frequently out of sight. The small end of the trunk and the branches usually point upstream; a swiftly flowing current tends to sharpen the points of the lurking tentacles. In days of wooden ships these spearlike objects would often hook into an oncoming steamer and would tend either to pierce the vessel's hull or to rip apart a plank from the keel or side. A snag was, therefore, very dangerous, and in time the early river pilots came to know these underwater devils by name, as for example, the well-known Umatilla Snag. Mayne recalled,

Upon one occasion, when I was going up the river in the "Enterprise," no less than three times after we had struggled past the snag the strong current caught and swung us broadside across the stream; and it was only by running the vessel's bow into the muddy bank without a moment's hesitation, and holding her there by the nose, as it were, until she recovered breath to make another effort, that we escaped impalement.[12]

Mayne relates how in such a situation the communications between the captain at the wheel in the pilot room and the engineer down in the engine room became highly exciting as they would shout to each other through a sound tube.

"Ho! Frank, how much steam have you?"

Frank shouts the number of pounds.

"Guess you must give her ten pounds more, or we shan't get past that infernal snag."

---

[9] Mills, *Stern-wheelers Up Columbia*, p. 140.

[10] Mayne, *Four Years in British Columbia and Vancouver Island*, p. 90.

[11] *Ibid.*   [12] *Ibid.*, p. 91.

Frantic stoking is now heard below. Uneasy passengers on the deck know what this might mean. An explosion! Yes, eternity!

"All ready, Cap'en: can't give her any more!" yells the engineer.

"Stand by, then!" orders the skipper. "Let go!"

". . . . ting! ting! ting!" goes the bell in the engine room, and that means full steam ahead. Every part of the little ship now creaks and trembles; the passengers watch eagerly. This time, thank goodness, she makes it safely by the snag and all aboard give a sigh of relief—until the next danger point is reached. The Yankee skippers who operated so many of the Fraser River vessels received from Commander Mayne a warm compliment for their perseverance.[13]

The temptation to race was ever present among steamship captains. When a new ship would enter the service it was only natural that its skipper would wish to prove how outmoded his rivals' were. Sometimes such races were formally arranged; at other times they came about by chance as two vessels might be chugging along in the water abreast each other at some wide portion of the river. The passengers, who invariably loved a close race, always did their best to urge their skipper on to greater speeds even though added pounds of pressure might mean another of those "terrible explosions." Mere explosions, however, the travelers left to fortuitous circumstances, and enthusiastically supported any chance race. "There isn't much you can do about such a thing as a ship blowing up," they would say calmly, knowing full well there was much that might have been done by the engineers who built the boilers.

Across the blue stretch of water between Victoria and New Westminster, on a pleasant April day, the then old steamer *Beaver* set out. She had just been overhauled from stem to stern, but she was the first steamer afloat in Pacific waters. At the same time from near-by docks the steamer *Julia* steamed out. It looked like a race. It was! Odds were against the *Beaver* because of her age. She drew ten feet of water and would not take advantage of shallows. But odds or no odds, money was wagered. The *Beaver* was in the lead, but the *Julia*, "Well, she hadn't gotten warmed up yet. You'll see." But not so. The *Beaver* churned away full steam ahead toward New Westminster. Never once did she give ground to the *Julia*, which, much to the chagrin of her confident backers, arrived in port thirty-five minutes behind the venerable old Hudson's Bay Company ship. "We understand," concludes Victoria's *Colonist*, "that considerable money changed hands on the occasion."[14]

---

[13] Mayne, *Four Years in British Columbia and Vancouver Island*, pp. 91–92. For a good description of a steam trip down the Fraser River see A. G. Doughty and Gustave Lanctot, eds., *Cheadle's Journal of Trip Across Canada, 1862–1863* (Ottawa, 1931), p. 235.

[14] *British Colonist*, April 3, 1860.

Another chance race is graphically recorded by R. Byron Johnson when aboard ship bound for Yale. The captain of Johnson's steamer, seeing his rival approach, was determined to "lick 'er or bust!" Gulping down two or three extra drinks, he was ready for action. Into the tube the captain shouted:

"Say, below thar, you 'tarnal skunks, jes' you wire in, will yer!"

"Wire in yerself, old man, and don't stand thar blowin'; . . . . we're kinder played out," came the retort.

Seeing himself thus thwarted the skipper offered any man aboard five dollars if he would go below and "take a turn at them fires!" Volunteers rushed forward, with a "Here y'ar cap'n!"

"I'm thar old hoss!"

"That'll du, you bet!"

Even so, the opponent crept closer and closer. What could the skipper do? Was he going to take a lickin' for the first time? All of a sudden he thought of a shipment of bacon and ham that had been taken aboard. Calling this to the attention of the men in the hold, he shouted:

"Pass it along to the firemen, sharp!"

"All right, cap."

Several sacks of bacon were added hastily to the wood, resin, and pitch that had already been fed into the firebox. It was the pork that turned the trick. Now the wired-down steam gauge read 160 pounds pressure! Forty more than the law allowed this ship to have.

Neck and neck raced the ships; but, concludes Johnson: "Fate was not with us, however; for suddenly a fearful shock and crash were felt and heard, and we stood stock still, with a snag run through the bottom of our hull; while the rival boat passed us with jeers. . . . ."[15]

There were other races; many of them. But a championship race, the most exciting of all, came but once in a decade. Such a one took place between the two new top-notch steamers, the *Olympia* and the *North Pacific*, in June 1871.

The *Olympia* belonged to George S. Wright, who with his brother had at this time an upper hand in Puget Sound navigation. The *Olympia*[16] had been built in New York City at a cost to Wright of $200,000. Certainly no ship would challenge her for a long time to come, her owner must have thought to himself as this beautiful side-wheeler made its initial run from Olympia to Victoria.

But down at Portland, L. M. and E. A. Starr had amassed a fortune in the manufacture of rye whiskey. They were now turning to new fields to conquer, and chose steamship navigation in Puget Sound.

---

15 Johnson, *Very Far West Indeed*, pp. 63–66.
16 This ship later became the Hudson's Bay Company's *Princess Louise*.

Nothing but the best would ever take the business from the Wrights, so the Starr brothers had built at San Francisco, at a cost of $100,000, a very graceful side-wheeler which they named the *North Pacific*.

Then followed the cutthroat competitive service, something the people of Puget Sound welcomed. Down went the fares until on one run they were reduced from $16 to 50 cents. Then finally: "free transportation, free meals," and a free lithograph of the ship.

This could not go on forever. There had to be a showdown, a race between the *Olympia* and the *North Pacific* from Victoria to Port Townsend. It was announced well in advance. Arguments ensued; bets were placed; excitement ran high. Aboard ship everything was placed in order —the boilers cleaned, the hulls scraped, easily combustible tar and resin were added to the fuel supply. And with discretion thrown to the winds, heavy weights were hung upon the safety valves of the boilers to assure maximum steam pressure.

Most of Victoria's population was down at the docks to see the take-off. Both vessels were laden with excited passengers eager for the start. Then amidst great shouting there came the start. As soon as the two ships vanished from view "every available vehicle," writes the *Colonist*, "was brought into requisition" as the people hastened down the road and over to Beacon Hill where they could snatch a final last glimpse of the racing ships.

At first there was little noticeable difference in the pace of the two contestants. They seemed even. But as they approached Port Townsend, the San Francisco-built *North Pacific* heaved a final extra spurt and beat her adversary to the goal by three minutes. She had made the run in two hours and forty-one minutes.

Defeat was hard to take for the Wright brothers. They now decided to dispose of their interests to the Starrs and withdraw from the field.

It was a memorable race.[17]

The old Mississippi River, the Missouri, the rivers of California—none of these had priorities on steamboat wrecks and explosions. They happened in the Pacific Northwest with startling frequency. Lewis and Dryden's stupendous catalogue and chronicle of ships has its pages only too well sprinkled with these prosaically told, but none-the-less tragic, stories:

"The boiler of the *Caledonia* exploded November 2, 1859, while on a trip from Victoria to Fraser River, killing the fireman, Charles Green. . . . ."

---

[17] *British Colonist*, June 28, 1871; Hacking, "Marine History of British Columbia," pp. 97–100.

"The year 1860 opened with another terrible wreck on the route between San Francisco and the Northwest, the antiquated *Northerner* going to pieces near Cape Mendocino, sacrificing nearly forty lives, and proving that the warning . . . . was still unheeded, and that inspection laws were lax indeed. . . . ."

"Two well known coasters came to grief in 1864, the barks *Iwanowa* and *Ocean Bird.*" The latter left Port Madison on March 19, encountered a gale on April 3, and capsized.

"A mournful tale of death and disaster darkened the pages of marine history in 1865, and, with the single exception of the loss of the steamship *Pacific* ten years later, no such terrible calamity has ever happened on the Pacific coast." The account then goes on to relate how the steamship *Brother Jonathan*, long known in the Pacific Northwest, ran onto rocks near Crescent City. "The greatest confusion reigned on board. The steamer was poorly equipped with life-saving apparatus. . . . ." The sea was heavy. Only one lifeboat with nineteen aboard reached Crescent City safely. These were the only passengers saved out of the nearly two hundred aboard.[18]

Scarcely a section of the Pacific Northwest escaped such tragedies. Repeatedly, newspaper editorials decried the laxity of the inspection laws, the foolhardy racing, the shipbuilding engineers who designed the engines. But all this was apparently of little avail in this age of reckless free enterprise. In the case of the *Brother Jonathan*, the captain's warning that the ship was overloaded went scornfully unheeded by the agent of the steamship company. If the captain objected to taking the steamer out, the company's official could always find another who would not object.[19]

"Within the last eighteen months," wrote the *Colonist*, "we have had three of our steamboats blown up. Two became total wrecks. The loss of life through these explosions has been from twenty to twenty-five persons, and nearly . . . . as many have been wounded."[20] This British Columbia newspaper declared many of its steamers to be "floating coffins" and felt that operators had given Victoria some of the poorest vessels.[21]

In Portland Harbor the well-known steamer *Senator* exploded with the loss of six lives,[22] but this tragedy was overshadowed by what was the greatest disaster in the marine history of the Pacific Northwest, the loss of the steamer *Pacific*, November 4 of this same year, 1875.

---

[18] *Lewis & Dryden's Marine History*, pp. 89, 95, 130, 131–33.
[19] *Ibid.*, p. 132.   [20] *British Colonist*, August 3, 1861.
[21] *Ibid.*, March 22, 1863.   [22] *Vancouver Register*, May 7, 1875.

The *Pacific* had steamed out of Victoria Harbor with about two hundred passengers and a crew of fifty aboard. Only two persons lived to tell what happened to this ship within the next few hours. Their names were Neil Henley, ship's quartermaster, and Henry F. Jelley, a passenger. Of the two, the latter was the only one awake when the accident happened, and the statements were conflicting. Later, however, it was confirmed that the *Pacific* had been fatally hit by another steamer, the *Orpheus*, but that Captain Charles A. Sawyer of this vessel had sailed away and left the multitude of survivors to drown.

The loss of the *Pacific* was a tragic blow, especially to Victoria, since so many of those aboard were residents of that city. Wrote the *Colonist*:

We have no heart to dwell to-day, on the disaster that has hurried into eternity so many of our fellow-citizens with whom only a few brief hours ago we mingled in the streets. . . . . The catastrophe is so far-reaching that there is scarcely a household in Victoria but has lost one or more of its members. . . . .[23]

One woman's body washed ashore just a short distance from her Victoria house.

In spite of disasters and reverses, the shipping business of the Pacific Northwest emerged from the 'fifties upon a firm footing. It was meeting very definite needs, which with the absence of railroads could hardly have been met any other way. One scarcely can escape the conclusion that the many services offered by the shipping interests, chiefly the transportation of passengers, freight, express, and mails, hastened the growth of civilization in the Pacific Northwest, thereby paving the way for the coming of the iron horse. Not until the closing decade of the ruggedly individualistic nineteenth century did a new, more modern, and better-regulated era of Pacific Northwest navigation begin.

---

[23] *Vancouver Register*, May 7, 1875; *British Colonist*, November 9, 1875, and September 30, 1881; *Lewis & Dryden's Marine History*, pp. 223–27.

CHAPTER XVIII

STAGECOACH AND EXPRESS MONOPOLIES

Powerful and grasping as was the Oregon Steam Navigation Company, it did not stand alone as a monopoly-seeking organization. In the Puget Sound and on the Fraser River there were smaller steamship businesses which frankly aspired to imitate the example of their big sister on the Columbia. The Pacific Mail Steamship Company had long enjoyed the lion's share of the coastwise mail contracts, and the California Steam Navigation Company had for all intents and purposes a monopoly of the California river shipping.

While the steamship interests set the pace for mergers or consolidations, those associated with staging and express were not slow to follow. The first evidence of rather highly co-ordinated staging operations in Oregon came in 1860 when the monopolistic California Stage Company extended its services to Portland. But this was merely a taste of what was to come.

Hardly had the California Stage Company begun its Oregon service when it fell on evil days. For a time it was confronted with a shortage of horses, and after scouring the Oregon market importations were made from the East at high cost.[1] Then during the winter of 1861–1862 a "most disastrous" flood so impaired the traffic that service over the Oregon-California line was halted for months.[2] This company, moreover, found it difficult to handle the steadily increasing volume of United States mail at the stipulated rate of $90,000 per annum. In view of this situation the company (it being the only bidder) felt compelled to ask the government for $250,000 per annum compensation when in 1864 it came time to make a new bid. This amount the postal department thought excessive, and only a short-term grant from September 15, 1864, to June 30, 1865, was awarded. In the meantime new bids were required, and again the California Stage Company, the only bidder, asked a sum of $300,000 per annum. This time the government refused to make an award and instead proceeded to make arrangements with outside interests headed by James Reeside who was to receive $225,000 per annum compensation for carrying the mails between Lincoln, California (forty-one miles north of Sacramento) and Portland.[3] Thus failing to obtain a

---

[1] "Reminiscences of H. C. Ward."

[2] Clark, *Willamette Valley*, p. 500.

[3] *House Executive Documents*, 39 Cong., 1 sess., doc. 1, p. 3; *Sacramento Daily Union*, October 23, 1865.

renewal of the contract on satisfactory terms, the California Stage Company declined to continue with its Oregon service "except by temporary arrangement for public accomodation [sic]."[4]

The failure to secure a favorable contract for the Oregon extension appears to have had a disastrous effect upon the entire California Stage Company business. While it did continue to operate stages between Oregon and California after the expiration of its mail contract on June 30, 1865, the concern disintegrated during the autumn of that year. This may have been augmented by the steady extension of railroad lines within California which compelled the stage firm to discontinue branch lines.

It was at this time of weakness that the door was opened for Louis McLane, president of the Overland Mail Company and general agent for Wells, Fargo and Company, to step in and assume control. The extent to which Wells, Fargo and Company owned the Overland Mail Company is not precisely known, but that the express concern was a heavy investor is definitely established.[5] In any event, during October 1865, McLane and a small group of San Francisco capitalists purchased sufficient California Stage Company stock for McLane to assume direction of the line.[6] Since the $179,000 United States contract for carrying mail between Portland and Lincoln went to the Henry W. Corbett Company of Portland,[7] McLane withdrew in 1866 from the Oregon field.

The proprietor, Henry W. Corbett, was a native of Massachusetts. He had come to Portland in 1851 and had made a considerable fortune as a retail and wholesale merchant. Later he became a partner with Harvey W. Scott and Henry L. Pittock as publisher of the Portland *Oregonian*. He was possessed, wrote a contemporary, of "a fair share of energy, tact, thrift, and abundance of prudent judgment."[8] He was very amiable and his success as a stagecoach operator was instantaneous and so far-reaching that even though Corbett became a United States Senator from Oregon in 1867 his name is still more closely identified in the public mind of that state with transportation than with any other phase of his career.

On July 1, 1866, Corbett and Company began staging operations over the long stretch of road between Sacramento and Portland. What had previously been called the California and Oregon Stage Line was thenceforth named the Oregon Stage Company.

Corbett gave his new line a good send-off. Many reorganizations were made; there were personnel changes, and large varicolored placards

[4] *Sacramento Daily Union*, October 23, 1865.

[5] J. V. Frederick, *Ben Holladay: The Stagecoach King* (Glendale, California, 1940), p. 260.

[6] *Sacramento Daily Union*, October 23, 1865.

[7] *Daily Alta California*, April 10, 1866.   [8] *Sacramento Daily Union*, October 9, 1866.

PALACE STEAMER ON THE COLUMBIA RIVER

THE STEAMER "R. R. THOMPSON" ON THE UPPER COLUMBIA

were posted to advertise the "Oregon Line Stages" which go "Through in Six Days to Sacramento."[9] A traveler on the line wrote Corbett August 14, 1866, praising the organization very highly. "The Hostlers all seemed to be on hand, ... the Stock on the whole route in good order; in fact there was but little . . . . that could be complained of except bad bridges . . . . ."[10]

Although changes were subsequently made in organization, the Oregon Stage Company continued to control the stagecoach business between California and Oregon until these two states were linked by rail in 1887.[11]

It was not until the rush of population into Idaho and Montana during the early 'sixties that thought was even given to the establishment of stage lines east of the Cascades. And even so, stagecoach service there lagged somewhat behind the establishment of the packing and wagon-freighting businesses.

Walla Walla appears to have been the first to see its importance as a stagecoach entrepôt as well as a freighting center. Prospective passengers would in all likelihood disembark from their river steamers at Wallula, and accordingly two daily stages began services over the Wallula–Walla Walla road in 1863. From the latter town a line known as the George F. Thomas and Company was the following year projected over the emigrant road to Boise. This concern was also known as the Thomas and Ruckel Line, because Col. J. S. Ruckel, of the Oregon Steam Navigation Company, later became associated with Thomas. Similarly, a triweekly service was begun in July 1863, between The Dalles and Boise.[12]

Other lines came into existence during the following year. Henry Greathouse established a stagecoach service between the booming Idaho towns of Centreville, Placerville, and Idaho City,[13] whereas John Hailey ("Uncle John," active in politics, and the "most popular man in Idaho"), mentioned in connection with pioneer freighting, began, in the same year, a stage service between the Umatilla landing and Boise by way of La Grande, a distance of about 285 miles. An enthusiastic Hailey supporter living in La Grande wrote the editor of the Portland Oregonian, January 17, 1865, that Hailey and Company (also known as the Oregon and Idaho Stage Company, and again as Hailey and Ish) had been offering regular service between Umatilla and his home town and

[9] Red Bluff Independent, July 4, 1866; see also, Scott, Oregon Country, I, 50, 108; V, 183–88.

[10] Mae Hélène Bacon Boggs, comp., My Playhouse Was a Concord Coach (Oakland, California, 1942), p. 452.

[11] Clark, Willamette Valley, p. 522.

[12] Gilbert, Historic Sketches, pp. 230, 232; James H. Hawley, ed., History of Idaho: The Gem of the Mountains (Chicago, 1920), I, 415–16; Gill, "Oregon's First Railway," pp. 176–77.

[13] Bancroft, Washington, Idaho, and Montana, p. 421.

had *"never missed a single trip"* and that only one and a half days were consumed in the Umatilla to La Grande lap of the journey to Boise. The time involved in the entire trip was four days. ". . . . every body who travel the route are loud in their praise of every one connected with the Stage line, who are ever obliging and know no effort too great to accommodate their patrons," continues this letter.[14]

The first stagecoach used by Hailey and Ish was purchased at Shasta City, California, and was delivered by being driven to Portland over the regular California-Oregon route and then shipped by steamer to The Dalles. From there it was again driven to Umatilla. The time consumed was fifty-nine days. This method of delivery proved so successful that four other coaches were imported in the same manner. The fare between Umatilla and Boise was $100. Such other Idaho towns as Idaho City, Placerville, and Owyhee were served by Hailey and Ish.[15] Said a group of travelers in a joint letter to the Portland *Oregonian* in 1865 about the Hailey and Ish line: "We can cheerfully recommend this line to the traveling public, for we know it to be in competent hands, and entirely able to do what it agrees to. . . . ."[16] Added to this, the *Idaho World* assured the public that there were "no Indians along the road."[17]

Complaints, on the other hand, were made about the roadway. "From Idaho City to Boise," wrote one passenger, the road is "a confirmed nuisance. . . . . The road to Boise," he added, "is so confined to gulches that it is a continual annoyance to the stage. . . . . The passengers had to carry the stage out into the willows in knee-deep water, to make way for freight wagons."[18]

Throughout the 'sixties there existed a keen competition between the stage lines operating over the Wallula–Walla Walla–Boise route and those giving service over the Umatilla-Boise road. Both roads crossed the Blue Mountains within two miles of each other and intersected at what was known as Express Ranch on the Burnt River, Oregon, seventy miles from Umatilla. At that point transfers could be made, not only from one of these lines to the other, but also with Greathouse and Company which, it will be recalled, ran its line to Placerville.

Up to 1865 these three companies continued to be the chief ones serving the Boise Basin, although smaller lines did exist. Ward and Company operated over a thirty-six-mile line between Idaho City and Boise but later sold out to Greathouse and Company. The Barnes and Yates Line operated over the sixty-five-mile Boise and Silver City, Idaho, road

[14] *Oregonian*, January 17, 1866.

[15] Bancroft, *op. cit.*, pp. 423–24; Gilbert, *op. cit.*, p. 232; *The Idaho World*, February 4, 1865.

[16] *Oregonian*, April 7, 1865.

[17] *The Idaho World*, May 8, 1867.　　　　　　　[18] *Ibid.*, July 1, 1865.

until 1865 when Hill Beachy, also a pioneer stageman, purchased it. In 1865 William Ish sold out his interest in the Hailey-Ish concern and became a partner of his erstwhile competitor in the Thomas line, but before the year was over Hailey bought up most of the Thomas and Ish interests. This deal was in turn followed (1865) by a consolidation of Hailey, Beachy, Greathouse, and a new man named Kelly. This great concern now controlled practically all staging operations in the Boise Valley. Then in 1866 this newly consolidated outfit secured a subcontract for carrying mail between Boise and Virginia City, Nevada. Indian depredations, however, were so great that the new Company was forced to discontinue operations into Nevada. In 1867 the *Oregonian* announced the completion of an "air line" road from The Dalles to Umatilla. The distance was now eighty miles, and the famous ex-Californian, Henry Ward, was to operate stages between The Dalles and Umatilla in less time than the steamboats which would thereby deprive the Oregon Steam Navigation Company of some of its business. A further extension of this road from Umatilla to Walla Walla was contemplated, the entire distance to be 125 miles, or just one day's ride by stage, and this would offer further competition with the monopolistic steamship company.[19]

In this Idaho-Nevada venture the foregoing gentleman did not stand alone. At this juncture none other than Captain John Mullan, the great road builder, entered the picture. On March 24, 1866, Mullan, long interested in establishing a stage line in the Inland Empire, announced his opening of the Chico–Silver City, Nevada line, a route over which he had already offered intermittent stage service during the preceding year.[20] The Mullan line was to be known as the California and Idaho Stage Line and offered to bring Californians much closer to the Idaho gold fields than did the roundabout service via Portland. The latter route was described as three times as far and twice as costly. "This route," says the *Chico Weekly Courant*, "has the advantage of all other routes to Idaho from the fact that it passes through a series of the richest mining Districts on the Pacific Coast."[21] The following is a newspaper announcement about this service:

IDAHO STAGE LINE!
THROUGH DIRECT
FROM
CHICO TO BOISE CITY

Carrying the United States Mail and Wells Fargo & Co's Express—Hurrah for the California and Idaho Stage Line!!! . . . .

---

[19] Hawley, *History of Idaho*, I, 415–19; *Oregonian*, June 12, 1867; Bancroft, *Washington, Idaho, and Montana*, pp. 435–36.

[20] *The Idaho World*, September 9, 1865; *Chico Weekly Courant*, March 24, 1866.

[21] *Chico Weekly Courant*, September 8, 1866.

Will go through in seven days [to Boise] . . . . The webfoot route may reap the fruits this season, but it will be the last. . . . . People need not risk their lives and their all by the dangerous ocean route any more. . . . . The overland stage will hereafter take the travel. Hurrah for the California and Idaho Stage Company![22]

The fare over this route, Chico to Ruby City, was sixty dollars, and the time involved four days.[23]

Well conceived and much needed as was this direct stagecoach connection between Idaho and California, Indian troubles from the very start presented terrific obstacles. Captain Mullan was able to secure a military escort,[24] but depredations along the line of travel continued to be considerable.[25]

The presence of the great Continental Divide between the Boise and Deer Lodge valleys handicapped stagecoach and express communication between the two equally thriving mining regions. Montana re-established her pack train communication with Idaho, Washington, and Oregon by means of the Mullan Road, but stagecoach connections were made only by indirect travel via the Oregon Trail. Not until the extension of the vast Holladay Overland Stage line into the Pacific Northwest July 1, 1864, was Montana provided with more or less direct stagecoach communication with her Western neighbors.

The Montana mining camps, on the other hand, early established direct and regular stagecoach and express connections with Fort Benton, the upper Missouri steamship port, and with Salt Lake City. Granville Stuart, writing his observations, recalled that in August 1863, A. J. Oliver and Company operated a mail and stage service between Virginia City, Bannack, and Salt Lake City.[26] Previous to this mails were carried by pony to points on the Oregon Trail, according to the recollections of a pioneer.[27] Note, for example, the following Virginia City, Montana, 1864 advertisement of Oliver and Company's Express, which, incidentally, also carried passengers:

A. J. Oliver & Co's
Express Line

Will Leave Virginia City for Great Salt Lake City, Utah every Tuesday and Saturday. . . . .

Nearest Route by
70 Miles
Time   4 Days!!

. . . .   D. W. Tilton & Co., agents.[28]

[22] *Chico Weekly Courant*, June 30, 1866.   [23] *Ibid.*, August 25, 1866.
[24] *Idaho Weekly Statesman*, September 10 and 16, 1865; Bancroft, *op. cit.*, pp. 435–36.
[25] Hawley, *History of Idaho*, I, 419.   [26] *Journals of Granville Stuart*, I, 264; II, 22.
[27] *The Anaconda Standard* (Butte, Montana), November 25, 1914.
[28] *Montana Post*, September 24, 1864.

The same *Montana Post* carried a dispatch to the effect that: "Oliver & Co's [stage] arrived on Monday, September 19th, three days and ten hours from Salt Lake City with four passengers and 800 lbs of peaches. That's good time Oliver."[29]

Irrespective of the Holladay system, to which reference will presently be made, many independent stage and express lines continued to flourish. The *Rocky Mountain Gazette* stated that for a given period, May to October 1866, no less than 2,500 passengers were carried by way of Fort Benton and Helena.[30]

Oregon stagemen, anxious to have their share of the Montana trade, organized the Oregon and Montana Transportation Company, which in conjunction with the Oregon Steam Navigation Company offered in 1866 through steamship-stagecoach service between Portland and the Montana mining camps.

Eastbound passengers over this very unusual route would travel by steamer up the Columbia River from Portland to White Bluffs and from there by stagecoach to a point on Pend d'Oreille Lake; across the Lake and up Clark's (or Clarke's) Fork to Cabinet Landing, Montana, passage was secured on the specially built *Mary Moody*; there still another portage was made by stagecoach to the mouth of the Jocko River from which point roads diverged to the various Montana mining camps. Seven to eight days were required for this remarkable trip from Portland to Jocko. When one takes into account the extremely wooded and mountainous character of this route it is no wonder that the *Oregonian* wrote with pride: "Too much cannot be said in praise of the gentlemen who have thus far pushed this gigantic enterprise to a successful end."[31]

With the beginning of exploitation of the Fraser River and Cariboo gold regions in 1858, another green pasture was opened to the express and stage business. Wells, Fargo and Company was in the best position to capitalize upon the British Columbia market, as it had established an office in Victoria, fully three years before the Fraser River gold rush began.[32] In 1859 the company's agent in Victoria was C. C. Pendergast, and it was largely through his office that the volume of express from up the Fraser and from Cariboo was funneled.

Offering some competition to Wells, Fargo and Company in British Columbia were the Freeman and Company New York and California Express, McDonald and Company's Express, and such purely local concerns as Yale's British Columbia Express which operated between Vic-

---

[29] *Ibid.*

[30] *Rocky Mountain Gazette,* October 20, 1866.

[31] *Oregonian,* June 2, 1866; Bancroft, *Washington, Idaho, and Montana,* p. 729 n.

[32] Winther, *Express and Stagecoach Days,* p. 142 n.

toria, Douglas, Hope, and Yale. William T. Ballou's Express, serving the Victoria-Lillooet region, pioneered by canoes and mules to the mines, and Jeffray and Company operated along the Fraser River.[33]

Some indication as to the volume of business performed by the leading express concerns may be had from a published statement of gold shipments to San Francisco up to September 4, 1860. Through 1858, Wells, Fargo and Company apparently handled all outgoing commercial shipments to San Francisco and the amount was $337,765. For 1859 this concern transported $951,489 in gold, whereas the McDonald and Freeman concerns shipped $199,815 and $60,000 respectively. The total for this year was $1,211,304. Then for the first eight months of 1860, Wells, Fargo and Company appears to have been again the only shipper, and the amount was $782,950, making a grand total[34] of $2,332,019.

In contrast with express, staging concerns remained local and independent in character. Not until 1861 did the first Concord coach appear in British Columbia. It had been imported from San Francisco by the True Briton Stage Line. "It is capable of accomodating twelve persons," wrote the *Colonist*, somewhat in amazement, "and is very light and at the same time a substantial looking affair." It was believed slated for the Harrison-Lillooet route.[35] One concern known as the Royal Mail Company's Stage Line operated between Douglas and Lillooet[36] in 1861. By the middle 'sixties the best-known and best-liked staging firm was F. K. Barnard's Express which connected with the steamer *Enterprise* at Clinton for the mouth of the Quesnelle River. From this point, according to an issue of the *Colonist* of April 1865, Barnard also promised coach service "to *Cottonwood* just as soon as the road is opened" and saddle trains from there to the Cariboo. In 1864 this company seems to have had bad luck, between precarious roads, unmanageable animals, and irresponsible drivers, for several references are made in contemporary news accounts to narrow escapes. The blame for one accident was laid to the driver being intoxicated and whipping the horses into a full gallop. At this clip the stage struck stone, the tongue broke, and, as a natural consequence, the horses ran away, turning the vehicle over on a high bank and injuring several passengers.[37]

While stage and express services were late in coming to the British

[33] *British Colonist*, April 9, 1859, April 14, 1860, October 4 and 14, 1861; *The Victoria Gazette*, July 30, 1859; Howay, Sage and Angus, *British Columbia and the United States*, p. 144.

[34] *British Colonist*, September 15, 1860.

[35] *Ibid.*, September 3, 1861.

[36] *Ibid.*, September 18, 1861.

[37] *Ibid.*, March 8 and September 12, 1864, April 4, 1865.

portion of the Oregon country, they persisted there long after the rail-road had replaced horse-drawn vehicles south of the forty-ninth parallel.

The problem of establishing adequate transportation facilities within the Pacific Northwest was one thing; to bind this vast region to the Union with adequate lines of overland communication was another task. It will be recalled that the United States government had taken measures to establish mail and passenger service between the Atlantic states and California during the 'fifties; as a result there was inaugurated in 1858 the famous Butterfield stage line (Overland Mail Company) between St. Louis and San Francisco. Then in 1860 the California Stage Company, already connecting with the Butterfield system, extended its facilities to include Portland, Oregon. This marked the Pacific Northwest's first direct transportation connection with the East, but the vast distances involved were such as to make extensive use of this system highly impractical.

Next came the Civil War which disrupted the Butterfield line and it was at this juncture that a remarkable man stepped into the foreground in the world of transportation. This person was Ben Holladay. Born in Kentucky, Holladay in 1820 had gone to St. Louis at the early age of sixteen. J. V. Frederick's biography describes the youthful Ben as "a rangy and sandy-haired" lad with "little education but from a good family." He stood six feet tall, was muscular and handsome. Hard work and native business acumen soon found him successively store clerk at Weston, Missouri, a liquor vendor, a tavern keeper, and, at twenty-one local postmaster and proprietor of a small hotel. Before another decade passed, the future stagecoach magnate was to become proprietor of a general store and owner of a factory. "Everything known of Ben Holladay at this time bespeaks those qualities which later brought him nation-wide prestige," wrote Frederick. He was "exceedingly ambitious and a dynamo of energy," quick-tempered, and at the same time well liked by many.[38]

It was the Mexican War in 1846 that caused Ben Holladay to become interested in transportation, securing as he did a contract to supply General Stephen W. Kearny with wagons and foodstuffs. The California Gold Rush offered new opportunities and in this connection Holladay formed a partnership with Theodore W. Warner for hauling supplies to Salt Lake City where their produce was sold at a good profit. In Utah Holladay used his money to purchase cattle which he drove to California and sold to the Panama Steamship Company. He repeated this venture and also organized some freighting concerns in California during the

---

[38] Frederick, *Ben Holladay*, pp. 20–24.

'fifties. After the Mormon War of 1857, for instance, Holladay became associated with the famous Russell, Majors and Waddell freighting firm that operated on the plains, and in this connection capitalized on the Pike's Peak gold rush in Colorado at the close of the decade.[39] Thus with the outbreak of the war and the resultant disruption of the Butterfield line, it was Ben Holladay who was ready, both from the standpoint of financial resources and personal experience, to capitalize on David Butterfield's misadventure.

It would be outside the scope of this work to delve into a detailed history of stagecoach and mail service in the central plains area. Suffice it to say that as early as 1848 an overland pack mule express had been organized between California and the Mississippi River by Samuel Brannan, but this venture did not outlast the year.[40] Two years later Samuel H. Woodson, who secured a United States government contract, began monthly mail service between Independence and Salt Lake City. Then in 1851 George Chorpenning and Absalom Woodward, likewise armed with a government contract, opened a similar service between the Mormon capital and Sacramento. In this form overland service was maintained until John Butterfield established his Overland Mail in 1858.

Good as it was, the establishment of the Butterfield service did not quiet the demand for faster and more frequent service over the central plains region. The simultaneous discovery of gold near Pike's Peak made frequent stagecoach service to that region imperative. Accordingly, William H. Russell of the Russell, Majors and Waddell firm and John S. Jones organized the Leavenworth and Pike's Peak Express which began operations May 17, 1859. This firm soon established regular communication between Missouri and Utah. Reverses due to the slackening of the Colorado gold rush caused the Russell, Majors and Waddell firm to take over the Leavenworth and Pike's Peak Express. In 1860 this firm was reorganized under a Kansas Territory charter and a new name was given it. It was to be known as the Central Overland California and Pike's Peak Express Company, and this firm was soon to operate the spectacular Pony Express, from April 1860, until the completion of the transcontinental telegraph line in the autumn of 1861.

Then, as has been stated, the Civil War disrupted the original Butterfield line in the south; in fact, military engagement very quickly took place in areas through which the Butterfield stage actually passed. Even before the Lincoln administration had taken office (March 2, 1861), Postmaster General Joseph Holt, with Congressional authority, provided

[39] Frederick, *Ben Holladay*, pp. 26–42.

[40] Winther, *Express and Stagecoach Days*, p. 19.

for a new mail contract for the transfer of the Butterfield mail to the central route. This was to go "from some point on the Missouri River connected with the East," to Placerville, California. Interestingly enough, in this new contract of 1861 the Central Overland California and Pike's Peak Express was to share with the Butterfield company. It was now arranged that the former would carry the mail between Atchison and Salt Lake City; Butterfield would take it between the Mormon capital and Placerville. On this new basis service began July 1, 1861, from St. Joseph, arriving in San Francisco on the evening of July 18.

In all these transactions Ben Holladay was in the background, but in an important way. His association with Russell, Majors and Waddell, owners of the Central Overland California and Pike's Peak Express, widened as the financial stringency of his three associates increased. The new central overland mail and passenger service, unfortunately, failed to pay expenses and on March 21, 1862, its assets were offered for sale at public auction at Atchison. And it was Ben Holladay, already one of the Company's partners and mortgagers, who, in an effort to protect his own investment, made the highest bid of $100,000. By this transaction the irrepressible Ben Holladay found himself in possession of over 1,200 miles of nonprofit stage lines.

Holladay dared not and did not rest upon his oars. He hastily revamped his main line between Atchison and Salt Lake City. The name Overland Stage Line was adopted (in 1866 to be changed to Holladay Overland Mail & Express Company); new and up-to-date coaches were ordered from the Abbot-Downing Company; faster livestock was purchased; personnel changes were made; and the main route itself was altered to provide cut-offs and to meet recent population shifts. Most important of all, Holladay secured favorable contracts from the United States government for carrying the mails over his line.[41]

The new king of the Central Overland was quick to capitalize on the great flow of miners into the Inland Empire. It is known that as early as March 1864, Holladay had secured a mail contract and had plans laid for an extension of the Atchison–Salt Lake City line to run over the familiar Corinne Road from Salt Lake City to Virginia City, Montana Territory (three hundred miles), and on July 1, 1864, a triweekly service was actually begun which passed old Fort Hall. Later, as the following advertisement[42] shows, this service was extended to other mining towns in the Montana district.

---

[41] Frederick, *op. cit.*, pp. 45 ff. For a general discussion see Frank A. Root and William E. Connelley, *The Overland Stage to California* (Topeka, 1901); LeRoy R. Hafen, *The Overland Mail* (Cleveland, 1926), chaps. 9–10.

[42] *Montana Post*, December 3, 1864.

OVERLAND STAGE LINE
Ben. Holladay, Proprietor
Carrying the Great Through Mail Between
Atlantic and Pacific States
This line is now running in connection with the Daily Coaches between

ATCHISON, KANSAS, & PLACERVILLE, CAL.

Tri-weekly Coaches between
Salt Lake City and Walla Walla,
Via Boise City, West Bannack, and

TRI-WEEKLY COACHES
between
Great Salt Lake City and Virginia City,
Montana, via Bannack City,

CARRYING THE U.S. MAIL,
Passengers, and Express Matter.

Also, tri-weekly coaches between Virginia City and Bannack City. Coaches for Great Salt Lake City and Bannack City, leave Virginia City every

TUESDAY, THURSDAY & SUNDAY MORNING,

connecting at Fort Hall with coaches to Boise and Walla Walla, and at Great Salt Lake City, with the daily lines to the:

ATLANTIC STATES, NEVADA AND CALIFORNIA,

Express matter carried in charge of competent and trustworthy messengers.
For further particulars apply at offices.

NAT STEIN, Agent.
Virginia City, Montana Territory.

There seemed to be no halting for Holladay. In fact, his mail contract called for similar triweekly service between Salt Lake City and the Boise Valley and finally Walla Walla, Umatilla, and The Dalles. At any of the last three points passengers and mail could be transferred to river steamers for delivery at Portland, Oregon, or vice versa. Fort Hall again became an important junction in that the Idaho, Washington, and Oregon-bound stages there turned west from the aforementioned Salt Lake City–Montana route. The contract called for service over this section to begin September 30, 1864. Holladay let a subcontract to Thomas and Company to operate between Boise City and The Dalles until 1866 when Hailey and Greathouse bought out the Thomas line and assumed the subcontract. The distance from Salt Lake City was about 1,000 miles. The fare at first over this stretch was $100 from Salt Lake City to Boise, $240, Salt Lake City to The Dalles; this, of course, was added to $300 fare from Atchison to Salt Lake City.[43]

---

[43] Hawley, *History of Idaho*, I, 412–13; Frederick, *op. cit.*, pp. 145–48, 154.

In its final organization as of 1866 the Holladay system was a vast and highly successful enterprise. Its importance to the Pacific Northwest was tremendous in that now, at long last, there were fast and, by 1866, daily stagecoach connections (involving a distance of about two thousand miles and less than three weeks' travel from the steamship landing at The Dalles to Atchison)[44] between this remote Oregon frontier and the Atlantic states.

What an elaborate transportation empire the Holladay system was! It is little wonder that its crafty creator has been called the "Napoleon of the West." He operated a main line of stages across the prairies from Atchison, Kansas, to Salt Lake City, a distance of 1,250 miles. From the capital of the Saints his subsidiary lines fanned out 950 miles northwest into Montana, Idaho, and Oregon to The Dalles. His mail contracts for these lines totaled $650,000 per year.

Operational costs were enormous. Over the full extent of the Holladay network stations and stables at ten- to fifteen-mile intervals, with large granaries and corrals, were maintained. Supplies, especially for the desert stations, had to be transported several hundred miles at great cost. In one year alone Holladay suffered a $1,500,000 loss from Indian depredations.

Holladay traveled extensively over his own lines, but in so doing, wrote a contemporary, he "passes over it with a rapidity and disregard of expense and rules, characteristic of his irrepressible nature." On one occasion he had himself driven from Salt Lake to Atchison in six and one-half days, a record run that cost the owner an estimated $20,000 in wear and tear on his stock.[45] But for its cost, it was a smooth-working organization that gave the Pacific Northwest its first direct stagecoach connection with the East.

Developments in the express field were closely knit to those of staging. The failure in California of Adams and Company Express in 1855 left no question about the supremacy of Wells, Fargo and Company in the express business on the Pacific Coast. San Francisco continued to be the headquarters for its Pacific Coast operations. In 1860 the company maintained 147 express offices in California, but that the firm was then securing a foothold in the Pacific Northwest is indicated by the presence of offices at Portland, Port Orford, Umpqua City, and Prairie City in Oregon; Seattle, Olympia, Steilacoom, Port Townsend, and Whatcom in Washington; and at Victoria and Fraser River in British Columbia. A financial statement published by the company in 1860 shows a gross

[44] *Idaho Weekly Statesman*, April 29, 1866.
[45] Bowles, *Across the Continent*, pp. 51–55.

revenue of $395,187.70 and a net income of $151,128.47 on express operations.[46]

Through the 'sixties and 'seventies Wells, Fargo and Company continued to expand its activities in the Pacific Northwest, noticeably so when the mining frontier advanced into the Inland Empire. In the absence of a special express office, the firm continued to follow a practice, long tried in California, of appointing local stagecoach operators as its agents. In nearly every town to which there were stagecoach connections one usually finds the advertisements regarding passenger service also carrying the words: "and Wells, Fargo & Co.'s Express."[47] As a tribute to the business ingenuity of this firm the *Oregonian* has this to say :

The people of all new sections are indebted a great deal to Wells, Fargo & Co., for the facilities afforded by their express to hear from the outside world. Before any mail facilities can be established in the regions that become suddenly peopled through the discovery of gold, and opened up to the commercial and mercantile communities, Wells, Fargo, & Co. send their messengers on ahead and become the medium through which business to the amount of millions is transacted. Even after mails are established, this express continues to be the most reliable means of communication for years. Their rates of carrying are greater, but there is no uncertainty about the matter. Just now, Wells, Fargo & Co. are all we have to depend upon for obtaining our exchanges, letters, etc., in this valley. We could not hear from the Capital, or any interior town on the overland route, were it not for them, and we are greatly indebted to them for favors. A community like this can appreciate Wells, Fargo, & Co., even at the expense of a Government, which they have contributed, and are still contributing daily, to support.[48]

The Wells, Fargo and Company office had come to be regarded on the West Coast as an institution, and in the mind of one writer, as much a part of any Western town as a billiard saloon and a restaurant. "They forward goods everywhere," adds this person, "convey nearly all the 'treasure' in gold or silver, do a general banking business, and are infinitely more trusted by the public with the transmission of mail matter than the Government Postoffice."[49] With regard to the letter-carrying it must be recalled that express companies wishing to carry the United States mails had first to pay the regular government postage charges and then add their own express franks. Nevertheless, the Wells, Fargo and Company sold $86,407.55 worth of express franks[50] in 1860, and in 1864

---

[46] "Wells, Fargo and Company Records," pp. 45, *passim.*

[47] See for example the *Puget Sound Business Directory . . . . 1872 (Olympia,* n. d.).

[48] *Oregonian,* September 15, 1865.

[49] Frederick Whymper, *Travel and Adventure in the Territory of Alaska . . . .* (New York, 1869), p. 317.

[50] "Wells, Fargo and Company Records," *passim.*

the firm is reported to have purchased no less than 2,500,000 three-cent stamps and 125,000 of higher value.[51]

Having acquired what was an unquestioned monopoly of the express business on the Pacific Coast, as well as a flourishing banking business, the Wells, Fargo and Company looked for new fields to conquer. Logically enough it turned to the stagecoach business with which it had always had the closest connections. William G. Fargo along with William B. Dinsmore were, in fact, co-recipients with John Butterfield for the so-called Butterfield mail contract awarded by Postmaster General Brown in 1857, a contract which by its very specifications called for stagecoach operations.[52] Later this famous express house felt compelled to consider further entrance into the staging business due to its inability to come to terms with Ben Holladay with regard to shipping express over his lines. The firm, first having failed by exerting pressure on Holladay, threatened in 1866 to establish a competing line between Salt Lake City (through its Butterfield interests it already had connections between Sacramento and the Mormon capital) and Denver. It was this situation that led to far-reaching consequences.

Holladay was not a person easily high-pressured. Having by 1866 gained full control of all competing lines as far as Salt Lake City, he reportedly burst out to his secretary: "Answer those express companies and tell them to stock [a competing line] and be d--d!"[53] Behind this bravado Holladay knew full well that with the completion of the Union Pacific–Central Pacific railroad his stagecoach system would be badly shattered. He knew, therefore, that if the Wells, Fargo and Company would buy his system, the decision to sell would be a wise one. And such happened to be the case. On November 1, 1866, Louis McLane, representing Wells, Fargo and Company, purchased from this erstwhile "King" the entire Holladay Overland Mail and Express system. For his holdings Ben Holladay received $1,500,000 in cash and $300,000 of Wells, Fargo and Company stock, and a directorship in the latter firm. Twelve days following the purchase, stockholders of the express firm met and changed the corporate name of Holladay Overland Mail and Express to Wells, Fargo and Company.[54]

Wells, Fargo and Company now reigned supreme, not alone in the field of express but in the stagecoach business as well. The importance of this transaction was nation-wide, but to the Pacific Northwest it had a very special meaning. It meant that now practically every department of its transportation facilities was controlled by three giant concerns:

---

[51] Whymper, *op. cit.*, p. 317.

[52] *House Executive Documents*, 35 Cong., 1 sess., vol. II, pt. 3, p. 986.

[53] Frederick, *Ben Holladay*, p. 252. [54] *Ibid.*, pp. 260–61.

the Oregon Steam Navigation Company, the Pacific Mail Steamship Company, and now the Wells, Fargo and Company. The day of monopolies had definitely arrived.

Did monopoly bring better service at lower costs? The answer, so far as stagecoach and express service was concerned is "No." There were complaints that Wells, Fargo and Company had ceased to be the efficient and much-liked public servant it had been for so long. From Helena came the report that Wells, Fargo and Company stages had slowed down their schedule and had restricted the service. "There is no sufficient reason," complained the *Helena Weekly Herald*, why her city should not have daily rather than triweekly service.[55]

And from *The Idaho World* came this damning complaint about the company's carelessness with the mails:

> The Overland Mail Evil—Ever since the Overland Mail was first instituted very serious evils have been connected with its operation. Chief among these evils is that most culpable one—the abandonment or destruction of whole sacks of mail matter by the roadside. It is charged by passengers who have made the overland trip in the mail stages, and their statements are corroborated by drivers who have been in the employ of the Company [Wells, Fargo and Company] that it is customary all along the route to cast away sacks of newspaper mails, in the streams, in swampy places, in mireholes, and other spots where the sacks are likely soon to sink out of sight, so that the trouble and labor of transporting them in the stages shall be spared. It is further alleged that the paper mail sacks are frequently opened on the way. . . . .[56]

What was even more damning to the reputation of Wells, Fargo and Company was a published letter, signed by four men, to the effect that they had observed that Wells, Fargo and Company mail carriers were careless with the mailbags and had lost some of them, and that they as stage passengers were (1867) obliged to travel from Denver to Salt Lake City in a lumber wagon rather than a coach, asking: "Is this proper treatment for the public to receive at the hand of a firm who are so largely compensated by the United States for a duty that they perform so badly?"[57]

To this *The Idaho World* replied: "Wells, Fargo & Co. are the contractors for carrying this Overland Mail. They contract to carry it safely and expeditiously," adding that this makes them "responsible for the faithfull fulfillment of their contract."[58]

Greater troubles than public complaints faced the Wells, Fargo and Company, when on May 10, 1869, the Union Pacific and Central Pacific railroads met at Promontory Point. Staging along the central route was,

---

[55] *Helena Weekly Herald*, November 28, and December 5, 1867.

[56] *The Idaho World*, May 11, 1867.

[57] *Ibid.*, June 1, 1867.   [58] *Ibid.*

for all intents and purposes, over. So far as the Union Pacific Company was concerned, Wells Fargo was out of luck. The exclusive privilege of handling express over this line went to the United States Express Company.

Then what about the Central Pacific? To the surprise, if not consternation, of most interested parties the Central Pacific Railroad Company, on September 25, 1869, granted the Pacific Express Company an exclusive monopoly to handle express over its facilities for a period of ten years. The chief reason for this arrangement may well be explained by the fact that the Central Pacific Railroad Company owned three-fifths of the stock of the Pacific Express.

Such a situation seemed ruinous to Wells Fargo, and officers of the company lost no time seeking an arrangement with their competitors. A joint meeting of directors of both companies met at Omaha on October 4. D. O. Mills and Lloyd Tevis were there representing the Pacific Express; none other than William G. Fargo, Charles Fargo, and A. H. Barney were there in person to represent the badly cornered but none the less powerful Wells Fargo concern. At this momentous Omaha conference Wells, Fargo and Company, for the consideration of $5,000,000, was given the exclusive privilege of handling express over the Central Pacific. The agreement also provided for the retirement from business of the Pacific Express Company.

A stormy meeting of Wells, Fargo and Company stockholders was held on November 25 to discuss how to raise the $5,000,000. Accounts vary somewhat, but it would appear that this huge sum was produced by increasing the capital stock of the company from $10,000,000 to $15,000,000. The price paid seemed like financial extortion to some of the stockholders at the time, but the decision proved sound from the long-range point of view. As the Central, and later the Southern Pacific, railroad systems expanded throughout the West and on south into Mexico, Wells, Fargo and Company expanded with it. Had the company not made this investment, its express services might well have gone the way of its stagecoach line and passed into the limbo of pleasant and exciting memories.[59]

The coming of railway express offered a challenge for the improvement of service which, happily, was accepted. Express transportation remained the same by definition, but within its sphere many new services were offered at far greater speed. "They will pay taxes on property thousands of miles from here," wrote *The Expressman's Monthly*; "if you die away from home they'll bury you anywhere you wish; they will

---

[59] Schaffer, "Early History of the Wells Fargo Express," pp. 99–111; Harlow, *Old Waybills*, chap. 14.

advance money to people in distress" and "provide them with tickets." They also offered to carry government money, supplies, and munitions, handle the shipment of fresh vegetables, and even look for lost or stolen treasures.[60] Having a highly skilled detective staff to combat road agents, the company considered this just a part of the day's work.

For many years after the coming of the transcontinental railroad, horse-drawn stagecoaches and express wagons continued to connect with the trains. The *Wells, Fargo & Co.'s Express Directory* for 1880 lists no less than seventy-six Wells, Fargo and Company offices in the five Pacific Northwest states. Many of these were still along stagecoach lines; some served as transfer points at stage and rail connections; and some were identified solely with railroad lines. Taken as a whole, this *Directory* listing reveals how widely scattered were the Wells Fargo offices, and how, by 1880, the company was in a good position to serve the entire Pacific Northwest.[61]

---

[60] *The Expressman's Monthly,* II (February 1877), 97–119.

[61] *Wells, Fargo & Co's Express Directory* (San Francisco, 1880).

THE MOUNTAIN HOUSE HOTEL, LORANE, OREGON
One of the better stage stations in the 'sixties

PORTAGE RAILROAD AT CELILO

CHAPTER XIX

STAGECOACH TRAVEL

In olden days the stagecoach was regarded as a public menace. When it was first introduced in Europe during the sixteenth century people thought it a dangerous innovation. People might be hurt by such fast-going contrivances, but what was even worse, wrote the Duke of Brunswick in 1588: "Young and old, have dared to give themselves up to indolence, and to riding in coaches."[1] In England one writer went so far as to denounce staging because he thought it the cause of the Gunpowder Plot. The coach, he held, was "a closed hypocrite; for it hath a cover for knavery, and curtains to vaile and shadow any wickedness."[2]

The coach was too useful a contrivance for mankind to spurn, and in time it gained wide popularity. Toward the close of the American Colonial period the stagecoach was in great demand, so that by the time the railroad came, stagecoach lines literally interlaced the entire settled portion of the United States.

In the Pacific Northwest local dependence upon the stagecoach continued long after its greatest usefulness had passed in the East. Until the completion of the Northern Pacific Railroad it remained an essential link between the Oregon country and the East. To a New Yorker, for example, who in 1860 wished to reach Portland in the fastest possible time, there would have been at his disposal Missouri-bound railway trains which even to Horace Greeley afforded "more exercise to the mile" than any other form of transportation. In the year 1860, a traveler from the East could make a transfer at Syracuse, Missouri, from a Pacific Railroad coach to one of Butterfield's coaches for a 3,500-mile trip to Portland via El Paso and Los Angeles. Two years later, with the establishment of the Holladay branch lines to the Columbia, this same New Yorker would undoubtedly have traveled a route which followed very closely the old Oregon Trail.

Whatever the route, the trip would not have been an easy one. Horace Greeley, upon the conclusion of his famous stagecoach ride to Placerville, wrote " . . . . it is a balm for many bruises to know I am at last in CALIFORNIA."[3]

It was at least some comfort to the overland travelers to know that,

---

[1] *Bulletin of the Business Historical Society*, III (September 1929), 11.

[2] *Ibid.*

[3] Horace Greeley, *An Overland Journey* (New York, 1860), p. 282; Conkling and Conkling, *The Butterfield Overland Mail*, I, 166.

difficult as it may have been to ride great distances in horse-drawn vehicles, the stagecoaches then in use were probably the best ever devised by man. Whether it was over the Butterfield or the Holladay lines that people traveled, they would in all likelihood have ridden in sturdy, up-to-date coaches, such as Concords made by J. S. Abbot and Sons (or by 1865, the Abbot-Downing and Company), Concord, New Hampshire; Troys made by Eaton, Gilbert and Company, Troy, New York; or Celerity Wagons made by James Goold Coach Company, Albany, New York.

The Concord coach, which had been on the market since 1813, was very sturdily built. The running gear was strongly held together with parts of iron, while the body was made of well-seasoned ash. The body of the coach rested upon two thick and equally strong thorough braces, straps which extended between the front and rear axles from curved arms. This construction enabled the passenger compartment to roll rather than bounce and jerk whenever the vehicle hit the countless inevitable holes and ruts in the roads.

The center of gravity was lower than on many other makes of coaches and therefore the Concord was less subject to tipping. Moreover, these coaches were so commodious that nine could be accommodated inside (three seats, each with room for three passengers, the middle one being a drop seat which lifted up at the ends to allow passengers to enter the front or rear seats), two on the driver's seat, and a dozen or more could find places on the top where often "dickey" seats were provided.[4] An iron railing was frequently placed around the flat top to secure the baggage. Whether the top was used for passengers or baggage, access to this part of the coach had to be made by the use of a step attached in front of the brake block. A portable step could be attached to the body below the door to aid passengers entering the coach.[5]

In the rear was the "boot" which in transportation parlance meant a leather-covered triangular-shaped rack which was used to convey mail, express, and the passengers' luggage. Then under the driver's seat was a compartment sufficiently large to contain the prized express box. A Concord coach weighed at least a ton, was pulled by either four or six horses, and covered from five to ten miles per hour. A good Concord cost $1,000 to $1,500 delivered on the Pacific Coast. To operate a Concord coach was, therefore, no casual matter, as is well illustrated by local

---

[4] Winther, *Express and Stagecoach Days*, pp. 97–98; Conkling and Conkling, *op. cit.*, I, 131–32; II, 377–83.

[5] "Reminiscences of H. C. Ward"; Oscar Osburn Winther, ed., "Stage-coach Days in California: Reminiscences of H. C. Ward," *California Historical Society Quarterly*, XIII (September 1934), 260 n.

staging concerns which, if they owned such vehicles, seldom failed to stress the fact in their advertisements. Here, for example, is an announcement of what is purported to be Oregon's first Concord coach: "In the Oregon Stage Company's line of stages is one Concord coach, (running between Oregon City, *via* Salem, and Corvallis,) the only one in Oregon. Its cost 'laid down' in Oregon, was $1100."[6]

Even on the main lines there were exceptions to the use of Concord coaches. For instance, over extremely rough and mountainous roads the "mud wagons" were preferred. These were springless wagons, or coaches. The body of the coach rested squarely on the axles. This was done in order to provide a lower center of gravity and thereby lessen the chances of tipping. Spring seats were used to absorb the shocks, and to these the driver and the passengers were strapped to avoid being thrown out when the wheels would sink suddenly into mudholes of indeterminate depths.

Still a third type of vehicle used in Western commercial transportation was the "jerky." This was a two-seated wagon and was in one respect distinguished from a coach in that the latter had three seats.[7]

To drive a stagecoach over the corduroy and dirt roads of the plains or of the Pacific Northwest was a matter requiring dexterity and skill. A considerable folklore has evolved around stagecoach drivers, and certainly many are deserving of a certain amount of lasting fame.[8] Referring to drivers of the Idaho country, Brigadier General James F. Rusling held that they were close-lipped when on the box, but loquacious when off. Moreover, Rusling believed they were extremely fond of both tobacco and whiskey, and also of "pondrous oaths." Coming upon a wagon freight, their greeting was something like this: "Clar the road! Get out of the way thar with your bull teams!"[9]

In such an extraordinary cast of characters it might seem difficult to single out certain men who, because of their special idiosyncracies, stand out above their fellows. But such is farthest from the truth. On the West Coast Hank Monk still remains King of the "knights." Among the court favorites are certainly Alfred, a mulatto, who is supposed to have "driven" more illustrious people than any other "knight," "Baldy" Green, Billy Hamilton, "Mr. Church," Clark Foss ("Old Foss" as he was later known) who had a reputation for being the most reckless driver on the coast, "Buck" Jones, Charlie McConnell, "Buffalo Jim,"

[6] *The Oregon Statesman*, June 14, 1859. For an account of Concord coaches see Banning and Banning, *Six Horses*, pp. 23–26.

[7] *Pacific Christian Advocate*, November 3, 1855.

[8] Oscar Osburn Winther, *Via Western Express & Stagecoach* (Stanford University, 1945), chap. 5.

[9] Rusling, *Across America*, pp. 42–43.

Geyser Bob, Hill Beachy, Henry Ward, and many others. Among the last to drive over the Siskiyous was still another group of drivers whose names live on, among them "Ab" Geddings, Dan Cawley, Nort Eddings, "Charley" Laird, "Hank" Geddings, George Chase, and "Buck" Montgomery (also a "shot-gun messenger").[10] Most of these are perhaps more identified with California than with the Oregon country, although they had a tendency to show up wherever there were roads for stage travel.

Major Truman recalled, for instance, that "Buffalo Jim," who drove out from Portland, had a runaway in the Willamette Valley. "The harness was getting shaky," begins the story, "and two of the traces had given away, but the undergear, the brake, and the lines, remained all right . . . . ." After much bucking, kicking, and going "like the wind" with the Major's wife and sister inside the coach, the four horses finally wore themselves down in the deep sandy soil over which they were fortunate enough to drive.

Hill Beachy was likewise well known in Oregon and Idaho, in fact became a proprietor of lines there before he died. It seems that his chief claim to fame was capturing and bringing to justice in 1863 three murderers in flight from an Idaho mining town with $100,000 in gold.

"Geyser" Bob drove in and out of Yellowstone and was called "Geyser" because he had apparently convinced some Englishmen whom he felt were too inquisitive that he had on many occasions driven down into Old Faithful and had come out at the Beehive.[11] Passengers were often a source of annoyance and there were various ways of dealing with this situation. If the ladies should get out of hand, the driver could, of course, shout "Indians!" and "that," said one old Idaho whip, "quieted them quicker than 40-rod whiskey does a man."[12]

Charlie McConnell drove on the California and Oregon Stage Line, and is referred to as the "prince of drivers." Wallis Nash, who sat in the box beside him on his way to Portland, wrote: "He handled his horses, and worked the heavy brake, and smoked cigars, and chatted unceasingly to his two box-seat passengers, doing all equally well."[13]

Famous in the annals of the Pacific Northwest staging is Henry C. Ward who began his career in September 1849, as one of the very first drivers in California. To an amazed public Ward proved that stages could be run between San Francisco and San Jose, a distance of about

---

[10] Scott, *Oregon Country*, III, see illustration opposite p. 60; see also Winther, *Via Western Express & Stagecoach*, chap. 5.

[11] Ben C. Truman, "Knights of the Lash: Old Time Stage Drivers of the West Coast," *Overland Monthly*, second series, XXXI (March 1898), 222, 317–18.

[12] Brown, *Fort Hall*, p. 355.

[13] Wallis Nash, *Oregon: There and Back in 1877* (London, 1878), p. 90.

fifty miles, in nine hours. Then in 1860 it was this same H. C. Ward who came to Portland to operate stages over the Oregon-California Line. Later his name became connected with pioneer staging into Idaho. Toward the end of his life Ward was the Portland stable superintendent for the Wells, Fargo and Company Express,[14] and it was this company that finally cared for him until his death in 1904.

Stagecoach service on the California and Oregon Line was about the best of its day. Over a period of years it also enjoyed the heaviest patronage. The opening in 1860 of this line between Portland and Sacramento was then considered a matter of national importance in view of the fact that it at last connected Oregon with her sister states both in the South and in the East. To use the words of the *Sacramento Daily Union*: "A person . . . . who has no desire to risk his life on the rough coast of Oregon can take a quiet seat in the stage, pass through a most interesting section of the country, and reach Portland at his leisure."[15]

It is, therefore, to those who traveled over this particular stage line that one might turn for descriptive accounts of stagecoach travel in Oregon. Reactions varied greatly. Some enjoyed it; some thought it a "serious matter" to be traveling in a stage from San Francisco to Portland "when one knows what a stage is, and what the roads are." If riding in the box on the top, there was always the fear of dozing and falling off the stage. And riding inside was no better, thought Nash. On the inside "your head strikes against the wooden supports of the leather sides." Legs, too, appear to have been in the way for there was never quite room enough for them. Then, added the disgruntled Nash, "just as you can hold up no longer, and sleep is stealing over you, creak, gur-r-r, crack go the hind wheels just under you, as the brake comes violently into play down hill, and the stones fly. And the dust!"[16]

Even to the more critical there was always something about a stagecoach journey that attracted favorable comment and this same passenger could not refrain from comments upon the wide tracts of undulating country of southern Oregon, "green everywhere with woods and copses," the "wide slopes of corn-land and grass-fields ripening into summer yellow."

If it was not the country that attracted comment, then it was the towns and the people in them. By the middle of day Nash reached Jacksonville, a town of 1,000 to 1,500 inhabitants. "The day being Sunday," he reports, "the town was in absolute quiet; had we been in Scotland there could not have been a more perfect rest from all worldly pursuits.

---

[14] "Reminiscences of H. C. Ward"; Winther, "Stage-coach Days in California," p. 255.

[15] *Sacramento Daily Union*, September 15, 1860.

[16] Nash, *Oregon*, pp. 86–87.

On the road as we drew near the town we passed waggons full of the country people on their way to church or chapel . . . . ."[17]

Passing through the Rogue River Valley the stage next came into the valley of the Umpqua which reminded Nash of the "Happy Valley of *Rasselas*" because of its green fields, snug homesteads and white farmhouses, its apple orchards and scattered chestnut trees. It gave him a sense of quiet and laziness, "as of a perpetual Sunday afternoon."[18] Soon he reached Roseburg, in 1870 a city of about eight hundred, and in conclusion he wrote:

> And so we passed through a good many miles, till the little town of Roseburg came into view, its white houses and church steeple shining in the bright morning sun. The stage pulled up at the inn before driving on to the post-office to deliver over the mailbags, and we got down to stretch and shake our stiff and weary limbs.
>
> To look back on the journey seemed to pass in review weeks of travelling, and hundreds of miles of distance. One would have thought no less if distance or time could have accounted for such aching bones, tired heads, bloodshot eyes, and travel-stained garments.
>
> The journey from California into Oregon was accomplished, and we had safely arrived in the land we had come so far to see.[19]

What Nash had to say of staging through southern Oregon is on the whole corroborated by other travelers. Murphy in his *Rambles* (1870's) comments at some length on this very same route lying between Roseburg and Jacksonville. From Murphy, however, something is learned about the road which through the Umpqua Canyon lay eight hundred feet above the river. To climb to this height "six horses toiled and struggled for nearly an hour." It was daylight when Murphy reached the summit which seemed to have filled him with "mysterious awe" and caused him "to involuntarily recoil from its brink." The road, he says, was only wide enough to allow one carriage to pass comfortably over it at a time, and "it was so full of curves as to seem a series of *culs-de-sac* . . . . ."[20]

Progress through the Willamette Valley was relatively fast, and as *The Oregon Statesman* put it: "It reminds one of the old fashioned days of stage travel, before the railroads grid-ironed the States, and sent the traveler whirling over the country at a 'head-swim' pace."[21] Nevertheless, the stagecoach made frequent stops to change horses and permit passengers to eat. For years the old Hoffman Hotel at Eugene City was the stopping place for stages, and if they did not stay there, J. K. Goldbaugh

---

[17] Nash, *Oregon*, p. 101.

[18] *Ibid.*, pp. 104–5.   [19] *Ibid.*, p. 107.

[20] John Mortimer Murphy, *Rambles in North-Western America From the Pacific Ocean to the Rocky Mountains* (London, 1879), p. 76.

[21] *The Oregon Statesman*, June 14, 1859.

would give to the traveling public "all the conveniences of a modern eating house."[22]

Portland, the metropolis of Oregon today, was then only a small town. On the eve of Oregon's statehood (1859) this city's population numbered 1,280, and a local chronicler states with pride that its assessed valuation had then reached the one and a third million mark. Not until 1861 did the *Oregonian* issue its first daily. But Portland was destined to experience an astonishing growth during the 'sixties and 'seventies. "Eighteen months ago," wrote the *Oregonian* in 1862, "any number of houses could be obtained for use, but today scarcely a shell can be found to shelter a family. . . . . The town is full of people and more are coming in." In that year the city boasted two bankers, six billiard rooms, twenty-two lawyers, twelve restaurants, fourteen hotels, and five livery stables, not to mention fifty-five retail liquor dealers and ninety-one retail merchants.[23] In 1866 a contemporary writer refers to Portland as a "pleasant, straggling, growing city" of 5,000 population located on a "smooth, glassy transparent river." Its wharves harbored ships from all parts of the world and its streets were rapidly becoming lined with brick buildings, "graceful" churches, spacious frame dwellings which graded off into an "irregular fringe of little cottages and rough cabins, scattered far up among hill-side stumps."[24]

It was at this flourishing city of the Pacific Northwest, noted even in those days for its roses blooming the year round, that most travelers terminated their long, weary six- to seven-day stage ride from Sacramento, or even worse, month's journey from Missouri. Any one of the city's numerous hotels and inns might have been a godsend at this time. Then as now the hotels made a strong bid for tourist business: for example, Portland's Metropolitan, on the corner of First and Yamhill, which claimed "as good accommodations to either permanent or transient boarders as any in the city." Board and lodging for singles was eight dollars per week and the proprietor promised "satisfaction to all who may be pleased to favor him with their patronage."[25]

Thus far all comments on staging in Oregon have been made with reference to ideal weather conditions. During the winter months the roads were, as one correspondent wrote in 1866, "inconceivably bad, for winter in Oregon means rain, not frost."[26] Even at this early date Oregonians were satirically referred to by their light-hearted neigh-

[22] *The People's Press*, October 1, 1859.   [23] Gaston, *Portland*, I, 241.
[24] Albert D. Richardson, "Oregon and Washington," *Beadle's Monthly*, II (September 1866), 184.
[25] *Portland Daily Advertiser*, October 13, 1859.
[26] Richardson, "Oregon and Washington," p. 181.

bors to the south as "Webfeet." It was the opinion of this same correspondent that in winter travelers in Oregon really paid "for the privilege
of being jounced in mud-wagons, or dislocated on horseback, or mired on
foot." It was even rumored that stagecoach passengers had died of old
age during their winter journeys from Sacramento to Portland.[27] During
midwinter no traffic over the California road occurred at all, and it was
about the middle of April before the first California Stage Company
coach came through to Portland.[28]

Transportation by stagecoach in Washington Territory was for a long
time subordinate to inland waterway travel. In going from Portland to
points in the Puget Sound area, the traveler almost invariably started by
boat. He would sail down the Willamette River to its mouth, then on
down the Columbia to the entrance of the Cowlitz River and up that river
to Cowlitz Landing, or some other desired point. With the beginning of
railroad developments in the Puget Sound area, this procedure was gradually modified so that one could go by boat from Portland to Kalama
(laid out in 1870 as headquarters for the future Northern Pacific Railroad) where one could entrain for Puget Sound. ". . . . but when I first
wended my weary way in that direction," wrote Murphy thinking about
the early 'seventies, "I was forced to travel by canoe up rapid rivers, and
by stage over heart-breaking corduroy roads, through mud several feet
deep, and through trackless forests . . . . ."[29]

The extent of the discomfort endured by early-day travelers in Wash-
ington Territory may be deduced from the following letter written in
Monticello, Washington, December 23, 1866, and addressed to Horace
Greeley's *New York Tribune*:

I'm in great luck sure, for I'm here alive. . . . . And if human nature ever gets
into a condition to appreciate and properly value a soft clean bed, or a clean cloth
bountifully spread with everything good, it is at this end of the stage line from
Olympia. . . . . At every step of his progress, the question arises, how is relief of
this intolerable suffering to be obtained. . . . . The great want of the Territory is
the want of roads, and *the road* of all other roads most needed is this from Olympia
to the Columbia river. . . . .[30]

In Washington, as in Oregon, there were rapid improvements. Population was on the increase and places which had most modest beginnings
were by the decade of the 'seventies enjoying a mushroom growth and
might then aptly be designated as cities. In 1872 Washington's capital
city, Olympia, announced a population of 1,800, and according to a directory for that year possessed "fine broad streets, shaded by the beautiful

[27] Richardson, "Oregon and Washington," p. 181. [28] *Oregonian*, April 14, 1864.
[29] Murphy, *Rambles*, p. 107. [30] Bancroft, *Scraps: Washington*, p. 157.

maple peculiar to the country." It had several churches, two public schools, a "female academy," and, of course, newspapers. It was into Olympia that stagecoaches came, because there was the head of Puget Sound navigation, and connections could be made, although irregularly, with all parts of the country. Every day stages left for the Columbia River and less frequently for other parts. Here, reads the *Puget Sound Business Directory*, travelers would find the hotels "comfortable" and free from disturbances, this being attributed to the character of the city's population, "the most quiet, perhaps, on the continent." In contrast with other cities, travelers coming to Olympia could be spared the sight of "riotous drunkenness," "assaults," "shooting affrays and kindred crimes." "A moral tone, stringent in its judgment, seems to pervade the community . . . . ," concludes this statement.[31]

As early as 1862 stagecoach connections were made between Olympia and the California and Oregon Stage Company at Portland. The old stage road meandered from Vancouver, Washington (a permanent military post), to Monticello and northward. It came into Steilacoom, which in 1872 had ceased to be a military post but was a town of about three hundred inhabitants not counting the inmates of the penitentiary there. Next came the embryonic town of Tacoma (established in 1870) and then Seattle which in 1872 was equal in size to Olympia. It possessed a good harbor, a few factories, "good" hotels, the territorial university, and two "live" newspapers.[32] From Seattle the road led northward, ending at Bellingham Bay.

Samuel Bowles visited Washington on his trip to the Far West during the summer of 1865. He had taken a steamer from Portland to Monticello where he boarded an open wagon stage, apparently the best then available. There were eleven passengers in his party, and since only eight could be crowded into the wagon, three rode horseback. To Bowles his ride through Washington Territory was the most "unpoetical" of his entire 3,000-mile stage trip. The road, he pointed out, was "rough beyond description" and three to four miles an hour was their rate of speed. For miles the wagon rumbled over trees and sticks which provided a kind of corduroy road over swampy land. At best it was an ungraded swath cut through a great virgin forest. Wrote Bowles:

We occasionally struck a narrow prairie or a thread-like valley; perhaps once in ten miles a clearing of an acre or two, rugged and rough in its half-redemption from primitive forest; but for the most part it was a continuous ride through forests, so high and thick that the sun could not reach the road, so unpeopled and

---

    31 *Puget Sound Business Directory, 1872*, section on Olympia, n.p.; Bancroft, *Scraps: Washington*, p. 157; Hewitt, *Across the Plains*, p. 516.
    32 *Puget Sound Business Directory, 1872.*

untouched, that the very spirit of Solitude reigned supreme, and made us feel its presence as never upon Ocean or Plain.[33]

It has previously been shown what wagon communications existed between western Washington and Walla Walla, but the two regions appear to have been devoid of any direct stagecoach connection before the 'eighties. Travel between eastern and western Washington was generally done by taking a stagecoach to a Columbia River landing and then continuing by steamship to places desired. Once a Columbia upriver landing was reached, the stagecoach connections with interior points could be made.

In the sagebrush country east of the Cascade Mountains there existed independently the far-flung staging system in the Inland Empire. It tied together Idaho, Montana, and eastern Oregon; it extended farther south to Nevada and California; and, as explained, it became a part of the great Holladay stagecoach system that connected the West with the railroading East. Walla Walla early became an important and also typical staging center, although in this respect not unlike Boise, Idaho, and Bannack and Virginia City, Montana. For the year 1862 Randall Hewitt has left this description of Washington's eastern metropolis, so often referred to in connection with other phases of transportation:

The city of Walla Walla . . . . was a straggling, disorderly looking place, located near the river of the same name, on a small stream called Mill Creek, an affluent of the Walla Walla River. This being the last outfitting frontier point from the Pacific side, made it a place of business importance. The dirty streets were crowded with freighting wagons and teams and pack animals and a considerable army of rough men. One would naturally conclude, to judge from the numerous places where gambling was in progress, day and night, with an orchestra and free lunch as additional attractions in each establishment, that this was the chief occupation, other things and exorbitant prices only ordinary adjuncts; all the games known to the guild were running in full blast unceasingly.[34]

Lord's description of Walla Walla does not conflict with the foregoing one. He thought it was a wild town where at the "shortest notice drinks can be indulged in; for all classes in Walla-Walla city, if in possession of the all-powerful dollar, take drinks." If the Goddess of Liberty had been seen strolling through this city's streets, Lord feels certain she would have been asked to take "an eye-opener." Second in importance as a lounging place, reported Lord, was the sutler's store and this was due not so much to the benches around the stove as to the fact that the sutler sold drinks "on the sly."[35]

It was over the facilities of the Oregon Steam Navigation Company that Caroline C. Leighton, a typical traveler, had come to Walla Walla

[33] Bowles, *Across the Continent*, pp. 199–200.
[34] Hewitt, *op. cit.*, p. 463.   [35] Lord, *Wilderness*, pp. 25–28.

from Seattle in 1866. The ultimate destination was Fort Colvile, and one might well turn to her for a vivid description of stagecoach travel to the scene of the first gold rush in the Inland Empire.

The journey from Walla Walla to Fort Colvile took eleven days and nights, points out Leighton. During these eleven days not one meal was eaten in a house and the sight of a bed was not experienced. "For several days," this lady observed, "we saw only great sleepy-looking hills, stretching in endless succession, as far as the horizon extended, from morning till night. . . . ." To her this inland country had real charm. She loved the hills and did not mind the sagebrush and bunch grass which then as now abounded in the region, and commented with pleasure upon the presence of flowers in unbelievable shades. At night the cry of coyotes added a weird note to what was an altogether different type of journey than any experienced in the Puget Sound area.[36]

To travel from Walla Walla to Boise Valley was somewhat different, and for an account of a stagecoach trip over this route one might be grateful to Murphy who, during the 'seventies (the same time he was in the Willamette Valley), extended his travels to include parts of the Inland Empire. The Idaho roads or "trails" Murphy described as rough and adds that "every jolt in the cumbrous vehicle, or every pitch into a rut, hurls the sleepy passenger from side to side, or sends him bounding towards the ceiling, and when he returns to his seat it is with an involuntary grunt of torture." When wide awake, he admitted to the contrary, one might well enjoy the "expansive" scenery around Boise, be animated by the bracing mountain air, and be thrilled by traveling "through a country almost as primeval as it was thousands of years ago."[37]

Beginning with 1864, it will be recalled, the Inland Empire became a part of Ben Holladay's, and subsequently Wells, Fargo and Company's, great network of stage lines which then served the West. From then on immigrants and travelers came in large numbers into the Pacific Northwest over the Holladay lines. It was in November 1866, that Brigadier General Rusling came into the Boise Valley over what was by then a Wells, Fargo and Company line, this concern having purchased the Holladay system November 1 of that year. From his reminiscences a vivid and striking description of travel on this, a supposedly de luxe line, may be secured. General Rusling's account of coming into the Boise Valley on November 11, 1866, may best be told in his own words. Once across the Divide they neared Boise where:

. . . . we found ranches and farms everywhere thickening up. Horses and cattle were out grazing by the roadside in considerable numbers, and down in the bottoms

---

[36] Caroline C. Leighton, *Life at Puget Sound* . . . . (Boston, 1884), pp. 44–56.
[37] Murphy, *Rambles*, pp. 173–74.

frequent squads of stacks indicated, that goodly crops of hay and grain had been cut and harvested. Wagons now appeared again on the road, ... We made one hundred and twenty miles, in the last twenty-two hours out from Boisè City, and rolled up to the Overland House with our last team as fresh and gamey as stallions.
. . . . We had mattrasses along, which we carried on top by day, and at night arranged into a passable bed. So, too, we had india-rubber pillows, and robes and blankets in abundance. . . . . We left Bear River about 10 P.M., in an ugly storm of rain and sleet, well tucked in for a night's ride; but in an hour or so were roused up by the stage coming to a dead-halt, and the driver singing out—it sounded half-maliciously—"Good place to walk, gents! Bad place ahead!" Out we got for a dismal walk of a mile or more, through a soft and yielding bottom, where the horses could hardly pull the empty coach through, and then in again, with muddy boots and disgusted feelings generally. Just before daybreak, we struck a long and steep "divide," where the sleet had thickened into snow, without stiffening the ground enough to bear the coach up, and here again we had another cheerful walk of a couple of miles or so, to relieve the blown horses. At King Hill, the last serious "divide" before reaching Boisè, we had another promenade of a mile or two, through five or six inches of snow, just after midnight; but I managed to stick by the stage. . . . . At night our mattrasses proved too narrow for three, after all, and Halsey's shoulders or knees were constantly punching into either L. or me. He and L. usually slept right along all night, but I got scarcely a genteel wink from Bear River to Boisè. By sunrise ordinarily we were up, and then came a general smoke and talk over the night's experience. . . . . By nine or ten A.M. we halted for breakfast, which usually consisted of chicory coffee, stringy beef or bacon, and saleratus-biscuit. Sometimes we got fried potatoes in addition—which helped the meal out somewhat—but not often. . . . . Bilious and aguish with that accursed mountain-fever still hanging about me, I need scarcely say, I had little relish for such a bill of fare, and indeed scarcely ate a "square meal" from Bear River to Boisè.[38]

The General enjoyed his stay in the present Idaho capital. He spoke of its mushroom growth, its log frame buildings housing its 3,000 inhabitants, and of "ebullient prosperity." The men were bearded, wore red shirts, expansive hats, and every man, related General Rusling, carried his bowie knife and revolver. At the time of this visit, it appeared that Boise's chief businesses were those of whiskey drinking and gambling.

The General's next objective was Umatilla on the Columbia River. But going was slow along this lap of his journey and they traveled at what he termed a "natural creep" which may be explained by the fact that his coach was being pulled by a four-mule team. Not until they reached a "bit of extra good road" on a downhill slope could the driver with the aid of "pounding and profanity" persuade his mules to go at a "mild trot." At Umatilla the General's stage ride was over, for there he boarded a Portland steamship. But by that time he had had enough of

---

[38] Rusling, *Across America*, pp. 219–21.

stagecoach travel, and admitted that the romance of this form of travel "was long since gone."[39]

Until the coming of the Holladay Concord stages into Montana in 1864, the people there had to be content to travel in almost anything that answered the description of a vehicle, and on anything that would get them from one place to another. One person recalled that even as late as 1873 he experienced no less than four modes of transportation while going from Corinne, Utah, to Helena, Montana. "Starting out in a sledge," he relates, "I was transferred to a coach, then to a 'jerky,' and finally reached Helena in a mudwagon."[40] There was little of the sandy desert on the Montana side of the Continental Divide and the roads were apparently more than usually rough. One woman related how difficult it was to sleep on the Montana coaches. She told how at one time she traveled from Virginia City, Montana, to Helena and was jolted so badly that sleep was about impossible, but then revealed that at the psychological moment a totally strange male passenger turned to her and said politely:

"Madam, I think you would rest better if you would rest your head on my shoulder."

"Did you try it?" she was asked by another woman when relating this experience.

"Indeed I did," was her quick reply, "and so would you under similar circumstances."[41]

It may be said that stagecoach travel in Montana was, as one local historian phrased it, "precarious, uncertain and dangerous."[42] But that was in a measure true elsewhere. In general, traveling by stagecoach was anything but comfortable. When making long trips it was possible for the passengers to stay overnight at an inn or hotel and proceed the next day, if there happened to be a daily schedule of coaches. Usually they operated on a triweekly basis and then there was always the likelihood that the next coach would have its full complement of passengers. For that reason passengers preferred to continue in the same coach which exchanged for fresh horses about every ten to twelve miles. Night travel was done practically without illumination on the roadway. The only light on a Concord came from small and weak lamps fastened in brackets on either side of the coach just behind the driver's seat. These could be pulled out of their sockets and used as torches, the elongated kerosene container being used as a handle. In their proper positions the lamps

[39] *Ibid.*, pp. 223–24, 234, 248.
[40] *Philipsburg Mail*, June 27, 1924.
[41] *Ibid.*   [42] Sanders, *A History of Montana*, I, 285.

enabled the driver to see if the horses were on the road, and they also served as a warning to oncoming vehicles.[43]

Another inconvenience associated with stagecoach travel were the infrequent, but always exciting, holdups, which often occurred without warning. Stagecoach robbers were known in the West as "road agents" and, ironically, some of them were remembered long after stage-line proprietors were forgotten. There is, for instance, the story of Stove Pipe Sam, on the Snake River bend. Stove Pipe Sam had done "poorly at cards" and had found "little or nothing at the diggings." In desperation Sam decided, about 1869, to rob the Wells Fargo stage. He chose his spot well. Desert Station, his careful choice, was two and one-half miles west of present-day Twin Falls, Idaho. From sagebrush and driftwood the resourceful Sam rigged up two dummies and strategically placed them near the edge of the road. It was dusk when the stage came creaking and rolling around the bend, the horses jogging along at the customary trot. Near his dummies stood Stove Pipe Sam. Reputedly unarmed, but in "a firm voice" he shouted: "Halt! Throw out the treasure box." This was language any jehu understood, and in face of such apparently overwhelming odds there was little reason to protest. The bewildered driver tossed out the little wooden Wells Fargo express box from under the seat, and off the jehu dashed as fast as the four-horse team could tear until he was lost in the dust of the desert trail.

All might have gone well for this apprentice knight of the road had he continued to play a lone hand. Unfortunately Sam confided in his card-playing pal, known only as Frederickson, to whom he offered half of the $1,500 of loot if Frederickson would help market the "dust." Such a proposition might have been acceptable to Sam's erstwhile "pard" had a tempting reward of $750 for the conviction of the robber not been posted. Frederickson figured wisely that it was equally profitable and much safer to turn Stove Pipe Sam over to the authorities.

Later at the Boise penitentiary this convicted road agent turned his interests from robbery to religion. He prayed vociferously and sang hymns fervently. With such a record he was not long in becoming known to his fellow inmates as "Preaching Sam." This supposed change of heart won him the sympathy of the local ministers, who secured a parole for their psalm-singing convert[44] in 1875.

Luckily in the case of Stove Pipe Sam no one was hurt, but such was not always the rule. One day at Hell's Acre near old Fort Hall no less than six or seven armed robbers dashed out from the sagebrush to halt

---

[43] *Humboldt Star and Silver State Post*, June 7, 1934.

[44] Charles S. Walgamott, *Reminiscences of Early Days* . . . . (Twin Falls, Idaho [1926]), pp. 9–11.

an approaching overland stage coming down the lower road. What action the driver contemplated is not known, for in this instance passengers opened fire. Simultaneously the robbers "returned volleys of buckshot into the coach" and at Frank Williams, the driver. Four of the passengers were killed and the driver was wounded. Two passengers escaped uninjured and ran into near-by brush, while still another, named William Carpenter, remained as yet untouched in the bottom of the coach. Covered with the blood of his fellow passengers Carpenter pretended that he was breathing his last. "Gentlemen," he said, "I am dying, don't mutilate my face. . . . ." He also begged them to spare William Brown, whose help Carpenter needed in his dying moments. The thugs obliged, and rode off with what was reported to be $60,000 in loot, leaving Brown and Carpenter with the dead.[45]

The cases of robbery were numerous in Idaho and they occurred frequently over a long period of time. In 1880 the Salisbury, Gilmore and Company stage, carrying Wells Fargo treasure, was robbed at Glenn's Snake River Ferry near Boise. It was after dark and the southbound stage was overdue. The hostler had just hung out a lantern when into the station jumped two armed men. They bound and gagged the hostler and threw him into a stable. When the stage arrived the road agents ordered the driver and one sole passenger from the box and then proceeded to loot the express box, mailbags, and the station. Their job accomplished, the two highwaymen vanished into the darkness as mysteriously as they had come.

Wells, Fargo and Company lost no time going in pursuit. They had such a good description of the men that within one week the guilty ones were hailed into Judge H. E. Prickett's federal court at Boise. The trial was expeditious; the men were found guilty of robbing the mails and jeopardizing human lives. The sentence was for life in the penitentiary.[46]

Legal justice was not always attained with such dispatch in Idaho. When the established forces of law and order failed, citizens tended to take such matters into their own hands. Vigilance committees were formed and justice, as miners understood it, was administered in extralegal fashion.

Not infrequently a simple statement such as the following would appear in local newspapers: "David English, Nelson Scott and Wm. Peoples who were arrested here a week or two since on charges of highway robbery were hung by the citizens of Lewiston, on Saturday night last." Then, as if a moral justification were needed, the newspaper added:

[45] *Washington Statesman,* July 28, 1865; Sanders, *A History of Montana,* I, 285–86.
[46] Hawley, *History of Idaho,* I, 420–21.

"If guilty the retribution was just—that they were guilty there was not the remotest doubt."[47]

In the face of such rough treatment one who called himself "A Retired Road Agent" made the following remonstrance in a letter to the *Washington Statesman*:

I observe that dangerous innovations are creeping into our system of jurisprudence. . . . . We [road agents] are the main pillars in the social fabric. . . . . Without us . . . . the social edifice would dissolve "and vanish . . . . ;" parties of pleasure would be robbed of their brightest ornaments; the ladies of their most elegant beaux and *beau monde* [would] be numbered with the things that were.

In answer to this epistle came the following editorial reply addressed to "Sage-Brush Jack": "You *may* be a 'retired road agent,' but your retiracy from the valley would make the thing appear plausible."[48]

Wherever there was gold dust in circulation there were robbers, and travelers were frequently forewarned to go prepared for the worst. Road agents are "getting quite numerous in these parts," observed *The Weekly Mountaineer* of The Dalles, Oregon: "Winter is coming on and these poor devils are laying in their winter supplies. Persons traveling had better keep their eyes peeled and if possible carry their howitzers with them loaded with grape and cannisters, ready to serve."[49]

There were road agents everywhere in the West, but in no place were they so vicious and bold as in Montana. Established governmental machinery failed to cope with the crime wave that swept along Montana's many lonely trails. It is not surprising, therefore, that many of the citizenry of the territory organized a Committee of Safety, and invoked what they called the Mountain Code. In the opinion of one local historian, this Montana Committee was "as necessary in the early days . . . . as are the legal tribunals of to-day. . . . ."[50] The achievements of the vigilantes are, to say the least, impressive. Between December 21, 1863, and the close of 1865, thirty-two road agents died "with their boots on."[51]

Heading the list was George Ives, who with Frank Parish held up the Peabody and Caldwell coach between Virginia City and Bannack in October 1863. One passenger named Dan McFadden, but popularly known as "Bummer Dan," reportedly lost $7,000. Others reluctantly contributed lesser sums, except one, who turned out to be a member of the hold-up gang.[52]

The culprits were not at first known, and scarcely a month passed

[47] *Washington Statesman*, November 15, 1862.　　　[48] *Ibid.*, February 17, 1865.

[49] *The Weekly Mountaineer*, October 28, 1871.

[50] [Michael A. Leeson, ed.], *History of Montana* (Chicago, 1885), p. 265.

[51] Thomas J. Dimsdale, *The Vigilantes of Montana* . . . . (Helena, Montana, n.d.), pp. 281–82.　　　[52] *Ibid.*, pp. 49–54; Leeson, *op. cit.*, pp. 268–71.

before Ives (this time in company with "Whiskey Bill" Graves and Bob Zachary) halted the Salt Lake Mail coach out from Virginia City. The affair had been carefully planned. The three robbers were on horseback, each armed with shotguns, pretending to be hunters. As the stage approached them Ives and his cohorts wheeled around and drew a bead on the driver and the passengers. The occupants of the coach were ordered out and searched. The job done, Ives simply said: "Get up and 'skedaddle'." Driver Thomas C. Caldwell obeyed, but when he thought it safe turned for a good look at the robbers. This was exasperating to Ives whose parting shout was: "If you don't turn round, and mind your business, I'll shoot the top of your head off." Caldwell promptly obeyed. As the coach vanished from sight the road agents gathered their loot amounting to $500 in cash and notes.[53]

As these holdups continued in such methodical fashion without anyone being brought to justice, suspicion belatedly turned upon suave Henry Plummer, the sheriff of the Bannack and Virginia City districts. Distrust of the sheriff was amply justified. He was actually the evil genius under whose businesslike direction a gang (known as "The Innocents") of about one hundred highwaymen, cattle rustlers, horse thieves, and murderers operated with precision, deftness, and skill. The organization of this group was amazingly intricate. There were various grades of officers, each office being filled according to the capability and aptitude of each man. Plummer was naturally first in command, with Billy Bunton probably as gangster Number Two. George Ives, Ned Ray, and Buck Stinson held high ratings by their chiefs.

Suspicion of Sheriff Plummer reached a climax with his lassitude in the Thomas Caldwell robbery. Immediately following this event a group of about twenty-five irate citizens gathered and then set forth in search of the "Robbers' Roost." The place was found and suspects, including one culprit, were arrested.

Ives's trial came first. It was held outdoors and the public was free to attend. After all witnesses were heard, as well as the arguments of the counsel and prosecutor, the judge, seated upon a wagon, gave the case to the jury which consisted of twenty-four men. Within thirty minutes a verdict was returned. Twenty-three jurors declared Ives guilty of murder and robbery; one dissented.

It was then moved as an alternative that the assembly adopt the verdict of the vigilantes that Ives was guilty. This motion carried, and after some haggling among the crowd, Ives was led ten yards from the scene of trial and was hanged. "Thus," wrote Dimsdale, "George Ives 'died in his boots'."[54]

---

[53] Dimsdale, *op. cit.*, pp. 63–65. [54] *Ibid.*, pp. 69–83.

Out of these incidents came the more formal organization of a Vigilance Committee. The climax came early when Plummer was caught unarmed. He begged for mercy, but was told: "It is useless for you to beg for your life; . . . . You are to be hanged." They took him to a scaffold where two of his comrades, Ned Ray and Buck Stinson, were swinging by the hemp. Plummer requested that he be given a "good drop" and this was granted so far as possible. The noose was placed around Plummer's neck and the vigilantes lifted him with their arms as high as they could reach, and then let go. "He died quickly and without a struggle"[55] on January 10, 1864.[56]

Between the hanging of Ives in 1863, and that of James Daniel in 1866, thirty-two road agents died through the increasing activity of the Montana vigilantes. Others were banned, so that no doubt remained that the Plummer gang, probably the most vicious in the West, was thoroughly and effectively stamped out. Before that time came, however, lawlessness had cost the lives of at least 102 persons killed by the organized gang of cutthroats.

It remains a sad commentary upon the West that society failed to establish a legal government strong enough to cope with outlaws, that peace-loving people felt obliged, instead, to turn over the problem of law and order to an extra-legal Committee of Safety.

For information on robberies involving loss of Wells, Fargo and Company treasure, one turns to the *Report* of James B. Hume, the Wells, Fargo and Company detective who trapped "Black Bart," the West's most infamous stage robber. Among the cases reported by Hume were Tom Brown alias "Tom Foster," George Bouldin, and Benjamin Berry. There was also William Briscoe, a deputy sheriff, who robbed the Wells, Fargo and Company's express on a stage going from Grants Pass to Jacksonville on January 18, 1884. For this he was given an eight-year term in Oregon's state penitentiary. Briscoe had two accomplices, one of whom, Charles Bassett, received a similar sentence. Charles Chambers robbed a Wells, Fargo and Company stage near Boise in 1881; W. S. Horrell did the same three years later. Frank Johnson chose Baker, Oregon, for a similar act, as did also Al Priest; J. H. Maxon chose Pendleton; John W. Miller and Tarlton B. Scott, alias "Scotty," successfully selected Silver City, Idaho, for the lone-hand robbery of Wells Fargo stages.[57]

There were other Wells, Fargo and Company robberies in the Pacific Northwest, but the bulk of express holdups occurred in California. Up

[55] Dimsdale, *op. cit.*, pp. 110–11.   [56] Quiett, *Pay Dirt*, p. 230.

[57] Report of James B. Hume and John N. Thacker, *Wells, Fargo & Co.'s Express* . . . . (San Francisco, 1885), pp. 18 ff.

to the time of Hume's *Report* in 1885, Wells, Fargo and Company paid over $73,000 in rewards. It secured no less than 206 convictions for robbery throughout the areas in which it operated. Eleven road agents were killed resisting arrest, and seven others were hanged. Only four passengers and four stage drivers were killed while riding in or driving Wells Fargo stages, which in ratio with the thousands of passengers and thousands of miles of travel was very small.[58] Of course, not all stage lines carried Wells Fargo treasure, and not all stages were operated by this company. This report, therefore, is very incomplete and merely shows what happened to one major concern engaged in transportation in the West.

With or without holdups, stagecoach passengers had to eat and sleep. Stagecoach travel whetted the appetite and contributed to enjoyment of a good night's sleep. Usually at ten- to fifteen-mile intervals along the country roads there were stations. Some of these were merely places where horses were hastily exchanged, but frequently they passed for what in old New England would have been cozy taverns and inns. In the Far West simple, often rude, farmhouses where overworked housewives "took in boarders" served the purpose. At such places the passengers hastened to get off to stretch their cramped legs, and if it were at mealtime or late at night they partook of whatever services such places had to offer.

Here the hungry and much bounced-about traveler was, to quote Nash, "fed chiefly on small, square bits of tough, fried meat, with fried potatoes, and sometimes pie. (This last you would eat of more freely were it not for the legions of house-flies, which dispute with you every mouthful!)"[59] Even Nash admitted that there were exceptions to bad fare and that at times the meals were even very good. He often spoke of being refreshed by tea or coffee when stopping at a roadside inn, and once of being "fed with abundance of cream and wild strawberries."[60] Rusling referred to "excellent meals at not unreasonable prices, all things considered," although at times the water, to use the words of an Idaho settler, was "a heap alkali and right smart warm."[61]

In Montana it was the observation of Helen F. Sanders that stage stations were conspicuous for their lack of accommodations, and such a name as "Dirty Woman's Ranch" was not uncommonly applied by facetious stage drivers. At one station when Colonel Wilbur Fisk Sanders, a Montana pioneer, looked somewhat disgruntled, the proprietor blurted out:

"Colonel, ain't your egg hard enough?"

[58] *Ibid.*, pp. 3–5.   [59] Nash, *Oregon*, p. 87.
[60] *Ibid.*, pp. 95 ff.   [61] Rusling, *Across America*, pp. 215, 225.

Replied the Colonel: "The whole damned breakfast is hard enough."[62]

Some of the more courageous and long-suffering souls made no stopovers for the night, choosing to continue their journey without interruption until the welcome end was reached. These passengers had to make the most of their opportunities. Sometimes the mailbags were piled high enough in the bottom of the coach so that travelers might stretch out and catch a few hours of uneasy sleep.

However, large numbers of the traveling public in those early days stayed overnight at the inns. When possible they chose for stopovers the towns and villages where some choice in accommodations might luckily be available. Local newspapers carried advertisements offering the traveling public "every attention," a "Ladies sitting room . . . . in good style," "live and let live" service, "private rooms," "good beds," a "bar always supplied with the best liquors and cigars," and just plain "food."[63] Goldbaugh, the Eugene City hotel proprietor, declared his table to be "furnished with the best the market affords," and that he was prepared "to furnish beds to those who may favor him with a call. Will you call, one and all?"[64]

Much of the glamour and drama associated with stagecoach travel is a fiction of the modern mind, heedless of the bruises and strain which the traveler of an earlier age had to endure. There were, nevertheless, those who were loath to give up the Concord, willing to take the jolts rather than submit to the greater monotony aboard the steam and rail train. "Railroads and steam-boats are all very well," if a person wants to be rushed through on business, to use the words of one old-timer, "but for comfort and pleasure give me the old Coach, when the day is fine, and the road is hard, ... and the horses go to their collars with a will. . . . ."[65]

[62] Sanders, *A History of Montana*, I, 285.

[63] *Pioneer and Democrat*, July 22, 1854; *Portland Daily Advertiser*, October 13, 1859; *Occidental Messenger*, September 27, 1857.

[64] *The People's Press*, October 1, 1859.

[65] Doings [pseud.], "Staging," *Hutchings' California Magazine*, IV (1860), 365.

CHAPTER XX

RAILROAD CONSTRUCTION*

In Hell Gate Valley near the summit of the Rocky Mountains an impressive ceremony was held on September 8, 1883. There it was that President Henry Villard drove the last spike signalizing the completion of the Northern Pacific Railroad from Duluth to Tacoma. The new road was immediately opened for traffic, and at long last the old Oregon country was joined with the East by rail.[1]

The completion of the Northern Pacific Railroad, and that of the Canadian Pacific two years later, followed by the Great Northern in 1893, were truly symbolic of a century of progress in the Pacific Northwest.

Before construction of transcontinental railroads began, there had been some local railroad building. Reference has been made previously to Bradford and Company, which in 1851 began work on a wooden portage tramway along the north bank of the Columbia River Cascades. Four years later, it will be recalled, Colonel Joseph S. Ruckel began building the portage wagon road on the south bank of the Cascades. On this roadbed the Oregon Portage Railroad later operated. These portage lines were controlled by the Oregon Steam Navigation Company. This concern, in 1863, completed an iron-railed road along what had previously been known as Thompson's Portage, on The Dalles-Celilo portage railroad. Added improvements were made on this vital portage, most notable of which was the transfer from the Oregon Portage line of the compact little steam locomotive, the "Oregon Pony," and for three years this engine saw service along the banks of the Columbia River.[2]

The first railroad in the Inland Empire was the Walla Walla and Columbia, about thirty-two miles long, built by the ingenious Dr. Dorsey S. Baker, one of the early Oregon pioneers. It was very much a homemade road. The rails were of fir, spiked to mortised ties. Later the rails were reinforced with iron straps. The rolling stock was of the crudest type, including a locomotive imported from Pittsburgh in 1872. This line, because of its spirited builder and singularity, was variously called

---

* The railroad history of the Pacific Northwest deserves a separate volume. The account given here discusses local developments (not national aspects) which tie in with the major theme, namely, prerailroad transportation.

[1] [Eugene V. Smalley and Henry J. Winser], *The Great Northwest: A Guide-Book and Itinerary* . . . . (St. Paul, 1888), pp. 18–19.

[2] Gill, "Oregon's First Railway," pp. 171 ff.; Clark, *Willamette Valley*, pp. 508–10; *supra*, chap. 18.

"Dr. Baker's road," the "strap iron road," and the "rawhide road." In 1875 the road was completed. Staggering profits were made from this enterprise, but this is not surprising when one observes that the freight rates on the thirty-two-mile line were from $4.50 to $6.00 per ton. Moreover, in 1878 Dr. Baker sold his fortune-making railroad to the Oregon Steam Navigation Company[3] for $321,132.00.

Some indication as to the number and size of scattered railroad lines in the Columbia River region was revealed when in 1879 the Oregon Steam Navigation Company agreed to sell its properties to Henry Villard. The famous steamship firm listed among its assets: (1) the Cascade Portage Railroad, Washington Territory, six miles of roadbed and track, along with sidings, turntables, shops, etc., three locomotives, three passenger cars, and thirty-five boxcars, all valued at $300,000; (2) the Oregon Portage Railroad, five miles of grading and trestle, seven miles of telegraph line, and miscellaneous other equipment with a total value of $75,000; (3) The Dalles and Ce!ilo Railroad, fourteen and a half miles of roadbed, track and sidings, turntables, three locomotives, twenty-seven boxcars, nineteen flatcars, two passenger cars, etc., valued at $700,000; (4) the Walla Walla and Columbia Railroad, formerly Dr. Baker's, with new steel rails added and valued at $600,000; (5) miscellaneous equipment necessary for rail operations, such as 250 miles of telegraph line between Walla Walla and Portland, valued at $25,000, and machine shops and equipment[4] worth $15,000.

The early settlers in the Willamette Valley who clamored so vociferously for railroad construction were without the financial means to bring their wishes to fruition. Help was needed from outside sources, and such was to come, not from Wall Street, but from financial interests in California.

During the 'sixties in California numerous "bonanza railroads" were under construction. The "Big Four," Leland Stanford, Collis P. Huntington, Charles Crocker, and Mark Hopkins, had organized the Central Pacific Railroad, and in 1864 construction of the first transcontinental rail line had begun. Among the multitude of projected routes was one which would connect California with Portland, Oregon.

Taking the initiative in this move for a California-Oregon railroad was an energetic surveying engineer named Simon G. Elliott from California. Supporting Elliott were several lawyers, businessmen, and politicians from both California and Oregon, men who stood to gain from

---

[3] Johansen, "Capitalism on the Far-Western Frontier," pp. 234–44; Fuller, *Pacific Northwest*, pp. 317–18; Scott, *Oregon Country*, IV, 212–13, 369.

[4] "Notes on Meetings of the Executive Committee of the Oregon Railway and Navigation Company," Economics Records Library, Reed College.

such a project. In all there were about seventy individuals who were actively interested, and at the once-bustling boom town of Jacksonville, Oregon, there was incorporated on October 13, 1863, the California and Columbia River Railroad Company.[5]

From the outset Portlanders, though interested, looked with suspicion on these developments, because they foresaw much of Portland's trade with southern Oregon falling into the laps of California competitors. Among the Portlanders most concerned was Joseph Gaston. Bitter dissenions arose over this and other issues. Before the year was out a faction from within the original group, led by Elliott, formed a second company to be called the California and Oregon Railroad Company,[6] whereas Gaston remained as leader of those who stayed with the original organization.

Both companies proceeded to make surveys. The survey for the first, or California and Columbia River Railroad Company, was made by Colonel Charles Barry. It was completed in October 1864, and is known as the "Barry Survey." The route outlined began at Jacksonville; it passed through the Umpqua Mountains and Valley; it crossed the Calapooya Mountains at Applegate Pass and thence ran along the west side of the Willamette River, and through the Tualatin Plains to Portland. Gaston naturally supported this project and it was he who hastened to present the Barry Survey to the Oregon legislature in an effort to obtain aid.

The survey for the second company, the California and Oregon Railroad Company, was made under the direction of Elliott. The proposed route through northern California followed the Sacramento and Shasta rivers, passed through the thriving mining town of Yreka, followed Willow Creek until crossing the Klamath River, and then went over the Siskiyou Mountains. Through Oregon this route went through Bear Creek Valley to Jacksonville; from there it followed first the Rogue River, then the Umpqua River to Roseburg. Entering the Willamette Valley, it passed successively through Eugene City, Corvallis, Albany, Jefferson, Salem, and thence to Portland.

Unlike its competitor, the California and Oregon Company looked to the federal government for aid rather than to the Oregon legislature. To facilitate this procedure there was formed on July 13, 1865, what might be called a sister organization, known as the Oregon and California Rail-

---

[5] Oswald Garrison Villard, ed., *The Early History of Transportation in Oregon*, by Henry Villard (Eugene, Oregon, 1944), p. 1; John Tilson Ganoe, "The History of the Oregon and California Railroad," *The Quarterly of the Oregon Historical Society*, XXV (September 1924), 239–40.

[6] This new company was incorporated at Sacramento under the laws of California on June 29, 1865; Clark, *Willamette Valley*, p. 510.

road Company. It was in reality the Elliott concern with its name reversed. Accordingly, in 1866, Congress passed a measure which gave to the California and Oregon Railroad Company and to whatever concern the Oregon legislature might designate, twenty alternate sections of public land for each mile of railroad to be constructed.[7]

This liberal Congressional act left no doubt as to who should receive the grant within California, but the door was still left wide open as to who would get it in Oregon. Which company would the Oregon legislature designate? That was the question. Would it be the Oregon and California Railroad Company? The California and Columbia River Company? Or would it be another company as yet unformed?

These questions became subjects of torrid controversy in Oregon political circles. As it turned out, Gaston's California and Columbia River concern ceased to exist, but during October 1866, there emerged in its place (still under Gaston's leadership) a new organization known as the Oregon Central Railroad Company. And to the surprise of many it was this new concern that the Oregon legislature chose to recognize as the one eligible to receive the liberal land grant proffered by the federal government.

Here, unfortunately, matters did not rest. A mad scramble for power arose within the victor's camp. One group rallied around Gaston, long a supporter of Barry and the so-called west-side route. The opponents of Gaston joined I. R. Moores, who favored a union with Elliott's Californians and the adoption of the Elliott route projected to follow the east side (or bank) of the Willamette River. Thenceforth the two concerns became known, respectively, as the West Side Company and the East Side Company.

Each considered itself to be legitimate successor of the Oregon Central Railroad Company, and as such the rightful heir to the land grant. During April 1868, both companies began construction of a railroad out of Portland, each thinking that this evidence of good deeds would further strengthen claim with the state lawmakers.

What happened was a race for survival between two concerns, each greatly handicapped by lack of funds. For a while it looked as if the West Siders would win. In the nick of time, however, the rival East Siders were saved by the arrival on the scene of the audacious and, according to his enemies, villainous Ben Holladay.[8]

A partnership was formed between Holladay and Elliott, and from

[7] Ganoe, *op. cit.*, pp. 241–49; Clark, *op. cit.*, p. 512.

[8] Villard, *op. cit.*, pp. 4–16; Clark, *op. cit.*, pp. 512–14; Ganoe, *op. cit.*, pp. 250–73; Joseph Gaston, "The Genesis of the Oregon Railway System," *The Quarterly of the Oregon Historical Society*, VII (June 1906), 105–32.

this point on the question as to which one of the two contesting companies was legally and legitimately entitled to official recognition was purely academic. To the ruthless Holladay such quibbling was a waste of time when lavish entertainment, bribery, and bullying proved infinitely more expeditious as a means of attaining desired ends.

When in 1868 the resourceful Ben Holladay arrived in Oregon, he was not only the undisputed "Stagecoach King" of America, but also a powerful figure in Pacific Coast steamship circles. He was a personality not easily pushed aside, and it is not surprising that in October 1868, the Oregon legislature designated the East Side Company, Holladay's group, as the one entitled to receive the coveted plum of 3,800,000 acres of public land.

In the face of such utter humiliation there was nothing left for Gaston's West Side Company to do but to capitulate. During August 1870, the West Siders transferred their control to Holladay, and the latter proceeded to merge the two Willamette railroad projects into one. To his reorganized and reincorporated concern Holladay gave the familiar name of Oregon and California Railroad Company.[9]

Leadership under Holladay left much to be desired, both from the standpoint of the investors and of the Oregon public as a whole. Holladay lost no time in quarreling with Elliott, and in removing this erstwhile promoter as superintendent of construction. However, according to Henry Villard, "this riddance did not really improve the situation." Financial problems multiplied for Holladay as work on the roadbed and the laying of new track proceeded. By January 1870, about $800,000 had already been spent on the project and much more would be needed to complete the road to Eugene City, at the upper end of the Willamette Valley. To secure needed funds Holladay recklessly sold bonds at 60 to 75 percent of par value, the takers of which were very largely German investors.

With funds thus secured, though at ruinous discount rates, Holladay plunged ahead with abandon. Railroad construction was stepped up. In order to eliminate river competition, Holladay bought out at least nine small local steamship lines as well as the Oregon City portage.

Bold as the entire scheme was, a plan which would certainly give to the Oregon and California Railroad Company monopolistic control over Willamette Valley transportation, the race with time was a losing one. Bond sales slackened, and the German holders of previously sold securities became increasingly restive when in 1873 interest payment failed to materialize.

---

[9] Villard, *op. cit.*, pp. 15–16; Scott, *Oregon Country*, I, 103; *Oregonian*, December 13, 1870.

It was at this point that the affairs of Holladay reached their crest, and from 1873 on this swashbuckling American rugged individualist was on his way out. And as the fortunes of Holladay waned, those of Henry Villard were definitely in the ascendancy.[10]

Villard, a German immigrant and successful journalist, entered railroading somewhat unwittingly. While recuperating in Germany in 1872 from an illness, he was asked by German investors in the Oregon and California Railroad Company to represent their interests. Thus armed, and assisted by Richard Koehler of Germany, Villard arrived in Portland in 1878. Wrote Villard:

My first business was to assume control of the several companies and then to have them take the necessary action to comply with the several requirements of the settlement with Holladay. The promised resignations of Holladay as president and director and of his fellow directors, and the promised proxies to vote all his stock at the annual meeting then convened of the Oregon & California stockholders, were ready and were delivered to me.[11]

As an executive officer, Villard was quick to see both the limitations and the golden opportunities for his newly re-formed companies. By themselves the Oregon Steamship Company and the Oregon and California Railroad Company had a doubtful and, at best, a limited future. The coastal steamship operations earned "millions net," to use Villard's own phrase, but not the railroads in their present form.[12] But if combined with the extensive facilities of the Oregon Steam Navigation Company, and if in turn direct railroad connections could be established between California and the East, then a great future was in store for the entire network. It was in pursuit of this dangling, elusive, golden apple that Villard, the new transportation king of Oregon, pointed his staff.

Acquisition of the Holladay interests was followed by numerous and involved financial manipulations which in 1879 led to the purchase by Villard of the Oregon Steam Navigation Company (see chapter xvi). Being in possession of these new holdings, Villard, on June 13, 1879, organized and became president of the Oregon Railway and Navigation Company which for all intents and purposes was a new name for the old Oregon Steam Navigation Company. The newly organized firm had authority to issue $12,000,000 of bonds and stocks for paying off its indebtedness. Plans called for the building of a trunk line along the south bank of the Columbia River with "fan-like" feeder lines

---

[10] Villard, *op. cit.*, pp. 17–34.

[11] Villard, *Early History of Transportation in Oregon*, p. 56; Henry Villard, *Memoirs of Henry Villard* (Boston, New York, 1904), II, 273; James B. Hedges, *Henry Villard and the Railways of the Northwest* (New Haven, 1930), pp. 13–15.

[12] Villard, *Early History of Transportation in Oregon*, pp. 64, 85; Ganoe, "Oregon and California Railroad," pp. 332–33.

extending into eastern Oregon and eastern Washington Territory. During 1880 construction on these lines began. By 1883 the Oregon Railway and Navigation Company had spent over $20,000,000 in building over five hundred miles of standard-gauge road; moreover, this investment was well made, for in 1883 the Oregon Railway and Navigation Company was one of the most profitable lines in the United States.[13]

In acquiring these extensive holdings in the Pacific Northwest, Villard had in mind (very privately) securing control of the then inactive Northern Pacific Railroad Company. In December 1880, this was accomplished by an $8,000,000 subscription to a blind pool, and the following year Villard was elected president of the Northern Pacific Railroad.[14]

It was now possible for this remarkable financier to complete the construction of the Northern Pacific Railroad, and link it with the elaborate transportation network already in operation in the Pacific Northwest. The last costly stretch separating the East from the West followed the rugged Clark's Fork Valley through the Bitterroot Mountains, a route early familiar to the fur traders of the North West Company. Most difficult of all was construction through Hell Gate River Canyon. On September 8, 1883, near Gold Creek, seven miles west of Garrison, this gap was closed and the last spike driven.

Meanwhile, railroad construction south from Portland had reached Roseburg in 1872, and for the next eleven years it remained at a standstill. During this entire period the earning remained low.

Under Villard's direction construction toward the Oregon-California boundary was resumed in 1883. The line was completed as far south as Ashland by May of the following year, and some work had been done south of this city before Villard's insolvency brought operations to a stop. For a while the Oregon and California Railroad staved off bankruptcy, but the company went into receivership in 1885, and two years thereafter control of the line passed into the hands of the Southern Pacific Railroad Company.[15]

Previously, the Southern Pacific Company had acquired control of the old California and Oregon Railroad, and had completed construction of this line north to the Oregon border. Now with both the Oregon and the California lines under its control, the remaining gap was hastily closed. A tunnel for 3,700 feet through a part of the Siskiyou Mountains

[13] "Minutes of the Oregon Railway and Navigation Company"; Eugene V. Smalley, *History of the Northern Pacific Railroad* (New York, 1883), pp. 258–60.

[14] Villard, *Early History of Transportation in Oregon*, pp. 91–93; Hedges, *Henry Villard*, chap. 4; *Clark County Register*, December 27, 1883; Winther, *The Great Northwest*, pp. 264–66.

[15] Ganoe, "Oregon and California Railroad," pp. 333–38.

near Ashland was the last piece of construction. But, according to the
Ashland *Tidings*, rail connections were established on December 17,
1887, and a northbound construction train "was run upon the Oregon
and California road."[16] A formal celebration at Ashland followed later
in the day during which Charles Crocker, one of California's "Big Four,"
drove the traditional golden spike.

The hour was getting late, relates the Ashland *Tidings*, and Crocker
executed his part of the program with dispatch. "I hold in my hand the
last spike," said Crocker. There were cries of "Hold it up!" "With this
golden spike I propose now to unite the rails between California and
Oregon, and I hope it will be the means of cementing the friendship
of the two States and make them as one people." He pointed out how
the driving of this spike would unite Portland and New Orleans, and
how Oregon had now become a part of the longest railroad system in
the world, controlled by the Southern Pacific Railroad Company.[17]

This line was 3,336 miles in length, with branches totaling 5,000
miles.[18] Crocker neglected to say that by the driving of this last spike
at Ashland the entire United States of America was encircled by rails, that
the Pacific Northwest now ceased to be an isolated frontier region and
was at last an important segment of this mammoth band of steel. The
editor of the Ashland *Tidings*, in anticipating this event, expressed well
the feeling of the people of this region when he wrote: "It means material
development—more rapid progress toward the population and general
wealth of the older states. . . . . To Oregon and California it means
greater facility for interchange of trade and products, which will be to
the advantage to both."[19]

The completion of the Oregon and California Railroad did not mean
the end of horse transportation. Until the coming of motor vehicles,
stagecoaches and wagon freighters remained familiar objects in regions
not served directly by the iron horse. The pioneer livery concern opened
by Eli Bangs well illustrates the stubborn persistence of the older methods
of travel and communication. Established at Eugene City about 1885,
Bangs joined with Earl McNutt and Judge C. P. Barnard to organize
the Eugene and Mapleton Stage Line connecting with stops at Elmira,
Hales's place in Elk Prairie, old Joe Fowler's at Walton, and Swisshome.
Well into the present century one could still transfer at Eugene City
from the fairly comfortable red plush seats of a Southern Pacific passenger coach to a three-seated mud wagon of a type familiar to pioneer

---

16 *Tidings*, December 23, 1887.

17 *Ibid.*   18 *Ibid.*   19 *Ibid.*, December 9, 1887.

travelers of the 'fifties. Within two hours one would be traveling across lonely prairie lands and then over some of the roughest mountain roads ever known to the West.

"In good, dry weather," reminisced Sam Winther, driver over this route, "it usually took about fourteen hours to go from Eugene to Mapleton, but during the rainy season . . . . well, it all depended on how many trees had fallen across the road, how flooded the streams might have been." Long stretches of the road were corduroy, and so rough was it that frequently passengers had to be tied to their seats to keep them from falling out of the coach and down the embankment into the raging Siuslaw River.[20]

Certainly not until a half-century had followed the driving of the last spike at Ashland could it be said that a system of transportation developed in the sixteenth century was about to become a memory in the West.

During the century that preceded the coming of railroads the Oregon country passed through stages of development not unlike those of other sections in North America.

A native economy was exploited, principally by the British and Americans, who were eager to profit from the fur trade. In the conduct of this trade rivalries were keen, but on the whole the British, who possessed greater training, experience, skill, and resources, gained mastery in this field.

Under the dominance of British fur companies, especially under the imaginative direction of the Hudson's Bay Company, there emerged a business organization that was breath-taking in scope; surprisingly humane, but by no means philanthropic, in relations with the natives; and, considering time and place, unswerving in its adherence to established business principles. The Americans, for their part, exhibited no less energy and perspicacity. Sharp Yankee coastal traders outstripped their rivals in the trans-Pacific sea-otter trade, but so far as the interior was concerned, American successes were sporadic. American presence in the Oregon country was never taken lightly by the great British monopoly, but at no time did the American inland fur traders constitute a serious threat to British supremacy.

The real enemies of the fur traders—British and American alike— were the settlers. Until the discovery of gold in British Columbia, the Hudson's Bay Company possessed sufficient political power and stratagem to control the immigration of British subjects, but all efforts to stem the accelerating tide of advancing American pioneer farmers proved futile.

---

[20] Sam Winther to the author.

Even before the settlement of the Oregon boundary question in 1846 the Hudson's Bay Company had recognized the inevitable and had begun what turned out to be a steady retreat northward.

To the agricultural communities both south and north of the Columbia River the problems attending trade, transportation, and travel remained critical until the coming of the railroads. Heroic efforts were made to provide new arrivals from across the plains with an all-land route in order to circumvent the perilous voyage down the Columbia River. The Barlow Road and the Applegate Cut-off were such routes. An old fur traders' trail connecting the Willamette Valley with Spanish California was made suitable for wagon traffic. And throughout the period under review the construction of corduroy, graveled and plain dirt roads, the building of bridges, the establishment of ferry service, and extension of steamship communication occupied the efforts of the Americans and British alike. In road development federal, state, and local governments were interested parties, but road-making in those days was also a private business venture, with profit as a motive.

Roads and, of course, water routes became the essential avenues of commerce. Packing, wagon freighting, stagecoaching, mail and express service, and travel for business and pleasure emerged, increased, and expanded somewhat in proportion to which transportation facilities became available. At no time, though, did the absence of roads deter settlers from pushing back the frontier. Also with complete abandon the Argonauts of the Northwest ventured into remote mountain recesses, seemingly without thought about the problem of supply.

As a rule such problems were overcome. The transportation of goods from major entrepôts to such distant mining camps as those on the upper Fraser River, in the Cariboo region, in Idaho and Montana, gave rise to major business enterprises.

Some of these transportation businesses proved to be highly profitable. From modest beginnings they frequently emerged into large and powerful consolidations which sought, and frequently achieved, monopoly status. Such concerns were the Oregon Steam Navigation Company, Wells, Fargo and Company Express, and the California and Oregon Stage Company. Out of these highly successful transportation ventures came a certain unity, though not, as in the case of the Oregon Steam Navigation Company and the Holladay interests, without some public abuse. Large personal fortunes were made out of the profits from operations, and these in turn made their influence felt in other fields of endeavor.

As a whole, the history of transportation before 1890 had a profound effect upon the lives of people who lived in and helped to build an important region—the Pacific Northwest.

BIBLIOGRAPHY

BIBLIOGRAPHY

MANUSCRIPTS

"Agreement between the Hudson[']s Bay Company and the Russian American Fur Company, 1839." Transcript, Archives of British Columbia, Victoria, British Columbia.

ALBRIGHT, ROBERT EDWIN. "The Relations of Montana with the Federal Government, 1864–1889." Ph.D. dissertation, Stanford University Library, Stanford, California, 1933.

ALLAN, ALEXANDER. "Cariboo and the Miners of British Columbia, Victoria, 1878." Bancroft Library, Berkeley, California.

"Archives of the Provisional Governments of Oregon." Oregon Historical Society Library, Portland, Oregon.

"Articles of Incorporation of the Oregon Steam Navigation Company." Leo J. Hanley Collection, Economics Records Library, Reed College, Portland, Oregon.

"Autobiography of Roderick Finlayson, 1818–1891." Archives of British Columbia, Victoria, British Columbia.

"B. G. [sic] Dowell, packer, to Hd. Qts., 1st Reg., Ore. Vol. Jan. 17, 1856." B. F. Dowell Collection, Henry E. Huntington Library, San Marino, California.

BUCHANAN, IVA LUELLA. "An Economic History of Kitsap County, Washington, To 1889." Ph.D. dissertation, University of Washington Library, Seattle, Washington, 1930.

"Chatham Journal, 1792." Transcript, Archives of British Columbia, Victoria, British Columbia.

"Commissioner of Indian Affairs, Department of Interior, Washington, D.C., to B. F. Dowell, February 12, 1867." B. F. Dowell Collection, Henry E. Huntington Library, San Marino, California.

"Correspondence Relating to Fort Langley from the Hudson's Bay Company's Archives, 1830–1858." Transcript, Archives of British Columbia, Victoria, British Columbia.

DAMON, JOHN F. "Journal, Victoria, 1859." Henry E. Huntington Library, San Marino, California.

DEE, HENRY D. "John Work: A Chronicle of His Life and a Digest of His Journals." M.A. thesis, University of British Columbia Library, Vancouver, British Columbia, 1943.

"Diary of Mrs. Ashmun J. Butler." G. S. Butler, Ashland, Oregon.

DOUGLAS, JAMES. "Diary of a Trip to the Northwest Coast, April 22–October 2, 1840." Archives of British Columbia, Victoria, British Columbia.

"Fort Langley Correspondence." Archives of British Columbia, Victoria, British Columbia.

"Fort McLoughlin Account Book, 1840–1841." Henry E. Huntington Library, San Marino, California.

"Fort Nisqually Account Book, 1841–1842." Henry E. Huntington Library, San Marino, California.

"Fort Nisqually Journal of Occurrences, 1835–1836." Henry E. Huntington Library, San Marino, California.

"Fort Nisqually: Miscellaneous Papers, 1835 and After." Henry E. Huntington Library, San Marino, California.

"Fort Simpson Correspondence, 1859–1871." Transcript, Archives of British Columbia, Victoria, British Columbia.

"Fort Vancouver Correspondence." Archives of British Columbia, Victoria, British Columbia.

FRASER, SIMON. "Letters from the Rocky Mountains, 1806–1807." Transcript, Archives of British Columbia, Victoria, British Columbia.

"General Joel Palmer Manuscript." Bancroft Library, Berkeley, California.

GILL, FRANK B. "An Unfinished History of Transportation in Oregon and Washington." Northwest Collection, University of Washington Library, Seattle, Washington; copy in Robert S. Ellison Collection, Indiana University Library, Bloomington, Indiana.

HACKING, NORMAN. "Early Marine History of British Columbia." Archives of British Columbia, Victoria, British Columbia.

"Hudson's Bay Company Returns—New Caledonia, 1856." Archives of British Columbia, Victoria, British Columbia.

HURST, BEULAH. "History of Mountain Passes." Files of the Oregon Writers' Project, Portland, Oregon.

———. "Water Transportation." Files of the Oregon Writers' Project, Portland, Oregon.

"James Clyman Diary." Henry E. Huntington Library, San Marino, California.

"James Douglas to James Yale, March 23, 1848." Archives of British Columbia, Victoria, British Columbia.

"James Douglas to Sir George Simpson, August 7, 1855." Archives of British Columbia, Victoria, British Columbia.

"James McMillan Journal, 1828." Transcript, Archives of British Columbia, Victoria, British Columbia.

JOHANSEN, DOROTHY O. "Capitalism on the Far-Western Frontier: The Oregon Steam Navigation Company." Ph.D. dissertation, University of Washington Library, Seattle, Washington, 1941.

"John C. Ainsworth Statement." Bancroft Library, Berkeley, California.

"John Green." Josephine Green Emmerick, Baltimore, Maryland. Courtesy of Robert Emmerick.

"John Jacob Astor to James Madison, July 27, 1813." William R. Coe Collection, Yale University Library, New Haven, Connecticut.

"John Jacob Astor to James Monroe, July [?], 1813." William R. Coe Collection, Yale University Library, New Haven, Connecticut.

"John Work Journals." Archives of British Columbia, Victoria, British Columbia.

"Joseph Lane Autobiography." Bancroft Library, Berkeley, California.

LAING, F. W. "Early Agriculture in British Columbia." Archives of British Columbia, Victoria, British Columbia.

———. "A Few Notes on the Early History of Fruit Growing on the Pacific Coast." Archives of British Columbia, Victoria, British Columbia.

[MACKENZIE, RODERICK, OR WENTZELL, F.]. "Sketch of the Indian Trade of Canada." Transcript, Archives of British Columbia, Victoria, British Columbia.

MINER, WILLIAM D. "Jesse Applegate: Oregon Pioneer." M.A. thesis, Indiana University Library, Bloomington, Indiana, 1948.

"Minutes of the Oregon Railway and Navigation Company." Northern Pacific Railroad Company, Portland, Oregon.

"Minutes of the Oregon Steam Navigation Company." Office of the Northern Pacific Railroad Company, Portland, Oregon.

MUNRO, J. B. "Agricultural Beginnings in the Interior of British Columbia." Archives of British Columbia, Victoria, British Columbia.

"Notes on Meetings of the Executive Committee of the Oregon Railway and Navigation Company." Economics Records Library, Reed College, Portland, Oregon.

"Record of Achievement by an Oregon Monopoly, A." Donald H. Bates Collection, Board of Trade Building, Portland, Oregon.

"Records of the Siskiyou Wagon Road Company." Robert E. Dodge, Ashland, Oregon.

"Reminiscences of H. C. Ward." Borel Collection, Stanford University Library, Stanford, California.

"Returns, Columbia District and New Caledonia, 1825–1857." Archives of British Columbia, Victoria, British Columbia.

ROBERSON, JOSEPH S. "History of Wells, Fargo & Co. and the Pony Express." Stanford University Library, Stanford, California.

Robert M. Graham, "Memoir." Yakima Library, Yakima, Washington.

SCHAFFER, JOHN GODFREY. "The Early History of Wells Fargo Express." M.A. thesis, University of California Library, Berkeley, California, 1922.

"Simeon G. Reed Statement." Bancroft Library, Berkeley, California.

"Steamer Beaver Fur Trade Journal." Archives of British Columbia, Victoria, British Columbia.

STRANGE, JAMES. "Narrative of a Voyage to the North West Coast of America, 1786–1787." Transcript, Archives of British Columbia, Victoria, British Columbia.

WALES, ELDON MAX. "The History of Hudson's Bay Company, 1670–1713." M.A. thesis, Indiana University Library, Bloomington, Indiana, 1929.

"Wells, Fargo and Company Miscellaneous Manuscripts." Wells Fargo Historical Museum, Wells Fargo Bank and Union Trust Company Building, San Francisco, California.

"Wells, Fargo and Company Records." Wells Fargo Historical Museum, Wells Fargo Bank and Union Trust Company Building, San Francisco, California.

[WENTZELL, F., OR MACKENZIE, RODERICK]. "Sketch of the Indian Trade of Canada." Transcript, Archives of British Columbia, Victoria, British Columbia. Original in Royal Colonial Institute, London.

"W. H. McNeill to John Work, May 15, 1855." Archives of British Columbia, Victoria, British Columbia.

WILLIAMS, HENRY B. "Pacific Mail Steamship Company." Bancroft Library, Berkeley, California.

WRINCH, LEONARD A. "Land Policy of the Colony of Vancouver Island, 1849–1866." M.A. thesis, University of British Columbia Library, Vancouver, British Columbia, 1932.

UNITED STATES AND STATE GOVERNMENT DOCUMENTS

"Archives of the Provisional Government of Oregon." See under "Manuscripts."

DEADY, M. P., compiler. *Organic and Other General Laws of Oregon, 1845–1864* (Portland, Oregon, 1866).

DEADY, M. P., AND LANE, LAFAYETTE. *The Organic and Other General Laws of Oregon.* . . . . Eugene, Oregon, 1874.

Laws of the Territory of Idaho. Lewiston, Boise, Idaho, 1864–1890.

Statutes of the Territory of Washington. Olympia, Washington, 1854–1859.

Statutes of the Territory of Washington. Olympia, Washington, 1855–1888.

[UNITED STATES]. "Message of the President," *Executive Documents,* 30 Cong., 2 sess., doc. 1.

———. *House Documents,* 31 Cong., 1 sess., doc. 348.

———. *House Documents,* 32 Cong., 1 sess., vol. VIII, doc. 56.

———. *House Executive Documents,* 33 Cong., 2 sess., doc. 2.

———. *House Documents,* 33 Cong., 2 sess., doc. 91.

———. *House Executive Documents,* 34 Cong., 3 sess., doc. 1.

———. *House Executive Documents,* 35 Cong., 1 sess., vol. II, pt. 3.

———. *House Executive Documents,* 36 Cong., 2 sess., vol. VIII, doc. 44.

———. *House Executive Documents,* 39 Cong., 1 sess., doc. 1.

———. Captain John Mullan, U.S.A., "Report on the Construction of a Military Road from Fort Walla-Walla to Fort Benton," *Senate Documents,* 37 Cong., 3 sess., doc. 43.

———. "Memorial of William A. Slacum," *Senate Documents,* 25 Cong., 2 sess., vol. I, doc. 24.

———. *Ninth Census of the United States* (Washington, 1872).

———. Rossiter W. Raymond, "Statistics of Mines and Mining in the States and Territories West of the Rocky Mountains," *House Executive Documents,* 41 Cong., 2 sess., doc. 207.

———. *Reports of Committees,* 31 Cong., 2 sess., doc. 95.

———. *Reports of Committees,* 32 Cong., 2 sess., doc. 2.

———. *Senate Documents,* 33 Cong., 1 sess., doc. 1.

———. *Senate Executive Documents,* 36 Cong., 2 sess., vol. III, doc. 1.

———. *Senate Documents,* 37 Cong., 3 sess., doc. 43.

———. *Senate Journal,* 29 Cong., 1 sess.

[UNITED STATES DEPARTMENT OF STATE]. *Treaties and Conventions,* . . . . Washington, 1873.

NEWSPAPERS*

The Anaconda Standard (Butte, Montana).

The California Farmer (San Francisco, California).

The Chico Weekly Courant (Chico, California).

Clark County Register (Vancouver, Washington Territory).

The Columbian (Olympia, Washington Territory).

Daily Alta California (San Francisco, California).

Daily British Colonist (Victoria, British Columbia).

Daily California Chronicle (San Francisco, California).

Daily Evening Bulletin (San Francisco, California).

The Democratic Crisis (Corvallis, Oregon Territory).

Democratic Standard (Portland, Oregon Territory).

Evening Picayune (San Francisco, California).

Helena Weekly Herald (Helena, Montana).

Humboldt Star and Silver State (Winnemucca, Nevada).

---

* The periods covered by each newspaper are omitted here. Definite citations appear in the notes.

Idaho Weekly Statesman (Boise City, Idaho).
The Idaho World (Idaho City, Idaho).
Montana Post (Virginia City, Montana).
New York Times (New York, New York).
Occidental Messenger (Corvallis, Oregon).
The Oregon Argus (Oregon City, Oregon Territory).
Oregon Spectator (Oregon City, Oregon Territory).
The Oregon Statesman (Oregon City, Oregon Territory).
Oregon Union (Corvallis, Oregon).
Oregon Weekly Times (Portland, Oregon Territory).
The Oregonian (Portland, Oregon).
Pacific Christian Advocate (Salem, Oregon Territory).
The People's Press (Eugene City, Oregon Territory).
Philipsburg Mail (Philipsburg, Montana).
Pioneer and Democrat (Olympia, Washington Territory).
Portland Daily Advertiser (Portland, Oregon).
Red Bluff Independent (Red Bluff, California).
Rocky Mountain Gazette (Helena, Montana Territory).
Sacramento Daily Union (Sacramento, California).
San Francisco Herald (San Francisco, California).
Seattle Post (Seattle, Washington).
Tidings (Ashland, Oregon).
Vancouver Telegraph (Vancouver, Washington Territory).
Victoria Daily Chronicle (Victoria, British Columbia).
The Victoria Gazette (Victoria, British Columbia).
Walla Walla Statesman (Walla Walla, Washington).
Washington Pioneer (Olympia, Washington Territory).
Washington Statesman (Walla Walla, Washington Territory).
The Weekly Mountaineer (The Dalles, Oregon Territory).
The Western Star (Milwaukie, Oregon Territory).

PERIODICAL LITERATURE

ABEL-HENDERSON, ANNE H., AND BARRY, J. NEILSON, editors. "General B. L. E. Bonneville," *The Washington Historical Quarterly*, XVIII (July 1927), 207–30.

AMBLER, CHARLES H. "The Oregon Country, 1810–1830: A Chapter in Territorial Expansion," *The Mississippi Valley Historical Review*, XXX (June 1943), 3–24.

APPLEGATE, LINDSAY. "Notes and Reminiscences of Laying Out and Establishing the Old Emigrant Road into Southern Oregon in the Year 1846," *The Quarterly of the Oregon Historical Society*, XXII (March 1921), 12–45.

BAILEY, WALTER. "The Barlow Road," *The Quarterly of the Oregon Historical Society*, XIII (September 1912), 287–96.

BARLOW, MARY S. "History of the Barlow Road," *The Quarterly of the Oregon Historical Society*, III (March 1902), 71–81.

BARRY, J. NEILSON. "Early Oregon Country Forts: A Chronological List," *Oregon Historical Quarterly*, XLVI (June 1945), 101–11.

———. "Spaniards in Early Oregon," *The Washington Historical Quarterly*, XXIII (January 1932), 25–34.

BEMIS, SAMUEL FLAGG. "Captain John Mullan and the Engineers' Frontier," *Washington Historical Quarterly*, XIV (July 1923), 201–5.

BERREMAN, JOEL V. "Tribal Distribution in Oregon," *Memoirs of the American Anthropological Association*, Nos. 46–49 (March 1937).

BRACKETT, WILLIAM S. "Bonneville and Bridger," *Contributions to the Historical Society of Montana*, III (1900), 175–200.

BRADLEY, HAROLD W. "The Hawaiian Islands and the Pacific Fur Trade, 1785–1813," *The Pacific Northwest Quarterly*, XXX (July 1939), 275–99.

BRADLEY, MARIE MERRIMAN. "Political Beginnings in Oregon," *The Quarterly of the Oregon Historical Society*, IX (March 1908), 42–72.

BUCKLAND, F. M. "The Hudson's Bay Brigade Trail," *The Sixth Report of the Okanagan Historical Society, 1935* (Vernon, 1936).

CARPENTER, E. W. "A Glimpse of Montana," *The Overland Monthly*, II (April 1869), 378–86.

CAYWOOD, LOUIS R. "The Archeological Excavation of Fort Vancouver," *Oregon Historical Quarterly*, XLIX (June 1948), 99–116.

[CHAMPNESS, W.]. "To Cariboo and Back: An Emigrant's Journey to the Gold-Fields in British Columbia," *The Leisure Hour*, Nos. 692–96 (April 1865), p. 203.

CHITTENDEN, HIRAM M. "The Ancient Town of Fort Benton in Montana," *Magazine of American History*, XXIV (December 1890), 409–25.

[COWDIN, E. C., AND STURGIS, WILLIAM]. "The Northwest Fur Trade," *Hunt's Merchants' Magazine*, XIV (June 1846), 532–39.

CRANDALL, LULU DONNELL. "The 'Colonel Wright'," *The Washington Historical Quarterly*, VII (April 1916), 126–32.

DAY, A. GROVE. "The Earliest Explorer-Traders of the Northwest Coast," *United States Naval Institute Proceedings*, CLVII (December 1941), 1677–83.

DODMAN, A. E., "Hudson's Bay 'Point' Blankets," *The Beaver*, Outfit 257 (December 1926), pp. 22–24.

EATON, W. CLEMENT. "Nathaniel Wyeth's Oregon Expeditions," *The Pacific Historical Review*, IV (June 1935), 101–13.

ELLIOTT, T. C. "The Earliest Travelers on the Oregon Trail," *The Quarterly of the Oregon Historical Society*, XIII (March 1912), 71–84.

———. "The Fur Trade in the Columbia River Basin Prior to 1811," *The Washington Historical Quarterly*, VI (January 1915), 3–10.

———, editor. "George Simpson to H. W. Addington, December 31, 1825," *The Quarterly of the Oregon Historical Society*, XX (December 1919), 333–39.

———. "The Mullan Road: Its Local History and Significance," *The Washington Historical Quarterly*, XIV (July 1923), 206–9.

———. "Peter Skene Ogden, Fur Trader," *The Quarterly of the Oregon Historical Society*, XI (September 1910), 229–78.

FRENCH, C. H. "H. B. C. Pioneer Steamer Ruled West Coast Trade 20 Years," *The Beaver*, I (February 1921), 2–4.

GANOE, JOHN TILSON. "The History of the Oregon and California Railroad," *The Quarterly of the Oregon Historical Society*, XXV (September and December, 1924), 236–83, 330–52.

GASTON, JOSEPH. "The Genesis of the Oregon Railway System," *The Quarterly of the Oregon Historical Society*, VII (June 1906), 105–32.

GILL, FRANK B. "Oregon's First Railway," *The Quarterly of the Oregon Historical Society*, XXV (September 1924), 171–235.

GILLETTE, P. W. "A Brief History of the Oregon Steam Navigation Company," *The Quarterly of the Oregon Historical Society*, V (June 1904), 120–32.

GUNTHER, ERNA. "An Analysis of the First Salmon Ceremony," *American Anthropologist*, n.s., XXVIII (October–December, 1926), 605–17.

HACKING, NORMAN R. "British Columbia Steamboat Days, 1870–1883," *The British Columbia Historical Quarterly*, XI (April 1947), 69–111.

———. "Paddle Wheels and British Oak on the North Pacific," *The Beaver*, Outfit 265 (March 1935), pp. 25–28.

———. "Steamboat 'Round the Bend," *The British Columbia Historical Quarterly*, VIII (October 1944), 255–80.

HASTINGS, LOREN B. "Diary of Loren B. Hastings," *Transactions of the Fifty-first Annual Reunion of the Oregon Pioneer Association, June 21, 1923* (Portland, 1926), pp. 13–26.

HOLMAN, FREDERICK V. "A Brief History of the Oregon Provisional Government and What Caused Its Formation," *The Quarterly of the Oregon Historical Society*, XIII (June 1912), 89–139.

———. "Some Important Results from the Expeditions of John Jacob Astor to, and from the Oregon Country," *The Quarterly of the Oregon Historical Society*, XII (September 1911), 206–19.

HOWARD, ADDISON. "Captain John Mullan," *The Washington Historical Quarterly*, XXV (July 1934), 185–202.

HOWAY, F. W. "British Columbia Brigade Trails," *The Beaver*, Outfit 269 (June 1938), pp. 48–51.

———. "International Aspects of the Maritime Fur-Trade," *Proceedings and Transactions of the Royal Society of Canada*, third series, XXXVI (May 1942), 59–78.

———., editor. "Letters Concerning Voyages of British Vessels to the Northwest Coast of America, 1786–1809." *The Oregon Historical Quarterly*, Vol. XXXIX (September 1938).

———. "A List of Trading Vessels in Maritime Fur Trade, 1785–1794," *Transactions of the Royal Society of Canada*, third series, Vol. XXIV (May 1930), Sec. II, pp. 111–34.

———. "The Loss of the 'Tonquin'," *The Washington Historical Quarterly*, XIII (April 1922), 83–92.

———, editor. "The Spanish Settlement at Nootka," *The Washington Historical Quarterly*, VIII (July 1917), 163–71.

———, editor. "William Sturgis: The Northwest Fur Trade," *The British Columbia Historical Quarterly*, VIII (January 1944), 11–25.

HUGGINS, EDWARD. "Puget Sound Pioneer Vessels," *The Washington Historian*, I (July 1900), 197.

JACKSON, W. TURRENTINE. "Federal Road Building Grants For Early Oregon," *Oregon Historical Quarterly*, L (March 1949), 3–29.

JOHANSEN, DOROTHY O. "The Oregon Steam Navigation Company: An Example of Capitalism on the Frontier," *Pacific Historical Review*, X (June 1941), 179–88.

———. "William Fraser Tolmie of the Hudson's Bay Company, 1833–1870," *The Beaver*, Outfit 268 (September 1937), pp. 29–32.

JOHNSON, F. HENRY. "Fur-trading Days at Kamloops," *The British Columbia Historical Quarterly*, I (July 1937), 171–85.

KINGSTON, C. S. "Introduction of Cattle into the Pacific Northwest," *The Washington Historical Quarterly*, XIV (July 1923), 163–85.

KINGSTON, C. S. "Spokane House State Park in Retrospect," *Pacific Northwest Quarterly*, XXXIX (April 1948), 185–88.

LAING, F. W. "Some Pioneers of the Cattle Industry," *The British Columbia Historical Quarterly*, VI (October 1942), 257–75.

LAMB, W. KAYE. "The Advent of the 'Beaver'," *The British Columbia Historical Quarterly*, II (July 1938), 163–84.

———. "The Founding of Fort Victoria," *The British Columbia Historical Quarterly*, VII (April 1943), 71–92.

LAWRENCE, ELEANOR. "Mule Trains and Muleteers on Early California Roads," *Touring Topics*, XXIV (July 1932), 16–18, 55.

LEWIS, WILLIAM S. "The Camel Pack Trains in the Mining Camps of the West," *The Washington Historical Quarterly*, XIX (October 1928), 271–84.

———, editor. "Experiences of a Packer in Washington Territory Mining Camps During the Sixties," by James W. Watt, *The Washington Historical Quarterly*, XIX (July and October, 1928), 206–13, 285–93; XX (January 1929), 36–53.

———. "Information Concerning the Estab[l]ishment of Fort Colvile," *The Washington Historical Quarterly*, XVI (April 1925), 102–7.

LYMAN, H. S. "Reminiscences of F. X. Matthieu," *The Quarterly of the Oregon Historical Society*, I (March 1900), 73–104.

McKELVIE, B. A. "The Founding of Nanaimo," *The British Columbia Historical Quarterly*, VIII (July 1944), 169–88.

MacLEOD, WILLIAM C. "Economic Aspects of Indigenous American Slavery," *American Anthropologist*, n.s., XXX (October–December, 1928), 632–50.

MALONEY, ALICE B. "Hudson's Bay Company in California," *The Oregon Historical Quarterly*, XXXVII (March 1936), 9–23.

MARIAGER, DAGMAR. "Nomadic Experiences of a Frontierswoman," *The Overland Monthly*, second series, X (September 1887), 316–26.

MASON, OTIS T. "Aboriginal American Basketry," *Annual Report . . . . of the Smithsonian Institution, 1902.* Washington, D.C., 1904.

MEANY, EDMOND S., "The Cowlitz Convention: Inception of Washington Territory," *The Washington Historical Quarterly*, XIII (January 1922), 6–8.

MERK, FREDERICK. "The Oregon Pioneers and the Boundary," *The American Historical Review*, XXIX (July 1924), 681–99.

———. "Snake Country Expedition, 1824–25," *The Oregon Historical Quarterly*, XXXV (June 1934), 93–122.

MOBERLY, WALTER. "History of Cariboo Wagon Road," *Art, Historical and Scientific Association Publication, 1907–1908 Session.* Vancouver, n.d.

MORTON, ARTHUR S. "The North West Company's Columbian Enterprise and David Thompson," *Canadian Historical Review*, XVII (September 1936), 266–88.

OLIPHANT, J. ORIN. "Old Fort Colville," *The Washington Historical Quarterly*, XVI (January and April, 1925), 29–48, 83–101.

———. "Winter Losses of Cattle in the Oregon Country, 1847–1890," *The Washington Historical Quarterly*, XXIII (January 1932), 3–17.

OLSON, R. L. "Adze, Canoe, and House Types of the Northwest Coast," *University of Washington Publications in Anthropology*, II (1929), 1–38.

O'MERA, JAMES. "An Early Steamboating Era on the Willamette," *The Oregon Historical Quarterly*, XLIV (June 1943), 140–46.

O'NEIL, MARION. "The Maritime Activities of the North West Company, 1813–1821," *The Washington Historical Quarterly*, XXI (October 1930), 243–67.

OVERMEYER, PHILIP HENRY. "Members of First Wyeth Expedition," *The Oregon Historical Quarterly*, XXXVI (March 1935), 95–101.

OVIATT, ALTON B. "Steamboat Traffic on the Upper Missouri River, 1859–1869," *Pacific Northwest Quarterly*, XL (April 1949), 93–105.

PALMER, LIEUTENANT HENRY S. "The Geography of British Columbia and the Condition of the Cariboo Gold District," *Royal Geographical Society Proceedings*, VIII (1864), 87–90.

PARRISH, EDWARD EVANS. "Crossing the Plains in 1844." *Transactions of the Oregon Pioneer Association for 1888* (1889), pp. 83–122.

PERRINE, FRED S. "Early Days on the Willamette," *The Quarterly of the Oregon Historical Society*, XXV (December 1924), 295–312.

PIERS, SIR CHARLES. "Pioneer Ships on Pacific Coast (From Eighteen Hundred to Early Eighties)," *The Beaver*, Outfit 258 (June 1927), pp. 24–25.

POPPLETON, IRENE LINCOLN. "Oregon's First Monopoly—The O. S. N. Co.," *The Quarterly of the Oregon Historical Society*, IX (September 1908), 274–304.

POWELL, F. W. "Bibliography of Hall J. Kelley." *The Quarterly of the Oregon Historical Society*, VIII (December 1907), 375–86.

PROSCH, THOMAS W. "The Military Roads of Washington Territory," *The Washington Historical Quarterly*, II (January 1908), 118–26.

———. "The Political Beginnings of Washington Territory," *The Quarterly of the Oregon Historical Society*, VI (June 1905), 147–50.

REID, ROBIE L. "Early Days at Old Fort Langley: Economic Beginnings in British Columbia," *The British Columbia Historical Quarterly*, I (April 1937), 71–85.

RICE, WILLIAM B., editor. "Early Freighting on the Salt Lake–San Bernardino Trail," *The Pacific Historical Review*, XI (March 1942), 73–75.

RICHARDSON, ALBERT D. "Oregon and Washington," *Beadle's Monthly*, II (September 1866), 181–92.

RICKARD, T. A. "The Use of Iron and Copper by the Indians of British Columbia," *The British Columbia Historical Quarterly*, III (January 1939), 25–50.

RIDEING, WILLIAM H. "An American Enterprise," *Harper's Magazine*, LI (1875), 314–26.

RYDELL, RUTH. "Tributaries of the Willamette: Yamhill, Santiam, Calapooya," *The Oregon Historical Quarterly*, XLIV (June 1943), 147–56.

SAGE, WALTER N. "Life at a Fur Trading Post in British Columbia a Century Ago," *The Washington Historical Quarterly*, XXV (January 1934), 11–22.

———. "The Place of Fort Vancouver in the History of the Northwest," *Pacific Northwest Quarterly*, XXXIX (April 1948), 83–102.

SARGENT, ALICE APPLEGATE. "A Sketch of the Rogue River Valley and Southern Oregon History," *The Quarterly of the Oregon Historical Society*, XXII (March 1921), 1–11.

SCHEFFER, VICTOR B. "The Sea Otter on the Washington Coast," *The Pacific Northwest Quarterly*, XXXI (October 1940), 371–87.

SPERLIN, O. B. "Washington Forts of the Fur Trade Regime," *The Washington Historical Quarterly*, VIII (April 1917), 102–13.

STONE, BUENA COBB. "Southern Route into Oregon: Notes and a New Map," *Oregon Historical Quarterly*, XLVII (June 1948), 135–54.

TALKINGTON, HENRY L. "Mullan Road," *The Washington Historical Quarterly,* VII (October 1916), 301–6.

THORNILEY, WILLIAM O. "Famous Pioneer Steamboats of Puget Sound," *Marine Digest,* XXII (April 22, 1944), 2.

TODD, RONALD. "The Steamer 'Beaver'," *The Pacific Northwest Quarterly,* XXVII (October 1936), 367–68.

TRUMAN, MAJOR BEN. C. "Knights of the Lash: Old Time Stage Drivers of the West Coast," *Overland Monthly,* XXXI (March and April 1898), 218–26, 308–18.

TURNEY-HIGH, HARRY. "The Diffusion of the Horse to the Flatheads," *Man,* XXXV (December 1935), 183–85.

VICTOR, FRANCES FULLER. "Flotsom and Jetsom of the Pacific—the Owyhee, the Sultana, and the May Dacre," *The Quarterly of the Oregon Historical Society,* II (March 1901), 36–54.

WEST, WILLIS J. "Staging and Stage Hold-ups in the Cariboo," *The British Columbia Historical Quarterly,* XII (July 1948), 185–209.

WINTHER, OSCAR OSBURN. "Commercial Routes from 1792 to 1843 by Sea and Overland," *The Oregon Historical Quarterly,* XLII (September 1941), 231–46.

——. "Inland Transportation and Communication in Washington, 1844–1859," *The Pacific Northwest Quarterly,* XXX (October 1939), 371–77.

——, editor. "Stage-coach Days in California: Reminiscences of H. C. Ward," *California Historical Society Quarterly,* XIII (September 1934), 255–61.

WINTHER, OSCAR OSBURN, AND GALEY, ROSA DODGE, editors. "Mrs. Butler's 1853 Diary of Rogue River Valley," *The Oregon Historical Quarterly,* XLI (December 1940), 337–66.

WRINCH, LEONARD A. "The Formation of the Puget's Sound Agricultural Company," *The Washington Historical Quarterly,* XXIV (January 1933), 3–8.

WYETH, JOHN A. "Nathaniel J. Wyeth, and the Struggle for Oregon," *Harper's New Monthly Magazine,* LXXXV (November 1892), 835–47.

[——]. "Bradley Manuscript—Book II," *Contributions to the Historical Society of Montana,* VIII (1917), 105–96.

[——]. "The Census of Vancouver Island, 1855," *The British Columbia Historical Quarterly,* IV (January 1940), 51–58.

[——]. "Early Navigation of the Upper Missouri River," *Contributions to the Historical Society of Montana,* VII (1910), 253–56.

[——]. *The Expressman's Monthly,* II (February 1877), 97–119.

[——]. "Fort Langley Correspondence," *The British Columbia Historical Quarterly,* I (July 1937), 187–94.

[——]. *Hutchings' Illustrated California Magazine,* I (December 1856), 241–46.

[——]. "Journal of Occurrences at Nisqually in 1870," *The Washington Historical Quarterly,* XXV (January 1934), 60–64.

[——]. *Niles' National Register,* LCVIII (May 31, 1845), 203–4.

[——]. "Puget's Sound Agricultural Company: Prospectus," *The Quarterly of the Oregon Historical Society,* XIX (December 1918), 345–49.

[——]. "S. S. Beaver," *The Beaver,* Outfit 260 (June 1929), pp. 206–8.

[——]. "Steamboat Arrivals at Fort Benton, Montana, and Vicinity," *Contributions to the Historical Society of Montana,* I (1876), 317–25.

[——]. "The Value of Oregon," *Hunt's Merchants' Magazine,* XIV (May 1846), 435–39.

BOOKS, PRINTED DOCUMENTS,* BOOKLETS, BROCHURES, ENCYCLOPEDIAS, DIRECTORIES, GUIDES, AND SCRAPBOOKS

ANDERSON, EVA G. *Chief Seattle.* Caldwell, Idaho, 1943.

ANGUS, H. F., editor. *British Columbia and the United States: The North Pacific Slope from Fur Trade to Aviation,* by F. W. Howay, W. N. Sage, and H. F. Angus. Toronto, 1942.

APPLEGATE, JESSE A. *Recollections of My Boyhood.* Roseburg, Oregon, 1914.

[ATCHESON, NATHANIEL]. *On the Origin and Progress of the North-West Company of Canada.* London, 1811.

BAGLEY, CLARENCE B. *History of Seattle from the Earliest Settlement to the Present Time.* 3 vols. Chicago, 1916.

BAILEY, PHILIP A. *Golden Mirages.* New York, 1940.

BAILEY, THOMAS A. *A Diplomatic History of the American People.* New York, 1940.

BANCROFT, HUBERT HOWE. *History of the Northwest Coast.* 2 vols. San Francisco, 1886.

——. *History of Oregon, 1834–1888.* 2 vols. San Francisco, 1886–1888.

——. *History of Washington, Idaho, and Montana, 1845–1889.* San Francisco, 1890.

——. *The Native Races.* 5 vols. San Francisco, 1883.

——. *Scraps: Montana Miscellany.* Bancroft Library, Berkeley, California.

——. *Scraps: Oregon Miscellany.* 2 vols. Bancroft Library, Berkeley, California.

——. *Scraps: Washington Miscellany.* Bancroft Library, Berkeley, California.

BANNING, CAPTAIN WILLIAM, AND BANNING, GEORGE HUGH. *Six Horses.* New York, London, 1928.

BARKER, BURT BROWN, editor. *Letters of Dr. John McLoughlin, Written at Fort Vancouver, 1829–1832.* Portland, Oregon, 1948.

BEAL, M. D. *A History of Southeastern Idaho.* Caldwell, Idaho, 1942.

BEGG, ALEXANDER. *History of British Columbia From Its Earliest Discovery to the Present Time.* Toronto, 1894.

——. *History of the North-West.* 3 vols. Toronto, 1894–1895.

BELL, JAMES CHRISTY, JR. *Opening a Highway to the Pacific, 1838–1846.* New York, 1921.

BIRD, ANNIE LAURIE. *Boise: The Peace Valley.* Caldwell, Idaho, 1934.

BOGGS, MAE HÉLÈNE BACON, compiler. *My Playhouse Was a Concord Coach, An Anthology of Newspaper Clippings and Documents Relating to Those Who Made California History During the Years 1822–1888.* Oakland, California, 1942.

BOLTON, HERBERT EUGENE. *Outpost of Empire: The Story of the Founding of San Francisco.* New York, 1939.

BOWLES, SAMUEL. *Across the Continent: A Summer's Journey to the Rocky Mountains, the Mormons, and the Pacific States, with Speaker Colfax.* Springfield, Massachusetts, 1866.

BRADLEY, HAROLD WHITMAN. *The American Frontier in Hawaii: The Pioneers, 1789–1843.* Stanford, California, 1942.

BRIGGS, HAROLD E. *Frontiers of the Northwest: A History of the Upper Missouri Valley.* New York, 1940.

---

* Except for government documents listed under "United States and State Government Documents" (pp. 307–8).

BROWN, JENNIE BROUGHTON. *Fort Hall on the Oregon Trail*. Caldwell, Idaho, 1932.

BURLINGAME, MERRILL G. *The Montana Frontier*. Helena, Montana, 1942.

BURPEE, LAWRENCE J., editor. *Journals and Letters of Pierre Gaultier de Varennes de la Vérendrye and His Sons*. Toronto, 1927.

———. *The Search for the Western Sea: The Story of the Exploration of North-Western America*. . . . . 2 vols. New York, 1936.

CAMPBELL, [J. L.]. *The Great Agricultural and Mineral West; A Hand-book and Guide for the Emigrant* . . . . Chicago [1866].

CAREY, CHARLES H. *A General History of Oregon Prior to 1861*. 2 vols. Portland, 1935-[1936].

CAUGHEY, JOHN WALTON. *History of the Pacific Coast of North America*. Los Angeles, 1933.

CHAPMAN, CHARLES E. *A History of California: The Spanish Period*. New York, 1936.

CHITTENDEN, HIRAM MARTIN. *The American Fur Trade of the Far West*. 3 vols. New York, 1902.

CLARK, ARTHUR H. *The Clipper Ship Era: An Epitome of Famous American and British Clipper Ships; Their Owners, Builders, Commanders and Crews, 1843-1869*. New York, London, 1910.

CLARK, PAL, editor. *Journal From Fort Dalles O. T. to Fort Wallah Wallah W. T. July 1858. Lieut. John Mullan, U.S. Army*. Missoula, Montana, 1932.

CLARK, ROBERT CARLTON. *History of the Willamette Valley, Oregon*. Chicago, 1927.

CLARKE, S. A. *Pioneer Days of Oregon History*. 2 vols. Portland, 1905.

CLELAND, ROBERT G. *The Cattle on a Thousand Hills: Southern California, 1850-1870*. San Marino, California, 1941.

———. *Pathfinders*. Los Angeles, 1929.

COLVILLE, SAMUEL, compiler. *City Directory of Sacramento for the Year 1854-55*. Sacramento, 1854.

CONKLING, ROSCOE P., AND CONKLING, MARGARET B. *The Butterfield Overland Mail, 1857-1869* . . . . . 3 vols. Glendale, California, 1947.

COOK, JAMES, AND KING, JAMES. *A Voyage to the Pacific Ocean* . . . . 3 vols. London, 1784.

CORNING, HOWARD MCKINLEY. *Willamette Landings*. Portland, 1947.

COUES, ELLIOTT. *History of the Expedition of Lewis and Clark*. New York, 1893.

COX, ROSS. *Adventures on the Columbia River, Including the Narrative of a Residence of Six Years on the Western Side of the Rocky Mountains* . . . . 2 vols. London, 1831.

COY, OWEN C. *The Humboldt Bay Region, 1850-1875*. Los Angeles, 1929.

CRUIKSHANK, E. A., editor. *The Correspondence of Lieut. Governor John Graves Simcoe*. 5 vols. Toronto, 1925.

DAVIDSON, GORDON CHARLES. *The North West Company*. Berkeley, California, 1918.

DEE, HENRY D., editor. *The Journal of John Work, January to October, 1835*. Victoria, 1945.

DENNY, ARTHUR A. *Pioneer Days on Puget Sound*. Seattle, 1908.

DE VOTO, BERNARD. *The Year of Decision: 1846*. Boston, 1943.

DIMSDALE, THOMAS J. *The Vigilantes of Montana; or, Popular Justice in the Rocky Mountains*. Virginia City, Montana, 1921.

DOMER, JOHN. *A Guide to British Columbia and Vancouver Island.* London [1858].

DONALDSON, THOMAS. *Idaho of Yesterday.* Caldwell, Idaho, 1941.

DOUGHTY, ARTHUR G., editor and compiler. "First Journal of Simon Fraser From April 12th to July 18th, 1806," *Dominion of Canada Report of the Public Archives for the Year 1929.* Ottawa, 1930.

DOUGHTY, ARTHUR G., AND LANCTOT, GUSTAVE, editors. *Cheadle's Journal of a Trip Across Canada, 1862–1863.* Ottawa, 1931.

DRIGGS, HOWARD R., editor. *The Bullwhacker: Adventures of a Frontier Freighter,* by William F. Hooker. New York, 1924.

DuBOIS, CORA. *The Feather Cult of the Middle Columbia.* General Series in Anthropology, No. 7. Menasha, Wisconsin, 1938.

DUNN, JOHN. *The Oregon Territory, and the British North American Fur Trade.* Philadelphia, 1845.

DURHAM, N. W. *History of the City of Spokane and Spokane Country, Washington, from Its Earliest Settlement to the Present Time.* 3 vols. Spokane, Chicago, Philadelphia, 1912.

[EVANS, ELWOOD, compiler]. *History of the Pacific Northwest: Oregon and Washington.* 2 vols. Portland, 1889.

FABENS, JOSEPH W. *The Uses of the Camel: Considered with a View to His Introduction into Our Western States and Territories.* New York, 1865.

FARNHAM, THOMAS J. *Traveling in the Great Western Prairies, the Anahuac and Rocky Mountains, and the Oregon Territory.* N.p. [1844].

FILCHER, J. A. *Untold Tales of California: Short Stories Illustrating Phases of Life Peculiar to Early Days in the West.* N.p., 1903.

FOSTER, SIR WILLIAM. *England's Quest of Eastern Trade.* London, 1933.

FRANCHÈRE, GABRIEL. *Narrative of a Voyage to the Northwest Coast of America in the Years 1811, 1812, 1813, and 1814.* New York, 1854.

FREDERICK, J. V. *Ben Holladay: The Stagecoach King. A Chapter in the Development of Transcontinental Transportation.* Glendale, California, 1940.

FRÉMONT, JOHN C. *Narrative of the Exploring Expedition to the Rocky Mountains, in the Year 1842, and to Oregon and North California, in the Years 1843–44.* London, 1846.

FRENCH, HIRAM T. *History of Idaho: A Narrative Account of Its Historical Progress, Its People and Its Principal Interests.* 3 vols. Chicago, New York, 1914.

FULLER, GEORGE W. *A History of the Pacific Northwest.* New York, 1931.

———. *The Inland Empire of the Pacific Northwest: A History.* 4 vols. Spokane, Washington; Denver, Colorado, 1928.

GASTON, JOSEPH. *Portland, Oregon: Its History and Builders.* Chicago, Portland, 1911.

GAY, THERESSA. *Life and Letters of Mrs. Jason Lee.* Portland, 1936.

GHENT, W. J. *The Road to Oregon: A Chronicle of the Great Emigrant Trail.* New York, 1929.

GILBERT, FRANK T. *Historic Sketches of Walla Walla, Whitman, Columbia and Garfield Counties, Washington Territory.* Portland, 1882.

GODDARD, PLINY EARLE. *Indians of the Northwest Coast.* New York, 1924.

GOLDER, F. A. *Russian Expansion on the Pacific, 1641–1850: An Account of the Earliest and Later Expeditions Made by the Russians Along the Pacific Coast of Asia and North America; Including Some Related Expeditions to the Arctic Regions.* Cleveland, 1914.

GRAY, WILLIAM HENRY. *A History of Oregon, 1792–1849, Drawn From Personal Observation and Authentic Information.* Portland, Oregon, 1870.

GREELEY, HORACE. *An Overland Journey, From New York to San Francisco, In The Summer Of 1859.* New York, 1860.

GREENBIE, SYDNEY, AND GREENBIE, MARJORIE BARSTOW. *Gold of Ophir: The China Trade in the Making of America.* New York, 1937.

GUINN, JAMES M. *A History of California and An Extended History of Los Angeles and Environs.* 3 vols. Los Angeles, 1915.

HAFEN, LE ROY R. *The Overland Mail 1849–1869: Promoter of Settlement; Precursor of Railroads.* Cleveland, 1926.

HAILEY, JOHN. *The History of Idaho.* Boise, Idaho, 1910.

HARLOW, ALVIN F. *Old Waybills: The Romance of the Express Companies.* New York, 1934.

HARMON, DANIEL WILLIAMS. *A Journal of Voyages and Travels in the Interiour of North America.* Andover, Massachusetts, 1819.

HASTINGS, LANSFORD W. *The Emigrants' Guide, to Oregon and California . . . .* Cincinnati, 1845.

HAWLEY, JAMES H., editor. *History of Idaho, The Gem of the Mountains.* 4 vols. Chicago, 1920.

HAZLITT, WILLIAM CAREW. *The Great Gold Fields of Cariboo; With an Authentic Description, Brought Down to the Latest Period, of British Columbia and Vancouver Island.* London, New York, 1862.

HEDGES, JAMES B. *Henry Villard and the Railways of the Northwest.* New Haven, Connecticut, 1930.

HELPER, HINTON R. *The Land of Gold: Reality Versus Fiction.* Baltimore, 1855.

HEWITT, RANDALL H. *Across the Plains and Over the Divide; A Mule Train Journey from East to West in 1862, and Incidents Connected Therewith.* New York, 1906.

HICKMAN, E. "William George Fargo," *Dictionary of American Biography,* VI, 271–72.

HINES, GUSTAVUS. *Life on the Plains of the Pacific. Oregon: Its History, Condition and Prospects . . . .* Buffalo, 1851.

HITTELL, JOHN SHERSTER. *The Commerce and Industries of the Pacific Coast of North America.* San Francisco, 1882.

———. *A History of the City of San Francisco and Incidentally the State of California.* San Francisco, 1878.

HOOKER, WILLIAM F. *The Bullwhacker: Adventures of a Frontier Freighter.* New York, 1924.

HOWAY, FREDERIC W. *British Columbia: The Making of a Province.* Toronto, 1928.

———, editor. *Voyages of the "Columbia" to the Northwest Coast, 1787–1790 and 1790–1793.* Boston, 1941.

HOWAY, F. W., SAGE, W. N., AND ANGUS, H. F. *British Columbia and the United States.* See Angus, H. F., editor.

HOWAY, FREDERIC W., AND SCHOLEFIELD, E. O. S. *British Columbia from the Earliest Times to the Present.* Vancouver, British Columbia, 1914.

[HUDSON'S BAY HOUSE]. *Hudson's Bay Company.* London, 1934.

HULBERT, ARCHER BUTLER, editor. *The Call of the Columbia: Iron Men and Saints Take to the Oregon Trail.* [Denver], 1934.

HULBERT, ARCHER BUTLER, AND HULBERT, DOROTHY PRINTUP, editors. *The Oregon Crusade. Across Land and Sea to Oregon.* [Denver], Colorado, 1935.

HUME, JAMES B., AND THACKER, JNO. N. *Wells, Fargo & Co.'s Express . . . . Giving Losses by Train Robbers, Stage Robbers, and Burglaries.* San Francisco, 1885.

HUNTER, J. MARVIN. *Old Camp Verde: The Home of the Camels, a Romantic Story of Jefferson Davis' Plan to Use Camels on the Texas Frontier.* Bandera, Texas, 1936.

HUNTINGTON, J. V., translator and editor. *Narrative of a Voyage to the Northwest Coast of America in the Years 1811, 1812, 1813, and 1814,* by Gabriel Franchère. New York, 1854.

HUTCHINGS, JAMES M. *In The Heart of the Sierras: The Yo Semite Valley Both Historical and Descriptive . . . .* Oakland, California, 1888.

INNIS, HAROLD ADAMS. *The Fur Trade in Canada.* Toronto, New Haven, 1930.
——. *Peter Pond: Fur Trader and Adventurer.* Toronto, 1930.

IRVING, WASHINGTON. *The Adventures of Captain Bonneville.* New York, 1883.
——. *Astoria, or Anecdotes of an Enterprise Beyond the Rocky Mountains.* 2 vols. Philadelphia, 1836.

JACOBS, MELVIN CLAY. *Winning Oregon: A Study of an Expansionist Movement.* Caldwell, Idaho, 1938.

JOHNSON, RICHARD BYRON. *Very Far West Indeed: A Few Rough Experiences on the North-West Pacific Coast.* London, 1872.

KEIR, MALCOLM. *The March of Commerce.* New Haven, Connecticut, 1927.

KELLEY, HALL J. *A Geographical Sketch of That Part of North America, Called Oregon.* Boston, 1830.

KEMBLE, JOHN HASKELL. *The Panama Route, 1848–1869.* Berkeley, California, 1943.

LANG, H. O., editor. *History of the Willamette Valley . . . . Together with Personal Reminiscences of Its Early Pioneers.* Portland, Oregon, 1885.

LA PÉROUSE, J. F. G. DE. *A Voyage Round the World, in the Years 1785, 1786, 1787, and 1788.* 3 vols. London, 1799.

LAUT, AGNES C. *The Cariboo Trail: A Chronicle of the Gold-fields of British Columbia.* Toronto, 1916.

LEDYARD, JOHN. *A Journal of Captain Cook's Last Voyage to the Pacific Ocean and in Quest of a North-West Passage Between Asia & America.* Hartford, Connecticut, 1783.

[LEESON, MICHAEL A., editor]. *History of Montana: 1739–1885.* Chicago, 1885.

LEIGHTON, CAROLINE C. *Life at Puget Sound with Sketches of Travel in Washington Territory, British Columbia, Oregon, and California, 1865–1881.* Boston, 1884.

LESLEY, LEWIS BURT, editor. *Uncle Sam's Camels: The Journal of May Humphreys Stacey Supplemented by the Report of Edward Fitzgerald Beale (1857–1858).* Cambridge, Massachusetts, 1929.

LEWIS, WILLIAM S., AND PHILLIPS, PAUL C., editors. *The Journal of John Work: A Chief Trader of the Hudson's Bay Co. During his Expedition from Vancouver to the Flatheads and Blackfeet of the Pacific Northwest.* Cleveland, Ohio, 1923.

LOMAX, ALFRED. *Pioneer Woolen Mills in Oregon: History of Wool and the Woolen Textile Industry in Oregon, 1811–1875.* Portland, 1941.

LORD, JOHN KEAST. *At Home in the Wilderness: What To Do There and How To Do It. A Handbook for Travellers and Emigrants.* London, 1876.

LYMAN, WILLIAM DENNISON. *History of Yakima Valley, Washington.* N.p., 1919.

MCARTHUR, LEWIS A. *Oregon Geographic Names.* Portland, 1928.

MCCONNELL, W. J. *Early History of Idaho.* Caldwell, Idaho, 1913.

MACFIE, MATTHEW. *Vancouver Island and British Columbia.* London, 1865.

MCGROARTY, JOHN S. *Los Angeles From the Mountains to the Sea.* 3 vols. Chicago, 1921.

MACKAY, DOUGLAS. *The Honourable Company: A History of the Hudson's Bay Company.* Indianapolis, Indiana, 1936.

MCKELVIE, B. A. *Early History of the Province of British Columbia.* Toronto, London, 1926.

MACKENZIE, ALEXANDER. *Voyages from Montreal, on the River St. Laurence, through the Continent of North America, to the Frozen and Pacific Oceans: in the Years 1789 and 1793.* London, 1801.

MCLEOD, MALCOLM, editor. *Peace River, A Canoe Voyage From Hudson's Bay to Pacific . . . . in 1828; Journal of the Late Chief Factor, Archibald McDonald,* by Sir George Simpson. Ottawa, 1872.

MACMULLEN, JERRY. *Paddle-Wheel Days in California.* Stanford University, Stanford, California, 1944.

MCNAUGHTON, MARGARET. *Overland to Cariboo.* Toronto, 1896.

MALONEY, ALICE BAY, editor. *Fur Brigade to the Ventura.* San Francisco, 1945.

MARQUIS, T. G. "The Period of Exploration," *Pacific Province.* 2 vols. Toronto, 1914.

MAYNE, COMMANDER R[ICHARD] C. *Four Years in British Columbia and Vancouver Island.* London, 1862.

MEARES, JOHN. *Voyages Made in the Years 1788 and 1789, From China to the North West Coast of America . . . .* London, 1790.

MEEKER, EZRA. *Pioneer Reminiscences of Puget Sound: The Tragedy of Leschi.* Seattle, Washington, 1905.

MERK, FREDERICK, editor. *Fur Trade and Empire: George Simpson's Journal, 1824–1825.* Cambridge, Massachusetts, 1931.

MILLS, RANDALL V. *Stern-Wheelers Up Columbia.* Palo Alto, California, 1947.

MONTGOMERY, RICHARD G. *The White Headed Eagle: John McLoughlin, Builder of an Empire.* New York, 1934.

MORICE, ADRIEN G. *The History of the Northern Interior of British Columbia: Formerly New Caledonia, 1660 to 1880.* Toronto, 1904.

MORISON, SAMUEL ELIOT. *The Maritime History of Massachusetts, 1783–1860.* Boston, New York, 1921.

MORRIS, ALEXANDER. *The Hudson's Bay and Pacific Territories. A Lecture.* Montreal, 1859.

MORTON, ARTHUR S. *A History of the Canadian West to 1870–71.* Toronto, n.d.

——, editor. *The Journal of Duncan M'Gillivray of the North West Company at Fort George on the Saskatchewan, 1794–5.* Toronto, 1929.

——. *Sir George Simpson.* Portland, 1944.

MULLAN, CAPTAIN JOHN. *Miners and Travelers' Guide to Oregon, Washington, Idaho, Montana, Wyoming, and Colorado. . . . .* New York, 1865.

MURPHY, JOHN MORTIMER. *Rambles in North-Western America from the Pacific Ocean to the Rocky Mountains From the Pacific Ocean to the Rocky Mountains.* London, 1879.

NASH, WALLIS. *Oregon: There and Back in 1877.* London, 1878.

NELSON, DENYS. *Fort Langley, 1827–1927: A Century of Settlement in the Valley of the Lower Fraser River.* Fort Langley, British Columbia, 1927.

NEVINS, ALLAN. *Frémont: Pathmarker of the West.* New York, 1939.

[NEW YORK CITY W.P.A. WRITERS' PROJECT]. *A Maritime History of New York.* New York, 1941.

NEWMARK, MAURICE H., AND NEWMARK, MARCO R., editors. *Sixty Years in Southern California, 1853–1913; Containing the Reminiscences of Harris Newmark.* Boston, 1930.

OGDEN, ADELE. *The California Sea Otter Trade.* Berkeley, California, 1941.

OTIS, F. N. *History of the Panama Railroad; and of the Pacific Mail Steamship Company.* New York, 1867.

PADEN, IRENE D. *The Wake of the Prairie Schooner.* New York, 1943.

PARKMAN, FRANCIS. *Pioneers of France in the New World.* Boston, 1901.

PAXSON, FREDERIC LOGAN. *History of the American Frontier, 1763–1893.* Boston, New York, 1924.

PHILLIPS, PAUL C., editor. *Forty Years on the Frontier: as Seen in the Journals and Reminiscences of Granville Stuart.* 2 vols. Cleveland, 1925.

PINKERTON, ROBERT E. *Hudson's Bay Company.* London, 1932.

PORTER, KENNETH WIGGINS. *John Jacob Astor: Business Man.* 2 vols. Cambridge, Massachusetts, 1931.

PORTLOCK, NATHANIEL. *A Voyage Round the World; But More Particularly to the North-West Coast of America . . . .* London, 1789.

POWELL, FRED WILBUR, editor. *Hall J. Kelley On Oregon.* Princeton, 1932.

PRENTISS, INGRAHAM, editor. *Seventy Years on the Frontier: Alexander Majors' Memoirs of a Lifetime on the Border.* Chicago, 1893.

PUTNAM, GEORGE GRANVILLE. *Salem Vessels and Their Voyages.* Salem, Massachusetts, 1925.

QUIETT, GLENN CHESNEY. *Pay Dirt: A Panorama of American Gold-Rushes.* New York, 1936.

RICH, E. E., editor. *Colin Robertson's Correspondence Book, September 1817 to September 1822.* The publications of the Champlain Society. Toronto, 1939.

——, editor. *The Letters of John McLoughlin From Fort Vancouver to the Governor and Committee, 1825–1846.* With an introduction by W. Kaye Lamb. 3 vols. Toronto, 1941, 1943, 1944.

——., editor. *Part of Dispatch from George Simpson Esqr: Governor of Ruperts Land . . . .* Toronto, 1947.

ROBINSON, NÔEL, AND [MOBERLY, WALTER]. *The Old Man Himself: Blazing the Trail Through the Rockies: The Story of Walter Moberly and His Share in the Making of Vancouver.* N.p., n.d.

ROLLINS, PHILIP ASHTON, editor. *The Discovery of the Oregon Trail; Robert Stuart's Narratives.* New York, London, 1935.

ROOT, FRANK A., AND CONNELLEY, WILLIAM E. *The Overland Stage to California.* Topeka, Kansas, 1901.

ROSS, ALEXANDER. *Adventures of the First Settlers on the Oregon or Columbia River: Being a Narrative of the Expedition Fitted Out by John Jacob Astor, to Establish the "Pacific Fur Company."* London, 1849.

——. *The Fur Hunters of the Far West; A Narrative of Adventures in the Oregon and Rocky Mountains.* 2 vols. London, 1855.

RUSLING, BRIGADIER GENERAL JAMES F. *Across America: or, The Great West and the Pacific Coast.* New York, 1874.

SAGE, WALTER N. *Sir James Douglas and British Columbia*. Toronto, 1930.

SANDERS, HELEN FITZGERALD. *A History of Montana*. 3 vols. Chicago, New York, 1913.

SCHOLEFIELD, E. O. S., AND GOSNELL, R. E. *A History of British Columbia*. 4 vols. Vancouver and Victoria, British Columbia, 1913.

SCHOOLING, SIR WILLIAM. *The Hudson's Bay Company, 1670–1920*. London, 1920.

SCOTT, LESLIE M., compiler. *History of the Oregon Country*, by Harvey W. Scott. 6 vols. Cambridge, Massachusetts, 1924.

SCRIVEN, GEORGE P. *The Story of the Hudson's Bay Company*. Washington, D.C., 1929.

SETTLE, RAYMOND W., AND SETTLE, MARY LUND. *Empire on Wheels*. Stanford, California, 1949.

SHERIDAN, PHILIP HENRY. *Personal Memoirs*. 2 vols. New York, 1888.

SMALLEY, EUGENE V. *History of the Northern Pacific Railroad*. New York, 1883.

[SMALLEY, EUGENE V., AND WINSER, HENRY J.] *The Great Northwest: A Guide-Book and Itinerary* . . . . St. Paul, Minnesota, 1888.

SOULÉ, FRANK, GIHON, JOHN H., AND NISBET, JAMES, compilers. *The Annals of San Francisco*. San Francisco, 1855.

SPARKS, JARED. *Life of John Ledyard, & the American Traveller*. Boston, 1847.

SPIER, LESLIE, editor. *The Sinkaietk or Southern Okanagon of Washington*. General Series in Anthropology, No. 6. Menasha, Wisconsin, 1938.

STIMSON, A. L. *History of the Express Business; Including the Origin of the Railway System in America*. New York, 1881.

——. *History of the Express Companies: and the Origin of American Railroads*. New York, 1858.

SULLIVAN, MAURICE S. *Jedediah Smith: Trader and Trail Breaker*. New York, 1936.

THORNTON, J. QUINN. *Oregon and California in 1848*. 2 vols. New York, 1855.

THWAITES, REUBEN G. *Early Western Travels, 1748–1846* . . . . 32 vols. Cleveland, 1904–1907.

TOPONCE, ALEXANDER. *Reminiscences of Alexander Toponce: Pioneer, 1839–1923*. Ogden, Utah, 1923.

TREAT, PAYSON J. *The Far East: A Political and Diplomatic History*. New York, 1928.

TRIMBLE, WILLIAM J. *The Mining Advance into the Inland Empire*. Madison, Wisconsin, 1914.

TYRRELL, J. B., editor. *David Thompson's Narrative of His Explorations in Western America, 1784–1812*. Toronto, 1916.

VILLARD, HENRY. *Memoirs of Henry Villard: Journalist and Financier, 1835–1900*. 2 vols. Boston, New York, 1904.

VILLARD, OSWALD GARRISON, editor. *The Early History of Transportation in Oregon*, by Henry Villard. Eugene, Oregon, 1944.

VINCENT, W. D. *The Northwest Company*. Pullman, Washington, 1927.

VISSCHER, WILLIAM LIGHTFOOT. *A Thrilling and Truthful History of The Pony Express or Blazing the Westward Way with Other Sketches and Incidents of Those Stirring Times*. Chicago, 1908.

VOORHIS, ERNEST, compiler. *Historic Forts and Trading Posts of the French Regime and of the English Fur Trading Companies*. Ottawa, 1930.

WADDINGTON, ALFRED. *The Fraser Mines Vindicated*. Victoria, 1858.

WAGNER, HENRY R. *Spanish Voyages to the Northwest Coast of America in the Sixteenth Century.* San Francisco, 1929.

WALGAMOTT, CHARLES S. *Reminiscences of Early Days: A Series of Historical Sketches and Happenings in the Early Days of Snake River Valley.* Twin Falls, Idaho [1926].

WALLACE, W. STEWART, editor. *Documents Relating to the North West Company.* Toronto, 1934.

WALLING, A. G. *History of Southern Oregon, Comprising Jackson, Josephine, Douglas, Curry and Coos Counties.* Portland, Oregon, 1884.

WATSON, DOUGLAS S., editor. *The Diary of Philip Leget Edwards: The Great Cattle Drive from California to Oregon in 1837.* San Francisco, 1932.

WATSON, ROBERT. *The Hudson's Bay Company.* Toronto, 1928.

WATT, ROBERTA FRYE. *The Story of Seattle.* Seattle, 1931.

WELLS, HENRY. *Sketch of the Rise, Progress and Present Conditions of the Express System.* Albany, New York, 1864.

WHYMANT, A. NEVILLE J. "Hudson's Bay Company," *Encyclopædia Britannica.* London, New York, 1929.

WHYMPER, FREDERICK. *Travel and Adventure in the Territory of Alaska.* . . . . New York, 1869.

WILKES, CHARLES. *Narrative of the United States Exploring Expedition, During the Years 1838, 1839, 1840, 1841, 1842.* 5 vols. Philadelphia, 1845.

WINTHER, OSCAR OSBURN. *Express and Stagecoach Days in California: From the Gold Rush to the Civil War.* Stanford, California, 1936, 1938.

———. *The Great Northwest.* New York, 1947.

———. "Transportation and Travel," *Dictionary of American History.* New York, 1940.

———. *Via Western Express & Stagecoach.* Stanford, California, 1945.

WRIGHT, E. W., editor. *Lewis & Dryden's Marine History of the Pacific Northwest.* Portland, Oregon, 1895.

WRIGHT, LYLE H., AND BYNUM, JOSEPHINE M., editors. *The Butterfield Overland Mail,* by Waterman L. Ormsby. San Marino, California, 1942.

WYETH, JOHN B. *Oregon; or a Short History of a Long Journey from the Atlantic Ocean to the Region of the Pacific, by Land.* Cambridge, Massachusetts. 1833.

YOUNG, F. G., editor. "The Correspondence and Journals of Captain Nathaniel J. Wyeth," *Sources of the History of Oregon.* Eugene, Oregon, 1899.

[———]. "Charter of the Governor and Company of Adventurers of England Tradeing into Hudsons Bay," May 2, 1670. Photostat, Public Archives of Canada, Ottawa, Ontario, Canada; also Indiana University Library, Bloomington, Indiana.

[———]. *Charters, Statutes, Orders in Council, etc. Relating to the Hudson's Bay Company.* London, 1931.

[———]. *Hudson's Bay Company Charter,* 1670. N.d., n.p.

[———]. *Prospectus of the Overland Camel Company.* N.p., n.d.

[———]. *Prospectus of the Puget's Sound Agricultural Company.* London, 1839.

[———]. *Puget Sound Business Directory, and Guide to Washington Territory, 1872* . . . . Olympia, Washington, n.d.

[———]. *Wells, Fargo & Co's Expdess Directory.* San Francisco, 1880.

INDEX

INDEX